Readings and Cases in International Human Resource Management

This fully updated and revised edition of this successful text retains all the favourite features from previous editions as well as adding a wealth of new ones. It features new readings and case studies alongside trusted "tried and true" readings and cases from past editions. The book is designed to sensitize students to the complexity of human resource issues in the era of globalization.

A wide variety of regions of the world are represented including Finland, France, Greece, Guyana, Israel, Japan, Mexico, Nepal, Paraguay, People's Republic of China, Senegal, Sweden, Thailand, United Kingdom, United States, and Vietnam. The readings and cases involve cross-cultural interactions between people and cultures and human resource systems.

Teaching Notes and supplemental material to enhance instructors' abilities to use the readings and cases with their students are available on the companion support site. Written to enable students to meet the international challenges that face them everyday, it will be an invaluable resource for all those studying International Human Resource Management. The accompanying website can be found at http://www.routledge.com/textbooks/9780415396882.

Mark E. Mendenhall is J. Burton Frierson Chair of Excellence in Business Leadership, University of Tennessee, Chattanooga, USA.

Gary R. Oddou is Professor of International Management and Global Business Management Program Director, California State University, San Marcos, USA.

Günter K. Stahl is Associate Professor of Organizational Behavior, INSEAD, France and Singapore.

Readings and Cases in International Human Resource Management

Fourth Edition

Edited by

Mark E. Mendenhall, Gary R. Oddou and Günter K. Stahl

Routledge
Taylor & Francis Group

LONDON AND NEW YORK

First published 1991 by PWS Kent Publishing Company
Second and third edition published 1995 and 2000 by South-Western College Publishing

This edition published 2007 by Routledge
2 Park Square, Milton Park, Abingdon, Oxon OX14 4RN

Simultaneously published in the USA and Canada
by Routledge
270 Madison Ave, New York, NY 10016

Reprinted 2008 (twice), 2009

Routledge is an imprint of the Taylor & Francis Group, an informa business

Typeset in Perpetua and Bell Gothic by
RefineCatch Limited, Bungay, Suffolk
Printed and bound in Great Britain by
TJ International Ltd, Padstow, Cornwall

British Library Cataloguing in Publication Data
A catalogue record for this book is available from the British Library

Library of Congress Cataloging in Publication Data
Readings and cases in international human resource management / edited by Mark E. Mendenhall,
Gary R. Oddou and Günter K. Stahl.—4th ed.
   p.   cm.
   Includes bibliographical references and index.
ISBN 0–415–39687–5 (hard cover)—ISBN 0–415–39688–3 (soft cover) 1. International business
enterprises—Personnel management. 2. Personnel management—Cross-cultural studies. 3. Intercultural
communication—Case studies. 4. Corporate culture—Cross-cultural studies. I. Mendenhall, Mark E.,
1956– II. Oddou, Gary R. III. Stahl, Günter K., 1966–
   HF5549.5.E45R43 2007
   658.3—dc22
   2006021516

ISBN10: 0–415–39687–5 (hbk)
ISBN10: 0–415–39688–3 (pbk)

ISBN13: 978–0–415–39687–5 (hbk)
ISBN13: 978–0–415–39688–2 (pbk)

Contents

PART 4

Challenges and trends in IHRM: employee relations, mergers and acquisitions and international joint ventures, global virtual teams and ethics

Cases:

Contributors

Nancy J. Adler
McGill University, Canada

Ruth V. Aguilera
University of Illinois at Urbana –
Champaign, USA

Barbara Bakhtari
USA

Schon Beechler
Duke Corporate Education, USA

Allan Bird
University of Missouri, St. Louis, USA

Ingmar Björkman
Swedish School of Economics, Finland

J. Stewart Black
INSEAD, Singapore and France

Jaime Bonache
Universidad Carlos III de Madrid,
Spain

David Bowen
Garvin School of International
Management (Thunderbird), USA

Charlotte Butler
INSEAD, France

Henri-Claude de Bettignies
INSEAD, France and Singapore

John C. Dencker
University of Illinois at Urbana –
Champaign, USA

Angelo S. DeNisi
Tulane University, USA

C. Brooklyn Derr
Brigham Young University, USA

Joerg Dietz
University of Western Ontario, Canada

Joseph J. DiStefano
International Institute for Management
Development (IMD), Switzerland

Christophe Falcoz
France

Zulima Fernández
Universidad Carlos III de Madrid,
Spain

Pedro Ferreira
Paraguay

Michelle Goffin
International AIDS Vaccine Initiative,
USA

Hal B. Gregersen
INSEAD, France

Roger Hallowell
The Center for Executive Development,
USA

Anne-Wil Harzing
The University of Melbourne, Australia

Martin Hilb
University of St. Gallen, Switzerland

Robert J. Jensen
University of Pennsylvania, USA

Carin-Isabel Knoop
Harvard University, USA

Alan Marr
Goldman Sachs, USA

Mark E. Mendenhall
University of Tennessee, Chattanooga,
USA

Hafiz Mirza
Bradford University School of
Management, UK

Evalde Mutabazi
Ecole de Management de Lyon, France

Barbara Myloni
Athens University of Economics and
Business, Greece

Ngo Minh Hang
National Economics University, Vietnam

Gary R. Oddou
California State University, San Marcos,
USA

Tom O'Neill
Brock University, Canada

Joyce S. Osland
California State University,
San José, USA

William H. Roof
IntelliDOT Corporation, USA

Sylvie Roussillon
Ecole de Management de Lyon,
France

Carol Saunders
University of Central Florida, USA

Günter K. Stahl
INSEAD, France and Singapore

Marja Tahvanainen
Helsinki School of Economics, Finland

Soo Min Toh
University of Toronto, Canada

Craig Van Slyke
University of Central Florida, USA

Douglas R. Vogel
City University of Hong Kong,
People's Republic of China

Acknowledgments

We would like to thank all those who have contributed to this book. Many of the authors willingly sent us cases, articles, manuscripts in progress and bibliographies that they had developed over the years. We regret that we could not include all the sources offered to us. However, many of them are listed and made available via the website associated with this book (see http://www.routledge.com/textbooks/9780415396882). Our thanks go primarily to two bastions of patience, perseverance and professionalism: Francesca Heslop and Emma Joyes. These two individuals literally made this book "happen" because of their understanding that instructors still need and want the convenience of a high-quality readings and case book for use in the classroom. A special thanks goes to our wives, Janet, Jane and Dorit, for their untiring support over the years as we have pursued our fascination with "things international" – they make all we accomplish possible, and our gratitude to them is eternal.

The publishers would like to thank the following for permission to reprint their material:

Academy of Management Executive: The Thinking Manager's Source for Roger Hallowell, David Bowen and Carin-Isabel Knoop, "Four Seasons goes to Paris", *Academy of Management Executive: The Thinking Manager's Source*, vol. 16, no. 4 (2002), pp. 7–23; Carol Saunders, Craig Van Slyke and Douglas R. Vogel, "My time or yours? Managing time visions in global virtual teams", *Academy of Management Executive: The Thinking Manager's Source*, vol. 18, no. 1 (2004), pp. 19–31; and Soo Min Toh and Angelo S. DeNisi, "A local perspective to expatriate success", *Academy of Management Executive: The Thinking Manager's Source*, vol. 19, no. 1 (2005), pp. 132–46.

Elsevier Inc. for Mark E. Mendenhall, J. Stewart Black, Robert J. Jensen and Hal B. Gregersen, "Seeing the elephant: human resource management challenges in the age of globalization", in *Organizational Dynamics*, vol. 32, no. 3 (2003), pp. 261–74; © Elsevier Inc. 2003.

Emerald Group Publishing Ltd for Nancy J. Adler, "Competitive frontiers: women managing across borders", *The Journal of Management Development*, vol. 13, no. 2 (1994), pp. 24–41.

Harvard Business School Publishing for J. Stewart Black and Hal B. Gregersen, "The right way to manage expats", Harvard Business Review, 1999, pp. 52–61.

INSEAD for Günter K. Stahl and Mark E. Mendenhall, "Andreas Weber's reward for success in an international assignment: a return to an uncertain future", 2003; © 2003 INSEAD, Singapore. All rights reserved.

INSEAD-EAC, France, for Charlotte Butler and Henri-Claude de Bettignies, "Changmai Corporation", 1999; © 1999 INSEAD-EAC, France. All rights reserved.

The International Institute for Management Development for Joseph J. DiStefano, "Johannes van den Bosch sends an email", 2000.

International Journal of Human Resource Management (http://www.tandf.co.uk) for Ruth V. Aguilera and John C. Dencker, "The role of human resource management in cross-border mergers and acquisitions", *International Journal of Human Resource Management*, vol. 15, no. 8 (2004), pp. 1355–70.

Ivey Publishing for Joerg Dietz, Michelle Goffin and Alan Marr, "Red Cross Children's Home: building capabilities in Guyana", 2002.

Sage Publications Ltd for Barbara Myloni, Anne-Wil Harzing and Hafiz Mirza, "Human resource management in Greece: have the colours of culture faded away?", reprinted by permission of Sage Publications Ltd from *International Journal of Cross Cultural Management*, vol. 4, no. 1 (2004), pp. 59–76 (© SAGE Publications 2004).

The Society for Applied Anthropology for Tom O'Neill, "Weaving wages, indebtedness, and remittances in the Nepalese carpet industry", reprinted by permission of the Society for Applied Anthropology from SfAA 2004, *Human Organization*, vol. 63, no. 2 (Summer 2004), pp. 211–20.

John Wiley & Sons Inc. for J. Stewart Black and Mark E. Mendenhall, "A practical but theory-based framework for selecting cross-cultural training methods", *Human Resource Management*, vol. 28, no. 4 (Winter 1989), pp. 511–39; and Marja Tahvanainen, "Expatriate performance management: the case of Nokia Telecommunications", *Human Resource Management*, vol. 39, nos 2–3 (Summer/Fall 2000), pp. 267–75.

We would also like to thank the following authors for continuing to allow us to reprint their contributions from previous editions of this reader: Allan Bird and Schon Beechler for "The link between business strategy and international human resource management practices"; Christophe Falcoz, Sylvie Roussillon and C. Brooklyn Derr for "Career management of highfliers at Alcatel"; Martin Hilb for "Computex Corporation"; Gary R. Oddou and Mark E. Mendenhall for "Expatriate performance appraisal: problems and solutions"; Joyce S. Osland and Pedro Ferreira for "Anatomy of a Paraguayan strike"; and William H. Roof and Barbara Bakhtari for "Recruiting a manager for BRB, Israel".

We would also like to thank the following authors whose work appears here for the first time: Ingmar Björkman for "Peter Hanson: building a world-class product development center for Hi Tech Systems in China"; J. Stewart Black for "Fred Bailey: an innocent abroad"; Jaime Bonache and Zulima Fernández for "Strategic staffing in multinational companies: a resource-based approach"; Evalde Mutabazi and C. Brooklyn Derr for "Socometal: rewarding African workers"; Ngo Minh Hang for "The case of ABB Transformer in Vietnam".

MARK E. MENDENHALL
Signal Mountain, Tennessee; USA

GARY R. ODDOU
Oceanside, California; USA

GÜNTER K. STAHL
Fontainebleau, France and Singapore

Mark E. Mendenhall, Gary R. Oddou and Günter K. Stahl

INTRODUCTION AND INTRODUCTORY READING AND CASE: "THE WHITE WATER RAPIDS OF ROBIN EARL"

WELCOME TO THE FOURTH edition of *Readings and Cases in International Human Resource Management*. If you are a long-time user of this text, we should like to take a moment to thank you for using the book in your teaching or consulting endeavors. Also, with this edition we welcome our association with a new publisher, Routledge. We originally put this book together because we couldn't find one ourselves, and we wanted such a book to use in our classes. Since then, with your help, the book has evolved and become a standby for teachers of international management/HRM/OB.

We think the best way to introduce the textbook is with an introductory reading/ case. It sets the tone of the book and, if you like, makes an excellent reading assignment to begin class with as well. We call it "The White Water Rapids of Robin Earl".

READING AND CASE: THE WHITE WATER RAPIDS OF ROBIN EARL

Business leaders of the present — let alone the future — need to possess international business skills par excellence in order to survive the chaotic world of international business. It also goes without saying that human resource managers will face new, unforeseen obstacles. Peter Vaill used the metaphor of "permanent white water" to describe the unpredictable, dynamic nature of doing business in the latter part of the twentieth century.

Most managers are taught to think of themselves as paddling their canoes on calm, still, lakes. . . . They're led to believe that they should be pretty much able to go where they want, when they want, using means that are under their control. Sure there will be temporary disruptions during changes of various sorts – periods when they will have to shoot the rapids in their canoes – but the disruptions will be temporary, and when things settle back down, they'll be back in a calm, still lake mode. But it has been my experience that they never get out of the rapids! No sooner do you begin to digest one change than another one comes along to keep things unstuck. In fact, there are usually lots of changes going on at once. The feeling is one of continuous upset and chaos.[1]

This metaphor aptly illustrates the world of international business. As Vaill notes, in the world of international business "things are only very partially under control, yet the effective navigator of the rapids is not behaving randomly or aimlessly. Intelligence, experience, and skill are being exercised, albeit in ways that we hardly know how to perceive, let alone describe" (p. 2). This book deals with the challenges that human resource managers will face in the twenty-first century. What will be the general nature of those challenges? Perhaps an example of a firm or individual would help illustrate these challenges. Let us consider the case of Robin Earl. Note that Robin Earl is a North American human resource manager in a North American company. However, she could just as easily be a manager in any medium-sized European, Asian, South or Central American, Australian or New Zealand, or African company. The issue is not her gender, her nationality or the nationality of her firm, but rather the challenges she faces due to globalization.

Robin Earl's "white water rapids"

Robin Earl is Director of Human Resources for BCN, a firm that among other things manufactures a line of semiconductors. BCN has been very successful in the last ten years. Sales have increased at an annual rate of 7 percent, and profits have correspondingly grown.

BCN has had overseas sales offices for the last seven years, exporting its products from its local manufacturing operations to South America and Southeast Asia. Recently, BCN's top management has been mulling over the possibility of developing manufacturing and distribution capabilities in South America and Asia – and possibly even in Europe. Doing so would allow BCN to take advantage of cheaper labor rates in some of these countries and to avoid export barriers in others. In addition, it could be more responsive to local demand for its products, and in the age of globalization move toward being a truly global firm.

Robin was asked by the firm's CEO to prepare an analysis (due on his desk in two weeks) of the human resource impact such moves would have on the firm. As Robin sat down at her desk, she began to jot down ideas. She found herself some-what baffled by this global angle of HRM, as she had no experience or training in managing human resources internationally. The following are some of her thoughts as she attempted to create an outline for her report.

I. How will international assignments fit into BCN's business strategy to become a truly global firm?

Do we have a clearly focused business strategy for becoming a multinational firm? She made a mental note to call John Fukumoto, the VP of Finance, to see how far the thinking of the top management team had progressed on that front. *How will the development of BCN's human resources fit into such a plan? I wonder why I am not on that planning team?* Robin wondered how she could insert herself into that process without being suspected of having ulterior motives.

What kind of perspective and experience should BCN's future top management have if they will be leading a true multinational firm? How will that experience be best-obtained – through international assignments or by the use of consultants? Am I going to be responsible for educating management regarding international issues? If so, it's the blind leading the blind, she thought, for she would not even be sure how to evaluate the validity of an external consultant's proposals. *I could always hire experts to evaluate the bid proposals of consulting firms,* she thought, *but that would run into serious budget squeezes for my department.*

Who should we send – our high potentials that are destined to lead the company in the next ten years or our non-designated personnel? How important will it be to have a global perspective at the top vs. having one throughout the levels of the company?

Robin began to think about the issue of dual-career couples as well. Just how hard will it be to attract our best people to go to a foreign country if their spouse has a good career here? she wondered. She had heard about some firms that had formed a consortium in the foreign country to help provide spouses of the expatriates with employment. Working together, they had more flexibility than if they were trying to go it alone.

Will local managers – if we use local managers – desire to be promoted to US headquarters? Will top management desire that? Fifteen years from now, what will, and what should, BCN's top management look like: an Asian managing a South American plant and a mixture of South Americans, Asians, Europeans and Americans at headquarters? The cost of hiring the numbers of new workers – not to mention well-qualified managers – is not going to be loose change. I hope they aren't ignoring the cost of hiring well-qualified managers and retaining them in their financial analyses, Robin thought. *How shall we retain the best and the brightest? What do Asians want in rewards? What do South Americans want? Is a good salary enough or are other factors involved?*

II. Which countries have cultures that best fit BCN's needs?

Robin remembered reading a newspaper article that mentioned that one of the factors important to Japanese firms locating in the US was finding compatible regional cultural norms. The Japanese liked the Southern US culture because of its regard for interpersonal relations in business settings, tradition, and respect for elders and persons in positions of authority. *Which countries have educational systems that would best-support the knowledge base that our personnel will need? Which countries have social systems that favor unions more than management? Which cultures within these regions are most favorable to American expatriates and their families? Most importantly, which cultures promote a strong work ethic?*

Which countries have governments that are stable and are not likely to change and upset the equilibrium of our workers' and managers' work schedules? What about the possibility of terrorism? Will I have to devise a terrorism-prevention training program? Which countries are friendly to us, not just businesswise but in their perceptions of Americans and their right to manage the local residents? I wonder how much kidnap insurance costs?

III. Should we send our own personnel overseas or hire locally?

Which countries in Asia, South America or Europe have qualified personnel to staff manufacturing operations from top to bottom? Do some countries have laws that require hiring a certain percentage of local workers? Robin remembered meeting a man once at a professional convention who had worked for a mining company in Africa. He reported having to hire local workers for all positions below middle-management level with the promise to phase out all Americans within ten years.

Can or should the subsidiary management come from BCN headquarters? If not, where would we find local managers to hire? The universities? Robin recalled reading once that in France the norm was to hire managers from the "grandes écoles" and not from the universities. *If we send our personnel, who should go? How long should their assignments be? How expensive will it be to house an American family at their accustomed standard of living in the new country? How should we select the Americans to send? Should we base our decisions on experience in the company, adaptability potential, or desire to relocate? What if nobody wants to go?*

IV. How shall we train employees for such assignments?

How much training will they need before they go? How in depth will it need to be? Do they need language training or is English good enough? Robin thought that most business people around the world speak English, so maybe this was not really an issue. *Will the firm budget my department the resources necessary to do quality training or shall I be left with a budget that will allow nothing more than bringing in a few local professors for a couple of hours each to do area briefings? Who can I call on to do the training?*

Robin felt somewhat relieved when she remembered reading about some cross-cultural training firms in the ad section of an HRM newsletter she reads. But her confidence ebbed when the following thought occurred to her: *How shall I know if the training these external consultants provide is valid and helpful or just a dog-and-pony show? Can I, with my staff, develop our own training program? What kind of time and money will such an endeavor require?* As Robin began mentally planning a strategy to develop training programs with her staff, her mind switched to yet another problem.

V. What are the career implications of foreign assignments?

Should the assignments be developmental or should slots simply be filled as they open up, regardless of whether or not the move will develop the employee? Robin was vaguely aware that companies such as IBM, Novartis and Philips view international assignments as an integral part of their management development for senior posts. *If the assignment is developmental, what shall we do when the employee returns?* Robin wondered if the company would give her authority to dictate what position returning managers should receive. She doubted they would give her that authority. But what would happen to these experienced internationalists if they didn't have a clear career path for them when they returned? *How shall we reintegrate these employees into BCN's home operations? We'll lose them*, Robin thought to herself, *if we can't offer them a good position when they return. How will the HRM department keep informed of the needs, concerns, performance and evaluation of the overseas employees? By phone? e-mail? video conferencing? fax? site visits?* Robin wondered whether she could justify trips to the Far East as site visits. They may be necessary, but might be viewed by others as a new perk for the HRM department.

The reentry part kept bothering Robin. Not only is there the position-transition issue to plan for; she also wondered how they might best capture their learnings about the foreign operations. *This could be really valuable*, she thought. *It could help us coordinate our efforts better, understand the challenges of our foreign operations, etc.*

VI. How productive will the cheap labor be?

If we do opt to set up in a country where the labor rates are inexpensive, can we introduce our management systems into the manufacturing plants? Will those systems be in harmony with the work culture of that country? I wonder if we will run into transfer-of-technology problems? Probably. Okay, so how do we train local workers to understand how we do things at BCN? Will I have to design those training programs, too?

I wonder if our managers will have to develop unique incentive systems to get their subordinates to work. No, probably not. Well, then again, maybe. After all, the people under me have different buttons that make them work harder; those buttons are not the same for everyone here in the US. Is it possible, Robin wondered, *for some cultures to have work norms that are antithetical to promotion and pay inducements? I think those would be universal motivators! Maybe this won't be a major problem. Maybe it will be more of a fine-tuning issue in terms of adapting our job design, incentive systems and motivational techniques to the country where we decide to set up shop.* Then the thought occurred to her, *What about motivating and evaluating the Americans overseas?*

VII. How should we do performance evaluation?

Can we just use the same forms, procedures and criteria, or is there something unique about a foreign assignment that requires unique performance-evaluation systems? When should we evaluate people? Robin remembered reading in a professional newsletter that expatriate employees require at least six months to settle into their overseas assignments. *Would it be fair to evaluate employees before six months? When would it be valid? After eight, ten or twelve months? This is getting very messy,* Robin sighed.

Should the criteria by which to judge performance in Asia and other places be *relative to the country in question, or should we use the same evaluation criteria everywhere?* The last thing Robin felt like doing was overseeing the development of a new performance-evaluation system! *We can get by with our current one,* she mentally noted. *Who should do the evaluating? Headquarters, the regional subsidiary superiors, peers, or a mixture of superiors and subordinates? Should the criteria revolve around bottom-line figures or personnel objectives? If financial-type performance criteria are emphasized, what happens if the dollar depreciates significantly against the local currency and wipes out the expatriate manager's cost savings and profits? How can the expatriate manager be evaluated, motivated and rewarded under such conditions?*

What about nationality differences in performance evaluation? If an American manager is being evaluated by a Peruvian subsidiary manager, will the evaluation be fair or is there potential for some sort of cultural bias? What if the American manager is a woman? Shall we be able to put together an attractive, but not too costly, compensation package for our expatriates? I wonder what such a package would look like. We need to offer something good to entice the employee to go, especially if the employee might lose the spouse's income; yet, if there's too great a difference in the package between the repatriate and local personnel, that will create we–them problems.

VIII. Will the unions be trouble?

Robin's thoughts were now racing between problems. *I remember reading somewhere,* she mused, *that in order to shut down a manufacturing facility in France (or was it Germany or Sweden?) management had to give the workers a full year's notice, retrain them, and then find them new jobs!* She knew the top management of her firm would find such a contingency troubling at best. *Well, maybe the Asian labor markets are less unionized and won't be as problematic.* Then Robin recalled meeting a public relations spokeswoman for a toy firm at a party, and the nightmare she had described.

It seems that the US management of her company had pressured the contract manufacturers in Hong Kong and the PRC to increase production dramatically in order to fill unforeseen demands during the Christmas season. The press had gotten hold of cases where female workers were working sixteen-hour days with no breaks; if they complained, they were terminated on the spot. Also, some of the women had miscarried. It was a public relations nightmare. *Maybe dealing with unions wouldn't be all bad. Maybe unions would protect us from questionable ethical nightmares,* Robin thought. But then she thought of codetermination laws in countries like Germany and workers' representatives sitting on the local boards of directors – that would not be easy for American managers to stomach. And what about managing people from other cultures? *We have a hard enough time in our California and Texas plants, let alone overseas!* As Robin put down her pen, the obvious complexity of the report loomed before her. She had just scratched the surface of the basic human resources issues associated with "globalization", and there seemed to be no end to the potential permutations around each problem. *This will be no easy task,* she concluded. As she left her office and made her way to the parking garage, she wondered, *Where can I go for help?*

BCN's situation closely parallels the initial path on which virtually all companies have had to tread in reaction to the issues, challenges and opportunities associated with the globalization of business. Within the globalization context of business operations, many business decisions become critical. While some of those decisions pertain to a firm's financial or physical resources, the most neglected and perhaps most important decisions to be made concern the management of the firm's international human resources. One of the greatest problems is the lack of a global perspective on the part of a firm's managerial cadre. As a member of one culture, the manager tends to see life from that perspective, to judge events from that perspective, and to make decisions based on that perspective. In an increasingly global business environment, such a perspective breeds failure.

Our principal objective for this book is to sensitize the reader to the complex human resource issues that exist in the global business environment. With this primary objective in mind, as stated previously, we have attempted to represent many regions of the world balanced by the quality of information and discussion potential of the reading or case.

Most publishing companies are turning to online creation of packets of readings and cases. Although a good idea in theory, it requires a great deal of research in case repositories and online journal systems to design a supplemental text of one's own. Most instructors are too busy with other obligations to spend the time necessary to design and create supplemental texts online, particularly if there is a good alternative, and we believe a book such as this one is just that alternative. We believe there is a need for books of "tried and true" cases and readings that provide stimulating and intellectually challenging material, yet written in ways that engage both the student and the instructor. If you are a new adopter of the book, we would like to thank you, and we look forward to your comments concerning your experience in using the book. Feel free to contact us with your feedback through the website that is associated with this book at http://www.routledge.com/textbooks/0415396883

In this new edition of our book we have kept the best cases from the previous editions and added new readings and cases that have the same type of "feel" as the old "tried and true" ones. The format of the book has changed slightly; however, the conceptual groupings of each major section of the book have essentially remained the same. We were reluctant to tamper with a conceptual format that so many people liked. Our field, however, is dynamic, and in order to be current we have updated many of the readings and some of the cases. However, a few of these readings and cases seemed to us to be classics. That is, the issues they address seem to transcend time (and copyright date!). We chose to keep these in the book, since we like to teach from them, and we know that most of you do as well.

This book can be used in a variety of ways in human resource management, management, and organizational behavior courses. It can stand alone, if the instructor's preference is to teach predominantly a case course. It can be used in tandem with other textbooks that have an IHRM, management, or organizational behavior focus, or as a supplement to them. Or the book can be used as a main text in human resource management or other related courses, and supplemented with other readings and texts with which the instructor is comfortable. A list of other readings that would be potentially useful in this regard is included on the website that is associated with this book (http://www.routledge.com/textbooks/0415396883)

The instructor's manual is available on this book's website (http://www.routledge.com/textbooks/0415396883). Contained in the instructor's manual are teaching notes for the cases, class discussion notes and guidelines for the readings, in-class and out-of-class assignments for the cases and readings, links to internet sites that relate to the cases and readings, Powerpoint slides that accompany the cases and readings, and lists of videos and feature films that present information that can add visual context to the readings and cases. Our goal is to support you as an instructor in all of your needs.

Our main objective for the book is simply this: to sensitize the reader to the complex human resource issues that exist in the global business environment. With this objective in mind, we have attempted to represent many regions of the world in terms of the locations in which the readings and cases are based: France, Israel, Paraguay, United States, Senegal, Finland, Japan, People's Republic of China, Vietnam, Greece, Mexico, Sweden, Guyana, Nepal and Thailand.

Additionally, our readings and cases involve cross-cultural interaction between people and cultures and human resource systems in the following combinations: Scandinavia – People's Republic of China, Canada – Guyana, United Kingdom – Thailand, United Kingdom – Israel, United States – Japan, Senegal – France, Germany – United States, Sweden – United States, Canada – France, Scandinavia – Vietnam, The Netherlands – Mexico.

However, in providing for this diversity of location and interaction, we chose not to "force fit" something into the book for the sake of regional or geographic representation. We included what we and our editors felt were quality readings and cases in the field of international human resource management. We do not view this book as a North American HR text nor as a European HR text. Our goal was to create a book of readings and cases that would focus on the points of confluence between cultures, human resource systems, and people in this era of globalization.

AN INTRODUCTION TO THE CASES AND READINGS

We have divided the book into four parts. The first section has readings and cases that illustrate issues germane to the context of international human resource management (IHRM).

Part 1: The context of IHRM: context, culture and strategy

This section begins with an article that was published in *Organizational Dynamics* by Mark E. Mendenhall and a group of his colleagues (J. S. Black, R. J. Jensen and H. Gregersen) entitled *"Seeing the elephant: human resource management challenges in the age of globalization"*. The latter part of the twentieth century and the beginning of the twenty-first century have been characterized by the inexorable emergence of globalization as a meta-context of virtually all social organizations. This article reports the perceptions of senior HR executives regarding the HR challenges that globalization is posing for them and their firms. The authors surveyed a group of elite senior HR executives regarding the challenges their companies were facing owing to globalization. The results of the survey provide the reader with a compelling snapshot of where companies have been and how they are trying to change in terms of their HR practices owing to the pressures of globalization. The authors provide guidance to companies wrestling with these challenges by providing lessons learned from best practices and from their experiences in consulting with firms in these areas. We chose this article to lead off the book because it provides students with a broad overview of the challenges facing IHRM in the twenty-first century, and through mini-case examples possible scenarios to solve the challenges are presented.

The second article in this section, *"The link between business strategy and international human resource management practices"*, was written especially for this book by two leading scholars in the field of international management, Allan Bird and Schon Beechler. They address the important issue of strategy as a context for IHRM practices in global firms. Too often, IHRM policies, practices and traditions are unattached to the primary global business strategy of the firm, and the two can often unintentionally work at cross-purposes. Bird and Beechler delineate cogent linkages between strategy and IHRM practice, and present implications for alignment between IHRM strategy and the overall strategy of the company. Strategy is an important context for IHRM practices, and the authors provide in this paper a useful framework for studying the conceptual linkages between practice and context.

The third article in this section, *"Human resource management in Greece: Have the colours of culture faded away?"* (by Barbara Myloni, Anne-Wil Harzing and Hafiz Mirza), explores another important context of IHRM, that of national culture. When firms set up operations in a country, to what degree must indigenous human resource issues be catered to, and to what degree can the firm socialize host national employees within the company's global corporate culture? To what degree have the effects of globalization homogenized human resource practices in Europe, and throughout the world? The authors explore this issue in the context of Greece, and provide useful insights into this important issue in the field.

To "put some flesh" on the conceptual issues associated with the context of IHRM, three cases were selected for inclusion in the text. The first, *"Peter Hanson: building a world-class product development center for Hi Tech Systems in China"*, focuses on the factors that influence the "integration versus localization" decision. Every global organization and international executive faces the issue of how and to what extent to adapt management practices to local circumstances. The case describes the challenges faced by Peter Hanson, a manager of a large and very successful Scandinavian high-tech company, who has been assigned the task of setting up a product development center in Beijing. What approach should he take with respect to HRM policies and practices in order to build a world-class product development center in China?

The second case, *"Red Cross Children's Home: building capabilities in Guyana"*, is a true story of a young woman's managerial experience in having to run an orphanage in Guyana and the role that culture played as an influencing agent on the efficacy of her change initiatives. The case describes her leadership decisions, human resource policy initiatives, and strategies for change, and their subsequent effects on the agency and its employees. A video accompanies this case where the expatriate is interviewed and questioned regarding the decisions she made, why she made them, and her analysis of their outcomes.

The setting of the third case in this section, *"Changmai Corporation"*, is Southeast Asia, specifically a pulp mill located in northern Thailand. It illustrates the cultural and ethical challenges in the minds of managers when Western and indigenous cultures clash. A Scottish manager believes he must pay a bribe to a government safety inspector to receive permission for his project to continue, as well as having to deal with differences in safety expectations between his company and local government regulations. Should Western business practices and ethics be superimposed upon host national projects, workers and governments? This case illustrates some of the ethical dilemmas that international managers are likely to encounter in their career and explores strategies for managing ethical conflicts.

Part 2: Identifying, selecting and managing the global workforce

"Strategic staffing in multinational companies" is probably one of the most conceptual papers in the book. It looks at organizations from a resource theory perspective and considers the role of the expatriate as a valuable, rare and inimitable

resource. Additionally, it looks at the roles of expatriates and how they relate to these resource systems. The authors advocate a much more strategic approach to the selection of expatriates given the potential importance of their roles. They also look at the work unit as a whole, and analyze the roles of expatriates within this context. The notion that the value of expatriates is often embedded into the system of the work unit is discussed as well.

Long-term international assignments are expensive, yet most companies get poor returns on this investment. J. Stewart Black and Hal B. Gregersen, two leading scholars in the field of IHRM, have studied the management of expatriates at more than 700 US, European and Japanese companies to determine where companies go wrong and what they need to improve in order to manage expatriates to their full advantage. In their article, *"The right way to manage expats"*, they show that effective companies share three general practices. First, they send people for the right reasons, meaning they send people abroad to generate new knowledge for the company or to develop their leadership skills. Second, they send the right people – successful companies select individuals that can succeed overseas. Finally, they end expatriate assignments with a deliberate repatriation process by providing them with career guidance and opportunities to put their international experience to work.

The third article in this section, *"Competitive frontiers: women managing across borders"*, examines the underlying assumptions that companies make about the role of women in global companies and the reasons why women continue to be under-represented in management in general and in international management in particular. We rate this as a "classic" reading. Though it was published in 1994, the issues Adler raises and the state of affairs regarding this topic have not changed drastically since the article was published. Based on numerous studies, Nancy J. Adler explores some of the traditional myths about women expatriates: that they do not want to be international managers and that foreign prejudice against women renders them ineffective. Her research found that women were interested in international assignments, were accepted by men even in cultures where local women were discriminated against, and were very successful when given the opportunity. However, another myth – that companies hesitate to send women abroad – is found to be true. Nancy J. Adler argues that competitive advantage in global organizations can only come from a combination of an increased representation of women and a recognition of differences as complementary.

"Career management of highfliers at Alcatel" is a case that poses very realistic and significant issues for any company that is going global. It deals with some very significant and interesting issues: how to manage a set of foreign firms that were previously independent and in some cases very nationalistic; how to develop your personnel to have a global mindset and one that will be able to manage a truly complex conglomerate representing many different foreign nationals. Embedded within these two major issues are questions about the appropriate degree of centralization in global firms: which parts to centralize and which aspects of the firm's operations should be decentralized? One of the major questions in the case is: How do you allow adequate autonomy for the firm to maintain its national identity while integrating it adequately to be part of a whole? The case presents three different

methods the firm is considering as ways to select individuals with the potential to manage Alcatel in the future. One represents the stereotypical and traditional "grande école" method in France. One represents the American "promotion based on merit" method, and the third represents the method that has been embedded within Alcatel and other large French enterprises: a feudal-type system where "who you know" counts for more than "what you know".

The second case in this section, "Recruiting a manager for BRB, Israel", reflects the often consternating trade-offs associated with the selection of expatriate managers on the part of headquarters staff. In this case a vice-president must recommend a regional manager to run the Israel subsidiary of his company. In recommending his selection, the vice-president of HR must take into consideration issues such as personality and managerial style fit between candidates and the president of the company, candidates' motives for desiring to work and relocate in Israel, age and experience vs. potential for future success on the part of the candidates, and cultural background differences amongst the candidates, to name a few. This case has been used with success in some of the most elite business schools in the world, and provides an effective background for the application of various human resource selection techniques.

Our final case in this section is a traditional favorite amongst past adopters of this text: "Fred Bailey: an innocent abroad". This is a classic tale of culture shock. The focus of this case is on the adaptation to both work and general life in Japan on the part of an expatriate couple, Fred and Jenny Bailey. The case traces the selection process, and also describes the subsequent experiences of Fred and Jenny in Tokyo. They run into cross-cultural challenges that are thorny and complex, and which significantly challenge them and their marriage. A true case (the names of the individuals in the case were changed, as well as the company, for purposes of anonymity), the instructor's manual provides information regarding the final outcome of Fred and Jenny's cross-cultural challenges.

Part 3: Training, performance management, appraisal and compensation issues for global managers

All companies use employee performance management (PM) practices; the question is: How effective are the practices that are employed? The purpose of PM practices is to ensure high levels of productivity on the part of employees. To date, the area of expatriate PM strategies has been an underresearched area in the field of international human resource management. In an attempt to gain more understanding of how PM programs influence expatriate productivity, in this article, "Expatriate performance management: the case of Nokia Telecommunications", Marja Tahvanainen studies the use of PM practices in Nokia for their expatriate cadre. Her findings have contributed significantly to the field's understanding of how expatriate PM processes should be enacted.

Traditionally, expatriate compensation packages in Western firms have been constructed to be financially attractive to expatriates in order to induce them to accept their overseas assignments. These financially attractive compensation packages, however, can cause a negative side-effect: a deep sense of inequity among host national managers who work for, or alongside, expatriate managers. In the second article in this section, *"A local perspective to expatriate success"*, Soo Min Toh and Angelo S. DeNisi argue that companies need to focus on developing HR practices and policies that provide equitable compensation to both expatriate and host national employees. On the surface, this seems to be a difficult, if not impossible, task to undertake; however, the authors offer insightful and creative ways by which this imbalance can be rectified. The article provides a rich catalyst for class discussion and an opportunity for students to analyze the viability of human resource change initiatives.

"Expatriate performance appraisal: problems and solutions" is a reading that has been a standard in the book since its beginning. The issues it raises are ongoing in firms that have an active expatriate program. It discusses the challenges in trying to develop an appropriate performance appraisal program when many domestic managers and human resource personnel don't really understand the additional challenges involved in working in a foreign country. Likewise, the evaluation of whatever criteria are developed is problematic. In most cases, the final evaluation of the expatriate is the employee's domestic manager. This is particularly true when the employee's superior is a foreigner. This raises specific issues of objectivity. How can a manager who is often thousands of miles away accurately measure an employee's performance? The difficulty of this leads typically to two different roads the evaluator takes: one road is simply giving the expatriate a very high evaluation out of ignorance and not really wanting to have to deal with an accurate measurement when the manager doesn't have the close contact necessary to do that; the other road involves basing the evaluation almost exclusively on objective criteria (sales volume, absence of problems created by the employee, profit margins, etc.), which poses a different set of problems.

The final reading of this section we rate as a "classic". Originally published in 1990, *"A practical but theory-based framework for selecting cross-cultural training methods"* delineates a framework for decision-making regarding the use of cross-cultural training programs based on principles associated with Social Learning Theory. J. S. Black and Mark E. Mendenhall discuss the critical situational variables associated with success in cross-cultural training programs (culture novelty, degree of cross-cultural interaction and job novelty) and their relationship to other critical training program design variables: training rigor and training duration. The contingency model offers practical yet theoretically sound principles for cross-cultural training program design, and remains as relevant today as when it was first published, when it received acclaim amongst practitioners and scholars in the field of international management.

Although far more European firms have African operations because of their history of colonization and subsequent political and trade relationships, African nations often manifest collectivist value clusters which are at odds with Western cultures. *"Socometal"* is an excellent case; its central issue relates to improving the productivity of West African employees of a European firm's subsidiary in Senegal.

The European management's approaches fail miserably in this regard, but then a local manager from Senegal, who was educated in France, takes on the challenge. His approach represents a consideration for collectivist cultural values, and it winds up working extremely well – beyond the expectations of any of the Europeans at the site. Unfortunately, the French manager who heads the subsidiary learns of it and, although the incentive–return relationship is clearly advantageous to both the employees and the firm, shuts down the program immediately. His mentality represents a very bureaucratic perspective and shows how ineffective rigidity is in trying to address the cultural needs of foreign employees.

The second case in this section, "*Andreas Weber's reward for success in an international assignment: a return to an uncertain future*", is a true story of a German bank executive on assignment in New York. The case illustrates some of the career issues facing expatriates and the problems that await them upon returning home. Andreas Weber is selected as a "high potential" employee in a large German bank, and is posted on an international assignment in the USA. After several years abroad, having progressed swiftly in his new job, he and his wife decide for family reasons to return to Germany, sure that Andreas' track record in New York would land him an attractive position in the company. Unfortunately, international assignments and repatriation do not always go as planned. In this case, Andreas' re-entry position is basically a demotion and not at all reflective of what he could offer the company. What went wrong and how should Andreas respond?

What do you do when you receive a letter or an email from a group of employees in an overseas subsidiary complaining about their expatriate manager and threatening to quit if conditions don't improve? In "*Computex Corporation*", Martin Hilb places the student behind the desk of an executive at headquarters who must deal with an international human resource emergency. Working with little contextual information, sparse information about the national and work cultures, and a paucity of specific knowledge about the personalities of the people involved, what strategy should the executive take to solve the problem before it escalates into a disaster? This case provides ample opportunity for students to apply theory and concepts learned in class to a real-world human resource emergency.

Part 4: Challenges and trends in IHRM: employee relations, mergers and acquisitions and international joint ventures, global virtual teams and ethics

The increase in merger and acquisition activity over the past twenty years evidences the trend of the use of this organizational approach to expand operations on the part of many firms. The merger and acquisition process is most often characterized by careful financial due diligence, a focus on potential product and system "synergies", and analyses of potential future financial profits. Lost in this process is a consideration of the human resource aspect of mergers and acquisitions. The first article, "*The role of human resource management in cross-border mergers and acquisitions"*, explores how human resource managers and practices can play a value-added role throughout the entire merger and acquisition process. The authors, Ruth V. Aguilera and John C. Dencker, offer a strategic framework that delineates the links between merger and acquisition strategic process and human resource strategic processes. All of these issues are explored in the context of cross-border mergers and acquisitions.

Globalization processes influence workers in all industries, at all levels, in all areas of the world. The impact of globalization on workers in developing countries is varied, but we introduce this issue to students via an excellent article, authored by Tom O'Neill, entitled *"Weaving wages, indebtedness, and remittances in the Nepalese carpet industry"*. As students explore the dynamics of child labor exploitation, domestic union vs. non-union systems of control and protection, worker indebtedness, remuneration of child laborers and their families, cost of living in urban centers, and purchasing vagaries of foreign companies, they will gain a better understanding of the complexity of the human resource implications of globalization, and the programs and initiatives that are being taken by differing organizations to ameliorate the needs of laborers in developing countries.

Global virtual teams provide many challenges to those working in them and to those who manage them. One of the significant challenges in global virtual teams has to do with the perception of time that team members from different cultures and nations hold. Individuals that hold differing perceptions about time enact different behaviors in time-related areas (deadlines, scheduling, measuring performance, etc.). In *"My time or yours? Managing time visions in global virtual teams"*, the authors (Carol Saunders, Craig Van Slyke and Douglas R. Vogel) map the typologies that exist associated with differing perceptions and mindsets on time. Their model and their recommendations for practice provide students with a rich framework from which to explore and analyze global virtual team processes.

Firms often acquire other firms in foreign countries or start up new operations in foreign countries. A question they all have to deal with in managing employees in the foreign locations is: To what degree should the acquiring firm force the employees to adapt to a common set of standards and practices to ensure uniformity across their operations? To what degree should they adapt to the local employees and the practices they are used to? *"Four Seasons goes to Paris"* chronicles a Canadian hotel chain with specific needs to standardize certain aspects of its operations so that customers worldwide will recognize the same elegance and hospitality from country to country. Yet its employees are largely indigenous to the country they work within. This reading looks at the decisions regarding employment and employee practices that Four Seasons standardized and decentralized.

Strikes are perhaps the most stressful and risky situations that domestic and global managers face in the workplace. In *"Anatomy of a Paraguayan strike"*, Joyce S. Osland and Pedro Ferreira describe in detail the build-up, dynamics and outcome of a strike initiated by two separate engineers' unions and a power company. This case does not involve an external multinational company; rather, it is a country-specific case that fleshes out the dynamics of a Paraguayan strike. This case offers students the opportunity to study labor relations in a specific culture, and to attempt to understand the values, norms and policies that drive labor relations processes in a country besides their own.

"*The case of ABB Transformer in Vietnam*" highlights the traps in doing international business without understanding the local employment practices, the role of the unions, and the role the media can play in creating perceptions of the goodness or badness of a foreign firm. ABB joined with a Vietnamese transformer firm and created what seemed to be a fruitful partnership. ABB brought the technology and experience, and the Vietnamese firm brought its market base and its knowledge of local customs and of the government. The representative of ABB who headed the joint venture made a business decision to lay off employees to try to reach a profitable balance sheet. The manner in which it was done was unacceptable to the employees, who then carried their story to the labor board and eventually to the media. The result was a terrible public relations catastrophe for ABB.

A Dutch executive, Johannes van den Bosch, has been having problems in coordinating with his Mexican counterpart to complete a project effectively. Exasperated, van den Bosch fires off an angry email to his Mexican colleague. After an hour, he decides to rewrite his email, and this second email details the facts and figures associated with the situation instead of venting his emotions. His expectations are that his Mexican colleague will provide specific assistance that he has requested in a timely manner. Subsequent events prove less than satisfactory, and "*Johannes van den Bosch sends an email*" provides students with an excellent opportunity to put themselves in the shoes of a virtual team and analyze the key factors that contribute to virtual teams' successes and failures.

NOTE

1   Peter Vaill, *Managing as a Performing Art: New Ideas for a World of Chaotic Change* (San Francisco, Calif.: Jossey-Bass, 1989), p. 2.

PART 1

The context of IHRM: context, culture and strategy

Readings:
- Mark E. Mendenhall, J. Stewart Black, Robert J. Jensen and Hal B. Gregersen
  SEEING THE ELEPHANT: HUMAN RESOURCE MANAGEMENT CHALLENGES IN THE AGE OF GLOBALIZATION

- Allan Bird and Schon Beechler
  THE LINK BETWEEN BUSINESS STRATEGY AND INTERNATIONAL HUMAN RESOURCE MANAGEMENT PRACTICES

- Barbara Myloni, Anne-Wil Harzing and Hafiz Mirza
  HUMAN RESOURCE MANAGEMENT IN GREECE: HAVE THE COLOURS OF CULTURE FADED AWAY?

Cases:
- Ingmar Björkman
  PETER HANSON: BUILDING A WORLD-CLASS PRODUCT DEVELOPMENT CENTER FOR HI TECH SYSTEMS IN CHINA

- Joerg Dietz, Michelle Goffin and Alan Marr
  RED CROSS CHILDREN'S HOME: BUILDING CAPABILITIES IN GUYANA

- Charlotte Butler and Henri-Claude de Bettignies
  CHANGMAI CORPORATION

Reading 1.1

Mark E. Mendenhall, J. Stewart Black, Robert J. Jensen and Hal B. Gregersen

SEEING THE ELEPHANT: HUMAN RESOURCE MANAGEMENT CHALLENGES IN THE AGE OF GLOBALIZATION

IN THE EARLY 1800s, an American farmer who had never seen an elephant decided to travel to a nearby town where a circus was scheduled to visit. Thinking to kill two birds with one stone, he loaded his wagon with vegetables, with the intent to sell them at the town's market after the performance of the circus. On the way to town he encountered the circus retinue, which was led by an elephant. The sight of the elephant terrified his team of horses, which promptly bolted – the result being an overturned wagon and spoiled vegetables littering the road. In response to this disaster, the farmer is said to have exclaimed: "I don't give a hang, for I have seen the elephant!"

In nineteenth-century America, "seeing the elephant" denoted the encountering of an exotic phenomenon, an unequaled experience, an adventure of a lifetime, or a particularly dangerous situation. Gold prospectors planning to travel west in the 1850s announced they were "going to see the elephant". Those who returned home without making it to California claimed they had seen the "elephant's tracks" or the "elephant's tail". Gold Rush-era Californians sometimes described the phenomenon as simply "the elephant".

What is the managerial "elephant" of the twenty-first century? Is there an unequaled, heretofore unknown, exotic sight, or some attractive, yet potentially overwhelming condition that can make or break people and organizations? There is. The elephant, *globalization*, has upset the cart of traditional business rules: the new rules of globalization are often vague, unstable, counterintuitive, and full of exceptions.

The elephant and HR: When chief executive officers (CEOs) try to aggressively position their companies to be global players, they often find their efforts frustrated due to a lack of global competencies in their managerial corps. As the former CEO of Brunswick Corp., Jack Riechert, put it, "We have all the financial, technical, and product resources we need to be a dominant global player. What we lack are the human resources. We just don't have the people we need who understand global markets and players." When CEOs turn to their human resource specialists for help in developing globally competent managers and globally sophisticated HR systems, how ready are HR managers to confront the "elephant" of globalization?

To get richer insights about the challenges of globalization for HR managers, we interviewed HR executives from over 30 companies and collected surveys from executives attending several sessions at the University of Michigan Senior Human Resource Executive Program (please see Appendix A for a description of our study). We will first look at how globalization is influencing the strategic trends of the companies of these HR executives, and then we will report, and offer solutions to, what they characterized as the primary HR challenges they are facing due to globalization.

Going global: Four years ago, we asked these HR executives to describe the overall strategic orientation of their company, and what the overall strategic orientation would be in 2004. As Figure 1 illustrates, their companies are migrating away from a domestic strategic focus and toward either a balanced or global focus. In the near term, most of this movement is from a domestic to a balanced focus (i.e., essentially equal focus on both domestic and international). However, by 2004 only 10 percent expected to remain focused primarily on domestic markets.

As one HR executive of a large discount retailer put it, "From our inception we have been a US company. However, this will not be the case going forward. Growth opportunities for us are in Europe, in Asia, and in Latin America. Also, our two biggest competitors are in Europe, and we need to beat them on their own turf."

Going from a domestic to balanced to global strategic focus is not an easy process and creates various HR challenges. A quick sketch of Black & Decker Corp.'s movement provides some initial insights. Prior to 1996, Black & Decker's eastern hemisphere regional headquarters was in Maryland. This

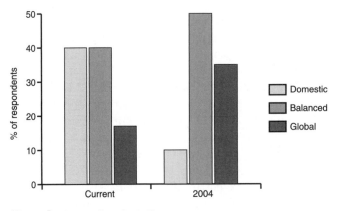

Figure 1. Strategic orientation

regional office was responsible for virtually all the countries along the Pacific Rim. The US location of their Asia Pacific regional office largely reflected the US, or domestic orientation of the company. Subsequently, Black & Decker moved the eastern hemisphere regional office, first to Singapore. This put the office closer to the regional action and increased the focus on the region. Black & Decker put a similar increase in focus on other regions of the world. This move to a more balanced (equal weight on global and domestic concerns) strategic focus involved numerous HR challenges, such as: moving people around the world on international assignments, determining the extent to which important processes such as performance management should be harmonized with head-quarters culture or with local business culture, determining cross-cultural issues associated with management development, and designing global compensation systems.

As senior executives within Black & Decker look forward to the future, they have determined that a balanced but separate domestic and international strategic focus is not ideal for the firm. While the current balance provides greater focus on global market opportunities (and competitors) the separation aspect creates duplication and does not work to capture synergies or economies of scale and scope. In the future, Black & Decker wants to better integrate its operations worldwide so that information, ideas, innovations, products, and people can move more seamlessly across the entire global organization.

How prepared are you?: Given that people and, in particular, leaders are critical to the successful movement of organizations from domestic business outlooks toward global strategic orientations, one naturally wonders how well HR executives and HR groups are prepared to meet this challenge. When asked about HR's competence at managing global issues, the executives we surveyed painted a picture that raises some concern: only about 1 percent of the executives surveyed thought that their HR staff at headquarters or in their business units were "world class" in managing global issues.

Becoming world class at managing HR issues is a challenge for even the most highly regarded companies. Even the best companies and well intentioned individuals can run aground on the unseen cultural reefs that lie in wait in the waters of global expansion. For example, when Jack Welch first took over as CEO of General Electric Co., only about 10 percent of its revenues were derived from international markets. It was a USA-centric organization. In addition to his mantra of be #1 or #2 (or get sold), he also pushed the major divisions to expand their strategic focus overseas. In response to this strategic shift, the Medical Systems division acquired companies in Japan and France. These acquisitions catapulted the division into the top position globally; however, things did not go well at first. Lack of international HR experience caused several missteps with GE's acquisition of Cie Générale de Radiologie in France. For example, during one of the initial integration meetings at a hotel in France, US managers put up English posters in the meeting room that declared, "GE is #1", and asked French managers to all wear T-shirts to the meeting with similar slogans on them. The French managers were insulted by these and other moves. As a result of these and other missteps, GE's new unit lost $25 million instead of making an anticipated $25 million in the first year after the acquisition. The second year also produced losses rather than anticipated profits. Today, the HR staff members at Medical Systems are considered to be some of the most capable anywhere. However, the case illustrates two critical points. First, even a great company can have HR staff who are not world class when it comes to global competencies. Second, lack of those competencies in advance of global strategic expansion can (and often does) lead to mistakes that cost the company money, morale, and momentum.

Bringing an HR group up to speed in terms of global competency development in time for them to enhance global strategy implementation is a stiff challenge. While a firm can decide to shift its strategic direction from a domestic to a global focus in the space of a few years, developing the required HR competencies may not be done as rapidly. It takes time for an individual HR staff or for an entire HR group to increase their global management capabilities and competencies, and this development needs to start *in advance* of the actual implementation of the firm's strategic shift. An executive with TRW Inc. pointed out the importance of this when he stressed that:

> . . . just because you have taken an international assignment to China does not mean you can effectively manage across multiple countries. For most [leaders] an international assignment is a critical developmental experience, but that is not all it takes to turn you into a global leader. This means that we must have HR people who are global long key point before we need business people; otherwise how will we identify, train, and develop business leaders?

For this HR executive, this realization came after taking part in a global leadership development program for high-potential executives in the company that involved – among other things – action-learning projects in China. The executive admitted that the experience "opened his eyes" to the real demands of managing global HR, especially in terms of leadership development. It is interesting to note that in another study we undertook a few years ago we found that only 11 percent of US HR executives had themselves lived or worked in a foreign country.

It is a troubling picture that these executives painted for us: Companies moving swiftly down the path to global strategy implementation, with HR systems and people who lack both system-wide and individual global expertise, and who have no time to adequately develop such expertise.

The "Big Five" global HR challenges: Regardless of how prepared companies are for global HR issues, they face them in real-time nevertheless. Consequently, we wanted to get a sense of what they felt were the biggest challenges they were currently wrestling with within the "context of ill preparation" discussed above. When we asked executives to identify the major challenges the HR function faced in terms of globalization concerns, the following five issues emerged:

- enhancing global business strategy
- aligning HR issues with business strategy
- designing and leading change

- building global corporate cultures
- developing global leaders

Just on the surface, these are incredible challenges, not easily met. For each one there is a long and steep learning curve; and to get to the top, you have to start early and climb hard. The question then becomes, "How do HR managers go about developing these competencies?"

DEALING WITH THE "BIG FIVE": ADVICE FOR ELEPHANT HANDLERS

From both the interviews and surveys, it was clear that these challenges were of significant importance to all executives. We start with the issue of enhancing business strategy, then move to the challenge of aligning HR practices with the strategy. From there we move to facilitating change efforts and creating effective cultures. We end where global strategies are made – with global leaders and their development.

Enhancing the creation of global business strategies

In order for the HR group to play a role in the creation and implementation of global business strategy, HR managers must focus on three important issues: (*a*) integrating global HR issues into the company's mission, (*b*) encouraging senior managers to be catalysts for integrating HR with global strategy development and implementation, and (*c*) keeping global HR issues on managers' radar screens throughout the strategy-building and implementation process.

Mission integration. Organizations that possess world-class global HR competencies ensure that the HR dimension is central to a company's global mission. "People" issues are integrated into every aspect of business operations. For example, at ExxonMobil Aviation (EMA), the managing director, John Bell, insisted from the start of the new organization that people be at the core of the mission. EMA sells a true commodity – jet fuel. Jet fuel is the same the world over. It is made to very exacting standards – so exacting that it is co-mingled at the airports in storage tanks. Shell, BP, ExxonMobil, TotalFinaElf and everyone else's jet fuel is mixed together. Consequently, as John Bell puts it, "People are our only differentiation". If EMA cannot differentiate by the quality of employees it selects and develops, it has little hope of beating competitors such as Shell or BP, which also have large refineries, pipelines, and on-airport refueling capabilities.

Another indicator of pure integration between global HR and global mission is the diminished distinction between domestic and international HR. In all aspects of its operations, Molex Inc., for example, has worked hard to break the old paradigm of domestic vs. international. It was one of the first US firms to do away with distinctions between the two concepts in the HR realm. Molex HR staffs around the world have the same titles. Its corporate culture views Molex as a global family of firms, rather than a US-based conglomerate.

Top management as catalysts. Many companies often espouse concern for global HR issues – and sometimes even mention it in their mission statements – but few companies actually have integrated that concern into their strategic planning and policy crafting processes. This integration begins with the CEO. Until Kofi Annan became the seventh Secretary-General of the United Nations, there was little concern in that organization regarding such basic human resource concerns as HR planning, staff development, or performance management. This, though the United Nations is a worldwide organization with a staff of 8,500 who represent the interests of people in 188 nations!

Since taking the reins, Secretary-General Annan has launched numerous reforms throughout the United Nations Office of Human Resources Management. Initiatives around succession planning, HR planning, managerial competency training, and performance management are now in place and are taking hold in an organizational culture that was not historically focused on employee development. All because the CEO led the change, and believed in its importance.

Keeping global HR on managers' radar screens. To lead global HR change initiatives, top management must first understand the link between organizational performance and the social capital of the firm. The senior HR staff must constantly reinforce this truth – even if the CEO and other senior executives "get it". As the HR director at a large Canadian steel company put it,

> Much of my job is capturing and keeping the attention of senior management. These guys are steel guys. They pay attention to hard things not soft, so I have to demonstrate to them that people issues deliver both hard financial losses when they are not right and tangible gains when they are.

This mantra must be communicated constantly – along with the hard evidence to support its claims. Over time, a constant focus on the inextricable relationship between HR issues and productivity will pay dividends, as has been demonstrated in a number of recent domestic and international academic studies.

Aligning HR processes and programs with overall global business strategy

The natural challenge that flows from a foundation of valuing social capital in an organization is the need to align HR processes and programs with global business strategies – and vice versa! To do so, it is critical to focus on three things: maintaining a global vs. a headquarters-based perspective, paying attention to HR issues during strategy implementation, and balancing local vs. global issues in HR policies.

Maintain a global perspective, not a headquarters-based perspective. Rather than respond in a region-specific way to economic fluctuations by downsizing or expanding its human capital, Molex views both its business operations and social capital from a truly global perspective. For example, from mid-1997 to mid-1998, the American and European regions of Molex's operations performed very well, while its Asian operations struggled. In the past, however, Molex's Asian operations had been cash cows. In responding to the Asian financial crisis, Molex's CEO, Frederick A. Krehbiel, addressed all Molex employees at the company's annual worldwide telecommunications meeting with the following message:

> Let us celebrate the advantages of being global. Despite the fact that the Southeast Asia operations are down, the company has made enough money elsewhere to give salary increases to everyone. There have been no layoffs. In fact, we have spent money in all of our regions to make needed improvements to operations. In the past, the productivity of our Asian operations allowed us to improve our operations in Europe and America. Now it is time for Europe and America to carry the rest of the world, as Asia carried them in the past. (Solomon, "Brace for Change", in *Workforce* [January 1999], p. 10)

Pay attention to HR issues during implementation of global strategy. The acquisition of Parker Pen by Gillette Co. in 1993 triggered a need to strategically restructure the organization of all units of Gillette (razors and toiletries, Duracell batteries, Oral-B dental care, and Braun appliances) into geographic units, each with a single sales force, to be more responsive to local needs. Gillette's senior executives wisely paid attention to human resource issues during the strategic planning and implementation of the restructuring, and because they did, the organizational transformation went more smoothly than it otherwise would have. For example, in Singapore, it was decided that all the Parker Pen and Gillette units were to be combined into one central "campus" rather than be spread out over the island. Parker employees who worked on the east side of the island threatened to quit if the campus was placed on the west side of the island, where the majority of the Gillette employees lived and worked. Conversely, the Gillette employees resented the idea that they might be asked to travel to the east side of the island to work. Rumors, fears, and poor morale began to fester, as everyone wondered what headquarters would do.

Rather than simply basing the location decision on the concentration of existing facilities, the preferences of senior managers, or the relative worth or power of dominant product units, Gillette senior management instead plotted on a map of Singapore the home of every single Gillette employee. The executives then chose a new site for the campus (rather than using existing facilities) based on the geographic location of all of Gillette's Singaporean employees. Valuable employees whose competencies (and customers!) could not easily be replaced were retained. Strategy and HR issues fused into the creation of a business decision that was more ideal than if it had been based on pragmatic organizational criteria alone.

Balance local vs. global issues in HR policy-making. A senior HR executive with DuPont Co., who has experience in Australia, USA, and several Asian countries, including Japan, explained that "even though DuPont has gone to global shared services in HR, it is impossible to have everything be the same the world over". Like many companies, DuPont has restructured human resources so that a vast majority of its activities are shared services done for all business units. While this works well in large countries with significant business operations, such as the US or Germany, it works less well in smaller countries where DuPont's businesses are not equally invested, such as Thailand. With market conditions so different in Thailand from, say, Japan, it is hard to run a shared recruiting service effectively out of a single regional office in Singapore. Yet the challenge of not duplicating activities, and therefore costs, is significant. In this case, DuPont has worked hard to balance these tensions. It has discovered that despite the differences at upper managerial levels where they typically use search firms to help them with external recruiting, it is best to do this on a coordinated basis across countries. In this way they can leverage their size to get better prices and service from search firms. It also helps them avoid reinventing the wheel on a country-by-country basis. However, when it comes to less skilled line employees, the benefits of a local approach outweigh those of coordination.

Assisting in leading global change initiatives

A primary role of the HR function in any organization is to assist in crafting and implementing organizational change initiatives. The development of policies that actually help people adjust to and learn the new skills required for global organizational change is absolutely necessary if a company is to be successful in the global marketplace. To pull this off, HR managers must focus on enabling people not only to carry out the change initiative, but also to take the lead in creating and implementing global HR change initiatives.

Enable people to change – don't just tell them to. China Light and Power (CLP) in Hong Kong is expanding from a domestic-oriented, government-controlled monopoly to a market-driven, global enterprise. It is a significant transformation, to say the least. The change in managers' focus from "what will the next set of government regulations be?" to "what are the market trends, who are our competitors, and what are they doing?" is a major challenge. It is, of course, not enough to say to these managers, "CHANGE!" Even if they all wanted to (and they don't), and even if they were all capable of changing on their own (and they're not), there is no guarantee they would move in the right direction.

Consequently, CLP implemented a set of new leadership competencies and communicated them to all managers. It then instituted a rather rigorous assessment program so that managers could get an idea of where they were relative to each of the competencies. Finally, those with the highest potential were put through a multi-phase, six-month program that included both traditional classroom education and study trips to deregulated electrical power markets, team projects, and an interactive (team-based) computer simulation of market competition. As a senior director of development explained, "If we don't show them the path and give them the tools, it's a bit unfair to let them go if they don't make the grade."

Taking the lead in creating and implementing global HR change initiatives. The corporate HR team of the Royal Dutch/Shell Group is an excellent example of an HR group that has created and led a global change initiative. In 1993, Shell, perceiving trouble among its expatriate staff, sent out a survey to 17,000 current and former Shell expatriates and their spouses. Two major problems were identified: loss of spouses' careers and separation from children who had to return to their home countries for secondary education. These two problems were causing significant damage to international mobility, productivity, and global leadership development.

Six Shell task forces attacked the problem and implemented major policy changes in 1995. To assist in expatriate children's schooling, Shell now selects a local primary school and works with the school to develop and adopt a curriculum that will prepare the expatriate children for secondary schooling in their home countries. Where this is not feasible and the number of expatriates in a specific location meet a threshold figure, Shell now builds and staffs a company elementary school. Traditionally, at the secondary school level, many expatriates had to send their children (from age 11) to boarding schools in their home countries. Shell has now contracted with International School Services to evaluate each locale and to strengthen existing schools by ensuring curriculum development, funding for lab equipment, etc. These curriculum-enhanced Shell programs are now in place at 800 secondary schools in 94 countries.

To meet the career needs of spouses and partners, Shell developed "The Outpost" in 1995. Located in The Hague, it now has 40 local hubs around the world. The Outpost hubs, run by spouses of Shell employees, provide a rich information network about job openings, career advice, and support services on a within-country and between-country basis. The central Outpost has a database of roughly 11,000 families who have indicated that they are willing to share their insights and experiences with others. The Outpost matches new expatriates with existing expatriates, organizes welcome committees for new expatriates, publishes a magazine to help expatriates, and provides books and materials on topics of interest to expatriate families.

The teams' work has freed high-potential managers to pursue assignments overseas, which enhances their global business skills. And building global business competencies among Shell's managers aids directly in the achievement of Shell's global business strategies.

Strategically assist in building global corporate cultures

The need to develop a global corporate culture that is strong enough to maintain a consistency of important company norms across nations, yet is also flexible enough to allow for local preferences in conducting business, is a difficult challenge. One way to achieve this balance is to focus on developing rituals that reinforce aspects of the corporate culture that top management wants to preserve. Another approach is to pay attention to local and cultural sensitivities and respect them despite the existence of a global, corporate culture.

Cement "global" rituals. People need symbolic reminders of the global scope and focus of the company because the vast majority of employees face local issues on a daily basis. Without the symbolic reminders, it is easy for day-to-day local demands to drive out global perspective. To tackle this dynamic, Molex has developed communications rituals to cement and reinforce the corporate norms they deem most important. Twice a month, each unit around the world has a communication meeting that lasts about an hour, but in some cases can go longer. Molex employees are informed of the status of the unit's performance and other issues that apply to that Molex unit.

Molex also conducts annual communication meetings. These meetings are attended in each unit by the chairman, the COO (chief operating officer), the executive vice president, the corporate vice president (VP) of HR, senior executives of the local entity, and senior executives from the region. Kathi Regas, corporate VP of HR for Molex, notes,

> Our annual communications meetings ensure that our employees know they're a part of something much bigger than their local entities. They know our history, our performance, and our plans for the future. This, combined with frequent contact among our employees from entities around the world, and common practices, helps maintain our culture and strengthens a global team of employees. (J. Laabs, "Molex Makes Global HR Look Easy", in *Workforce* [March 1999], p. 45)

Respect local cultural sensitivities. While great benefits can come from a unifying global corporate culture, local employees can and do resist the firm's culture if they view it as cultural imperialism vs. competitive unification. Although Black & Decker stumbled with its strategy for DeWalt power tools in Asia (which we describe just a bit later in this article), it was successful in folding Asia into one of the critical elements of its global corporate culture through sensitivity and respect for local values.

Black & Decker believed that one of the keys to its success had been a culture of direct and candid developmental feedback to managers. It used a 360-degree performance appraisal process for gathering feedback for managers on how they were doing relative to their bosses', their peers', and subordinates' perceptions. When it moved its eastern hemisphere headquarters from Maryland to Singapore, it also wanted to implement this developmental process.

As Black & Decker talked with local Asian employees, it became clear that it was a bit "counter-cultural" to give feedback (especially anything negative) to one's boss. When asked if employees felt bosses could benefit from the feedback, if employees wanted to give the feedback, and if they wanted to receive feedback, they almost universally said *yes*. The real cultural issue turned out to be face-to-face encounters and confidentiality. The HR director at the time, Robyn Mingle, created a system whereby comments from subordinates were submitted to HR, transcribed from hand to electronic format, and "scrubbed" to ensure that any hints in the comments as to who might have made them were removed. Then the original handwritten comments were shredded.

Black & Decker thus preserved a unifying element of its global corporate culture and values (i.e., 360-degree feedback and constant improvement) and at the same time respected the elements of the local culture that did not fit the exact way the practice was implemented in the US. As Robyn Mingle put it, "The critical thing is the end result – do you preserve the fundamental value? The fact that we had to implement it a bit differently in Asia than the US is fine and in fact necessary."

Developing future leaders

It takes executives and managers with global mindsets, global competencies, and global experience to develop and implement global strategic initiatives. One major function of HR in the twenty-first century will be to transform domestic, ethnocentric managers into global managers.

Figure 2 provides an interesting perspective from our sample of HR executives regarding the influence of strategic focus on global leadership development. For example, executives whose companies currently have an international strategic focus view developing global leaders and managing an effective global corporate culture as being more important than those from companies with a domestic strategic focus. It is likely that global leaders were seen as the most important issue because – despite organizational structures, information systems, and the like – it is individual leaders and teams of executives that make decisions that either help or hurt the company's competitive position. In our talks with executives in these internationally focused companies, some general reasons surfaced that explained this state of affairs.

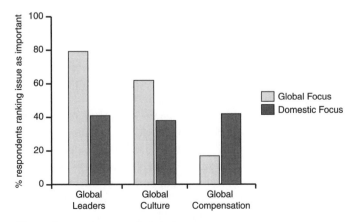

Figure 2. Importance of global issues

An HR executive from Black & Decker explained how the company suffered in Asia because the executives who were sent there had little previous international experience. As a consequence, in launching their leading power tool brand, DeWalt, in Asia they took the same approach that had worked miracles in the US.

The successful marketing strategy in the US called for taking the tools out to job sites and letting workers use the tools. This strategy "pulled" the tools into the market because after the firsthand experience with the tools either the workers bought the tools themselves or influenced their bosses to buy them. When done in Asia, literally hundreds of workers would come down off the construction sites and try out the tools. Like their American counterparts, they were also impressed with the tools' functionality. However, unlike American counterparts, they did not own or buy their tools, and they had zero influence over their bosses or the company's tool purchasing decisions. Consequently, while the marketing events generated large crowds, they did not generate sales.

Developing global leaders is critical to global business success. To a great extent, executives interviewed were of the opinion that the success of a company's efforts in a new region or country could be no greater than the international savvy of the key leaders making strategic decisions for that market. One of the capabilities consistently mentioned was being sensitive to cultural and business differences and recognizing that what worked in one country may not work in another.

How, then, can global leaders be developed?

Expatriate assignments as vehicles for global leadership development. A plethora of social science research clearly indicates that to develop global leadership competencies in people, companies must make sure that managers have real global experiences. Thus, the strategic use of expatriates is critical in the development of global leaders. In fact, in a separate study, international assignments were found to be the single most powerful development experience. This may be part of the reason that we have seen a number of companies – such as 3M, Chevron Corp., Citicorp, GE, Nokia AB oyj, Shell Oil Co., and Texas Instruments Inc. – add an international assignment as one of the experiences managers need in order to be promoted to senior, corporate executive positions. John Pepper, recent chairman of Procter & Gamble Co., put it this way, "My assignment to Italy when I was a young manager was one of the most important events in my entire career. It totally changed how I looked at the business. It also laid a solid foundation for when I later had responsibilities for our European operations. This in turn proved invaluable when I became CEO."

In particular, international assignments help leaders develop one of the most critical capabilities required in a global corporation – balancing global integration and local responsiveness. Mr. Pepper talked about his experience in Europe trying to introduce Visor laundry detergent into countries where there were different types of washing machines. Simplified, some countries had "top loaders" and others had "front loaders". While both cleaned clothes, the detergent tended to distribute unevenly in front loaders. Although they could have spent literally millions of dollars reformulating the detergent to work in front-loading washing machines, instead they created a perforated plastic ball into which the detergent was placed and then tossed in with the clothes at the beginning of the wash cycle. As the ball tumbled with the clothes, the detergent flowed out. This invention allowed P&G to meet local differences and at the same time spread the development costs over a much larger revenue base and thus bring the per-unit development costs down.

Mr. Pepper explained that without these sorts of experiences as a leader outside your home market, you either take an imperial perspective as a CEO that your way can and should work everywhere in the world, or a fortress mentality that assumes that nothing from the outside can possibly be right for your market.

Create training programs that simulate expatriate assignments. Many companies are beginning to pay attention to developing leaders who have global competencies. Nokia, Shell, Unilever Bestfoods, TRW Inc., 3M, and the United Nations are examples of just a few companies that are consciously trying to develop global leadership competencies in their managers. One of the more novel approaches is that of the Union Bank of Switzerland (UBS).

Managers of the Union Bank of Switzerland have participated in a project named *Seiten Wechsel* ("PerspectiveChange"), established by the Schweizerische Gemeinnützige Gesellschaft, a nonprofit organization that brings together business executives with less privileged members of society, with the goal to further their mutual understanding. The purpose of this program is to expose managers to subcultures within their own country during short, compressed time periods. Managers of UBS were for a short period of time (usually about two weeks) assigned to social welfare projects that required them to look after homeless people, work with juvenile delinquents, care for HIV-patients who were terminally ill, or live together with immigrants seeking asylum. All involved benefited from the program – the people received much needed support and help, while the managers learned how to perceive the world through the eyes of people quite different from them.

According to the managers who participated in the program, "PerspectiveChange" helped them to reduce subjective barriers and prejudices, learn more about themselves, broaden their horizons, and increase their interpersonal skills – all competencies of global leadership. In addition, the program motivated managers to assume greater responsibility for those who need help; 60 percent of participants have supported the institution in which they volunteered after the program ended.

By exposing employees to subcultures within their own country, a foreign assignment can be simulated – they are immersed in a foreign culture at a relatively deep level, and they have to integrate into a different social system, function effectively in a strange environment, and deal with cultural diversity.

CONCLUSION

Clearly, some have seen the elephant of globalization and are hard at work changing themselves and their companies. However, there is increasing evidence that those who have not seen the elephant may not have a choice to avoid it for much longer. Given the steep and long learning curve for mastering international challenges such as enhancing strategy, aligning the organization with the strategy, facilitating global changes, creating an effective global culture, and developing global leaders, HR executives must lead – not lag – the global strategic focus of their firms.

To the extent that people are key to effective globalization and to the extent that international assignments are one of the most powerful developmental experiences, our research identified a shortage of HR executives with international assignment backgrounds. Some HR executives whom we interviewed suggested that this shortage existed in their companies because HR had been treated largely as a "local issue" (i.e., hiring and paying local employees). Others suggested that the perceived value of HR just did not offset the costs of sending an HR executive on an international assignment. Whatever the reasons for HR executives not having international assignment experience, it seems that this is a specific issue to change in the future.

Finally, to the extent that capable global leaders formulate strategy, implement structures, align the organization, champion needed changes, and determine and reinforce a unifying global culture, it is little wonder that those HR executives most experienced with globalization also ranked the challenge of global leader development as most important. The process of identifying and developing global leaders cannot be implemented overnight, nor will the results magically appear the next quarter. Consequently, building global leadership is perhaps the most important and hardest of the challenges, because working on it almost always precedes the obvious organizational need for it. It is quite easy to get people to jump off a burning oilrig platform, but much harder when they cannot yet smell smoke. This inherent resistance may in fact be why HR competency usually lags strategic focus.

Thus HR executives must lead globalization in part by example. If they have not identified and developed competent global HR talent, how much credibility – in advance of globalization – will they have for creating and implementing systems that identify and develop global leaders? Yet, if HR executives wait for the globalization demand to fully manifest itself as the company moves into new markets, acquires foreign companies, enters into joint ventures with partners abroad and then sees those efforts fail, HR executives will likely find their capabilities falling short of the demands. As "people problems" are identified as key causes for faltering globalization efforts, HR executives report to us that they increasingly see the finger of blame pointing at them.

Fundamentally, what we conclude from this study is that the largest globalization challenge HR executives confront is anticipatory change – changing before there is clear demand. While the challenges of anticipatory change are not unique to globalization, the need for it that globalization creates is nevertheless inescapable.

APPENDIX A. SIDEBAR: DESCRIPTION OF STUDY

The data presented here were gathered from both interviews and surveys. We interviewed HR executives in 30 firms headquartered in Europe (7 firms), North America (18), and Asia (5). These firms were selected based on ratings of a separate academic group and executive committee of a leading human resource professional association. We also conducted a survey commissioned by the Human Resource Planning Society. The survey was conducted at three sessions of the Senior HR Executive Program at the University of Michigan. HR executives from 84 out of 95 companies represented at the program participated in the study. The 84 companies had an average number of employees of 73,000 per company. The average firm size, in terms of annual revenue, was approximately $18 billion per year; all companies had operations outside of their home country, and most had substantial global operations. Of the respondents, 59.5 percent represented companies based in North America; 21.4 percent were based in Europe; and 16.7 percent were based in Asia, Australia, and South America.

ACKNOWLEDGMENT

The authors appreciate the funding provided for this research project by the Human Resource Planning Society and Brigham Young University's Center for International Business Education and Research (CIBER).

SELECTED BIBLIOGRAPHY

For a comprehensive discussion of the importance of human resource management functions in globalizing managerial cadres, see: J. S. Black, A. Morrison, and H. B. Gregersen, *Global Explorers: The Next Generation of Leaders* (New York: Routledge, 1999); P. Evans, V. Pucik, and J. Barsoux, *The Global Challenge: Frameworks for International Human Resource Management* (New York: McGraw-Hill, 2002); M. E. Mendenhall, T. M. Kühlmann, and G. K. Stahl, *Developing Global Business Leaders: Policies, Processes, and Innovations* (Westport, Conn.: Quorum Books, 2001).

For a detailed account of the relationship between HR issues and productivity, as has been demonstrated in a number of recent domestic and international academic studies, please see B. E. Becker and B. Gerhart, "Human Resources and Organizational Performance: Progress and Prospects", *Academy of Management Journal*, 39(4) (special issue: *Human Resources and Organizational Performance*), 779–801. See also B. E. Becker and M. A. Huselid, "High Performance Work Systems and Firm Performance: A Synthesis of Research and Managerial Implications", *Research in Personnel and Human Resources Management*, 1998, 16, 53–101; B. E. Becker, M. A. Huselid, P. S. Pickus, and M. Spratt, "HR as a Source of Shareholder Value: Research and Recommendations", *Human Resource Management*, 1997, 36, 39–47; M. Carpenter, G. Sanders, and H. B. Gregersen, "Bundling Human Capital: The Impact of International Assignment Experience on CEO Pay and Multinational Firm Performance", *Academy of Management Journal*, 2001, 44(3), 493–512; and M. A. Huselid, S. E. Jackson, and R. S. Schuler, "Technical and Strategic Human Resource Management Effectiveness as Determinants of Firm Performance", *Academy of Management Journal*, 1997, 40, 171–88.

To read more about some of the case examples described in this article, see: J. S. Black, H. Gregersen, M. Mendenhall, and L. Stroh, *Globalizing People through International Assignments* (New York: Addison-Wesley, 1999); C. M. Solomon, "Brace for Change", *Workforce*, January, 1999, 6–10; R. M. Kanter and T. D. Dretler, "Global Strategy and Its Impact on Local Operations: Lessons from Gillette Singapore", *Academy of Management Executive*, 1998, 12(4), 60–8; V. Frazee, "Tearing Down Roadblocks", *Workforce*, February, 1998, 50–5; J. Laabs, "Molex Makes Global HR Look Easy", *Workforce*, March, 1999, 42–6; C. Bingham, T. Felin, and J. S. Black, "An Interview with John Pepper: What it Takes to Be a Global Leader", *Human Resource Management*, 2000, 39 (Summer/Fall), 287–92; and M. E. Mendenhall and G. K. Stahl, "Expatriate Training and Development: Where Do We Go from Here?" *Human Resource Management*, 2000, 39 (Summer/Fall), 251–65.

Finally, for more information regarding the historical phenomenon of "seeing the elephant", please see: J. Levy, *They Saw the Elephant: Women in the California Gold Rush* (Norman, Okla: University of Oklahoma Press, 1992).

Reading 1.2

Allan Bird and Schon Beechler

THE LINK BETWEEN BUSINESS STRATEGY AND INTERNATIONAL HUMAN RESOURCE MANAGEMENT PRACTICES

INTRODUCTION

RESEARCH ON INTERNATIONAL HRM has blossomed in recent years yet much of this research has been in the area of staffing. Reasons for focusing almost exclusively on this area, especially among practitioners, appear to stem from the high costs of making poor staffing decisions. Two issues which have been extensively researched are these: (1) staffing of parent country nationals vs. host or third country nationals; and (2) appropriate criteria for selecting expatriates. Some limited attention has also been directed at related expatriate issues, including compensation and type of training for expatriates.

In addition to research on expatriates, a few writers have examined the role of HRM in formulating and implementing business strategy at an international level. The focus of this work is on HRM's role in the formal design of business strategy, as well as its role as an enhancer of strategy, concentrating specifically on HRM's role in implementation.

In the general literature most work linking strategy and HRM has been prescriptive and focused on domestic settings, yet clear associations between strategy and human resource activities have been found. We can classify studies of linkages between human resource management practices and business strategy into two categories. The first group conceptualizes strategy–HRM linkages in a broad, macro perspective. These authors use one of a variety of strategic typologies and then relate specific strategies to general categories of HRM policy.

Porter, for example, identifies two generic strategies: (1) overall cost leadership; and (2) differentiation. In his discussion of the skills, resources, and organizational requirements needed for each strategy, Porter alludes to a strategy–manager match and considers some of the HRM policy implications that grow out of this match. A *cost leadership strategy* is based on the experience cost curve concept. This strategy places the company in a low-cost position where it can earn above-average returns despite strong competition. Under a cost leadership strategy, job requirements are those of establishing tight cost controls, making frequent reports, enforcing strict rules, and establishing incentives based on quantitative methods.

By contrast, a *differentiation strategy* is a strategy based on distinguishing the company's products or services from those of competitors. By providing unique and distinctive non-price value, the company can insulate itself through customer loyalty. A differentiation strategy requires an emphasis on coordination, incentives based on qualitative methods, and the maintenance of quality and technological leadership.

Macro perspectives, such as Porter's, are useful in delineating possible strategy–human resources linkages, yet they lack specificity and fall short in their regard for the myriad details of HRM policy and practice. A remedy to this shortcoming is found in studies that have a micro perspective, attempting to trace relationships between strategy and individual HRM policies. Micro research, for example, proposes specific linkages between business strategies and selection practices or staffing and training practices that are likely to be found under different career systems. Mainstream HRM has adopted a micro perspective, attempting to trace relationships between strategy and individual HRM policies. Studies in this category often utilize one of the macro perspectives as a foundation for their more specific analyses.

However, while the existing research employing a macro perspective lacks specificity, studies in the second category of micro-focused approaches suffer a shortcoming of their own. They seek to identify linkages which extend from business strategy down to actual human resource policy applications; however, generally they focus only on a single function, failing to take into account how business strategy might influence other, related HRM functions.

BACKGROUND

Both micro and macro approaches linking strategy and HRM fail to explicitly recognize the assumptions upon which they are predicated. There are two general assumptions which underlie all models connecting HRM practices and business strategy. First, it is assumed that the selection and mix of human resource practices are determined by the specific strategy a firm adopts, which is itself influenced by environmental constraints such as government regulations, competitor actions, etc. Second, it is assumed that firms achieving a tighter fit between alignment of environmental constraints, strategy requirements, and HRM practices will perform better than those that do not.

Failure to recognize these two assumptions has led researchers to ignore some of the complexities inherent in multinational firms. For example, consistency found between a parent company and its foreign subsidiaries with regard to business strategy and HRM policies has often been assumed. Differences between the environment of a parent organization and those of its foreign subsidiaries, however, may create strong pressures for the firm to modify its local operations in each country. This is particularly true with respect to HRM policies. Labor markets, union influence, worker skill level and skill variety, along with legal requirements relating to hiring, compensation, and dismissal practices are all likely to differ significantly from one country to the next.

The second contingency assumption specifies that effective performance is a result of the alignment of internal operations to the external environment. Given the potential cross-national variations cited above, multinational firms that achieve internal consistency (between parent and foreign subsidiary) would appear to run a high risk of misalignment with the external environment. Looking at these two assumptions together, the implication for multinational firms is one of competing pressures: internal pressures for consistency between strategy and HRM practices, and external pressures for consistency between HRM practices and the environment.

Recognition of competing pressures on HRM practices is a return to the well-documented dilemma of "standardization versus differentiation" that pervades debates of how to administer international operations. There is a dynamic tension between the need for the overseas affiliate to adapt to local conditions versus the need to integrate across the MNE as a whole. To date, most approaches have suggested that resolution of this dilemma is determined by the relative strength of the competing forces.

A STRATEGIC FRAMEWORK

We propose an alternative approach that focuses on the *extent to which a MNE firm requires consistency* between parent and subsidiary business strategy and between parent and subsidiary HRM practices. In doing so, we suggest that these twin needs for consistency are determined by (1) the strategies that firms adopt; and (2) the nature of the international competition in which they are involved. Internal and external pressures are filtered by two strategic choices that MNEs make. Firms decide on the strategy they will pursue and the domain within which they will pursue it.

The environment–business strategy match

One way of viewing the external environment of MNEs is to identify the nature of international competition in the industry in which a firm is involved. There are two types of industry competition. A *multidomestic* industry is one in which competition in a given country is essentially independent of competition in other countries. For example, the soft drink industry in Japan is not influenced by competition in the soft drink industry in China. Insurance and retailing are characteristic multidomestic industries. By contrast, an industry such as that of commercial aircraft manufacturing involves competition where activities in one country have a significant influence on activities in another. For example, competition in the petroleum industry occurs across nations, with oil wells in one country, refineries and processing facilities in another, and various end-users located in those two countries as well as others. Industries of this type are labeled *global*.

Differences between the two types of competition are reflected in the varying demands for coordination that each imposes. Global industries exhibit greater coordination needs than do multidomestic industries. The need for coordination implies pressure for internal consistency.

While MNE environments can be classified into global versus multidomestic types, firms' strategic orientations can also be classified in terms of orientation with regard to two broad types: *cost leadership* and *product differentiation*. A cost leadership strategy, as alluded to earlier, seeks to achieve competitive advantage by being the least-cost producer of a product, while a product differentiation strategy seeks competitive advantage by providing unique value to a product.

Originally these two strategic archetypes were put forward as mutually exclusive. A firm could pursue a cost leadership strategy, for example, only at the exclusion of a product differentiation strategy. Indeed, "being stuck in the middle" was considered one of the weakest positions a firm could occupy. However, recent research concludes that a single firm can successfully pursue both strategies.

Simultaneous efforts at cost leadership and product differentiation do not, however, suggest equal weighting between the two. Indeed, though changes in environmental pressures may encourage firms to adopt a combined strategy, organizational imprinting – locking into a particular view of the environment early in an organization's life – and the development of distinctive competencies within a firm may result in a persistent bias toward one or the other. For example, Sony and Matsushita both seek to compete on the basis of cost and product variety. Nevertheless, Sony's roots and corporate culture help maintain a preference for differentiation over cost. Similarly, when push comes to shove for Matsushita, the choice is in favor of cost.

Because the cost-differentiation distinction remains persistent in practice, it can be usefully employed in discussions if cost leadership and product differentiation are thought of as opposite ends of a continuum. Consequently, firms may locate themselves at any point along the continuum that reflects the mix of cost and differentiation strategies they are pursuing.

Since a strategy of cost leadership seeks to achieve competitive advantage by being the least-cost producer of a product, then this strategy requires a firm to focus on functional policies. Under a cost leadership strategy, internal operations of a firm command attention and the drive is for internal efficiency.

A product differentiation strategy, on the other hand, seeks competitive advantage through the ability of a firm to provide unique value to a product, one that will be more localized in terms of its appeal to a particular foreign market or segment. Using a strategy of differentiation, firms are less concerned with cost and more concerned with identifying what special value they are able to add. A differentiation strategy requires a firm to develop an external focus, to be intimately aware of what its customers desire.

When a MNE's strategic orientation is considered in combination with the type of international competition in which it is involved, we can map out the requirements for consistency. As shown in Figure 1, the four combinations of MNE strategic orientation and international competition exhibit their own unique requirements for consistency between the parent company and the overseas subsidiary.

Pursuing a cost leadership strategy in an industry characterized by multi-domestic competition generates the highest levels of stress on the parent–subsidiary relationship. The strategy of cost leadership, and its accompanying internal focus on efficiency, creates strong pressures for standardization in the business unit's strategy across countries. At the same time, the multi-domestic nature of the industry provides strong encouragement for the firm to adapt to local conditions in order to compete with local and multinational competitors.

Firms pursuing a cost leadership strategy in an industry where competition is global, though experiencing strong pressures for internal consistency, will feel lower levels of pressure to conform to the myriad local external environments of its subsidiary operations. This is not to suggest that environmental constraints and pressures will be unimportant for MNEs in this quadrant. Rather, pressures will be lower relative to firms in the multidomestic–cost leadership quadrant which must respond to local competitor actions.

STRATEGIC ORIENTATION

	Cost	**Differentiation**
Multidomestic	• Strong pressure for consistency between parent and subsidiary strategy; • Strong pressure for consistency with local external environments	• Weak pressure for consistency between parent and subsidiary strategy; • Strong pressure for consistency with local external environments
International competition		
Global	• Strong pressure for consistency between parent and subsidiary strategy; • Weak pressure for consistency with local external environments	• Weak pressure for consistency between parent and subsidiary strategy; • Weak pressure for consistency with local external environments

Figure 1. The pressures for consistency resulting from MNE strategic orientation and the nature of international competition

Pursuing a differentiation strategy in an industry characterized by multi-domestic competition leads to low levels of stress on the parent–subsidiary relationship. The strategy of differentiation and its accompanying external focus aimed at providing unique value to its customers generate weaker pressures for standardization across countries. At the same time, the multidomestic nature of competition suggests that a firm should adapt to local conditions.

By contrast, a differentiation strategy in an industry where competition is global affords MNEs with the widest range of latitude in consistency requirements. Internal pressures for alignment of parent and subsidiary strategy are lower than for firms following a cost leadership strategy. Simultaneously, the global nature of the industry in which the MNE competes suggests that pressures to adapt to the local external environment will also be relatively weak.

Regardless of whether a firm competes in a multidomestic or global competitive environment, the efficiency orientation of a cost leadership strategy places greater emphasis on internal consistency than does a differentiation strategy. Second, localization pressures associated with a multidomestic competitive environment make it harder for MNEs to achieve consistency than in a global competitive environment. Therefore, consistency between parent and subsidiary business strategies will have a greater impact on firm performance in MNEs employing a cost leadership rather than a differentiation strategy. Moreover, firms competing in a multidomestic competitive environment will experience greater difficulty in achieving consistency between parent and subsidiary business strategies than firms competing in a global competitive environment.

The business strategy–HRM strategy match

If a MNE's performance is based on its capacity to internally align its operations in a way that allows it to match environmental constraints, then there must be a way to determine whether or not a firm is properly aligned with its environment. More than any other function within a MNE, the management of human resources is decentralized. With the exception of matters related to expatriates and international assignments, the vast majority of HRM affairs are handled at the level of the subsidiary. Consequently, a consideration of business strategy–HRM strategy linkages must necessarily shift attention away from a MNE's business strategy at the parent level and its position in international competition to a focus on how these two factors interact with subsidiary-level business strategy to influence the choice of HRM strategy.

At the subsidiary level, the requirement for internal consistency may be interpreted as the degree of integration with the parent company necessary for success. For example, due to strong pressures for internal consistency and relatively weak pressures for external consistency we would expect subsidiaries of MNEs competing in global industries with a cost leadership strategy to be highly integrated with the parent. On the other hand, subsidiaries of MNEs pursuing a product differentiation strategy in multidomestic industries are more likely to be less integrated with the parent.

Human resource management strategies

Business strategy determines how a firm competes in a given business. Firms select business strategies in accordance both with evaluations they make about the environment in which they wish to compete and the resources available within the firm. In order to develop and implement a business strategy, however, it is necessary to break it down into its various components or to develop functional strategies. These functional strategies are further decomposed into policies which, when implemented, become practice.

Policies can be thought of as decision rules. They are procedures that organization members are expected to follow. Practices, on the other hand, are less formal than policies and can be thought of as the actual decisions taken by organization members. Practices thus reflect those procedures that are actually carried out. In the international context, for example, a MNE may have a worldwide policy of equitable pay schemes for all of its employees, but how that policy is translated locally can vary from country to country. Thus, for a single firm, practices may differ across countries while the policy remains consistent.

Our framework predicts that if a firm's strategy is congruent with the external environment, firm performance will be higher than if its strategy does not match the environment. However, consistency between a plan (strategy) and the external environment is only a first step. It does not directly predict firm performance. Rather, firm performance is determined by the application of the plan, through the implementation of functional policies, including those contained in a HRM strategy.

A number of classification schemes have been suggested for categorizing HRM strategies. One widely used typology defines three types of HRM strategies. A *utilizer strategy* deploys the human resources of the firm as efficiently as possible through: (1) the acquisition and dismissal of personnel in accordance with the short-term needs of the firm; (2) the matching of employee skill to specific task requirements. An *accumulator strategy* builds up the human resources of the firm through: (1) the acquisition of personnel with large, latent potential; (2) the development of that latent potential over time in a manner consistent with the needs of the organization. A *facilitator strategy* is focused on new knowedge and new knowledge creation. It seeks to develop the human resources of the firm as effectively as possible through the acquisition of self-motivated personnel and the encouragement and support of personnel to develop, on their own, the skills and knowledge which they, the employees, believe are important.

Determination of the appropriate HRM strategy for a given subsidiary can be achieved by assessing the intersection of a subsidiary's business strategy with its degree of integration with the parent. Appropriate combinations are shown in Figure 2.

Because a utilizer HRM strategy helps to maintain a lean workforce by acquiring or dismissing employees as and when skills are required, this strategy is more appropriate to a cost leadership business strategy. The utilizer strategy is effective not only because of its efficiency orientation, but also because of its high level of flexibility, making it easier to fit subsidiary human resources with the demands of the parent (high integration). With decreasing integration, the

STRATEGIC ORIENTATION

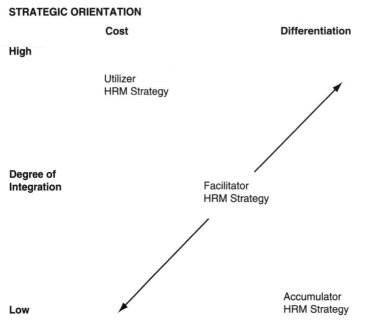

Figure 2. The implications for HRM strategy of subsidiary strategic orientation and degree of integration between subsidiary and MNE

utilizer strategy may still remain somewhat effective. However, as pressures for local adaptation increase, the subsidiary is less able to implement a utilizer strategy, particularly if it is not in line with local norms and customs.

A facilitator strategy is appropriate in a wide range of circumstances because it can handle HRM demands along both dimensions. The facilitator is qualitatively different from the utilizer and the accumulator in that it seeks to support new knowledge creation. Complex and evolving human resource demands, resulting from strong pressures in opposing directions for both strategic orientation and integration, call for an evolutionary, learning orientation.

An accumulator HRM strategy facilitates the flexibility required under a differentiation strategy by providing an excess pool of employees with latent potential which can be tapped as needed. An effective accumulator strategy would be easiest to pursue under conditions of low need for integration with the parent. As the demand for integration rises, the accumulator strategy breaks down because of the increasing influence of the parent company which stem from its desire to exercise tighter control as a result of the subsidiary's increased centrality to the MNE's overall operations.

We would expect that those subsidiaries which match their HRM strategy to their combination of business strategy and degree of integration with the parent will perform better than those that do not. The following briefly summarizes the main ideas developed so far:

1. Among subsidiaries employing cost leadership business strategies and having a high degree of integration with the parent, those which adopt a

utilizer HRM strategy will perform better than those that employ an accumulator or facilitator HRM strategy.

2. In subsidiaries employing product differentiation business strategies and having a low degree of integration with the parent, those which adopt an accumulator HRM strategy will perform better than those that employ a utilizer or facilitator HRM strategy.

3. Finally, for subsidiaries pursuing both cost leadership and differentiation strategies, those which adopt a facilitator HRM strategy will perform better than those that employ a utilizer or accumulator HRM strategy.

CONSISTENCY IN PARENT–SUBSIDIARY HRM STRATEGY ALIGNMENT

Although HRM constitutes the most decentralized of all MNE functions, it is also true that the increasing globalization of MNEs has brought about an increased desire and need for greater coordination and consistency between parent and subsidiary. Application of the above framework in assessing HRM practices in both the parent and subsidiary provides a means by which to determine the extent to which the two are in alignment. Moreover, the relationships in Figure 1 indicate that the need for parent–subsidiary alignment of HRM activities may vary depending on the strategic orientation of the MNE and the nature of international competition for the industry in which it competes.

Firms pursuing a cost leadership strategy in industries characterized by multidomestic competition will strive for consistency in HRM activities. However, they will do so in the face of strong pressures to modify their practices from one country to the next. In such a situation, consistency between parent and subsidiary in the application of a utilizer HRM strategy may not only be difficult to carry out, but lead to a loss of local competitiveness as well. For example, pressure to adapt locally is usually amplified for HRM practices because labor, blue- and white-collar combined, represents an area where cost reductions may make a significant contribution to implementing a cost leadership strategy. Adapting to local labor conditions in an attempt to obtain cost advantages, however, may introduce greater disparity between parent and subsidiary with accompanying increases in the cost of monitoring and managing the overseas operation.

By contrast, firms employing a cost leadership strategy in industries typified by global industries will seek consistency in a more amenable context. While experiencing internal demands similar to those of cost leadership firms in multidomestic industries, they pursue consistency in a setting more willing to forgive a measure of local insensitivity. Aligning a utilizer HRM strategy in both parent and subsidiary may be more easily achieved. Additionally, firms in this quadrant are likely to achieve a higher degree of parent–subsidiary alignment than are firms in the other three.

We can conclude that firms employing a cost leadership/utilizer combination competing in industries characterized by global competition will achieve a higher degree of integration between parent and subsidiary than firms with similar combinations competing in industries characterized by multi-domestic competition. Furthermore, firms employing a cost leadership/utilizer combination competing in industries characterized by global competition will perform better than firms with similar combinations competing in industries characterized by multidomestic competition.

MNEs with a differentiation strategy in industries characterized by multi-domestic competition will experience relatively weak internal demands for parent–subsidiary consistency. Simultaneously, pressures on subsidiaries to be sensitive to local conditions make it difficult to achieve alignment between parent and subsidiary HRM practices. Unlike a utilizer HRM strategy, however, an accumulator HRM strategy is more appropriate since it emphasizes the accumulation of resources and possesses more organizational slack and latent human resources potential. The result is greater flexibility in human resource activities and less stringent requirements for consistency. Firms in this quadrant exhibit a lower degree of consistency than firms in the other three quadrants but this also means that consistency requirements may be less important.

Firms employing a differentiation/accumulator combination competing in industries characterized by multidomestic competition achieve a lower degree of integration between parent and subsidiary than firms with similar combinations competing in industries characterized by global competition. By contrast, firms employing a differentiation/accumulator match competing in industries characterized by multidomestic competition will perform better than firms with similar combinations competing in industries challenged by global competition.

Finally, MNEs with a product differentiation strategy in an industry where competition is global confront internal pressures for alignment that are lower than for firms with a cost leadership strategy. Simultaneously, the global nature of the industry in which these firms compete indicates that local external environment pressures are also weak. Alignment of parent and subsidiary HRM activities for firms in this quadrant is less critical to firm performance than for firms employing a cost leadership strategy. This leads to the conclusion that firms employing a differentiation/accumulator combination competing in indus-tries characterized by global competition achieve a higher degree of integration between parent and subsidiary than firms with similar combinations competing in industries with multidomestic competition. Additionally, firms employing a differentiation/accumulator combination competing in industries characterized by global competition will perform better than firms with similar combinations competing in industries where competition is multidomestic.

CONCLUSION

This framework constitutes a model bridging macro and micro perspectives on the linkages between business strategy and HRM practice in MNEs. It con-cludes that there must be consistency between parent-level business strategy and subsidiary-level HRM strategy.

The framework also provides direction to HRM managers by clarifying the extent to which there is a need for consistency between parent and subsidiary in multinational operations. In doing so, it provides both a rationale and a means for them to sort through the dilemmas involved in trying to integrate parent and subsidiary operations.

Barbara Myloni, Anne-Wil Harzing and Hafiz Mirza

HUMAN RESOURCE MANAGEMENT IN GREECE: HAVE THE COLOURS OF CULTURE FADED AWAY?

INTRODUCTION

THIS ARTICLE INVESTIGATES WHETHER Human Resource Management (HRM) in Greece is maintaining its national character or whether it is converging towards an international model that potentially clashes with traditional societal values. We are addressing a critical issue in the convergence–divergence debate that has been the concern of many cross-cultural researchers, mainly in the area of human resource management, since, of all management processes, HRM practices seem to be the most susceptible to cultural differences (Gooderham and Brewster, 2003). The impact of national culture on the way HRM practices are developed and implemented within firms from different countries has been widely acknowledged (Ferner, 1997; Gooderham et al., 1999; Khilji, 2003; Newman and Nollen, 1996; Rosenzweig and Nohria, 1994; Schuler and Rogovsky, 1998; Yuen and Kee, 1993). On the other hand, some authors believe the logic of technology and markets to be a stronger force on organizations than societal values. This logic could eventually lead to the adoption of universally applicable management practices (Kidger, 1991). Using data collected from Greek firms and subsidiaries of multinationals (MNCs) located in Greece, we compare the two groups on specific HRM practices. The aim of this article is to show how HRM practices of Greek firms differ from those of MNC subsidiaries and examine the extent and way these HRM practices reflect Greek national culture.

Starting from the convergence–divergence debate, we focus on previous research that has established strong links between HRM and the cultural environment. This is followed by an analysis of Greek national culture, based on the empirical findings of the GLOBE project (Papalexandris et al., 2002), and the development of specific hypotheses to test the extent to which current HRM in Greece is compatible with the nation's values and culture. After a description of the study's methodology and sample characteristics, we present our comparative results and provide a discussion of the main findings. The article concludes by presenting the limitations of the study, as well as implications for cross-cultural management research and practice.

THEORETICAL FRAMEWORK

The convergence–divergence debate in HRM

The convergence–divergence debate has been an ongoing issue in international management for some time (Fenton-O'Creevy and Gooderham, 2003). During the 1950s and 1960s, when the internationalization of business led researchers to study the management of organizations in different countries, there was a belief that the principles of management hold universally (Gooderham and Brewster, 2003). The basic idea, which is known as the "convergence hypothesis", was that the "best management practices" could be applied everywhere, irrespective of the national environment. The principal logic behind this hypothesis is the notion that increasing industrialism affects business organizations in a homogenizing way, regardless of their country location (Kerr et al., 1960). Progress in the sciences, as well as increasingly advanced technological systems and production methods, will eventually lead all industrial societies towards similar structures. Convergence is based on the concept of "competitive isomorphism", which means that firms will eventually adopt similar, "best" management practices since they face increasingly similar globally competitive environments (Fenton-O'Creevy and Gooderham, 2003). Moreover, according to Locke et al. (1995), best management practices internationally were believed to derive from the US model.

However, the convergence hypothesis began to lose ground during the 1970s, giving way to a growing interest in national differences, stemming from cultural factors, among organizations. This shift of approach towards the concept of culture is recorded by Adler and Bartholomew (1996) in a survey of academic and professional journals. Of all international organizational behaviour and HRM articles published between 1985 and 1990, 71 per cent included the concept of culture. Almost all these articles (94 per cent) concluded that culture makes a difference to the issues studied. Hence, this research showed that by the second half of the 1980s there was general agreement, both inside and outside North America, that culture does matter. Indeed, as Adler and Bartholomew (1996: 20) suggest, "the verdict now appears to be cast in favour of divergence", that is to say, organizational and managerial behaviour is maintaining its distinctiveness across cultures.

Central to this cultural approach is that societies/countries are conspicuously different from each other and that this distinctiveness is reflected in the way that organizations are managed (Olie, 1995). Management and organization cannot be isolated from their particular cultural environment. According to some researchers, issues that relate to the types of interactions and behaviours, as well as the most appropriate relationships among people in organizations, stem from cultural assumptions and values. "This determines the information that managers notice, interpret and retain and therefore leads to different ways of seeing the same event and to different approaches to problem resolution and solution" (Sparrow and Wu, 1998: 27). As Hofstede (1980) and Schneider (1989) have shown, national culture can impact on the culture of an organization by selecting and framing the particular sets of organizational values, behaviours and norms that managers perceive as being consistent with their own basic assumptions that have been developed in their particular cultural context. In this way, cultural assumptions also influence the process of organizational decision-making.

Within the context of HRM, the debate has been stimulated by the recent internationalization of trade legislation and the formation of supranational institutions such as the European Union. In the latter case, it is believed that the introduction of common legislation and agreements between countries of the EU will eventually lead to harmonization of IR (Industrial Relations) and HRM systems across different national contexts (Brewster, 1994). Therefore, there are two versions of the convergence thesis in the context of this article: the traditional, market-technology driven convergence of management practices towards a US model, as well as the more specific convergence driven by institutional forces within the EU (Gooderham and Brewster, 2003). However, there is still a persistent belief that social, political and cultural differences between countries will continue to supersede the forces of globalization emanating from technologically driven markets or supranational agreements (Sparrow and Hiltrop, 1997). Furthermore, those in favour of the divergence thesis would even oppose the possibility of delayed convergence, since

> . . . they argue that national, and in some cases regional, institutional contexts are not only slow to change, partly because they derive from deep-seated beliefs and value-systems and partly because major re-distributions of power are involved, but, more importantly [. . .] even when change does occur this can only be understood in relation to the specific social context in which it occurs. (Gooderham and Brewster, 2003: 8)

The previous discussion may suggest that convergence or divergence happen over time; indeed, this debate tends to view HRM as a singularity that will either converge or diverge (Sparrow et al., 2003). Several studies have found evidence that both convergence and divergence are happening at the same time, but at different levels and rates (Clark, 1996; Smith and Meiksins, 1995; Tayeb, 1994). This might support Child's (1981) argument that convergence is occurring at the macro-level of the organization, such as functional and technological structures, while micro aspects, such as people's behaviour patterns, tend to diverge across countries. Even a single HR function operates at many levels, in terms of philosophy, policy, programme, practice and process (Schuler et al., 1993). Therefore, according to this argument, even if there are common elements of

HRM at the macro-level, there will still be divergence at the level of inter-pretation and application of these elements in different countries (Clark, 1996).

Cross-cultural comparisons of HRM

According to Laurent (1986) and Schneider (1988), of all management practices HRM practices seem to be the most vulnerable to cultural differences and hence the least likely to travel from one country to another. This is because they are often designed by members of one culture to handle members of that particular culture. As with most management practices, HRM practices are grounded in cultural beliefs that reflect the basic assumptions and values of the national culture in which organizations are embedded. Therefore, an HRM system may be meaningful and effective in one culture, but ineffective in another (Laurent, 1986).

A number of researchers have demonstrated the influence of national culture on HRM policies and practices (Easterby-Smith et al., 1995; Gooderham et al., 1999; Hofstede, 1993; Khilji, 2003; Newman and Nollen, 1996; Rosenzweig and Nohria, 1994; Schuler and Rogovsky, 1998; Sparrow et al., 1994; Yuen and Kee, 1993). Some of them have focused on how human resources are managed in different parts of the world and which specific issues of HRM have to be taken into consideration within a specific country. Others have been engaged in investigating the transfer of HRM practices in MNCs.

Past research has successfully attempted to explain some of the variance in HRM practices across cultures, using Hofstede's cultural dimensions (Erten-Buch and Mayrhoffer, 1998; Newman and Nollen, 1996; Schuler and Rogovski, 1998). However, the degree of cultural impact on HRM practices differs according to the specific practice, with some practices being more culture-bound than others (Easterby-Smith et al., 1995; Myloni, 2002; Sparrow and Wu, 1998; Vance et al., 1992; Weber et al., 1998; Yuen and Kee, 1993), although research has produced contradictory results. For example, in a comparative study of HRM practices in matched Chinese and UK companies, most differences were observed in the "softer" areas of HRM where relationships are important, such as performance appraisal, reward systems, selection criteria and unions–management relations (Easterby-Smith et al., 1995). Most of these differences could be linked clearly to strong cultural factors, such as the great concern that Chinese have for relationships and harmony and their fear of "losing face". On the other hand, practices that were found to be similar for the two samples (e.g. planning) were not considered culture sensitive and it was argued that other factors such as company size, industry, strategy etc. had a greater effect on them. In contrast, Sparrow and Wu (1998), who tried to link particular cultural beliefs and values with specific HRM preferences, could not identify a closer relation-ship between cultural values and "soft" areas of HRM. They found that the hard and more quantifiable practices such as planning, staffing and training are more culture-bound than the soft, behaviour/relationship-related ones like career development, performance appraisal, work design and pay and rewards systems. Lastly, Weber et al. (1998) found that training and development and pay/benefits were best explained by organizational factors, such as sector, size and corporate strategy, while selection and recruitment were strongly affected by cultural factors.

This discussion is of particular relevance to MNCs. Firms that operate in an international environment have to deal with different institutional frameworks and cultural diversity. Research evidence indicates that MNC subsidiaries are facing competing pressures for standardization and conformity to parent company practices on the one hand, and adaptation to local norms on the other (Jain et al., 1998; Milliman et al., 1991; Rosenzweig and Nohria, 1994). With regard to HRM, a variety of factors have been found critical in shaping practices in MNC subsidiaries (Bae et al., 1998; Beechler and Yang, 1994; Janssens et al., 1995; Newman and Nollen, 1996; Ngo et al., 1998; Rosenzweig and Nohria, 1994). These include the home and host country institutional and cultural environment, MNC strategy, organizational culture and control, subsidiary embeddedness and dependence, as well as contingency factors such as sector, size, age, ownership type etc. MNC responses to such pressures have resulted in the emergence of various hybrid forms of HRM practices (Fenton-O'Creevy and Gooderham, 2003; Myloni, 2002; Tayeb, 1998). In consequence, MNCs are considered an important vessel for the transfer of management practices between countries. At the same time, indigenous companies, through mimetic isomorphism, attempt to emulate management practices, especially in cases where such practices come from MNCs that originate from dominant economies (Tempel, 2001) and are considered as more efficient or competitive than local practices (Ball, 1992; Papalexandris, 1992).

In the context of the previous discussion, and given the possibility that convergence and divergence can happen simultaneously at different levels, this article examines the strength of the link between national culture and the way HRM is practised in Greek firms, and how this differs from practices used in foreign MNC subsidiaries in Greece. Based on an analysis of the Greek cultural environment, we formulate specific hypotheses that link HR practices such as HR planning, recruitment and performance appraisal,[1] to specific cultural values.

Greek culture and HRM practices

Very few studies have dealt with HRM in Greece (Papalexandris, 1987, 1991, 1992; Papalexandris et al., 2002). Among these, only Papalexandris (1987) has compared HRM in Greek firms and MNC subsidiaries. She found significant differences between the two samples and concluded that the use of systematic HR practices is lower in Greek firms compared to foreign subsidiaries, which have more sophisticated practices, often implementing guidelines directed from their parent companies. However, there was no systematic attempt to link cultural values with HR practices in Greek firms. A further step towards this end was made in terms of the GLOBE project (House et al., 1999). The principal aim of the GLOBE (Global Leadership and Organizational Behaviour Effectiveness) project is to develop measures of societal and organizational culture and establish their links with leadership attributes across cultures. The project involves 62 countries, including most of the EU member states. The study has identified nine dimensions of societal culture, which reflect perceptions of middle managers about society as it is now, as well as their preferences of how they would like it to be. Four of the dimensions, that were found to be most relevant to HR practices (Papalexandris et al., 2002), will be used for the purpose of this study, namely performance orientation, future orientation, family/in-group collectivism and power distance. Specifically, according to House et al. (1999: 192):

- *Performance orientation* refers to the extent to which an organization or society encourages and rewards group members for performance improvement and excellence. It has its roots in McClelland's (1985) work.
- *Future orientation* is the degree to which individuals in organizations or societies engage in future-oriented behaviours such as planning, investing in the future and delaying gratification. This dimension was derived from Kluckhohn and Strodtbeck (1961).
- *Family/in-group collectivism* reflects the degree to which individuals express pride, loyalty and cohesiveness in their families or organizations and was adopted from Triandis (1995).
- *Power distance* is defined as the degree to which members of an organization or society expect and agree that power should be unequally shared and has its origins in Hofstede's (1980) work.

The GLOBE project dimensions' mean scores for Greece and for the MNC's parent countries included in this study (taken from Ashkanasy et al., 2002; Papalexandris et al. 2002; Szabo et al., 2002) are given in Table 1. A comparison

Table 1. GLOBE project: mean scores of Greece and the MNCs' country of origin included in this study

Country	Performance orientation	Future orientation	Family/in-group collectivism	Power distance
Australia	4.36	4.09	4.17	4.74
Belgium**	n/a	n/a	n/a	n/a
Canada	4.49	4.44	4.26	4.82
Denmark	4.22	4.44	3.53	3.89
Finland	3.81	4.24	4.07	4.89
France	4.11	3.48	4.37	5.28
Germany*	4.25	4.27	4.02	5.25
Italy	3.58	3.25	4.94	5.43
Japan**	n/a	n/a	4.63	n/a
Netherlands	4.32	4.61	3.70	4.11
Switzerland	4.94	4.73	3.97	4.90
UK	4.08	4.28	4.08	5.15
USA	4.49	4.15	4.25	4.88
Greece	3.20	3.40	5.27	5.40

Notes: * Former West Germany. ** Published Globe data not available for these countries.

between the mean scores of Greece and the home countries of MNCs in the study reveals that in all dimensions Greece consistently scores either lower or higher than all other countries.[2]

Furthermore, according to Koopman et al. (1999), Greece (together with France and Italy) belongs to a separate cultural cluster in Europe, the South/East cluster as opposed to the North/West. They also suggest that the North/West cluster displays significantly higher scores on the dimensions of performance and future orientation, while the South/East cluster scored higher on family/in-group collectivism and power distance.

The GLOBE results are supported by other authors. Papalexandris et al. (2002) indicate that one of the main characteristics of Greek culture is strong family bonds. Even though in big cities there might have been a recent change in this respect, the extended family is still the norm in Greece. The father is the centre of the family, he is responsible for all its members and the one who makes the final decision. There is a strict hierarchy and younger members are expected to show respect to the older. Power is concentrated in a few hands, which is usually accepted although it does not go unquestioned. This is clearly reflected in the relatively high power distance score for Greece. Moreover, Greeks are generally characterized by a low level of trust towards people unless they belong to one's extended family, which sometimes could include close friends as well as relatives. According to an analysis by Triandis and Vassiliou (1972, cited in Georgas, 1993), Greeks showed a high degree of protection, support and devotion to their in-group, while being hostile and competitive with members outside of it. Georgas (1993) argues that family/in-group collectivism has critically affected the way Greek firms are organized and managed.

The majority of firms in Greece are family owned, where the manager (who is usually the owner) makes most of the decisions and is reluctant to delegate authority to his subordinates for fear of losing his power. Even in circumstances where the firm grows in size and scope, the owner-manager will prefer to hire people from the in-group, who may be inefficient, rather than to trust highly skilled professionals who are strangers (Makridakis et al., 1997). According to Papalexandris (1992), the value of *filotimo* (meaning the love of honour) helps employers to secure loyalty in their business. This may be also related to the low score in performance orientation in Greek society. The GLOBE results show that Greek society does not encourage high performance results and that there is mistrust towards those achieving individual goals. Regarding the future orientation dimension, Greece scores lower than most countries in our sample, except Italy. This reluctance for long-term planning is often attributed to continuous political and economic instability, war, as well as frequent changes in legislation (Makridakis et al., 1997). Arguably, this explains the short-term programming orientation of many Greek firms (Bourantas and Papadakis, 1996).

The above discussion leads us to expect that HR practices in Greek firms will remain in line with the cultural environment and thus will diverge from those practised in MNC subsidiaries. As previously mentioned, HRM is composed of a range of practices, some of which may converge while others remain divergent. For this reason, a variety of HR practices including HR strategy and planning, selection and recruitment, and performance appraisal were included in the study; and a set of hypotheses linking such practices with the four dimensions of societal culture were developed.

HR strategy and planning Due to the low levels of future orientation, we expect that HR planning in Greek firms will be less systematic and structured than MNC subsidiaries, so we hypothesize that:

Hypothesis 1a: Greek firms will be less likely to have a written HR strategy than MNC subsidiaries.

Hypothesis 1b: Greek firms will be less likely to have long-term planning of staffing requirements than MNC subsidiaries.

Hypothesis 1c: Greek firms will be less likely to have tight links between HR and corporate planning than MNC subsidiaries.

Hypothesis 1d: Greek firms will be less likely to have explicit planning procedures than MNC subsidiaries.

Selection and recruitment Due to the high levels of family/in-group orientation, we expect that Greek firms will show a preference for recruiting people they already know and trust and will base their selection on less objective criteria than MNC subsidiaries, so we hypothesize that:

Hypothesis 2a: Greek firms will be more likely to recruit internally than MNC subsidiaries.

Hypothesis 2b: Greek firms will be less likely to use standardized selection methods and make more use of references and recommendations than MNC subsidiaries.

Performance appraisal Due to a combination of high levels of family/in-group orientation and low levels of performance and future orientation, we expect that performance appraisal will be underdeveloped in Greek firms and will be based on subjective criteria. According to Papalexandris et al. (2002), appraisal is often used to justify promotion decisions that have already been taken. Moreover, we expect that the high levels of power distance will lead to less direct communication between supervisor and employee and that the supervisor's opinion will be more important in appraisal than that of the employee, peers or subordinates compared to MNC subsidiaries. Therefore, we hypothesize that:

Hypothesis 3a: Favouritism in performance appraisal will be more likely in Greek firms than in MNC subsidiaries.

Hypothesis 3b: Greek firms will be more likely to use performance appraisal for promotion purposes than career development compared to MNC subsidiaries.

Hypothesis 3c: Greek firms will be less likely to have written performance appraisal reports than MNC subsidiaries.

Hypothesis 3d: Interviews between supervisor and employee for the purpose of performance appraisal will be less likely in Greek firms than in MNC subsidiaries.

Hypothesis 3e: Employees, their peers or their subordinates will be less likely to participate in performance appraisal in Greek firms than in MNC subsidiaries.

In order to test these hypotheses, we conducted a comparative analysis between Greek firms and MNC subsidiaries, to which we will return after the methodology section.

METHODOLOGY

Using the survey method, we collected data from HR managers of Greek firms and MNC subsidiaries. A questionnaire, based on previous work by Schuler and Jackson (1987), as well as the Price Waterhouse Cranfield project (Brewster and Hegewisch, 1994), was developed to assess the various components of a firm's HRM system. This was translated into Greek, back-translated into English and pre-tested in a pilot study. The questions focused on HRM practices with respect to managerial employees only. Since HRM practices often differ between occupational groups (Bae et al., 1998), we chose to focus on a relatively narrow category of jobs to limit the need to repeat the questions for different categories, which would have made the questionnaire too long and complicated. As a consequence, our results may reveal larger differences between Greek firms and MNC subsidiaries, since research indicates that HRM practices for lower hierarchical levels are more localized in MNC subsidiaries (Lu and Bjorkman, 1997). For the purpose of this article, only questions that relate to HR strategy and planning, selection and performance appraisal practices were analysed.

Questionnaires were either completed during interviews or sent by post and completed in the absence of the researcher. We followed this mixed approach in order to ensure an acceptable number of replies, since mail surveys have a record of low response rates (Harzing, 1997). Our data collection process took place over a three-month period, between March and May 2000. In total, from the 269 companies we approached, 150 MNC subsidiaries and 119 Greek companies, 135 participated in our study, representing a 50 per cent response rate. Of the 135 questionnaires, 83 were completed during the interviews while 52 were completed in the absence of the researcher.[3]

Sample

The total number of responses from foreign subsidiaries was 82, while data about HRM in Greek companies were collected from 53 local firms. With regard to the subsidiary parent country, five countries are present in reasonable numbers, that is the US, the UK, Germany, France and the Netherlands. Table 2 shows a more detailed picture of the parent countries involved. Unfortunately, there is

Table 2. Sample characteristics

Subsidiary country	Responses (%)	Industry/services	Subsidiaries (%)	Greek firms (%)
Australia	1.2	Airlines	3.7	–
Belgium	2.4	Banks	13.4	9.4
Canada	1.2	Chemicals	11.0	–
Cyprus	1.2	Clothing	1.2	1.9
Denmark	1.2	Computer, office equipment	3.7	1.9
Finland	1.2	Consultancy	4.9	7.5
France	9.8	Electrical equipment	9.8	1.9
Germany	12.2	Food and beverages	11.0	22.6
Italy	3.7	Hotels	6.1	7.5
Japan	1.2	Insurance	3.7	7.5
Netherlands	12.2	Metals	2.4	5.7
Switzerland	3.7	Motor vehicles and parts	3.7	1.9
UK	18.3	Paper	1.2	5.7
USA	30.5	Petroleum and products	3.7	–
		Pharmaceuticals	9.8	9.4
		Supermarkets	2.4	–
		Telecommunications	3.7	1.9
		Other	4.9	15.1

no equal representation of all parent countries in the population and this is reflected in our sample. Greenfield sites represent 80 per cent of the sample, while the remainder are acquisitions.

In both MNC subsidiaries and Greek firms, there was an equal representation of manufacturing and services sectors, with the largest number of responses coming from firms operating in chemicals/pharmaceuticals, electronics, food/beverages, banks and hotels (Table 2). This is in line with the industry structure of the total population of companies in Greece (ICAP, 2001). The majority of both MNC subsidiaries and Greek firms have more than 200 employees, although Greek firms show a larger average size. Differences in size between the two samples are statistically significant. This is mainly due to the fact that almost half of the Greek firms have a production function[4] while only one third of the MNC subsidiaries have one. In terms of the average size (based on sales) of the total population of MNC subsidiaries, our sample frame includes slightly larger subsidiaries as around 40 per cent of our firms are placed within the top 200 largest industrial and commercial firms (ICAP, 2001). The same applies to the Greek firms sample. However, this selection was made on purpose, as we decided to target companies that were large enough to have an HRM department and developed HR strategy. Therefore, our sample is only representative of large Greek firms and not the entire population of firms. There are no statistically significant differences between responding and non-responding companies in terms of parent country, industry and size.

Measures

The questionnaire assessed the independent variables with questions about firm nationality (Greek firm or MNC subsidiary), industry (manufacturing or services), and size (total workforce).[5] From a list of several items, which capture aspects of most HRM practices, 11 questions were used to measure the constructs included in the hypotheses. A sample of key measures of HR planning, selection and recruitment, and performance appraisal, is provided in Appendix 1.

RESULTS AND DISCUSSION

In order to test the hypotheses, we compared the HRM practices in Greek firms and MNC subsidiaries. Chi-square tests were used for dichotomous variables, while t-tests were used for Likert-type variables.[6] Percentages, means and significance levels of the use of HR practices between Greek firms and MNC subsidiaries are presented in Table 3. We also conducted post-hoc analyses to test whether there were significant differences among manufacturing and services firms or large and small firms, since sector and size have been found to have considerable effects on HRM (Gooderham et al., 1999; Papalexandris, 1992). As can be seen in Table 3, these analyses revealed very few significant differences and only concerned specific selection and performance appraisal methods.

HR strategy and planning In line with *Hypothesis 1a*, significant differences were found between Greek firms and MNC subsidiaries as to whether there is a written or verbal HRM strategy or no strategy at all ($\chi^2 = 6.581$, $p = 0.018$). Our results show a more systematic approach on the part of foreign subsidiaries. Greek firms are nearly twice as likely to either have no strategy or only a verbal strategy. Table 3 presents information on how far ahead companies plan their staffing requirements. MNC subsidiaries use significantly more long-term planning than Greek firms ($\chi^2 = 4.624$, $p = 0.016$). Specifically, only 11.3 per cent of Greek firms make 2–5 year plans compared to 23.5 per cent of subsidiaries. In addition, none of the Greek firms used more than five years planning for staffing requirements. Thus *Hypothesis 1b* is also confirmed.

The type of link between human resources and corporate planning also differs significantly among companies ($t = -1.681$, $p = 0.048$). HR planning was found to be less tightly linked with corporate planning in Greek firms than in MNC subsidiaries. Greek firms also reported less explicit planning procedures and activities than subsidiaries, though the difference is only marginally significant ($t = -1.354$, $p = 0.089$). Although *Hypothesis 1c* and *Hypothesis 1d* were supported, we observe that quite a large number of Greek firms do use explicit planning procedures and show a tight link between HR and corporate planning. This could be the sign of a Greek HRM transition towards a more structured and planned system.

Selection and recruitment Contrary to our expectations (*Hypothesis 2a*), Greek firms were not found to recruit more internally compared to MNC subsidiaries ($t = -0.865$, $p = 0.194$). Although the majority of Greek firms preferred internal recruitment, MNC subsidiaries were also found to follow the same pattern. Here we could speculate that factors other than culture play a more important role, such as labour market conditions or firm size, although we did not find statistically significant differences for the latter. MNC subsidiaries' preference for internal recruitment may also imply an adaptation to the local practice.[7] On the other hand, as expected, selection methods are still under-developed in Greek companies. Table 3 shows that interviews with potential recruits and CV data are the most commonly used methods in both Greek firms and MNC subsidiaries, followed by references. However, the use of both inter-views and CV data are significantly higher in subsidiaries ($\chi^2 = 3.462$, $p = 0.031$ and $\chi^2 = 3.902$, $p = 0.024$ respectively). Group interviews and psychometric tests are the least used, with the latter being marginally significantly different between the two firm categories ($\chi^2 = 2.240$, $p = 0.067$). Interestingly, the use of references is quite high for both Greek firms and subsidiaries, while the importance of recommendation and personal acquaintance with the potential candidate is significantly higher in Greek firms ($t = -1.530$, $p = 0.040$). These results support *Hypothesis 2b*. At the same time, the low percentage of MNC subsidiaries that use standardized methods such as assessment centres and psychometric tests, as opposed to their considerable use of references and recommendations, might indicate a host country influence on MNCs' selection methods.

Performance appraisal Supporting *Hypothesis 3a*, the extent to which favouritism influences performance appraisal was found to be significantly higher in Greek firms than subsidiaries ($t = -2.80$, $p = 0.003$). However, the mean value for Greek firms is not very large. On the other hand, although the primary objective of employee appraisal in Greek firms was found to be promotion rather than career development, which is slightly more important for MNC subsidiaries, differences were not significant ($t = 1.126$, $p = 0.131$). Although *Hypothesis 3b* is not supported, the effects of culture might be argued to be quite strong in this case, since subsidiaries appear to follow the way performance appraisal is traditionally implemented in Greek firms.

The different methods for appraising employee performance used by Greek firms and MNC subsidiaries are presented in Table 3. As we can see, written reports are used more in MNC subsidiaries than Greek firms ($\chi^2 = 3.712$, $p = 0.026$), while personal interviews between supervisor and employee are marginally significantly more frequent in MNC subsidiaries ($\chi^2 = 1.876$, $p = 0.085$), thus supporting *Hypothesis 3c* and *Hypothesis 3d*. In relation to different actors' participation appraising employees' performance, Table 3 shows a quite different picture for the two categories of firms. The employee's supervisor is clearly the person responsible for appraisal in both cases, but there are significant differences on how important the employee's own view or their peers' or subordinates' views are for their appraisal. In line with *Hypothesis 3e*, employees, their peers or their subordinates are less likely to participate in performance

Table 3. Percentages, mean values and significance of the differences in the use of HR practices between Greek firms and MNC subsidiaries, and significant differences according to sector and size

HR practice		MNC subs %	Greek firms %	Sig.	Sector			Size (number of employees)				
					man	serv	Sig.	<100	100–200	201–500	>500	Sig.
HR Planning												
HRM strategy	Lack of strategy	3.7	7.5	**0.018**								
	Verbal strategy	19.5	37.7									
	Written strategy	76.8	54.7									
Planning of staffing requirements	No planning	3.7	9.4	**0.016**								
	<1 year	37.0	41.5									
	1–2 years	32.1	37.7									
	2–5 years	23.5	11.3									
	>5 years	3.7	–									
Link between HR and corporate planning*	Loose/tight	5.06*	4.60*	**0.048**								
Planning procedures*	Implicit/explicit	4.83*	4.47*	**0.089**								
Recruitment and Selection												
Recruitment*	Internal/external	3.52*	3.74*	0.194	50.0	22.6	0.000	5.9	47.8	48.8	39.1	0.009
Selection methods	Application forms	43.2	33.3	0.125								
	Assessment centres	34.6	25.9	0.144								
	Psychometric tests	32.1	20.4	**0.067**								

Category	Variable			p			p					p
Importance of recommendations*	Interviews	98.8	92.6	**0.031**								
	CV data	95.1	85.2	**0.024**								
	References	51.9	55.6	0.336	47.6	62.3	**0.046**					
	Group interviews	21.0	13.0	0.116								
	Low/high	3.54*	4.00*	**0.040**								
Performance Appraisal												
Performance appraisal favouritism*	Low/high	2.08*	2.63*	**0.003**								
Performance appraisal objective*	Promotion/career development	3.96*	3.69*	0.131								
Performance appraisal methods	Super-employ. interview	83.8	74.1	**0.085**				94.1	78.3	90.2	68.9	**0.018**
	Checklist forms	36.3	29.6	0.213								
	Non-written feedback	13.8	18.5	0.228								
	Written appraisal reports	75.0	59.3	**0.026**	63.0	77.4	**0.040**	64.7	47.8	80.5	68.9	**0.030**
Opinion importance in performance appraisal	Employee supervisor	100.0	98.1	0.111								
	Employee's own	82.5	48.1	**0.000**								
	Employee's peers	20.0	11.1	**0.086**								
	Employee's subordinate	16.3	5.6	**0.030**								

Note: * Indicates variables measured in 7-point Likert-type scales and mean values.

appraisal in Greek firms than in MNC subsidiaries ($\chi^2 = 17.679$, $p = 0.000$; $\chi^2 = 1.856$, $p = 0.086$ and $\chi^2 = 3.507$, $p = 0.030$ respectively). However, it is worth pointing out that it is not so common for peers and subordinates to express their opinion about such issues even in MNC subsidiaries, where percentages are rather low. Our empirical results show that performance appraisal practices in Greek firms reflect national culture to a great extent. Moreover, they indicate that MNC subsidiaries might have adapted their practices to be more in line with the Greek cultural environment.

CONCLUSIONS AND IMPLICATIONS

The previous analysis points to several differences between Greek firms and MNC subsidiaries concerning the use of specific HRM practices. The majority of differences are in the expected direction. Only one of the hypotheses we put forward (*Hypothesis 2a*) was not supported, while the relationship proposed in *Hypothesis 3b* was not significant. Therefore, the results indicate that the effect of national culture on HRM in Greece is quite prominent. HR practices, such as planning, recruitment and performance appraisal are to a great extent in accordance with the cultural values of Greek society, as identified by project GLOBE. It is evident that Greek firms show a high level of embeddedness in their cultural environment. Practices such as the use of recommendations in recruiting employees and a limited long-term HR planning are still common even in larger Greek companies. Such findings are partly in line with other recent research that examines the link between societal culture and HRM in Greece (Papalexandris et al., 2002). However, our study takes a step further by studying the cultural embeddedness of Greek firms in terms of their HRM practices vis-à-vis foreign subsidiaries. It is important to emphasize the fact that our Greek sample consists of larger companies (in terms of employment) compared to MNC subsidiaries; and we might expect such firms to be more convergent towards MNC subsidiaries' practices. Even so, differences still hold, and it can be argued that these differences would have been even stronger if we had included smaller Greek firms in our sample as well.

Despite the differences between practices in Greek firms and MNC subsidiaries, this study also shows certain similarities. Performance appraisal practices in both groups of companies are characterized by a less participative, more top-down approach, reflecting the high power distance and respect for authority in Greek society. Moreover the relatively high use of references and recommendations in selection and the preference for internal recruitment in both groups probably reflects the high level of in-group/family collectivism in Greece. This may suggest that MNC subsidiaries have adapted parent company HRM practices to the local environment up to a point. These practices might be characterized by high levels of cultural susceptibility and/or sensitivity to cultural differences.

In terms of the convergence–divergence debate, it is interesting to note that, for the range of HR practices examined, the primary tendency we find is for MNCs to adapt to local practices in some areas. However, there seems to be little adaptation by Greek firms. Therefore, in this particular context, we observe that the signs of divergence are more prominent than the signs of convergence. We could argue that this tendency can be explained by strong and persistent national cultural norms and values, although other reasons might explain the lack of convergence. For instance, timing might be a factor: it is possible that Greek firms still have some way to go in terms of facing direct global competition or that they are not consciously looking for "best practices" internationally. Nevertheless, the fact that some MNCs might have adapted to local norms does suggest that "divergence" can be an important factor.

Overall, it is apparent that some practices are more common in MNC subsidiaries, while others show limited applicability to the particular host country context and hence have to be adapted. These results could be helpful to MNC decision makers in deciding which practices are more easily transferred into the Greek socio-cultural context and which practices have to be adapted to a degree. Such considerations might be especially pertinent in cases of MNC acquisitions of Greek firms, joint ventures or other types of strategic alliance. Apart from these managerial implications, this article has contributed to the field of IHRM (International Human Resource Management) from both a comparative and international perspective. It has included subsidiaries from MNCs located in many different countries, both from Europe and the US, and constitutes a further step in exploring the under-explored area of HRM practices in Greece.

In terms of its limitations, the present research suffers from using HR managers as the sole respondent for companies in the sample. Although the "key-informant approach" is widely used (De Cieri and Dowling, 1999), it runs the risk of common method variance (Philips, 1981). The use of multiple respondents (other managers and employees at both headquarters and subsidiary level) would serve to validate the reports of HR managers, but such an approach was not practically feasible. However, the statistical tests that we undertook to assess the presence of common method variance in our results indicated that this issue is not likely to be a major concern in our study.[8] A further limitation is that we focused on HRM practices used only for white-collar employees; hence blue-collar workers were not included. Our decision in this respect was driven by the fact that it was impossible to collect information about all employees. However, as already mentioned, we would expect that HRM differences between Greek firms and MNC subsidiaries would be less prominent at blue-collar levels.

In conclusion, our comparison between the HRM practices used in Greek firms and MNC subsidiaries has revealed both differences and similarities. It has indicated that Greek companies are still embedded in their cultural environment to a considerable extent. At the same time, there is some evidence that MNC subsidiaries have adapted to the host country, embracing practices that are in line with the Greek cultural environment.

APPENDIX 1. SAMPLE OF KEY MEASURES FOR HR PRACTICES

HR strategy and planning

1   HRM strategy existence (written, verbal or no HRM strategy)
2   Planning of staffing requirements (<1 year, 1–2, 2–5, >5 years)
3   Loose/tight link between human resource planning and corporate planning (7-point Likert scale; loose – tight)

Selection and recruitment

1   Internal/external recruitment (7-point Likert scale; largely internally – largely externally)
2   Selection methods used (application forms, assessment centres, psychometric tests, interviews, CV data, references, group interviews)
3   Low/high importance of recommendation and/or personal acquaintance with the potential candidate (7-point Likert scale; not important – very important)

Performance appraisal

1   Method(s) used in appraising employee performance (personal interview between supervisor–subordinate, checklist forms, grades for various traits, informal/non-written feedback, written reports)
2   People that participate in employee performance appraisal (supervisor, employee him/herself, peers, subordinates)

NOTES

1   Given the paper length limitations, we have chosen to focus on only three groups of HR practices. We made sure to include practices from both hard (HR planning) and soft (selection, performance appraisal) areas of HRM (Easterby-Smith et al., 1995).
2   With the exception of Italy that scores lower in future orientation and higher in power distance. However, since there were only 3 Italian subsidiaries included in our sample, we can safely disregard this exception.
3   Since our questionnaires were completed in two different ways, we tested whether this had any systematic impact on responses. T-tests were performed separately for subsidiaries and local companies, and showed very few significant differences, indicating that responses did not differ substantially between the two research methods.
4   Firms with production plants are generally larger than firms with just a sales function.
5   We created four size groups: <100, 100–200, 201–500 and >500.
6   Although there are a large number of comparisons conducted through t-tests, we did not administer Bonferroni correction to adjust the alpha levels. There were two reasons for that. First, this type of correction is usually applied to multiple comparisons of "independent" variables, and much less frequently to multiple comparisons of "dependent"

variables. With regard to Bonferroni correction, this would normally only be applied if the dependent variables are conceptually linked or refer to the same construct. At a very high level of abstraction all our variables refer to HR transfer. At a lower level of abstraction, we have several variables referring to specific HR practices. However, we do not see our variables as different measures of the exact *same* construct. Moreover, it is also important to note that we have constructed very specific hypotheses, firmly grounded in the literature. As such, these comparisons are planned rather than *post hoc*.

7 HR managers in MNC subsidiaries might also have interpreted internal as internal to the MNC as a whole, not internal to the subsidiary. In this case, it might be quite logical that MNC subsidiaries have more internal recruitment, since they have a larger source of potential employees to draw on. However, we doubt this would have affected the answer to the internal recruitment question much, since expatriate presence in the sample subsidiaries is quite low and none of the HR managers interviewed mentioned international recruitment.

8 Such as *t*-tests, Harman's one-factor test (Podsakoff and Organ, 1986) etc.

REFERENCES

Adler, N. J. and Bartholomew, S. (1996) "Building Networks and Crossing Borders", in P. Joynt and M. Warner (eds) *Managing across Cultures: Issues and Perspectives*, pp: 7–32. London: International Thomson Business Press.

Ashkanasy, N. M., Trevor-Roberts, E. and Earnshaw, L. (2002) "The Anglo Cluster: Legacy of the British Empire", *Journal of World Business* 37(1): 28–39.

Bae, J., Chen, S. and Lawler, J. J. (1998) "Variations in Human Resource Management in Asian Countries: MNC Home-country and Host-country Effects", *The International Journal of Human Resource Management* 9(4): 653–70.

Ball, G. (1992) "Personnel Management in Greece: The Spartan Profession", *Personnel Management* September 1992: 40–4.

Beechler, S. and Yang, J. Z. (1994) "The Transfer of Japanese-style Management to American Subsidiaries: Contingencies, Constraints and Competencies", *Journal of International Business Studies* 25(3): 467–91.

Bourantas, D. and Papadakis, V. (1996) "Greek Management", *International Studies of Management and Organization* 26(3): 13–32.

Brewster, C. (1994) "European HRM: Reflection of, or Challenge to, the American Concept?", in P. S. Kirkbride (ed.) *Human Resource Management in Europe: Perspectives for the 1990s*, pp. 56–89. London/New York: Routledge.

Brewster, C. and Hegewisch, A. (eds) (1994) *Policy and Practice in European Human Resource Management – The Price Waterhouse Cranfield Survey*. London/New York: Routledge.

Child, J. (1981) "Culture, Contingencies and Capitalism in the Cross-national Study of Organizations", in L. L. Cummings and B. M. Staw (eds) *Research in Organizational Behavior 3*, pp. 303–56. Greenwich, Conn.: JAI Press.

Clark, T. (1996) "HRM: A Unified Understanding or a Multiplicity of Meanings?", in T. Clark (ed.) *European Human Resource Management: An Introduction to Comparative Theory and Practice*, pp. 244–62. Oxford: Blackwell Business.

De Cieri, H. and Dowling, P. J. (1999) "Strategic Human Resource Management in Multinational Enterprises: Theoretical and Empirical Developments", in P. M. Wright, L. D. Dyer, J. W. Boudreau and G. T. Milkovich (eds) *Research in*

Personnel and Human Resources Management: Strategic Human Resources Management in the Twenty-first Century, Supplement 4, pp. 305–27. Stamford Conn.: JAI Press.

Easterby-Smith, M., Malina, D. and Yuan, L. (1995) "How Culture-sensitive is HRM? A Comparative Analysis of Practice in Chinese and UK Companies", *International Journal of Human Resource Management* 6(1): 30–59.

Erten-Buch, C. and Mayrhoffer, W. (1998) "Human Resource Management and National Culture: Two Birds that Flock Together? Empirical Evidence from 13 European Countries", paper presented at the 24th Annual Conference of the EIBA, Israel, 13–15 December.

Fenton-O'Creevy, M. and Gooderham, P. N. (2003) "International Management of Human Resources", *Scandinavian Journal of Business Research* 17(1): 2–5.

Ferner, A. (1997) "Country of Origin Effects and HRM in Multinational Companies", *Human Resource Management Journal* 7(1): 19–37.

Georgas, J. (1993) "Management in Greece", in D. J. Hickson (ed.) *Management in Western Europe: Society, Culture and Organization in Twelve Nations*, pp. 109–24. Berlin: Walter de Gruyter.

Gooderham, P. N. and Brewster, C. (2003) "Convergence, Stasis or Divergence? Personnel Management in Europe", *Scandinavian Journal of Business Research* 17(1): 6–18.

Gooderham, P. N., Nordhaug, O. and Ringdal, K. (1999) "Institutional and Rational Determinants of Organisational Practices: Human Resource Management in European Firms", *Administrative Science Quarterly* 44(3): 507–31.

Harzing, A. W. K. (1997) "Response Rates in International Mail Surveys: Results of a 22-country Study", *International Business Review* 6(6): 641–65.

Hofstede, G. (1980) *Culture's Consequences: International Differences in Work-related Values*. London: Sage.

Hofstede, G. (1993) "Intercultural Conflict and Synergy in Europe", in D. J. Hickson (ed.) *Management in Western Europe: Society, Culture and Organization in Twelve Nations*, pp. 1–8. Berlin: Walter de Gruyter.

House, R. J., Hanges, P. J., Ruiz-Quintanilla, S. A., Dorfman, P. W., Javidan, M., Dickson, M. W., Gupta, V. and 159 co-authors (1999) "Cultural Influences on Leadership and Organisations: Project GLOBE", in W. Mobley, J. Gessner and V. Arnold (eds) *Advances in Global Leadership*, pp. 171–233. Stamford, Conn.: JAI Press.

ICAP (2001) *Greek Financial Directory 2001: Greece in Figures*. Athens: ICAP.

Jain, H. C., Lawler, J. J. and Morishima, M. (1998) "Multinational Corporations, Human Resource Management and Host-country Nationals", *The International Journal of Human Resource Management* 9(4): 553–66.

Janssens, M., Brett, J. M. and Smith, F. J. (1995) "Confirmatory Cross-cultural Research: Testing the Viability of a Corporation-wide Safety Policy", *The Academy of Management Journal* 38(2): 364–82.

Kerr, C., Dunlop, J. T., Harbison, F. and Myers, C. A. (1960) *Industrialism and Industrial Man*. Cambridge, Mass.: Harvard University Press.

Khilji, S.E. (2003) " 'To Adapt or not to Adapt' Exploring the Role of National Culture in HRM – A Study of Pakistan", *International Journal of Cross Cultural Management* 3(1): 109–32.

Kidger, P. J. (1991) "The Emergence of International Human Resource Management", *International Human Resource Management* 2(2): 149–63.

Kluckhohn, F. R. and Strodtbeck, F. L. (1961) *Variations in Value Orientations*. Evanston, Ill.: Row, Peterson & Co.

Koopman, P. L., Den Hartog, D. N., Konrad, E. and 50 co-authors (1999) "National Culture and Leadership Profiles in Europe: Some Results from the GLOBE Study", *European Journal of Work and Organizational Psychology* 8(4): 503–20.

Laurent, A. (1986) "The Cross-cultural Puzzle of International Human Resource Management", *Human Resource Management* 25(1): 91–102.

Locke, R., Piore, M. and Kochan, T. (1995) "Introduction", in R. Locke, M. Piore and T. Kochan (eds) *Employment Relations in a Changing World Economy*, pp. xiii–xxix. London: Sage.

Lu, Y. and Bjorkman, I. (1997) "HRM Practices in China–Western Joint Ventures: MNC Standardization Versus Localization", *International Journal of Human Resource Management* 8(5): 614–28.

McClelland, D. C. (1985) *Human Motivation*, Glensview, Ill.: Scott, Foresman.

Makridakis, S., Caloghirou, Y., Papagiannakis, L. and Trivellas, P. (1997) "The Dualism of Greek Firms and Management: Present State and Future Implications", *European Management Journal* 15(4): 381–402.

Milliman, J., Von Glinow, M. A. and Nathan, M. (1991) "Organizational Life-cycles and Strategic International Human Resource Management in MNCs: Implications for Congruence Theory", *Academy of Management Review* 6(2): 318–39.

Myloni, B. (2002) "The Transfer of Human Resource Management Practices within Multinational Companies in Greece – A Comparative Analysis of Human Resource Management Practices in Subsidiaries of European and US Multi-nationals and Greek Companies", unpublished PhD thesis, University of Bradford School of Management.

Newman, K. L. and Nollen, S. D. (1996) "Culture and Congruence: The Fit between Management Practices and National Culture", *Journal of International Business Studies* 27(4): 753–79.

Ngo, H., Turban, D., Lau, C. and Lui, S. (1998) "Human Resource Practices and Firm Performance of Multinational Corporations: Influences of Country Origin", *The International Journal of Human Resource Management* 9(4): 632–52.

Olie, R. (1995) "The 'Culture' Factor in Personnel and Organization Policies", in A. W. K. Harzing and J. Van Ruysseveldt (eds) *International Human Resource Management: An Integrated Approach*, pp. 124–43. London: Sage Publications.

Papalexandris, N. (1987) "Factors Affecting Management Staffing and Development: The Case of Greek Firms", *European Management Journal* 6(1): 67–72.

Papalexandris, N. (1991) "A Comparative Study of Human Resource Management in Selected Greek and Foreign-Owned Subsidiaries in Greece", in C. Brewster and S. Tyson (eds) *International Comparisons in Human Resource Management*, pp. 145–58. London: Pitman.

Papalexandris, N. (1992) "Human Resource Management in Greece", *Employee Relations* 14(4): 38–52.

Papalexandris, N., Chalikias, J. and Panayotopoulou, L. (2002) "Societal Culture and Human Resource Management: Exploring the Mutual Interaction in Greece", paper presented at the 2nd International Conference *Human Resource Management in Europe: Trends and Challenges*, Athens, Greece, 17–19 October.

Philips, L. W. (1981) "Assessing Measurement Error in Key Informant Reports. A Methodological Note on Organizational Analysis in Marketing", *Journal of Marketing Research* 18(4): 395–415.

Podsakoff, P. M. and Organ, D. W. (1986) "Self-Reports in Organizational Research: Problems and Prospects", *Journal of Management* 12(4): 531–44.

Rosenzweig, P. M. and Nohria, N. (1994) "Influences on HRM Practices in Multinational Corporations", *Journal of International Business Studies* 25(2): 229–51.

Schneider, S. C. (1988) "National vs. Corporate Culture: Implications for Human Resource Management", *Human Resource Management* 27(2): 231–45.

Schneider, S. C. (1989) "Strategy Formulation: The Impact of National Culture", *Organization Studies* 10(2): 149–68.

Schuler, R. S. and Jackson, S. E. (1987) "Linking Competitive Strategies with Human Resource Management Practices", *The Academy of Management Executive* 2(3): 207–19.

Schuler, R. S. and Rogovsky, N. (1998) "Understanding Compensation Practice Variations across Firms. The Impact of National Culture", *Journal of International Business Studies* 29(1): 159–77.

Schuler, R. S., Dowling, P. J. and De Cieri, H. (1993) "An Integrated Framework of Strategic International Human Resource Management", *The International Journal of Human Resource Management* 4(3): 717–64.

Smith, C. and Meiksins, P. (1995) "System, Society and Dominance Effects in Cross-national Organisational Analysis", *Work, Employment and Society* 9(2): 241–67.

Sparrow, P. R. and Hiltrop, J. (1997) "Redefining the Field of European Human Resource Management: A Battle between National Mindsets and Forces of Business Transition?", *Human Resource Management* 36(2): 201–19.

Sparrow, P. R. and Wu, P. (1998) "Does National Culture Really Matter? Predicting HRM Preferences of Taiwanese Employees", *Employee Relations* 20(1): 26–56.

Sparrow, P. R., Schuler, R. S. and Jackson, S. E. (1994) "Convergence or Divergence: Human Resource Practices and Policies for Competitive Advantage Worldwide", *The International Journal of Human Resource Management* 5(2): 267–99.

Sparrow, P. R., Harris, H. and Brewster, C. (2003) "Towards a New Model of Globalizing HRM", paper presented at the 7th International Human Resource Management Conference, Limerick, Ireland, 4–6 June.

Szabo, E., Brodbeck, F. C., Den Hartog, D. N., Reber, G., Weibler, J. and Wunderer, R. (2002) "The Germanic Europe Cluster: Where Employees have a Voice", *Journal of World Business* 37(1): 55–68.

Tayeb, M. H. (1994) "Organizations and National Culture Methodology Considered", *Organization Studies* 15(3): 429–46.

Tayeb, M. H. (1998) "Transfer of HRM Practices across Cultures: An American Company in Scotland", *International Journal of HRM* 9(2): 332–58.

Tempel, A. (2001) *The Cross-national Transfer of Human Resource Management Practices in German and British Multinational Companies.* Munich: Rainer Hampp Verlag.

Triandis, H. C. (1995) *Individualism and Collectivism.* Boulder, Colo.: Westview Press.

Vance, C. M., McClaine, S. R., Boje, D. M. and Stage, H. D. (1992) "An Examination of the Transferability of Traditional Performance Appraisal Principles across Cultural Boundaries", *Management International Review* 32(4): 313–26.

Weber, W., Kabst, R. and Gramley, C. (1998) "Human Resource Policies in European Organisations: Country vs. Company-specific Antecedents", paper presented at the 6th Conference on International Human Resource Management, Paderborn, 22–8 June.

Yuen, E. C. and Kee, H. T. (1993) "Headquarters, Host-culture and Organizational Influences on HRM Policies and Practices", *Management International Review* 33(4): 361–83.

Ingmar Björkman

PETER HANSON: BUILDING A WORLD-CLASS PRODUCT DEVELOPMENT CENTER FOR HI TECH SYSTEMS IN CHINA

INTRODUCTION

Peter Hanson, the head of the product development center (PDC) of Hi Tech Systems in Shanghai, had been in China for five months. He was the first person in the product development center when he arrived in Shanghai in April 2000. Thinking back at the period he had spent in China so far, he felt that things had gone quite well. The PDC was now up and running, and today, on September 12th, 2000, Peter welcomed its sixteenth employee.

None the less, Peter still had a number of concerns. The PDC was still rather small, and it was possible for him to interact with and influence all employees. As the PDC would grow significantly over the next year, he wanted to make sure to create a healthy and positive atmosphere and orientation toward work. His vision was to create a world-class PDC in Shanghai, but how to do that in a country that was mainly a recipient of technological know-how from abroad, and what measures should be taken to convince other parts of Hi Tech Systems to engage in joint development projects with his PDC? And, even if he managed to develop the competencies needed to build a world-class PDC through careful recruitment and selection as well as good investments in training and development, how were they to retain the employees in a market where job-hopping was common, money apparently an important reason why people switched jobs, and well-educated people had ample opportunities in other companies? Basically his question was: Would lessons on how to manage human resources obtained in North America and Europe apply also in the People's Republic of China?

PRODUCT DEVELOPMENT IN HI TECH SYSTEMS

Hi Tech Systems was established in Stockholm, Sweden, in 1976. Already, by the late 1980s, Hi Tech Systems had become known as one of Europe's most innovative firms in its industry. The growth continued in the 1990s with firm profitability remaining healthy. The company is currently one of the three largest firms in its industry. Hi Tech Systems's global manufacturing comprises six production facilities in five different countries on three different continents. Approximately 45 percent of sales come from Europe, but in particular the United States and also Japan and China have become important markets.

Product development is seen as key to the success of Hi Tech Systems. Almost 20 percent of Hi Tech Systems' employees are working in research and development. Hi Tech Systems has product development centers (PDCs) in Sweden, the United Kingdom, the United States, Japan, Hong Kong (China) and, most recently, Mainland China. There is a global PDC management group headed by Johan Lind that consists of all the PDC heads and convenes once a month. Johan Lind reports to the head of global product development in Hi Tech Systems, Anders Jonsson.

The responsibility for product development programs resides with the global business lines and the so-called "platforms" (such as Japanese user interface). Research programs within the business lines that lead to actual products also draw on the work being done within the platforms. In each PDC, people work on projects related to both Hi Tech Systems business lines and platforms.

A full-grown PDC has some 400–500 employees, a variety of competencies, and is expected to have the capability needed to develop an entire new product. There are several reasons why the company has established a whole portfolio of PDCs. First, different areas differ in terms of technologies and standards relevant for the business. Therefore, it makes sense to locate research and development activities in locations where the technologies reside. Second, by dispersing PDCs to different parts of the world, the company can move product-creation activities in response to environmental and market changes. Third, it enables Hi Tech Systems to draw on human resources not available in one location. Hi Tech Systems has traditionally done most of its product creation in Sweden, but as a result of the growth of Hi Tech Systems there are not enough engineering students in the whole country to satisfy its needs. Fourth, products need to be local-adapted and this is easier to carry out locally than in a distant PDC.

In a typical research program, most of the work on the key components of a new product is done within one single "core" PDC. Within each project there is a fairly clear distribution of responsibilities across the PDCs involved. Other, "peripheral" PDCs are typically involved in developing locally adapted variations of the product. Most of the work has typically already been done in the core PDC before the other PDCs get involved (although, in order to ensure that the necessary local adaptations of the final product can be made at a later stage, people from each of the geographical regions are involved in steering groups already during the conceptualization stage). The knowledge transfer mostly takes place through people from the PDCs who visit the core PDC for 1–3 months to work with the product development people before they return to their own units. At the point when the project has been established in the peripheral PDCs, the focal project leader reports to the global head of the focal product development project and to the head of the main PDC. Heavy emphasis is put on establishing and following up on project milestones.

HI TECH SYSTEMS IN CHINA

The People's Republic of China started opening up to the outside world in 1979. In 1992 the Hi Tech Systems group established a representative office in Shanghai, and in 1995 a first joint venture was established. By the beginning of 2000, Hi Tech Systems already had four joint ventures and wholly owned subsidiaries in China. Hi Tech Systems had become a significant player in the rapidly growing Chinese market where it was competing with other Western, Japanese but also increasingly strong local competitors. China had become one of Hi Tech Systems's most important markets. Most of the products sold in China were produced in the firm's local factories.

However, Hi Tech Systems had so far no product development center in China. Toward the end of the 1990s there was a growing consensus that this neglect had to be rectified. A decision to establish a PDC in Shanghai was made by Hi Tech Systems's management board in January 2000. Peter Hanson was chosen to head the PDC.

PETER HANSON

Peter Hanson was born in California in 1962. After graduating from college with a major in management his first job was with a major US industrial firm. As a part of his job, in 1989–90 he spent six months in Hong Kong. During his assignment in Hong Kong, he "fell in love with Asia and China. Since that moment he knew that he was going to return to Asia." Peter also met his future wife who moved with him to the United States. In 1991–3, Peter did an MBA and then started to work in a small start-up company. In late 1997, Peter was persuaded by one of his previous colleagues to join Hi Tech Systems. When joining Hi Tech Systems, Peter was appointed operations manager. After some months, he was asked to head the engineering unit of the new product development center that was built up in Philadelphia. Peter accepted the job, which meant that he would be responsible for the largest unit of the PDC. Peter and his new boss, Curtis O'Neill, soon became very close, with Peter acting as the second in charge of the PDC. Peter recalls:

> I learned a lot from Curtis. He was very people-oriented. He would make sure that you get an opportunity to get into an environment where you either learn or you don't. He gave people lots of challenges, lots of learning opportunities, where they could prove themselves. He would also quite directly point to areas of improvement. He also underlined the

importance of networking, how to build networks of people that you can draw on.

One of the things that Peter learned soon after joining Hi Tech Systems was the importance of having good personal contacts within the company. The Hi Tech Systems global product development worked to a significant extent through informal contacts across units, and it was crucial to be well connected. His choice of the five product line managers in his department reflected this view. While people in the Philadelphia unit expected and pressured him to choose local people for the positions, he selected three expatriates and only two local employees.

> People thought I was taking promotions away from Philadelphia. I had my own views in mind – we needed to be connected to the other centers. If you're well connected people trust you to do a good job within a research program, and it is also easier to get technical help if needed. I then used lots of interviews with the candidates to convince people about their capabilities and to get some buy-in from the other managers. I also made sure to tell people that the objective was to fill the positions with local people in two–three years. In fact, the line managers had as an explicit objective to develop a local replacement of themselves.

During the next eighteen months, Peter visited Sweden several times. He often took part in the global PDC group meetings as O'Neill's stand-in. The global PDC management also knew that he was interested in returning to Asia, something Peter had mentioned from the outset in his performance management discussions.

ESTABLISHING THE PRODUCT DEVELOPMENT CENTER

During the summer of 1999, the global PDC-management group decided that a feasibility study on the possible creation of a PDC in the People's Republic of China should be carried out. In October 1999, Peter was asked to become involved in the project. His task was to examine the data and write a report on whether or not a PDC should be established and, if so, where in China it should be located. By that time Peter also knew that he would be the preferred candidate as head of the PDC (if approved). In January 2000 the Hi Tech Systems global management board approved the establishment of a PDC in Shanghai. One of the advantages of Shanghai was that the PDC would be able to use the existing Hi Tech Systems organization in the city. It would be easier to learn from the experiences of Hi Tech Systems' largest Chinese production and its China headquarters, both of which were located in Shanghai. In February, Peter went to China on a pre-visit mainly to meet people in the Hi Tech Systems organization.

When it became clear that the PDC would be established, Peter started to look for people. There was no established policy for people management within the global product creation organization, but Peter was told to draw on the HR department at the Hi Tech Systems group in China for support. He thought he would initially need approximately ten positions for expatriates, and it would be of crucial importance to find suitable people for the key positions.

> It was networking all the way – the social networks were very important! There were many people who knew that I would do it, and some of them contacted me. I contacted and spoke to lots of people in all parts of the Hi Tech Systems organization. I wanted the candidates to have experience in launching Hi Tech Systems products in China. They should know the Chinese environment and culture. This meant that there were only a very small number of people who fulfilled my criteria. And they had to commit to staying at least two or even three years, which is not usual in Hi Tech Systems. Towards the end of the period they start hunting for another job anyhow.

Peter finally identified four people that he wanted: one Swede, and three people from the People's Republic of China who had studied and worked for several years abroad (two in the United States, one in Sweden). One of them he already knew in advance, the others he had identified through his networking activities. All the Chinese had a strong educational background, with degrees from top Chinese universities before leaving the country for overseas graduate studies. Everybody had at least some experience in leading teams.

> I talked a lot to them. Have they thought about living in China? Were they (the Chinese) conscious about the challenges involved in going back to China? For instance, people may be jealous of them making much more money, travelling abroad and having much higher positions than they themselves had? Have they realized that it's going to be a start-up operation, and that it may be difficult to get things started and people on board?

To persuade the people he wanted to accept relocating to China, Peter tried to create a positive and challenging vision for the PDC. To date, Hi Tech Systems had probably not done enough to meet the needs of the Chinese-speaking countries. Did they want to become a part of the process of creating a world-class PDC in China? The PDC would become responsible for the Chinese user interface-platform – did they want to participate in the challenge of its development? Being restricted by the company's expatriate compensation policy, which was built on a standardized job-grading system, he was able to offer competitive but not exceptional salaries. He finally managed to persuade all four candidates to accept a job in his PDC. They all knew each other from their previous jobs. During the late spring of 2000, he found some additional people in the global Hi Tech Systems organization who also agreed to take jobs in Shanghai.

A part of my strategy was to get people from different product development centers. By having these people in my organization we are able to
easily reach into the other PDCs which is particularly important in the
beginning as we are dependent on doing parts of larger projects in
collaboration with other centers. If we have good people who have
credibility from each of the other PDCs, we will be recognized and seen
as trustworthy.

But Peter did not see technical competence as the only important criterion. In his
view:

Eighty percent is attitude. It doesn't matter what you can do if you lack
drive. With drive you can always fill in the gaps. . . . Perhaps it has something to do with my own background. I have had to manage without an
engineering education in an organization and industry that are extremely
technology-intensive.

The PDC was to report to the global PDC management and to the Hi Tech Systems
China country management. As agreed upon with the global PDC management
group, PDC Shanghai would be responsible for product creation in the Chinese-
language area, including Mainland China, Hong Kong, Singapore and Taiwan. In the
beginning it would mostly do limited parts of larger products in collaboration with
other global PDCs, working on software and on Chinese-specific applications. The
long-term vision was eventually to have the competencies to even be able to build
new products in China.

THE START OF THE PRODUCT DEVELOPMENT CENTER

Peter and his family finally arrived in Shanghai on April 12th, 2000. The next
employee arrived from overseas in May, and already by September the unit had
sixteen employees, half of whom had been recruited from abroad. Peter's estimate
was that, long term, 15–20 percent of the employees would be from overseas but that
it would take three to four years to decrease the proportion of expatriates to that
level.

When you build a home, first you build the foundations. You need to make
sure that the foundations are in place – the recruitment process, human
resources management, finance. Then you need key managers to build the
organization around.

In the recruitment of local employees, the PDC was collaborating closely with Hi
Tech Systems's human resources (HR) department. After job descriptions and job
grade levels had been determined by the PDC, the HR department would announce

the position using both advertisements and the Hi Tech Systems home page, receive CVs, do a first screening of the candidates, and arrange for interviews and assessment of the applicants. The interviews were done by a minimum of two PDC managers, who also acted as observers in the assessment centers organized by the HR department. For the assessment of applicants in China, Hi Tech Systems used "The Space Shuttle". The Space Shuttle was a game where the applicants worked together in a group with the objective of reaching an agreement on how to build a space shuttle. By observing the applicants involved in a problem-solving situation where they also interacted with each other, the observers could draw their own conclusions about the applicants. Recruitment and selection of local employees largely resembled practices used elsewhere in the global Hi Tech Systems organization.

Some other Western firms had apparently made larger adjustments in their selection practices in China. For instance, Peter had heard that Shell had changed its selection practices based on an in-depth study of its existing Chinese managers and entry-level management trainees. Traditionally Shell focused on analytical and problem-solving abilities. However, when, for example, applicants were asked to identify the strengths and weaknesses of the Chinese educational system and then say what they would do to remedy deficiencies if they were the Minister of Education, if there were any responses at all they tended to be uniformly bland. It was also found that the kind of "Who would you throw out of the airplane?" question commonly used in the West also tended to engender a "learned helplessness effect" on the part of Chinese university graduates, who have excelled at clearly defined tasks in a familiar environment and who had "learned" to respond to the unfamiliar by simple freezing. Shell's system identified the Chinese education system as the chief culprit. The educational system is hierarchical, extremely competitive, and almost exclusively based on examination of rote learning. Problem-oriented interaction among strangers is unnatural and problematic for most Chinese. Therefore, to evaluate the decision-making skills, communication skills, analytical problem-solving abilities, and leadership capabilities of the applicants based on hypothetical cases solved in assessment situations may be very difficult. As a result, Shell's study recommended the use of real case studies rather than hypothetical questions.[1]

Competence development would probably be key to the success of the PDC both in terms of localizing its operations and in producing good results. By mid-September, the new employees had mostly worked on small projects, like setting up the IT system. A couple of people had also been sent to Hong Kong to work in the field with experienced engineers for three weeks. Formal training would be important, and the PDC would need to collaborate with Hi Tech Systems's HR unit on the course program offered to the PDC employees. To what extent should the Chinese employees receive the same content and delivery as Hi Tech Systems employees elsewhere? In China, the Confucianist and Communist-influenced Chinese educational system in which the learner is a mostly passive receiver who is obedient to the instructor tends to create linear rather than lateral thinking and precedent-based problem-solving where the focus is on getting the "right" answer.

None the less, hands-on on-the-job coaching would be even more important for the development of the new employees. Most of the responsibility for coaching would obviously be on the experienced Hi Tech Systems employees but it would also be important to bring in people from other PDCs for visits in Shanghai. Coaching on the part of the expatriates would be extremely important, Peter thought. He had already been discussing it at length with the managers that he had hired, but he was not sure whether or not that was enough, especially not when the unit would grow over the next couple of years. He certainly would not be able to coach all expatriates by himself.

In Hi Tech Systems's globally standardized performance management system, all employees should carry out performance management discussions with their superiors. Within this system, individual objectives are established and followed up. According to company policy, the individual's objectives must be specific, and if possible measurable, key activities for how to reach the objectives shall be specified, criteria for how to evaluate the performance agreed upon, and, finally, development plans decided upon. Peter's aim was that every new employee would do their first performance management discussion within a month after they joined the organization. All Hi Tech Systems superiors in China were trained in how to use the system, but there was still a question of how the "Western" system would be implemented in the Chinese culture characterized by respect for hierarchy, face, and harmonious personal relationships.

Peter had also given the question of the relationship between employee competence development and career progress quite a lot of thought. In Hi Tech Systems world-wide people achieved high status by having excellent technological knowledge and skills rather than by having made a successful career as a manager. However:

> In China especially the young people expect to get a new title every year; otherwise they had better start looking for another company. The speed of expected career progression clearly differs from the West. To develop the level of competence required for the next career step will be a challenge. Can they achieve it once a year? I think very few will.

The compensation of employees would follow the Hi Tech Systems policies. Managers and team leaders were compensated based on both business and individual performance. High-level executives and senior managers had a large business performance component in their bonus system, while the compensation of lower-level employees was mostly based on their individual performance. In the Shanghai PDC, individual performance would be evaluated based on 4–5 objectives. Peter required that the objectives had to be measurable on a ten-point scale. For instance, a manager's performance could be evaluated based on the manager's ability to fill positions in his/her group, employee satisfaction (as measured in company-wide surveys), employee turnover, the team's ability to stay within the budget, and some measure of quality (to be determined in discussions between the person and Peter). Each person's performance was evaluated every six months, and bonuses paid accordingly. The target bonus was 10 percent of the person's base salary, with 20 percent as maximum. People working on a specific development project were not evaluated every six months; the evaluation rather followed the milestones of the project. The bonus element was also somewhat larger for people working on projects than for other PDC members.

Peter believed that the compensation system would work well in China. Having clear objectives and rewards linked with their fulfillment would help send a clear message to the employees: your performance equals what you deliver – not the personal connections, or *guanxi*, that you have! None the less, at least in the start-up phase of the PDC it might be somewhat difficult to establish feasible objectives for the employees. Additionally, there had been reports from other foreign firms that there was a tendency among local employees to set objectives so that they would be reached by the subordinates.

LOOKING TOWARDS THE FUTURE

Analyzing the start-up phase of the PDC, Peter found that many things had gone quite smoothly. For instance, the two Chinese "returnees" who had joined the PDC so far (the third was still in Sweden but would relocate next month) seemed to do well. Although China had changed a lot since they left the country some ten years ago, their interaction with the local employees seemed to go well.

Managing the growth would certainly be a challenge in the next couple of years, Peter thought. For instance, local employees would have to be taught to manage themselves and to take responsibility – behaviors not automatically understood and accepted in the Chinese environment. While the Hi Tech Systems culture was non-hierarchical and meritocratic, the Chinese culture is hierarchical, and the "face" of superiors could be at stake if subordinates made their own initiatives rather than waiting for orders from their superiors. Furthermore, during the Communist regime since 1949 the Chinese had been discouraged from engaging in competitive and entrepreneurial behavior. The Chinese proverb "The early bird gets shot" aptly illustrates the reluctance on the part of Chinese employees to engage in the kind of innovative behavior that Peter wanted to see in the PDC. On the other hand, Peter had seen several Chinese changing their behavior significantly abroad. What should they do to promote this behavior also in the Shanghai PDC?

Peter was also looking for somebody to work closely with Hi Tech Systems' HR function. This person would work closely with him and the line managers to define future competence needs and how they could be met. "So far I guess I have fulfilled this role, but I'm afraid that neither me nor line managers will have time enough to pay sufficient attention to this issue in the future."

Finally, Peter was concerned about retention. "I have also been told by [a human resources expert] that a one Renminbi salary difference may make a person switch jobs." Peter believed that money would not be key to retaining the employees, though. To create a positive, family-like atmosphere might help. Peter had started a tradition of everyone in his unit meeting for a snack on Monday mornings. He also made a conscious effort to spend time talking to people in the department. Furthermore, he had invited people out for lunch and dinner. To maintain a positive relationship between the foreign and local employees, he tried to coach the expatriates not to mention how much money they made, how they lived, and how cheap they found most things to be in Shanghai (say "reasonable" instead, was his advice). All this had apparently contributed to the beginning of rumors that "things are done a bit differently in PDC". He was now thinking of whether to involve the employees' families in some way. Formal team-building exercises should probably also be done.

There were so many things to do. . . . Peter looked out of his window in one of the many new multistory buildings in the Pudong area of Shanghai. Where should he start?

NOTE

1   The Economist Intelligence Unit (1998): *China on the Couch*. September 28th, 3–4.

Joerg Dietz, Michelle Goffin and Alan Marr

RED CROSS CHILDREN'S HOME:

BUILDING CAPABILITIES IN GUYANA

Richard Ivey School of Business
The University of Western Ontario

It was February 28, 1998, and another oppressively hot night in Georgetown, Guyana. Michelle Goffin sat back at her desk and began to reflect on her recent experiences as director of the Guyana Red Cross Society's Children's Convalescent Home (CCH). While she felt that she had already initiated many positive changes in the past eight weeks, the CCH was still plagued by chronic absenteeism and morale problems. Five days ago, the situation had escalated. On Mashramani, Guyana's national holiday, none of her employees had shown up for work. In the following days, employees had fallen back into old unreliable work patterns and morale was as bad as ever. Goffin was frustrated and unsure how to proceed. She took a deep breath and pondered her next steps.

GUYANA – THE JEWEL OF THE BRITISH CROWN

Guyana is a small country on the northern coast of South America. It is about 215,000 square kilometers with a population of 700,000, of which 230,000 live in the capital Georgetown. Guyana boasts a Caribbean-type coastline, rainforests in the Amazon belt and rolling savannahs. Originally a Dutch colony, it became a British colony in 1831. The British colonialists established sugar and tobacco plantations, using African slaves to run them. Subsequent influxes of indentured laborers from various countries dramatically altered the ethnic makeup of Guyana. By the end of the 19th century, almost 40 per cent of the population was East Indian and 35 percent was of African descent. Chinese, Portuguese, American Indian and mixed races comprised the remaining 25 percent.

During the British reign, Georgetown's grand wooden buildings and sprawling gardens made it the garden city of the West Indies. The British colonists introduced education, health care and legal systems, and Guyana had the highest rates of literacy and wealth in South America. English was the official language, but Creolese, an English dialect with strong Indian and African influences, became the spoken language.

In 1966, Guyana achieved independence under Forbes Burnham. As a dictator, Burnham rigged elections, ignored human and civil rights and fostered government corruption, which became rampant. He established strong diplomatic ties with China, Cuba and other communist nations, nationalized the natural resources and took control of foreign trade. In the mid-1970s, as demand fell for sugar and bauxite (Guyana's largest exports), the already poor country slipped into severe poverty. Many educated and wealthy citizens emigrated to avoid property confiscation and to provide a future for their families.

In 1992, Dr. Cheddi Jagan became prime minister after winning internationally supervised elections. At this point, Guyana had been in a permanent recession for almost 20 years. Its health, education and legal systems were in shambles. More than half of Guyana's citizens lived abroad; those who stayed were poorly educated. Guyana was second only to Haiti as the poorest country in the Western Hemisphere.[1] With assistance from the World Bank and International Monetary Fund, Jagan began to rebuild Guyana and its infrastructure. Jagan, however, died in 1997, and subsequent political unrest slowed Guyana's development.

THE GUYANA RED CROSS SOCIETY

In 1968, the Guyana Red Cross Society (GRCS) severed its ties with the British Red Cross and became a member of the International Federation of the Red Cross (IFRC) (see Exhibit 1). Despite the loss of financial support, throughout the 1970s, the GRCS continued its many programs, such as Youth and Seniors Groups, First Aid, Health Education, Meals on Wheels and Community Assistance. As the country became poorer, the demand for programs by the GRCS increased, but its funding and volunteer membership decreased. By the 1980s, the GRCS could only fill a few roles and had sunk into helplessness and ineptitude.

By 1995, the GRCS board officially had more than 40 directors (see Exhibit 2). Twelve directors formed the executive committee to oversee operations for the secretary general (comparable to a chief executive officer). The executive committee was mandated to meet monthly and to act as an advisory committee and an auditor of daily GRCS activities. In reality, however, the board and the executive committee were ineffective; meetings were sparsely attended and reporting obligations were rarely met. In 1996, the secretary general, 91-year-old Ivor Robinson, was forced to resign due to health reasons. His departure left a succession problem: the youth officer, Eileen Lalljee, was 76; the welfare officer, Lucille Mongul, was 82 and the deputy secretary general, Belle Stevenson, had just passed away. The remaining volunteer corps had shrunk to a few largely uneducated individuals, many of whom were incapable of filling managerial roles. In December 1996, the executive committee recruited Dorothy Fraser as the new secretary general. The 55-year-old, Canadian-born Fraser had married a Guyanese and moved to Guyana 30 years ago. She had previously worked for another charitable project.

By 1997, Fraser and the board had become extremely concerned about the CCH, the largest funded program in the GRCS. Physical conditions in the home were deplorable. The CCH also had not been accountable for funds received or spent since 1993. The lack of proper accounting meant that the GRCS could not complete audited financial statements and faced expulsion from the IFRC.

THE CHILDREN'S CONVALESCENT HOME (CCH)

History

In conjunction with the Ministry of Health, the GRCS built the CCH in 1981. Its original purpose was to be a rehabilitation center for the many critically malnourished children (up to age four) discharged from the Georgetown Public Hospital. The needs of the country, however, were changing in the 1990s. The CCH became a home for the abandoned babies of young, unwed mothers, who often had been expelled by their families. The incidence of HIV, drug abuse and domestic violence had grown, further increasing the number of abandoned babies. Legally, the Ministry of Health served as the guardian for these children, but its social workers rarely communicated with the CCH. As a result, many children who desperately needed the CCH's care were not transferred from the public hospital.

Operations

The board of directors appointed the director of the CCH. This full-time position was responsible for administrative duties and supervised the matron, who ran the day-to-day operations. The matron worked with a staff of approximately 20 women. Most were between 18 and 24 years old and had not attended or completed secondary school. With the director's approval, the matron scheduled the women to work nine-hour shifts, six days per week. Despite this workload, the GRCS considered these women to be volunteers and gave them a monthly stipend of only US$30.[2] Moreover, although the matron scheduled three to five employees per shift, routinely only one staff member showed up to work. The average tenure of the volunteers was six months.

MICHELLE GOFFIN

Goffin was born in 1974 and raised near Toronto. In 1992, Goffin entered the Co-operative Education program at the University of Waterloo to pursue an honors degree in biochemistry and biotechnology. During her co-op work terms, she performed various jobs, including laboratory research for the Government of Canada, quality control in a chemical factory and instructional design work for her parents, who were management consultants. In May 1995, Goffin decided to use a work semester for volunteer work abroad, something she had been interested in for many years. A Toronto-based charity, the Canadian Foundation for World Development, posted her to Georgetown for a four-month volunteer position.

Goffin arrived in Georgetown in May 1995, and moved into an apartment attached to the CCH. She worked primarily at a nearby hospital, but she spent her mornings playing with the CCH children and taking them on excursions. The CCH had no running water, functioning toilets or washing machines. The resulting filth and lack of hygiene were shocking, even by Third World standards. The condition of the children, however, troubled Goffin even more. She commented:

> These children led a brutal life. They should have been energetic and full of life, but instead they were flat, hopeless and full of despair. They did not play with each other and the CCH staff did not play with them. They received proper nutrition, but absolutely no affection or stimulation. I have never seen children so unhappy.

BACK TO GUYANA

In her final year at university, the academic year 1996/97, Goffin learned through Dorothy Fraser's son (a fellow student) that Fraser had become the GRSC secretary general. She was having difficulties with the current CCH director and was looking for a replacement. Goffin contacted Fraser to apply for the job and, after several conversations, accepted the position as director in May 1997. She commented:

> I was excited about this job. After my first trip to Guyana, I knew that if I ever had a chance to go back, I would do so in order to "save" the children. Now, I had the opportunity.

Goffin spent the summer gathering donations for the CCH, researching and compiling resources on early childhood education and sorting out immigration issues. She left for Guyana on September 2, 1997.

Because Fraser had told Goffin that the previous CCH director and the matron would be discharged prior to her arrival, Goffin expected to immediately assume her position as director. When Goffin arrived at the CCH, however, the previous director prevented her from entering the facility. Goffin commented:

> I knew that Fraser wanted change and that she thought I could help, but she was powerless to remove the existing management. She had very deep personal and social ties to the old director and the GRCS executive committee. I sensed quickly that the political and family connections ran deep and that it would be months before anything changed.

Goffin spent the next four months working at the headquarters of the GRCS. She developed a community health program and a first-aid training program for the GRCS. Many CCH staff members attended this latter training. As a result, Goffin met many of them and became acquainted with their learning and working styles. Goffin also established a volunteer program in conjunction with the University of Waterloo and compiled training and policy manuals for volunteers. In January 1998, she finally took control of the CCH. Goffin said:

> Having to wait for another four months was a setback, but I made the best of it. I learned about the GRCS and its problems, but my goal was still to "save" the children.

TAKING OVER

Goffin's first visit to the CCH in January 1998 quickly proved that nothing had changed since 1995. The CCH, which was home to 14 children and had 20 employees, still did not have running water or working toilets. Termites had infested the 18-year-old wooden structure, resulting in so many holes in the floorboards that entire rooms had to be closed off. The roof was so leaky that, during the rainy season, the staff had to pile all the beds in one corner of the dormitory room so the children could stay dry. The weeds in the garbage-filled yard were about four feet high. Old, rusty swing sets and furniture littered the grounds and prevented the children from playing outside.

Because of the deplorable working conditions and long hours, absenteeism was rampant, resulting in double and triple shifts for the few conscientious workers who showed up. The workload was exhausting and soon these employees would not show up for shifts because they needed rest or because they felt they deserved a break. The lack of support meant that the workers had to prioritize. They fed and cleaned the children, but could do little else, including cleaning the facilities or playing with the children. They had little patience for unpredictable four-year-old children, and often used violence to discipline them.

Although the children were lifeless and emotionally neglected, Goffin did not blame the staff. Many had experienced difficult childhoods and did not understand how to play with children or why it was important. Moreover, because the matron continually scolded and demeaned the staff, they did not obey her instructions. To make matters worse, the previous director had used terror and bribes as her chief tools to motivate the matron and staff.

There was no meaningful process for selecting staff. Because they were technically volunteers, the previous CCH director and the matron could not decline applicants. Furthermore, with absenteeism and turnover so high, there was little incentive to turn down any pair of hands.

There was also no formal training program. Many of the women had their own children, which was seen as training enough. Inevitably, bad habits and poor childcare practices would surface at work. Goffin thought to herself:

> How can I expect caregivers to play with the children, when their parents probably never played with them? How are they supposed to know that playing is important for children?

Finally, compounding the employee issues was the lack of an overall system to measure and reward good childcare practices. Goffin said:

> The term "childcare" was just not part of the lexicon at the CCH. It was very difficult to drive consistent, positive behavior when there was literally no way to measure or monitor performance, good or bad, and there was no way to reward or address that performance.

After taking stock of the situation for a few days, Goffin began to realize exactly what she had gotten herself into:

> I knew that the situation was bad when I lived here in 1995, but it was overwhelming when it became my full-time responsibility. I had been there less than a week and I felt that I would need to be there for the rest of my life to fix everything.

ONE STEP AT A TIME

The first thing Goffin did was to try to improve the quality of care that the children received:

> I couldn't quantify what "happy" meant. I just wanted my kids to be happy. You know what a happy kid looks like and I did everything I could to convey that image to my staff.

Goffin started with her staff because they were around the children all of the time. She met the staff individually to assess their skills, their deficiencies and their commitment:

> I outlined what I expected of each of my staff and explained my vision for the home to them. I asked them what they needed from me to become happier in their jobs. Money came up time and time again. Some girls were paying more in transportation than they were earning in a month, which accounted for some of the absenteeism. By securing additional donations through sponsorship programs and fundraisers, I got approval from GRCS headquarters to double their reimbursement to $60 per month and to reduce their working week to five eight-hour shifts, which was standard in Guyana.

She provided basic training so that the employees understood the implications of everything from not showing up for work to how their interactions with the children affected the children's development and behaviors.

> It was a lot like teaching children. They didn't understand the consequences of their actions. I had to spell out, like an adult would to a child, that if they didn't do their job properly there could be fatal outcomes. An example of this was an incident when a worker did not report to me or the next shift that a young baby was vomiting and had fever. The baby nearly died and was hospitalized for five days because the worker did not do her job properly.

She also changed the scheduling system to better reflect the needs of the CCH and held regular, mandatory meetings with staff, seeking input and feedback. Goffin wanted to establish new work rules and tried to change the work environment:

> I tried to empower the staff by assigning responsibilities to teams rather than to individuals. I figured each shift was a team and each team was capable of deciding the most efficient way of doing the chores and making the children happy. Too often in the past I had seen an employee walk by a crying child because it was not her responsibility. So, I took away individual tasks and duties, instead ensuring that the team be responsible for the smooth running of the home and the well-being of the children. Moreover, I instituted an open door policy to my office.
>
> I did not believe that these girls were lazy. In the course of their lives, they just never had a chance to accomplish anything or had any power to control their lives. People are unmotivated when they feel powerless. I wanted to give them a feeling of accomplishment.

Goffin also began a campaign to improve the physical environment of the CCH:

Everybody pitched in when we cleaned up the building. I convinced a local businessman to send his men with a lawnmower to clear out our lawns so the children could play outside. When he came and saw the conditions of the rest of the CCH, he also offered to fix the plumbing. Before you knew it, we had running water, working toilets and even working washing machines.

After one month, Goffin began to see signs of hope and a turnaround. She said:

I was able to get more abandoned children from the public hospital transferred, so we had 30 children in total. I thought the employees were working hard and as a team. They looked happy; the children were going to be happy — it was a whole new era, a fresh start.

MASHRAMANI

February 23, 1998, was Guyana's national holiday — Mashramani. Not a single employee came to work. Goffin was extremely frustrated:

I knew about Mashramani, but with over a month of solid attendance and contributions from my employees, I didn't expect all of the no-shows. We had so much positive momentum, and nobody showing up was the old way of doing things. The absenteeism on "Mash day" set off another vicious cycle of absenteeism. All the positive team building fell apart and the employees stopped working with each other. If I did not directly supervise, they would not do their jobs. If I took a day off or had to leave the CCH to run an errand, they left work early or would lock the kids in the dorm, or they would just not show up at all.

After "Mash day", I felt so betrayed. It was as if my staff had just been humoring me all along. I asked them why they reverted to their old behaviors and what needed to change. All I got were blank looks. I was angry and discouraged. I had given them what they had asked for. I worked 12-hour days, six days a week, but every time I looked over my shoulder there was chaos and apathy. They didn't give me advice or suggestions on how to improve the place. All they did was grumble and complain when my back was turned. If problems arose, they waited until I discovered them rather than telling me about them.

What more could I do? I thought that I had made their work more fun. I doubled their salary. Why couldn't they see that if they were respectful and followed the rules, that we would all be happier? I wanted us to be a team. I wanted them to trust me. I wanted the kids to be happy and I wanted to believe that when I walked away at night, everything would be okay. I wanted my staff to be happy and to take control of their own lives. I just didn't understand why they wouldn't work with me. I didn't want to be the bad guy who had to walk around with a big stick and enforce the rules and regulations.

DESPERATE MEASURES FOR DESPERATE TIMES

Goffin felt that she had four options available to her. The first option was to admit defeat and return to Canada. Perhaps she was too young, too inexperienced and too foreign to effect lasting changes, and that it might be time to cut her losses.

The second option was to ask the GRCS for more resources. Despite their recent pay raise, the employees still took home less than half of the monthly cost of living. She thought that more money might encourage the employees to work harder. Additionally, Goffin thought of asking either Fraser or another member of the board to spend more time at the CCH to help manage the immediate problem and assess the situation. She expected that the staff would respect the commands of Fraser or a member of the board. Moreover, she felt that she could learn from Fraser or a member of the board about the employees' mindset.

The third option was to give the staff more responsibility. They had initially responded well to her changes, and more responsibility might keep the momentum going. Goffin thought that she could identify some key staff members and force them to make decisions and lead by example. She felt that this option was very risky, but if the staff responded positively, she might be able to finally break the cycle of hopelessness and apathy.

The fourth alternative was to discipline her staff. Perhaps she had been too lenient and had given the employees too much freedom. The staff had not partici- pated in decision-making before and they accepted discipline by their supervisors when they made mistakes. Perhaps they were simply unable to work in the environ- ment that Goffin had tried to establish and might react more favorably to taking orders from her.

Morale had been disheartening in the five days since Mashramani. Goffin needed to do something immediately before any bad habits returned for good.

EXHIBIT 1. ORGANIZATION OF THE RED CROSS AND RED CRESCENT MOVEMENT

The International Red Cross and Red Crescent Movement is composed of three arms: the International Federation of the Red Cross (IFRC), the International Com- mittee of the Red Cross (ICRC) and the 178 national societies. The red cross on a white background is the most recognized symbol worldwide. The movement is an impartial body, providing to those in need. In Islamic countries the Red Crescent is used in place of the Red Cross so there is no association with Christian-based religions.

Founded in 1919, the IFRC is the world's largest humanitarian organization. Its mission statement is "to provide assistance to the world's most vulnerable without discrimination as to nationality, race, religious beliefs, class or political opinions". The IFRC's work focuses on four core areas: promoting humanitarian values, disaster response, disaster preparedness, and health and community care. The IFRC is most visible during natural disasters such as drought, landslides and famine, as well as during the rebuilding of countries that have been devastated by war. The IFRC receives its funding primarily from the national-societies that campaign on its behalf.

Established in 1863, the ICRC has the mission to be an impartial, neutral and independent organization whose exclusively humanitarian mission is to protect the lives and dignity of victims of war and internal violence and to provide them with assistance. It directs and coordinates the international relief activities conducted by the movement in situations of conflict. It also endeavors to prevent suffering by promoting and strengthening humanitarian law and universal humanitarian principles.

The national societies are located in 178 countries worldwide and provide a network for both the ICRC and IFRC to carry out their missions worldwide. The main aims of the national societies are to promote the values of the Movement within a country, to train persons in first aid so they will be ready to assist in times of disaster, to assist the most vulnerable persons within their communities and to raise money for the ICRC and IFRC. The strength in this system can be seen in countries such as Canada and the United States where the Red Cross is visible through programs such as First Aid Water Safety and Blood Transfusion. In many European countries the societies were established by royalty or the elite and, as such, had access to the funds needed to promote their goals and to assist in disasters.

Source: International Committee of the Red Cross and Red Crescent Societies, www.icrc.org, August 2002.

EXHIBIT 2. ORGANIZATIONAL CHART OF THE GUYANA RED CROSS SOCIETY

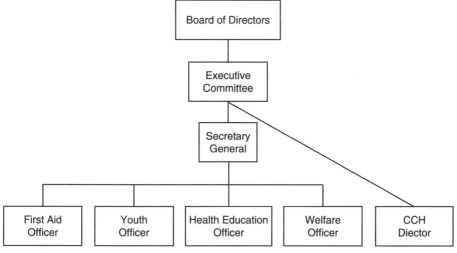

Note: The executive committee is made up of 12 members of the board of directors. If the secretary general is absent, a deputy secretary general acts as a substitute.

NOTES

1   By 1999, Guyana had an estimated per capita gross national product of only US$760.
2   The 1998 standard of living in Guyana was approximately US$100 per month.

Charlotte Butler and
Henri-Claude de Bettignies

CHANGMAI CORPORATION

David McLeod had been general manager of the All-Asia Paper Co. (AAP), part of the Changmai Corporation, for just two months. Previously, he had spent four years running a large and long-established pulp mill in South Africa. Bored by a job that had fallen into well-ordered routine, McLeod had eagerly responded to the challenge presented to him by Changmai's director of personnel, Barney Li: to take over as head of the five-year-old AAP pulp mill, one of the biggest in SE Asia, and double production within a year.

As Li explained, the ethnic Chinese owner of the Changmai group, Tommy Goh, was dissatisfied by the performance of the mill, then headed by a Malaysian expatriate and producing on average 21,500 tonnes of pulp per month. The mill contained state-of-the-art equipment which, Goh felt, was not being used to full capacity. He was therefore looking for an experienced Western manager to introduce a more professional approach and increase production. Time was of the essence as Goh's instinct, which had never failed him yet, told him that the volatile paper industry was about to undergo one of its periodic surges. When this happened, Goh wanted to be able to take full advantage of the rise in pulp prices. Currently, the mill's production costs ran at US$200 per ton of kraft pulp, for which the selling price was US$350 per ton. If, as Goh anticipated, the price climbed again to its previous high of US$700 per ton, he stood to make a real killing.

McLeod, a highly qualified engineer, had a wide experience gained in some of the most sophisticated pulp mills in the world. A Scotsman by birth, he had begun his career in Scandinavia before moving on to Canada, the US and finally South Africa. For him, the opportunity to work in Asia was an added attraction. When he finally met Goh, in a hotel room in Hong Kong, he was impressed both by the man and by his knowledge of the industry.

At age 45, the entrepreneurial Goh was head of a diversified empire. Building new businesses was his life's blood, so although rich and successful he remained restless, always searching for the next big opportunity. Closest to him, apart from two family members working in the Changmai group, were those dating from his early days in the tough world of street trading, where he made his first million by the age of 24. These people bore Goh unstinting loyalty.

Goh was a forceful personality, whose enthusiasm for what the mill could achieve made McLeod eager to get to work. His new boss, McLeod decided, was a man of some vision, clearly used to making fast decisions and seeing them implemented immediately. In meetings, Goh's impatience was signalled by the way he constantly checked his Rolex wristwatch, and barked orders to the young, smartly suited aide who relayed his chief's commands into a mobile phone. McLeod was surprised, therefore, when Goh invited him to lunch and then took him to a small backstreet restaurant that looked only one level up from a street stall, though the food was excellent. The incongruity of Goh, his aide and himself in such a setting whilst outside Roni, the waiting driver, leaned against the BMW eating a bowl of noodles, had struck McLeod forcefully. It was a memorable introduction to the cultural dissonances of this new world.

Goh's latest project was to build a rayon mill on the AAP site. Although the later chemical processes were different, pulp and rayon used the same wood and shared the initial production stages, so the synergies were obvious. To build the rayon mill, Goh had entered into a 50–50 joint venture with a Chicago-based US company whose representative, Dan Bailey, was permanently on site. McLeod was pleased to learn that he would find a fellow Westerner at AAP. Most of the workers on the site, said Li, were locals led by expatriate managers, mainly from the region.

Fired by his meeting with Goh, McLeod had gone to AAP full of energy and enthusiasm. His first sight of the mill was a rude shock. To his experienced eye, the five-year-old infant looked more like a battered old lady. On closer inspection it was clear that, although the mill was indeed equipped with the most modern technology, its maintenance had been dangerously neglected. A dozen urgent repairs leapt to McLeod's eye following his first tour of the mill, and every succeeding day he discovered more. In the first few months, McLeod worked eighteen hours a day, often being called out in the middle of the night to deal with some urgent breakdown. The local employees he found willing, but completely untrained. Safety precautions were rudimentary, and McLeod was undecided about whether or not to try and impose Western standards. However, in a preliminary effort to raise standards he had regularly toured the site and pointed out the most glaring breaches of safety regulations to the offending superintendents.

Until today McLeod had felt that, with effort and organisation, he could get the mill into shape and reach Goh's target. Then, at ten o'clock that morning, he had received a visit from Mr Lai, a government official from the Ministry of Safety and Environmental Control. McLeod knew that Lai had been inspecting the site for the past three days and had anticipated a reprimand from him as, judged by Western environmental standards, the mill had several defects. On the other hand, thought McLeod, no accidents had occurred whilst Lai was on site, which was a good sign, and perhaps an indication that his emphasis on obeying safety rules was having an effect. So he was relieved when a beaming Mr Lai said how pleased he was with his inspection and invited McLeod to walk with him down to the river into which waste water from the mill was emptied after passing through the two-level treatment plant. Goh had been very proud of this feature of the mill which, he had told McLeod, made environmental standards at AAP "the equal of those prevailing in Oregon". After primary treatment in a settling basin, the water passed through to a lagoon for secondary, bacteriological treatment in accordance with government standards. Only after two days of treatment in the lagoon was the water let out into the river.

As they walked along the muddy bank and discussed Lai's findings only minor infringements were mentioned, from which McLeod inferred that local enforcement of environmental regulations was indeed less stringent than in the West. "So, all in all," Lai concluded, "I would say that I could put in a favourable A1 report on environmental standards at the mill except", he paused, "for two small problems that I'm sure can be easily resolved given goodwill on both sides. The first concerns the broken filter in the waste water unit which, I understand from your foreman, should be fixed in the near future. However in the meantime, as I saw for myself, the water coming through the outlet pipe is quite polluted. Such a pity for the villagers who live on the other bank and fish in the river, especially coming after the unfortunate incident last year when, as I understand it, the lagoon dam collapsed and untreated waste water poured into the river, just at this very bend. I hear that several shacks were washed away, and that the river was poisoned. The villagers have told me how angry they were when they found dead fish floating in the river. They say the compensation they received was very small, hardly anything in fact; and now, seeing the brown water coming out of the outlet pipe, they greatly fear a repeat of this shocking incident.

"Just imagine, Mr McLeod, if one of the local newspapers decided to write about their fears, about how the poor villagers and their simple fishing life were threatened by a rich and powerful company. Such publicity would be most unwelcome to AAP, not to mention Mr Goh. It might even harm his plans for future projects involving government concessions. How angry he would be in such a case – and I hear that his anger can be terrible indeed for those around him. You would have my very great sympathy." And the smooth brown face of Mr Lai had looked anxiously up at McLeod, apparently in genuine concern.

"My other small concern", continued Mr Lai, "is the mill's long-term safety record. Really, I am sorry to see that so many grave accidents have occurred; two deaths by falling from a height, and another from being caught and mangled by machinery in motion. Then there are several reports of serious burns and blisters to people working in the lime kiln, an operator blinded in one eye after iron chips flew out of the spinning tank and another who lost an arm when he slipped on to the roller conveyor. Plus many other small accidents such as people being struck by falling objects or stepping on to nails with their bare feet. When you add up the number, Mr McLeod, the safety record does not look very harmonious.

"But do not look so worried, Mr McLeod," continued Lai. "I am sure we can find a solution if we put our heads together. I am returning to my hotel room in the village now, to write my report. It is my last task before I go on leave for a week. My wife has won money on a lottery ticket and is going to use it to make a pilgrimage to Lourdes. As Christians, it has always been our dearest wish to visit Lourdes together one day. It would have meant so much to us. But, sad to say, this will not be. I cannot accompany her as the lottery money will only pay for one person. So I must stay at home and look after our children." Lai sighed. "For someone like me on the salary of a humble government official, to visit Lourdes with my wife must remain just a dream. I was only just thinking to myself how wonderful it would be if I had a fairy godfather who could wave his wand, and make my dream come true."

McLeod felt sweat trickle down his back, not wholly because of the humid heat of the morning. The collapse of the lagoon dam, which had happened long before his arrival, he knew about. According to Goh, the contractors building the dam had cheated by using poor-quality cement. As a result, the dam had burst after a season of exceptionally heavy rains, with the consequences as recounted by Lai. However, Goh had assured McLeod that since then the lagoon had been rebuilt using the best-quality materials, and thoroughly tested. There was absolutely no possibility of such an incident being repeated. As for the filter, although it had been faulty for some time the pollution that resulted from it was really very minor, as proved by the fact that the daily effluent readings of the water passing through the pipe still fell within the safety range specified by the Ministry. A new filter had been ordered but, unfortunately, had not yet arrived. With so many other things on his mind, it had not occurred to McLeod to associate the past lagoon collapse with the present fault in the waste unit and Lai's official inspection. Now he cursed himself for not having seen the potential danger of their being connected. As he was only too well aware, if the incident was resurrected by Lai and the gossip he had picked up, exaggerated by stories of the present pollution, was repeated into the wrong ears, then the effects could be catastrophic both for AAP and for the Changmai group. Inevitably, Goh had business rivals who would be only too pleased to have ammunition with which to attack him.

As for the safety record, McLeod wondered where Lai had got his information, as not all the examples he gave were familiar to him. McLeod had been strictly monitoring the accident figures since his arrival and, although there had been the usual crop of minor injuries inevitably associated with high-tech machinery and an unskilled workforce, nothing major had occurred. Again, Lai must be using past history, for, as McLeod knew, in the early years of operations the mill's safety record had been very poor. As he tried vainly to think of a suitable reply, Lai turned to leave.

"You know where to find me," said Lai. "I will return to the Ministry tomorrow at nine thirty with my report, which I'm sure will be positive now we have had this little chat. I must say, I will be glad to get back to my family. We are quite worried about my eldest son. He has recently graduated from a small technical college in the south of England. It was a great sacrifice to send him, but we hoped that it would open up many opportunities for him. He is now a qualified mechanical engineer but so far has not been able to find a job that suited his talents. You know, it has occurred to me while touring this mill that here would be an ideal opening for my son. He would be very interested to work with your control distribution system. Computers have always fascinated him, and I'm sure he could very quickly learn to manage the system. What a good start it would be for him. Perhaps you have a suitable vacancy? If so, let me know tomorrow. Good day, Mr McLeod."

With a final beaming smile, Lai got into the company car that had been arranged for his use during his stay, and was driven off. His mind whirling, McLeod drove back to the office. This was the last thing he had expected. As he thought about what had passed, his shock was replaced by anger. How dare Lai try to blackmail him in this way. He would never give in to such demands. The thought of an inexperienced, unqualified person meddling in the computerised control distribution centre, one of the mill's most advanced features, made his hair stand on end. It was AAP's nerve centre, monitoring operations in all parts of the mill. Any breakdown there would be disastrous. Then he remembered Lai's comments about the damage that would be caused by a negative report that dug up the old scandal of the lagoon and hinted that history might repeat itself, or that highlighted AAP's early safety record, and the effects of all this on the villagers and on Goh. What was he going to do?

Just then his thoughts were interrupted by a knock, and his secretary, Anna, rushed into the room. "Quick," she said, "accident in the chemical area. Many people hurt." Grabbing his hard hat, McLeod rushed from the room and drove over to the plant where a crowd was gathering. He cursed. The chemical plant had been one of the worst-maintained areas and he had been renovating it as fast as he could.

The supervisor, Mr Budi, met him. "It's not as bad as we first thought," said Budi. "There was a loose valve and some of the chlorine leaked. But one of the workers panicked and started shouting, and then everyone began rushing about yelling it was 'another Bhopal'. Only one person has been hurt because of the leak – he inhaled the gas and so burned his throat. His hands and eyes also need medical attention. Two others were trampled in the rush to get out, but I think that the guards are getting things under control." McLeod looked out of the window. The security guards were trying to disperse the crowd, with some success. "Luckily, it's nearly lunch time," continued Budi. "That should help." McLeod inspected the leak. As Budi said, it was minor. But, given the lack of training among the staff and the reluctance to wear safety clothing, any incident could fast become a full-scale disaster. "I'll go and see the injured men in the clinic," said McLeod, "and then get back to the office. Let me know if you need me."

Back in his office, McLeod added "safety drill" to the long list of jobs he had to tackle in the very near future. He knew he should phone Goh and tell him what had happened, but he didn't yet feel strong enough. On impulse, he decided to go over to see Dan Bailey on the rayon site. He needed to talk to someone, a fellow Westerner. As he drove up, however, he saw that Dan, too, was having problems. He was arguing with a man McLeod recognised as one of the local contractors whose gang was part of the construction team. As McLeod arrived, the contractor shrugged and walked off.

"What's up, Dan?" said McLeod, seeing the anger in Dan's face.

"We've just had another man killed in a fall from the scaffolding," Bailey replied. "That makes ten since we started eight months ago. The man wasn't wearing boots, safety harness or a hard hat. I've told the contractors over and over again that they must provide the right equipment, it's even written into their contract. But they say 'yes, boss' and do nothing. They say they can't afford to, as Goh has negotiated such a tight contract. I spoke to Goh about it, but he says the workers don't belong to him, and that he cannot be held responsible for what the contractors do in his plant. His main concern is to get the mill finished fast and start production. Everyone squeezes everyone else, corners get cut, and as usual it's the poor at the bottom who pay for it. Have you seen the way they are living? There is no more room in the dormitories, so some containers have been temporarily converted by putting in wooden bunks. They have no running water, no electricity, they work up to their knees in mud in bare feet, and no one thinks anything of it. What a country!"

McLeod nodded in agreement. "The working conditions were the first thing that shocked me when I came to the site. I mentioned it to Goh, but he got really mad and told me the West had a nerve to try to interfere with other countries. He said to me, 'Look at your own history and see how you treated your workers in the past. Did any outsider tell you it was wicked? Look at conditions in your cities today – the drugs and violence, the crime and the homelessness – and then decide if you have a right to preach to others. I can't stand this Western pressure for labour rights in Asia, and your arguments about 'social dumping'. It's the same in China, where the Americans are always moaning about human rights. To us, trying to impose Western values seems just a dirty trick to protect your inefficient businesses. Don't condemn us before you take the beam out of your own eye." McLeod paused. "Goh must have learned that at mission school," he said with a smile. Then he went on to describe his encounter with Mr Lai.

Dan's reply was not comforting. "Sounds like you've got no choice, old buddy," he said. "But it just shows you how the attitude towards the enforcement of environmental standards, which is being monitored by powerful pressure groups, differs from the way safety legislation, which does not attract the same level of interest in the outside world, is more or less ignored. But if you think you've got problems listen to this." Bailey lowered his voice. "You know that our CEO, Howard Hartford, is visiting from Chicago on his annual tour of our operations in the region. I spent yesterday morning with him in a meeting with Goh – it was quite a combat. Anyway, that evening, as I was leaving the office, Benny Burdiman, who's heading procurement for the rayon project, poked his head round the door, apologised for disturbing me and asked me to sign a form so he could go to town next day and clear the new power boiler we've been expecting through customs. The form, from accounts, was a bill for 'R.S. Tax: US$35,000'. I was puzzled, as I thought everything had been paid for. I remembered authorising a cheque for the vendors a week ago. I hadn't a clue what this was for."

Bailey continued, "Well, you know what Benny is like. He has been with Goh from the beginning and is the sharpest negotiator in the region. He treated me like I was a backward child, and explained that the boiler was now in a bonded warehouse at the port. To get it, he had to give the director of customs a little present. He said it was quite normal, and that US $35,000 was the going rate. Apparently 'R.S. Tax' is a local joke – it stands for 'Reliable service tax'. Accounts keeps a special budget to pay it. 'You'll get used to it,' Benny said. Wanted me to sign at once, but I said, 'Now, hold on; I'll have to think about this. Let me get back to you tomorrow.' "

"So what did you do?" asked McLeod.

"I dumped it straight in the CEO's lap," said Bailey, with some satisfaction. "You know how outspoken he has always been in the press about the decline of moral values in business. Well, I told him the whole story last night over dinner and said that obviously, in the light of the circular he sent round to all operations six months ago, stating the company's commitment to conducting business round the world in a totally clean way and in the best traditions of US ethical business practice, backed by the threat of legal prosecution and instant dismissal for anyone contravening these standards etc. etc., there was no way I could do what Benny wanted. Then I also reminded him how vital the boiler was for the plant, and how far we already are behind schedule, and how there are half a dozen other important items to be delivered in the very near future. He looked quite dazed."

"So what did he decide?", asked McLeod.

"Haven't heard from him yet," said Bailey. "But he promised to call me before he left this evening".

McLeod turned to go. "See you in the bar after work then, Dan. Can't wait to hear how it ends."

He returned to the office and, to his relief, the rest of the afternoon passed without incident. Standing at the guesthouse bar later he reviewed his day; a near-riot and an attempt to blackmail him. Not quite what he had anticipated on taking the job. Still pondering his problems, McLeod took his drink over to a quiet corner but within a few minutes he was joined by Hari Tung, Financial Director of the Changmai Corp., and a Frenchman, Thierry Dupont.

Born locally, Harvard-trained Hari Tung was a very smart young man who worked closely with Goh. Thierry Dupont, who worked for a French multinational, was one of the many vendors to the rayon project, on site to check the machinery his company had supplied. He was holding a bottle of champagne. "Come, my friends," said Thierry, "celebrate with me. I just heard that I have won a *very* lucrative contract for my firm with, let's say, a large conglomerate in a country not far from here. And you know what? I got it because of my 'corruption skills'. I outbid and outdid German and US, even Japanese competition to get it. It was hard work, requiring a lot of creativity, but it was worth it, and tonight I am so proud."

"Proud!" exclaimed McLeod. "You can't be serious! You are corrupt, and you have corrupted someone else. What is there to be proud of in that?"

"My friend," said Thierry, "thanks to this contract, my company back home will have work for the next two years. With 13 per cent unemployment in France, anyone who creates jobs is a hero. In my opinion, corruption is a small price to pay to give work to Europeans. And, of course, there will be a nice little promotion in it for me. Now, stop making a fuss and have a drink."

"But David has a point," said Hari in his perfect English. "By your actions you are corrupting others. And, if you think about it, that is not the only way that you in the West are helping to corrupt the people of this region. It is something that I and my friends, who are the fathers of young children, often argue about. Look at the

Western values the young are absorbing while watching your films, full of sex and violence. What sort of heroes are they going to copy? I have always been glad to be part of a culture with such a strong sense of family. Take Mr Goh, whose family is extended to include all those who work for him. They know that the next generation will also find a place with him and so, secure in their 'iron rice bowl', they work together for the good of the group, not for the individual as I have seen people do in the West. But this sense of community is beginning to break down, and we Asians are allowing it to happen."

Hari continued, "Although we welcome the transfer of Western technological progress, we do not feel the same about your moral standards. As we see it, Western values are poisoning the local people who in the end, we fear, will be as morally bankrupt as people in your part of the world. You cannot stop the poison spreading. In every hotel, there is CNN showing the same images, encouraging the same materialist attitudes of want, want, want. Global products for global consumers, they claim. But where will it all end? Imagine, if each and every one of the 1.2 billion Chinese were to consume as much as Americans, it would mean 'goodbye, planet earth'. It could not support that degree of consumption and the pollution that would go with it. And we would all be responsible."

"What absolute rubbish," said Thierry. "It will never happen. Come on, let's talk about something more cheerful. Leave morality to the professors. While there's business to be done and a buck to be made, why should we worry?"

This case was written by Charlotte Butler, Research Associate, and Henri-Claude de Bettignies, Professor at INSEAD. It is intended to be used as a basis for class discussion rather than to illustrate effective or ineffective handling of a situation.

PART 2

Identifying, selecting and managing the global workforce

Jaime Bonache and Zulima Fernández

STRATEGIC STAFFING IN MULTINATIONAL COMPANIES: A RESOURCE-BASED APPROACH

INTRODUCTION

IN AN INFLUENTIAL PAPER in the international human resource management literature, Kobrin (1988) argued that US multinational enterprises (MNEs) were progressively reducing the number of international assignees in response to a need to reduce costs and due to the high rates of failure of expatriates. Some years later, it seems that this statement may not reflect the current practice of MNEs. According to the 2002 survey carried out by the consulting firm Organization Resources Counselors (ORC), from a sample of 775 MNEs the most common pattern among the majority of these companies, including the North Americans, is an increasing use of expatriates.

As a reflection of this increase in international assignees, there is an abundant number of studies about the way organizations manage their pool of expatriates. The studies cover different areas: selection, training, relocation and adjustment, pay and performance, career development, return. Of these practices, expatriate selection is perhaps the area that has received the most attention (see, for example, Tung 1981, 1982; Brewster 1991; Björkman and Gertsen 1993; Arthur and Bennett 1995; Gong 2003). Studies on expatriate selection have focused mainly on the criteria which MNEs apply when assessing candidates for global assignments, the methods they use for selecting these candidates and the barriers to international mobility. In spite of their interest, these studies are often accused of being merely descriptive, developed in relative isolation from other expatriation policies and failing to connect expatriate selection to the company's international strategy (Bonache et al. 2001).

In view of these limitations, we attempt to base expatriate selection on a theoretical approach that allows us to link this policy with both the firm's strategic goals and other expatriation policies. This study addresses a funda-mental question: What relationship exists between the MNE's international strategy and the expatriate's selection policy?

This question will be addressed within the conceptual framework of the resource-based view of the firm (e.g. Penrose 1959; Lippman and Rumelt 1982; Wernerfelt 1984; Barney 1991; Peteraf 1993). This theoretical model is chosen for two main reasons. First, because it enables us to provide a solid theoretical foundation for the expatriate selection policy; second, because of the importance this theory attributes to both resources and the strategic design of HR practices.

We begin with a brief description of the resource-based view of the multi-national firm. From this theoretical baseline, and relying on numerous examples from a set of Spanish multinationals, we will clarify the strategic role of inter-national assignments. We will then propose a series of hypotheses regarding the way in which expatriates will be selected depending on the role they play within an organization's internationalization process. We will conclude with a discussion regarding the contribution of our work to expatriate HRM.

RESOURCE-BASED VIEW OF THE MNE

The resource-based view of the firm is basically a strategic theory. As such, it analyses the conditions under which firms can achieve positions of competitive advantage. According to this view, competitive advantage can occur only in situations of firm resource heterogeneity (resources are unevenly distributed and deployed across firm) and firm resource immobility (they cannot be transferred easily from one firm to another). A sustainable competitive advantage is achieved when firms implement a value-creating strategy that is grounded in resources that are valuable, rare, imperfectly imitable and non-substitutable (Barney 1991).

In the resource-based view, each enterprise is seen as a bundle of resources. These encompass all input factors that are owned or controlled by the firm and enter into the production of goods and services to satisfy human needs (Amit and Schoemaker 1993; Lado and Wilson 1994). They can be both tangible (financial and physical resources) and intangible (technology, reputation, organizational culture, human resources).

Some resources that provide the company with a competitive advantage in the firm's home country are also useful in other countries. According to Penrose (1959), firms expand in an effort to utilize their resources efficiently in the search for rents. In addition to providing an opportunity to derive additional rents from existing resources, internationalization also provides learning opportunities through exposure of the company to new cultures, ideas, experi-ences, etc., which can be used to create new expertise that complements and leverages its current knowledge. Hence, the simultaneous efforts to earn income from existing resources and to seek new resources to generate future income define the two basic dimensions of multinational expansion (Tallman and

Fladmoe-Lindquist 1994). This view of internationalization is well illustrated by the expansion process of Zara, a Spanish textile company. In Spain this company developed the ability to complete a complex production process every fifteen days. This allowed it to offer stylish clothing every two weeks through its national network of shops at very reasonable prices. This capacity afforded Zara a leading position in its national market and became the driving force of its internationalization. The company expanded to those markets where demand for its products existed and where it could easily deploy its organizational resources (Belgium, France, Greece, Mexico, Portugal, USA). The company gradually enhanced its overall competitive capacity through the practices it learned in some of those markets (e.g. merchandising in New York). In sum, the company's resources – what it knows how to do better than its competitors – are what allowed and guided its international expansion.

During this exploitation and accumulation of resources, not all subsidiaries perform the same function. On the contrary, the literature on corporate internationalization has also pointed out that there is internal differentiation among subsidiaries making up an MNE (Barlett and Ghoshal 1989; Ghoshal and Nohria 1989; Martinez and Jarillo 1991; Gupta and Govindarajan 1991; Roth and Morrison 1992). Based on the extent (low versus high) to which subsidiaries develop the aforementioned two dimensions of internationalization, we can classify them into four categories: implementor, autonomous unit, learning unit, globally integrated unit (see Figure 1).

Implementor

Implementor subsidiaries apply the resources developed in the headquarters or other units of the organization to a specific geographic area. For example, the Spanish electrical firm Union Fenosa, which also provides consulting in the electrical sector, began its international expansion eight years ago and is now present on four continents and in a total of twenty-one countries. The firm's strategy is based on exporting knowledge and experience gained in providing consulting to electrical firms.

		Application of existing resources	
		High	Low
Creation of new resources	Low	Implementor	Autonomous unit
	High	Globally integrated unit	Learning unit

Figure 1. The strategic role of subsidiaries

Autonomous unit

Autonomous units are much less dependent on the human and organizational resources existing in the rest of the company's international network. In this case, internationalization is based more on the transfer of products or capital than on intangible assets (Gupta and Govindarajan 1991). The reason for this is that their environment is considered to be so idiosyncratic that the subsidiary has to develop expertise internally. This developed knowledge cannot then be transferred to other subsidiaries. Examples of this type of unit would be the Chinese subsidiary of the Spanish transportation company Alsa, or the subsidiary of the Banco Bilbao-Vizcaya-Argentaria (BBVA) in Cuba.

Learning unit

The learning unit acquires and develops new resources that may later be exported to other parts of the organization. An example of this type of unit is the US branch of Maphre, a Spanish insurance company. The reason for its location in the USA is the headquarter's interest in learning from the most competitive markets in order to transfer this knowledge to other units of the organization (including Spain).

Globally integrated unit

The globally integrated unit develops new expertise but also uses the resources generated in other subsidiaries or in the headquarters. Therefore, these subsidiaries best represent the modern subsidiary from a resource-based view. The Chilean subsidiary of the Spanish telephone company Telefónica belongs to this category. The company's management procedures were established in this subsidiary; yet the firm soon recognized the limitations of its domestic resources. This was due to the fact that the Chilean subsidiary had to operate within a free market context, an environment that the headquarters did not know due to the highly regulated Spanish telecommunications market. In this situation, learning was a major objective and a significant part of the experience. Given the recent liberalization of the Spanish telecommunications market, the capabilities (in marketing, customer service, etc.) that the company built in the Chilean subsidiary have proved to be highly useful in the domestic market.

Knowledge

So far we have seen that within the set of resources that is transferred among the different units of the MNE there are tangible resources (financial resources, physical assets) and intangible resources (human resources, technology). It is increasingly recognized that intangible resources are more important to the firm both in value and as a basis for competitive advantage, and that knowledge is the most strategically important intangible resource (Grant 1996). Knowledge is the resource that potentially best satisfies the characteristics, which are most important in establishing a competitive advantage over rivals (i.e. to be valuable, rare, imperfectly imitable and non-substitutable). Given that this concept plays an essential part in this work, it is necessary to define it with the utmost clarity.

In order to define knowledge some authors point to the meaning of this notion in philosophy (see, for example, Nonaka 1994; Grant 1996). As Nonaka (1994: 15) asserts: "The history of philosophy since the classical Greek period can be regarded as a never-ending search for the meaning of knowledge." Yet, the type of knowledge that is of interest in business does not necessarily agree with the type of knowledge with which philosophers are concerned. The latter – speculative knowledge – was clearly defined by Aristotle in *The Nicomachean Ethics*. This is focused on the understanding of the nature of things, simply for the sake of understanding. The "speculative man" aims to have his notions conforming to the truth of things, not to bring things into harmony with his notions. Aristotle contrasts speculative knowledge with that which he defines as productive knowledge. In this type of knowledge, man is not interested in the unalterable nature of things (the nature of space, for example, or freedom), except in so far as this knowledge may be necessary to help him to be productive.

In the scope of business it is productive knowledge that is of interest; this knowledge enables the firm to add value to the incoming factors of production (Gupta and Govindarajan 1991). It may refer to input processes (e.g. purchasing skills), throughput processes (e.g. product designs, process engineering, technological and organizational knowledge) or output processes (e.g. marketing know-how, merchandising). Thus understood, knowledge differs from information, which is simply a statement of facts (i.e. external market data about key customers, competitors or suppliers).

For the purposes of this work, it is important to point out that productive knowledge has a series of characteristics:

Tacit and explicit knowledge

Knowledge can be tacit or explicit. This distinction is drawn from Polanyi (1966) who distinguished between these two types of knowledge on the basis of the observation that "we can know more than we can tell". Explicit knowledge can be codified (expressed in words and numbers) and easily communicated and shared in the form of hard data, manuals, codified procedures or universal principles. In contrast, tacit knowledge is deeply rooted in an individual's experience and only revealed through its application ("learning by doing"). As a result, tacit knowledge is not easily visible and expressible, making it difficult to imitate and transmit.

Hierarchical knowledge

Knowledge is organized according to a hierarchical structure (Grant 1995).[1] Some knowledge is very concrete and involves performing a certain task, whereas other knowledge is the integration of different types of expertise of a more specific nature. For example, a hospital's knowledge that allows it to treat heart patients depends on the integration of different lower-level expertise such as diagnosis, cardiovascular surgery, post-operative care and other support know-how. In general, complex knowledge is more difficult to imitate and replicate in the market.

Generic and specific knowledge

Knowledge can be generic or specific. Generic knowledge can be applied in any company without losing value (for example, accounting expertise). Specific knowledge can be applied in the company proper but loses value in another organization. An example of this type of knowledge is an employee who knows a digit of the code that opens the company's safe. This information is highly valuable when combined with the knowledge of other employees, but its value diminishes outside the organization. As a result, the person who possesses this knowledge will lose most of his/her value upon abandoning the organization. Since a resource must be scarce and imperfectly mobile in order to be a source of competitive advantage, it holds that specific knowledge is more crucial than generic knowledge to explain the company's competitiveness and internationalization.

Context-specific and context-generalizable knowledge

Knowledge can be context specific and context generalizable. As noted earlier, internationalization exposes the company to multiple markets in which different knowledge can be applied and developed. Depending on its usefulness outside the location where it is developed, knowledge can be context specific or context generalizable. If it is confined to its place of origin, it is context specific. If it is effective across countries, it is context generalizable (Taylor et al. 1996).

Individual and collective knowledge

Knowledge can be held individually or collectively (Prahalad and Hamel 1990). The generation or building of a particular type of knowledge depends only on a single individual (i.e. the ability to work in a particular language). Collective knowledge is the outcome of knowledge integration. It is the product of the coordinated efforts of many individual specialists who possess many different but complementary skills (Grant 1996). Both collective and individual knowledge can be explicit and tacit. An example of explicit collective knowledge (and hence a type of knowledge that can be objectified) is the organization's established human resources practices (performance appraisal procedures, selection methods, etc.). The organization's culture is an example of tacit collective knowledge. It is something which is manifested in the practice of an organization, but which cannot be objectified. Similarly, whereas "numerical computation" is a case of explicit individual knowledge, "negotiation skills" are an example of tacit individual knowledge.

Knowledge acquisition and generation

The process of obtaining and generating knowledge is gradual. A minimum amount of time is required to generate and assimilate new knowledge – what Dierickx and Cool (1989) call "time compression diseconomies". This occurs even to acquire coded (and thus easily interpreted and transmitted) knowledge. In addition, acquisition of knowledge is path dependent, which means that the way in which the knowledge is gained affects the results that are eventually obtained.

Knowledge as information

Finally, Itami (1987) pointed out that knowledge, just like any other intangible asset, is characterized by the fact that its raw material is information possessed by the individuals and groups both within the organization and outside (for example, brand image and reputation become embodied in the company's customers and suppliers).

   The information and people are two essential elements of intangible assets in general and of knowledge in particular. It is the people who have the experience, information and knowledge, which are applied in the activities carried out by the company. From this perspective, we can discuss the role that expatriation policies play within corporate internationalization.

The strategic role of expatriation selection policy

The literature on the resource-based view has paid neither theoretical nor empirical attention to the strategic role of expatriation policies (see Gong 2003 for a notable exception). Therefore, the principal basis on which to discuss the role of these policies from this theoretical perspective comes from the domestic literature (Wright and McMahan 1992; Wright et al. 1994). Building on this domestic literature, we present a model suggesting that expatriation policies have two basic functions. The first is to identify and attract employees with the knowledge, skills and abilities required for the successful implementation of the strategy of the subsidiary. Having obtained this pool, the next aim of expatriation practices is to encourage expatriates to behave in a way that supports such a strategy. In this work we limit our attention to the first function of expatriation policies and, in particular, to expatriate selection.

In the analysis of expatriate selection we develop a contingency approach, which draws on the following reasoning. First, we argue that the type of subsidiary partly determines the expatriate's strategic role. Second, we maintain that each strategic role requires different types of knowledge, skills and abilities on the part of expatriates. Finally, assuming a rational view according to which expatriate selection aims at supporting the subsidiary strategic role, we argue that the company will carry out different selection choices according to the subsidiary to which the expatriate will be assigned.

Reasons for using expatriates

According to Black et al. (1992), expatriates play three main strategic roles in corporate internationalization: control and coordination of operations (management function), transfer of skills and knowledge, managerial development. Edstrom and Galbraith (1977) argued that expatriate roles depend on the company's international strategy. They noted that companies which integrated their operations globally assigned expatriates for reason of coordination, while those which followed a multi-domestic strategy chose expatriates for control reasons. Since our analysis is carried out at the subsidiary level, our objective at this point will be to correlate the reasons for using expatriates to the types of subsidiary. Along these lines, we argue that while many expatriations involve more than one role, the relative importance of each varies by type of subsidiary.

Implementor subsidiaries exploit knowledge from other units. Most of the knowledge that is transferred among units is tacit (for instance, the capacities of a company's managers and employees to launch new products). Given that such tacit knowledge cannot be codified or contained in manuals and can only be observed through its application, when a company decides to transfer tacit knowledge between different units it must assign employees to the foreign operations (Pucik 1992; Bonache et al. 2001). Therefore, skills and knowledge transfer is expected to be a critical reason for using expatriates in implementor subsidiaries.

A significant presence of these knowledge transfer expatriates is also to be expected in the globally integrated units since there is a considerable input of knowledge into these subsidiaries. Along with transfer of knowledge, co-ordination is another reason to assign expatriates in globally integrated subsidiaries. For example, in its first phase of internationalization the Spanish textile company Zara wanted to ensure that its activities were coordinated in order to exploit the economies of scale that result from selling standardized products to the same global market segment. The firm only produces articles that can be sold in the nine countries in which it does business. To do so the headquarters chose to assign expatriates to start up operations and transferred them to different units in order to increase their knowledge of the network, their awareness of the impact of their decisions and to develop multiple contacts which would allow them to act as links between interdependent units.

In autonomous subsidiaries, there is no relevant transfer of knowledge from the headquarters to the subsidiary or vice versa. Therefore, there is little basis for using expatriates to transfer know-how. Moreover, the fact that the expatriates' expertise is not well suited to the subsidiary environment, together with factors such as expatriate costs, the motivation and aspirations of local employees or local governmental pressures, will make international assignments seem less attractive to the multinational firm (Gong 2003). On this basis, it could be argued that these subsidiaries will tend to be directed not by expatriates but by local managers who speak the language, understand the country's culture and political system and generally belong to a social elite that permits the company more easily to penetrate the market. In addition, using local directors increases the company's acceptance by the government and trade unions in the host country.

In spite of these considerations, circumstances may exist (which can also be found in other types of subsidiaries) that force the company to opt for expatriate instead of local directors in order to ensure control of subsidiary. For example, in situations of political risk (where an event is likely to occur that will change the profitability prospect of a specific investment), or cultural risk (when there is a large cultural distance between headquarters and subsidiary), the head-quarters need to process a lot of information. This may lead to the assignment of "trustworthy" managers whose function will be to increase the channels of communication between the headquarters and subsidiary and to guarantee that head-office interests are well represented in the subsidiary (Boyacigiller 1990; Bonache and Pla 2005). Thus, maintaining control is the main reason why the management of BBVA assigned a Spanish expatriate to its subsidiary in Cuba.

Finally, learning units transfer knowledge from their units to other units. The dominant pattern of international transfer will be one of managers from these units to another country (Black et al. 1992). On other occasions international transfers involving learning units may be more similar to the typical parent-country expatriate pattern. This is the case of transfers to the US sub-sidiary of Maphre. Top management sees this subsidiary as the ideal unit for a management development process leading to organizational learning. What the manager learns about elements such as the US insurance market, local competitors and international competitors operating in a highly competitive market can later be transferred to Spain and other units and incorporated into future resources. Management development thus becomes the main reason for using expatriates in learning units.

Strategic choices in expatriate selection

Once we have analyzed the reasons that a firm might have for assigning expatriates to each of its subsidiaries, we can examine expatriate selection. This process involves choosing qualified individuals to fill positions in the organization's international network. The organization faces several strategic choices during the selection process:

- internal recruitment vs. external recruitment
- individual vs. teams
- technical qualifications vs. other selection criteria
- extrinsic rewards vs. intrinsic rewards

These are only an example of the choices that confront management when selecting expatriates. Other decisions, which we do not include in our analysis, would be, for example, whether to include the family in the selection process or whether psychological screening should be used. It is also important to note that these choices represent two opposite extremes on a continuum. The majority of the decisions fall somewhere in between these two extremes. Therefore, it becomes a question of emphasis, not exclusion. A review of the expatriation literature suggests the choices that are specified in Table 1.

Internal vs. external recruitment

An interesting finding by a recent study on expatriate selection is that there is a perceived shortage of international managers, primarily due to the growing resistance to international mobility (Scullion 1994). In addition to family and personal issues (i.e. the growing unwillingness to disrupt the education of children, the growing importance of quality of life considerations; Black et al. 1992; Shaffer et al. 1999), and the continued uncertainty regarding international terrorism and political and social unrest of certain destinations (Scullion 1994), it is well documented that the career implications of international assignments are often frustrating. A lack of respect for acquired skills, loss of status, and reverse culture shock upon return are recurring problems in many companies

Table 1. The strategic role of the subsidiary and selection of expatriates

	Implementor	Autonomous unit	Globally integrated unit	Learning unit
Main expatriates' roles	Transfer of knowledge	Control	Transfer of knowledge; coordination	Career development
Source of recruitment	Internal labor market	Internal labor market	Internal labor market	External labor market
Dominant selection criteria	Technical competence	Cultural adaptability; language skills	Technical competence; cross-cultural communication	Motivation and potential
Team vs. individuals	Teams and individuals	Individuals	Teams and individuals	Individuals
Rewards	Medium emphasis on extrinsic and intrinsic rewards	High emphasis on extrinsic rewards	High emphasis on intrinsic rewards	High emphasis on intrinsic rewards

Table 2. Reasons given for declining an international assignment

	Percentage of companies	
	Most common	Least common
Spousal/dual career issues	43	18
Concerns about children (e.g. education)	36	10
Compensation package not enough of an incentive	29	19
Expatriate career issues	28	18
Undesirable host location	27	21
Anxiety over culture shock (e.g. language, customs, foreign foods)	12	37
Decreased contact with family, friends, and community	11	36
Concerns about aging parents	6	42
Selected candidates rarely reject assignments	52	

Source: Based on 2002 *Worldwide Survey of International Assignment Policies and Practices*, European Edition, Organization Resources Counselors.

(Daily et al. 2000; Stahl et al. 2002). The most common reasons for assignment refusal, as set out in the 2002 ORC survey on international assignments, are shown in Table 2. The most common reasons given for declining an assignment are spousal/dual career issues, impact on the employee's career and concern about the compensation package or host location.

The shortage of international managers creates problems in selection. From an organization's viewpoint, the selection decision is ideally made in circumstances where an organization has a large number of applicants seeking an international assignment. However, given the limitation in the pool of candidates from which to choose, a selection process differs greatly from an ideal situation. In fact, availability seems to be the critical variable in the acceptance of an international assignment (Brewster and Scullion 1997).

In order to respond to this shortage the company can introduce external recruitment to fill management positions abroad. In spite of this possibility, it is well documented that the majority of firms rely almost exclusively on internal recruitment for foreign management positions (Torbiörn 1982; Scullion 1994). This selection option can be found even in markets where there is plenty of skilled labor (Boyacigiller 1990). This led us to pose the following question: Why is there not a greater emphasis on external recruitment?

To respond to this question, it is necessary to take into account the strategic role of expatriates in the different subsidiaries. Implementor and globally integrated subsidiaries exploit existing knowledge in other units of the organization. Much of the knowledge, which is transferred among units of an MNE firm, is not only tacit but also specific (Penrose 1959; Bartlett and Ghoshal 1995). Specific and tacit knowledge are of an idiosyncratic nature, referring to the specific way in which things are done and can only be acquired through observation and expertise within the company (i.e. advanced technological expertise or specific marketing activity). Therefore: (*a*) if the company's strategic advantage is usually found in the MNE's specific knowledge; (b) if this specific knowledge can only be acquired within the company; (c) if, because of its tacit nature, this specific knowledge can only be transferred by expatriates; then the basic recruitment source of expatriates will be the company itself and not the external labor market.

A reliance on internal employees is also justified if the strategic purpose of an assignment is coordination and control of operations. The coordination function of expatriates in globally integrated units requires the assignment of people with broad experience in the firm, including a wide array of contacts throughout the company (Black et al. 1992). The control function of expatriates in autonomous subsidiaries requires the assignment of trustworthy people to guarantee that the interests of headquarters are well represented in the subsidiary. From this point of view, it is also logical to look within the firm in order to fill the management position with an internal manager who has an established track record and proven loyalty to the company.

However, in the case of learning units, recruiting can be from the external labor market. External managers can be assigned to one unit from a country with special competencies in a certain area. Later, they can be assigned to other units in order to implement what they have learned. Resorting to external recruitment is not only a way of responding to the shortage of international managers, but is also consistent with the view that points to this recruitment source as one of the main methods of bringing into the organization individuals who have new skills and abilities and different ways of approaching job tasks (Baron and Kreps 1999).

Team vs. individual assignments

The function of control of expatriates in autonomous subsidiaries is highly individual. Just one expatriate in a key post can ensure that the interests of the headquarters are well represented in the subsidiary. This can also be said of expatriates in globally integrated subsidiaries who perform a coordination function. Similarly, assignments to learning units for management development purposes can be performed by a single individual.

Yet when we analyze assignments for the transfer of knowledge, which takes place in both implementors and globally integrated units, we get a different picture. As noted earlier, knowledge can be individual or collective. If the knowledge to be transferred is implicit individual knowledge (for instance, the knowledge of a brilliant intuitive stockbroker), the transfer will only involve that individual. On the other hand, collective knowledge is the product of the coordinated efforts of many individual specialists who possess different but complementary knowledge (Grant 1996). If this knowledge cannot be transferred upwards because of its tacit nature, then the transfer of such complex organizational knowledge may involve the transfer of the whole team. For example, the launching of new products involves the coordinated action of many individual specialists (i.e. market researchers, brand managers, advertising executives, sales representatives). The manager responsible for the launch knows only a fraction of what his subordinates know. For this reason, when a company wants to transfer this new product development capability to other subsidiaries it has to transfer a team, not just an individual (Bonache and Brewster 2002).

Technical qualifications vs. other selection criteria

One of the questions most studied in expatriate management is that of the criteria used to select international assignees. In the survey of Organization Resources Counselors (2002) technical and other professional qualifications were by far the most frequently cited criteria employed when selecting a person for a job overseas (see Table 3). This finding is consistent with other surveys on expatriate selection criteria (Mendenhall et al. 1987; Tung 1981, 1982: Björkman and Gertsen 1993).

Despite the emphasis on technical qualifications and domestic performance, there is abundant evidence that other factors also play a critical role in the success of international assignees. In a recent study on the relative importance of factors that contribute to the success of expatriates, as perceived by 338 international assignees, Arthur and Bennett (1995) classified them into five categories:

- job knowledge and motivation
- relational skills
- flexibility/adaptability
- extra-cultural openness
- family situation

The authors found that family situation (adaptability of spouse and family, stable marriage, willingness of spouse to live abroad) and flexibility/adaptability (tolerance of ambiguity, listening skills, ability to deal with stress) were perceived as the most important factors in the success of expatriates. An interesting

Table 3. Factors involved in selecting employees for international assignments

	Percentage of companies	
	Most important	Least important
Skills and competencies	66	0
Job performance	28	0
Job level	4	5
Prior international living experience or assignment	2	6
Language ability	1	9
Projected assignment cost for that individual	1	20
Familiarity with assignment country	0	6
Marital status	0	52

Source: Based on 2002 *Worldwide Survey of International Assignment Policies and Practices*, European Edition, Organization Resources Counselors.

question then becomes: Why does expatriate selection tend to focus on technical competence?

According to Tung (1981), the emphasis on technical competence is due to the fact that this is more easily identified than other factors such as cultural adaptability. Since technical competence is always an important element in any job, those making the selection prefer to play safe to minimize possible errors.

From a strategic perspective, the firm must first pay attention to defining the strategic role of the assignment and then to assessing the factors required to accomplish this role successfully. This approach provides us with a new reason for the emphasis on technical competence: the nature of certain international assignments. If the fundamental reason for using expatriates is to transfer the skills and knowledge that provide the company with a strategic advantage over competitors – a typical assignment of implementors and globally integrated units – it is logical that technical competence and domestic track record become the dominant selection criteria.

Yet if the strategic purpose of an international assignment is coordination – also a typical assignment in globally integrated units – then the candidate will have to possess or develop a wide array of contacts throughout the company. Although technical competence will also be relevant in performing this coordination role, the dominant selection criteria must be to possess good cross-cultural communication skills.

The success of autonomous subsidiaries depends more on the ability to adapt to local conditions than on the technical support received from headquarters. Therefore, cultural adaptability and language skills should be the criteria emphasized, rather than technical competence, when selecting expatriates to perform a control function in an autonomous unit. Similarly, given that management development is the main reason for assigning expatriates to learning units, motivation for learning and potential for advancement as a manager will be the criteria to emphasize.

Extrinsic vs. intrinsic rewards

This choice refers to the type of incentive offered by the organization to accept an international assignment. Such incentives can be extrinsic or intrinsic. Extrinsic rewards involve types of tangible or monetary reward, while intrinsic rewards are intangible gains such as the opportunity for professional development, security or recognition.

A situational factor that determines the emphasis of one type of reward or another is repatriation (Black et al. 1992; Black and Gregersen 1999; Toh and DeNisi 2003; Bonache 2005). Lack of respect for acquired skills, loss of status, and reverse culture shock are reported to be recurring problems upon repatriation. The gap between an expatriate's expectation and reality upon return may negatively affect his or her level of satisfaction (Guzzo et al. 1993; Strohl et al. 1998). This problem is very obvious to the rest of the organization's employees and can influence a multinational firm's ability to recruit new employees for future assignments.

The repatriation problem is minimized if expatriates are assured that international experience will positively affect their professional development. However, that is not the normal practice as the purpose of providing personnel for international assignments seems more to cover immediate human resource needs than to create a career development strategy for future corporate directors (Mendenhall *et al.* 1987).

Taking into account the context specificity and the value of expertise acquired abroad, not all assignments generate the same repatriation problems, nor do they have the same impact on professional careers (see Figure 2). If the knowledge gained abroad cannot be applied once the assignment is concluded (e.g. because it is context specific), repatriation problems will arise. This would explain the results of several investigations (Howard 1974; Harvey 1982) which demonstrate that skills developed abroad by expatriates are barely exploited. On the other hand, if this knowledge is of benefit once the assignment is concluded, repatriation will be easier. Also, the company's long-term competitive advantage depends on constant updating of the knowledge on which it is based (Tallman and Fladmoe-Linquist 1994). Consequently, the value of knowledge acquired abroad will increase as it continues to accumulate with knowledge that already exists in the country of origin. If this value is high, it will have a positive impact on professional development. Otherwise, the impact will be more uncertain.

Figure 2 shows how expatriation problems and the impact on professional career assignments determine the type of reward offered by the organization. Expatriates in autonomous units develop expertise that is totally heterogeneous with regard to that existing in any other unit. Therefore, those assignments result in more serious repatriation problems. In view of the uncertainty associated with repatriation, monetary incentives are strongly emphasized to attract human resources to the expatriation service (Adler and Ghadar 1990; Toh and DeNisi 2003).

In the other three kinds of subsidiary, knowledge is shared between units, which facilitates repatriation. However, the value of the knowledge acquired abroad varies among subsidiaries. Thus, globally integrated units and learning

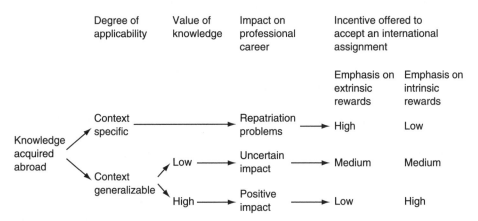

Figure 2. Knowledge acquired abroad, repatriation and type of reward

subsidiaries contribute heavily to the generation of new expertise in the country of origin. Under these conditions, the incentives offered by the firm to accept the international assignments could be less of a monetary type and related more to the intrinsic value involved in the opportunity to undertake a brilliant career within the organization. Thus, in strongly integrated companies such as Zara the condition for access to executive posts at headquarters is to have had at least one international assignment.

Finally, expatriates in implementor subsidiaries contribute very little to new know-how. An international assignment will therefore have a more indecisive impact on the professional career. As a result, the headquarters will also have to emphasize extrinsic rewards to motivate acceptance of the assignment.

CONCLUSION

Drawing on the theoretical notions of the resource-based view, in this paper we have attempted to explain the strategic content of expatriate selection. Although there is still much empirical work to be done in this area of research, we believe that our analysis makes a number of important contributions. First, it helps us to clarify the linkage between expatriates and competitive advantage: if the primary source of sustainable competitive advantage is tacit and specific knowledge which is owned by people; if a firm's internationalization is based on the transfer to other markets of competitive advantage that it possesses in the domestic market, other markets require the movement of the people who possess it; then it is safe to say that international assignments of employees play a critical strategic role in a firm's internationalization.

The second contribution of our study points to areas of research that so far have received very limited attention. In particular, this study has found that international assignments may involve the transfer of teams, not just individual managers. This is consistent with the heavy emphasis of business literature on team-based structures, but conflicts with the prevailing "individualistic" trend in the standard expatriation literature. Such a trend assumes that firms are hierarchical structures dominated by the superior knowledge of the senior management team. This conception can be questioned from two points of view. First, within a firm, different employees undertake different activities in the process of transforming inputs into outputs, and there is no reason to think a priori top management's view is privileged (Spender 1996). Second, to be imperfectly imitable is a requisite for a resource to be a source of sustainable competitive advantage. If knowledge is linked to an individual, competitor firms can imitate this advantage by hiring this individual. If the competitive advantage is a result of the integration of many cooperating individuals, it may not be apparent which personnel are responsible for it: in other words, there is causal ambiguity (Reed and DeFilippi 1990). This suggests that, instead of focusing exclusively on individuals as the basic unit of analysis, a more comprehensive theory of international assignments must also embrace teams.

In addition to these contributions, our analysis also has implications for the international competitiveness of MNEs. It is well documented that the majority of MNEs fail to adopt a systematic and coherent approach to selection and that most assignments are short-term, problem-solving experiences (Brewster and Scullion 1997). Arguably, this ad hoc approach to staffing has performance costs. In accordance with the prevailing thinking in strategic human resource management, the integration of human resource practices and corporate strategy results in improved corporate performance (Baron and Kreps 1999). Therefore, it can be expected that empirical research will show that companies which select their expatriates in connection with the subsidiary's strategic objectives, as we have attempted to show in this work, will obtain better performance than those that operate in this area on an ad hoc basis.

NOTE

1   Grant (1995) does not speak of knowledge but capabilities. However, these are no more than the knowledge that the company possesses regarding the way to combine resources to perform a productive activity.

REFERENCES

Adler, N. J. and Ghadar, F. (1990) "Strategic human resource management: a global perspective" in R. Pieper (ed.), *Human Resource Management: An International Comparison*, New York: De Gruyter.

Amit, R. and Schoemaker, P. J. (1993) "Strategic assets and organizational rent", *Strategic Management Journal* 14: 33–46.

Arthur, W. and Bennett, W. (1995) "The international assignee: the relative importance of factors perceived to contribute to success", *Personnel Psychology* 48: 99–114.

Barlett, C. A. and Ghoshal, S. (1989) "Managing across borders: new organizational responses", *Sloan Management Review* 10: 43–53.

Barlett, C. A. and Ghoshal, S. (1995) *Transnational Management*, 2nd edn, Boston, Mass.: Irwin.

Barney, L. (1991) "Firm resources and sustained competitive advantage", *Journal of Management* 17: 99–120.

Baron, J. and Kreps, D. (1999) *Strategic Human Resources: Frameworks for General Managers*, New York: John Wiley & Sons, Inc.

Björkman, I. and Gertsen, M. (1993) "Selecting and training Scandinavian expatriates: determinants of corporate practice", *Scandinavian Journal of Management* 9(2): 145–64.

Black, J. S., and Gregersen, H. B. (1999) "The right way to manage expats", *Harvard Business Review* 77(2): 52–63.

Black, J. S., Gregersen, H. B. and Mendenhall, M. (1992) *Global Assignments*, New York: Jossey Bass.

Bonache J. (2005) "Job satisfaction among expatriates, repatriates and domestic employees. The perceived impact of international assignments on work-related variables", *Personnel Review* 34(1).

Bonache, J. and Pla, J. (2005) "When are international managers a cost effective solution? The rationale of transaction cost theory applied to staffing decisions in MNCs", *Journal of Business Research* 58(10): 1320–9.

Bonache, J., Suutari, V. and Brewster, C. (2001) "A review and agenda for expatriate HRM", *Thunderbird International Management Review* 42(1): 3–21.

Boyacigiller, N. (1990) "Role of expatriates in the management of interdependence, complexity, and risk of MNEs", *Journal of International Business Studies*, third quarter: 257–78.

Brewster, C. (1991) *The Management of Expatriates*, London: Kogan Page.

Brewster, C. and Scullion, H. (1997) "A review and agenda for expatriate HRM", *Human Resource Management Journal* 7(3): 32–41.

Daily, C., Trevis, C. and Dalton, D. (2000) "International experience in the executive suite: The path to prosperity?", *Strategic Management Journal* 21: 515–23.

Dierickx, I. and Cool, K. (1989) "Asset stock accumulation and sustainability of competitive advantage", *Management Science* 35: 1504–11.

Edstrom, A. and Galbraith, J. (1977) "Transfer of managers as a coordination and control strategy in multinational organizations", *Administrative Science Quarterly* 22: 248–63.

Ghoshal, S. and Nohria, N. (1989) "Internal differentiation within multinational corporations", *Strategic Management Journal* 10(4): 323–37.

Gong, Y. (2003) "Subsidiary staffing in multinational enterprises: agency, resources, and performance", *Academy of Management Journal* 46(6): 728–39.

Grant, R. M (1995) *Contemporary Strategic Analysis*, Cambridge, Mass.: Blackwell.

Grant, R. M. (1996) "Toward a knowledge-based theory of the firm", *Strategic Management Journal* 17: 109–22.

Gupta, A. K. and Govindarajan, V. (1991) "Knowledge flows and the structure of control within multinational corporations", *Academy of Management Review* 16(4): 768–92.

Guzzo, R. A., Noonan, K. A. and Elron, E. (1993) "Employer influence on the expatriate experience: Limits and implications for retention in overseas assignments", *Research in Personnel and Human Resources Management*, suppl. 3, 323–38.

Harvey, M. (1982) "The other side of foreign assignment: dealing with the repatriation dilemma", *Colombia Journal of World Business* 1: 53–9.

Howard, C. G. (1974) "The returning overseas executive: cultural shock in reverse", *Human Resource Management* 13(2): 49–62.

Itami, H. (1987) *Mobilizing Invisible Assets*, Cambridge, Mass.: Harvard University Press.

Kobrin, S. J. (1988) "Expatriate reduction and strategic control in American multifunctional corporations", *Human Resource Management* 27(1): 63–75.

Lado, A. A. and Wilson, M. C. (1994) "Human resource systems and sustained competitive advantage", *Academy of Management Review* 19: 699–727.

Lippman, S. and Rumelt, R. P. (1982) "Uncertain imitability: an analysis of interfirm differences in profitability under competition", *Bell Journal of Economics* 13: 418–38.

Martinez, J. I. and Jarillo, J. C. (1991) "The evolution of research on coordination mechanisms in multinational corporations", *Journal of International Business Studies* 20(3): 389–514.

Mendenhall, M. E., Dunbar, E. and Oddou, G. R. (1987) "Expatriate selection, training and career pathing: a review and critique", *Human Resource Management* 26(3): 331–45.

Nohria, N. and Ghoshal, S. (1994) "Differentiated fit and shared values: alternatives for managing headquarters–subsidiary relations", *Strategic Management Journal* 15: 491–502.

Nonaka, I. (1994) "A dynamic theory of organizational knowledge creation", *Organization Science* 5: 14–37.

Organization Resources Counselors (2002) *Worldwide Survey of International Assignment Policies and Practices*, New York: Organization Resources Counselors, pp. 1–102.

Penrose, E. T. (1959) *The Theory of Growth of the Firm*, Oxford: Blackwell.

Peteraf, M. A. (1993) "The cornerstones of competitive advantage. A resource-based view", *Strategic Management Journal* 14: 179–91.

Polanyi, M. (1966) *Personal Knowledge: Towards a Post-Critical Philosophy*, Chicago, Ill.: University of Chicago Press.

Prahalad, C. K. and Hamel, G. (1990) "The core competence of the corporation", *Harvard Business Review* 68(3): 79–91.

Pucik, V. (1992) "Globalization and human resource management", in V. Pucik *et al.* *Globalizing Management*, Chichester: Wiley.

Reed, R. and DeFilippi, R. (1990) "Casual ambiguity, barriers to imitation, and sustainable competitive advantage", *Academy of Management Review* 15: 88–102.

Roth, K. and Morrison, A. J. (1992) "Implementing global strategy: characteristics of global subsidiary mandates", *Journal of International Business Studies* 23: 715–35.

Scullion, H. (1994) "Staffing policies and strategic control in British multinationals", *International Studies of Management and Organization* 24(3): 86–104.

Shaffer, M. A, Harrison, D. and Gilley, M. (1999) "Dimensions, determinants, and differences in the expatriate adjustment process", *Journal of International Business Studies* 30(3): 557–81.

Spender, G. (1996) "Making knowledge the basis of a dynamic theory of the firm", *Strategic Management Journal* 17: 45–62.

Stahl, G. K., Miller, E. and Tung, R. (2002) "Toward the bounderyless career: A closer look at the expatriate career concept and the perceived implications of an international assignment", *Journal of World Business* 37: 216–27.

Tallman, S. and Fladmoe-Lindquist, K. (1994) "A resource-based model of the multinational firm", paper presented at the Strategic Management Society Conference, Paris, France.

Taylor, S., Beechler, S. and Napier, N. (1996) "Toward an integrative model of strategic international human resource management", *Academy of Management Review* 21(4): 959–65.

Toh, S. M. and DeNisi, A. (2003) "Host country national reactions to expatriate pay policies: a model and implications", *Academy of Management Review* 28(4): 606–21.

Torbiörn, I. (1982) *Living Abroad: Personal Adjustment and Personnel Policy in Overseas Settings*, New York: Wiley.

Tung, R. (1981) "Selection and training of personnel for overseas assignments", *Columbia Journal of World Business* 16(1): 68–78.

Tung, R. (1982) "Selection and training procedures of US, European, and Japanese multinationals", *California Management Review* 25: 57–71.

Wernerfelt, B. (1984) "A resource-based view of the firm", *Strategic Management Journal* 5: 171–80.

Wright, P. M. and McMahan, G. C. (1992) "Theoretical perspectives for strategic human resource management", *Journal of Management* 18(2): 259–320.

Wright, P. M., McMahan, G. C. and McWilliams, A. (1994) "Human resources and sustained competitive advantage: a resource-based perspective", *International Journal of Human Resource Management* 5(2): 301–26.

J. Stewart Black and Hal B. Gregersen

THE RIGHT WAY TO MANAGE EXPATS

IN TODAY'S GLOBAL ECONOMY having a workforce that is fluent in the ways of the world isn't a luxury. It's a competitive necessity. No wonder nearly 80 percent of midsize and large companies currently send professionals abroad and 45 percent plan to increase the number they have on assignment.

But international assignments don't come cheap. On average, expatriates cost two to three times what they would in an equivalent position back home. A fully loaded expatriate package including benefits and cost-of-living adjustments costs anywhere from $300,000 to $1 million annually, probably the single largest expenditure most companies make on any one individual except for the CEO.

The fact is, however, that most companies get anemic returns on their expat investments. Over the past decade, we have studied the management of expatriates at about 750 US, European, and Japanese companies. We asked both the expatriates themselves and the executives who sent them abroad to evaluate their experiences. In addition, we looked at what happened after expatriates returned home. Was their tenure worthwhile from a personal and organizational standpoint?

Overall, the results of our research were alarming. We found that between 10 percent and 20 percent of all US managers sent abroad returned early because of job dissatisfaction or difficulties in adjusting to a foreign country. Of those who stayed for the duration, nearly one-third did not perform up to the expectations of their superiors. And, perhaps most problematic, one-fourth of those who completed an assignment left their company, often to join a competitor, within one year after repatriation. That's a turnover rate double that of managers who did not go abroad.

If getting the most out of your expats is so important, why do so many companies get it so wrong? The main reason seems to be that many executives assume that the rules of good business are the same everywhere. In other words, they don't believe they need to – or should have to – engage in special efforts for their expats.

Take the expat assignment process. Executives know that negotiation tactics and marketing strategies can vary from culture to culture. Most do not believe, however, that the variance is sufficient to warrant the expense of programs designed to select or train candidates for international assignments.

Further, once expats are in place, executives back home usually are not inclined to coddle their well-paid representatives. When people are issued first-class tickets on a luxury liner, they're not supposed to complain about being at sea.

Finally, people at the home office find it difficult to imagine that returning expats need help readjusting after just a few years away. They don't see why people who've been given an extended period to explore the Left Bank or the Forbidden City should get a hero's welcome. As a result of such thinking, the only time companies pay special attention to their expats is when something goes spectacularly wrong. And by then it's too little, too late.

Of course, some companies do engage in serious efforts to make foreign assignments beneficial both for the employees and the organization. Very often, however, such companies consign the responsibility of expat selection, training, and support to the human resources department. Few HR managers – only 11 percent, according to our research – have ever worked abroad themselves; most have little understanding of a global assignment's unique personal and professional challenges. As a result, they often get bogged down in the adminis-trative minutiae of international assignments instead of capturing strategic opportunities.

Over the past several years, we have concentrated on examining the small number of companies that have compiled a winning track record in the process of managing their expats. Their people overseas report a high degree of job satisfaction and back that up with strong performance. These companies also hold on to their expats long after they return home. GE Medical Systems, for example, has all but eliminated unwanted turnover after repatriation and has seen its international sales expand from 10 percent to more than 50 percent of its total sales during the last ten years.

The companies that manage their expats effectively come in many sizes and from a wide range of industries. Yet we have found that they all follow three general practices:

When making international assignments, they focus on knowledge creation and global leadership development. Many companies send people abroad to reward them, to get them out of the way, or to fill an immedi-ate business need. At companies that manage the international assignment pro-cess well, however, people are given foreign posts for two related reasons: to generate and transfer knowledge, to develop their global leadership skills, or to do both.

They assign overseas posts to people whose technical skills are matched or exceeded by their cross-cultural abilities. Companies that manage expats wisely do not assume that people who have succeeded at home will repeat that success abroad. They assign international posts to individuals who not only have the necessary technical skills but also have indicated that they would be likely to live comfortably in different cultures.

They end expatriate assignments with a deliberate repatriation process. Most executives who oversee expat employees view their return home as a nonissue. The truth is, repatriation is a time of major upheaval, professionally and personally, for two-thirds of expats. Companies that recognize this fact help their returning people by providing them with career guidance and enabling them to put their international experience to work.

Let's explore the practices in turn, illustrating them with companies that have put them to good use over the past several years.

SENDING PEOPLE FOR THE RIGHT REASONS

For as long as companies have been sending people abroad, many have been doing so for the wrong reasons, that is, for reasons that make little long-term business sense. Foreign assignments in glamorous locales such as Paris and London have been used to reward favored employees; posts to distant lands have been used as dumping grounds for the mediocre. But in most cases companies send people abroad to fill a burning business need: to fight a competitor gaining market share in Brazil, to open a factory in China, to keep the computers running in Portugal.

Immediate business demands cannot be ignored. But the companies that manage their expats effectively view foreign assignments with an eye on the long term. Even when people are sent abroad to extinguish fires, they are expected to plant forests when the embers are cool. They are expected to go beyond pressing problems either to generate new knowledge for the organization or to acquire skills that will help them become leaders.

Imagine a large Canadian company that wants to open a telephone-making plant in Vietnam. It would certainly send a manager who knows how to manufacture phones and how to get a greenfield facility up and running quickly. The manager's performance rating and compensation would reflect those objectives, but that's where most companies would stop. Companies that manage their expats effectively, however, would require more of the manager in Vietnam. Once the plant was established, he would be expected to transfer his knowledge to local professionals and to learn from them, too. Together, they would be expected to generate innovative ideas.

Nokia, the world's second-largest manufacturer of mobile phones, is a good example of a company that effectively uses international assignments to generate knowledge. Unlike most large technology companies, Nokia does not rely on a central R&D function. Instead, it operates 36 centers in 11 countries – from Finland to China to the United States. Senior executives scan their global workforce for engineers and designers who are likely to generate new ideas when combined into a team. They bring these people together in a R&D center for assignments of up to two years, with the explicit objective of inventing new products. The approach works well: Nokia continues to grab global market share by rapidly turning new ideas into successful commercial products, such as the Nokia 6100 series mobile telephones that were launched last year in Beijing and have quickly captured a leading position in markets around the world.

Other companies have more need to focus on the second reason for international assignments: to develop global leadership skills. Such companies would concur with a recent observation by GE's CEO: "The Jack Welch of the future cannot be like me. I've spent my entire career in the United States. The next head of GE will be somebody who has spent time in Bombay, in Hong Kong, in Buenos Aires." An executive cannot develop a global perspective on business or become comfortable with foreign cultures by staying at headquarters or taking short business trips abroad. Such intangibles come instead as a result of having spent more than one sustained period working abroad.

Indeed, the only way to change fundamentally how people think about doing business globally is by having them work abroad for several months at a time. Everyone has a mental map of the world – a set of ingrained assumptions about what people are like and how the world works. But our maps may not be able to point us in the right direction when we try to use them in uncharted territory. Consider the case of a tall American businessman who, during a recent trip to Japan, dined at a traditional restaurant. Upon entering, he bumped his head on the doorjamb. The next day, the same thing happened. It was only on the third time that he remembered to duck. People on international assignments hit their heads on doorjambs many times over the years. Eventually, they learn to duck – to expect that the world abroad will be different from the one they had imagined. Hard experience has rearranged their mental maps or, at the very least, expanded the boundaries on their maps.

It is with such a broadened view of the world that global leaders are made. A vice president for Disney, for example, was posted in 1993 to EuroDisney, the company's struggling theme park just outside Paris. Stephen Burke arrived in France with the same mental map of the company as the senior managers at home. He believed, for instance, that families and alcohol do not mix at Disney theme parks. But after living in France for several months Burke came to see what an affront EuroDisney's no-alcohol policy was to most of its potential local customers. A glass of wine with lunch was as French as a cheeseburger was American. Further, Burke came to see that Disney's lack of focus on tour operators – a more important distribution channel in Europe than in North America – made it inconvenient to book reservations for complete vacation packages, which many Europeans prefer to arrange.

With his new perspective on the local market, Burke pushed hard to persuade Disney's top management to sell wine at its French park and to create complete vacation packages for tour operators. He succeeded. Because of those and other changes, attendance and hotel occupancy soon skyrocketed, and EuroDisney posted its first operational profit. Burke told us afterward, "The assignment to EuroDisney caused me to challenge long-held assumptions that were based on my experiences and career at Disney. After living in France, I came to look at the world quite differently."

The two principal goals of international assignments — generation of knowledge and development of global leaders — are not mutually exclusive. But it is unlikely that an international posting will allow a company to achieve both goals in every case or to an equal degree. Not every employee going abroad has abundant knowledge to share or the right stuff to be the company's future CEO. What matters, however, is that executives explicitly know beforehand why they are sending a person overseas — and that the reason goes beyond an immediate business problem.

Just as important, it is critical that expats themselves know the rationale for their assignments. Are they being sent abroad to generate knowledge or to develop their leadership skills? At the effective companies we studied, this kind of information helps expats focus on the right objectives in the right measure. For example, a communications company recently transferred one of its top lean-manufacturing experts from Asia to the United States. His task was to help managers understand and implement the practices that had been perfected in Singapore and Japan. The company's senior executives did not expect him to hone his leadership capabilities because they did not believe that he would ascend the corporate ranks. Knowing the main purpose of his posting, the expert was able to focus his energy on downloading his knowledge to other managers. Moreover, he did not build up unrealistic expectations that he would be promoted after returning home.

Companies with foreign operations will always face unexpected crises from time to time. But the companies that reap the most from sending their people abroad recognize that international assignments can't just be about sending in the medics. They must also be about ensuring the organization's health over the long term.

SENDING THE RIGHT PEOPLE

Just as managers often send people abroad for the wrong reasons, they frequently send the wrong people. Not because they send people who don't have the necessary technical skills. Indeed, technical skill is frequently the main reason that people are selected for open posts. But managers often send people who lack the ability to adjust to different customs, perspectives, and business practices. In other words, they send people who are capable but culturally illiterate.

Companies that have a strong track record with expats put a candidate's openness to new cultures on an equal footing with the person's technical know-how. After all, successfully navigating within your own business environment and culture does not guarantee that you can maneuver successfully in another one. We know, for instance, of a senior manager at a US carmaker who was an expert at negotiating contracts with his company's steel suppliers. When transferred to Korea to conduct similar deals, the man's confrontational style did nothing but offend the consensus-minded Koreans – to the point where suppliers would not even speak to him directly. What was worse, the man was unwilling to change his way of doing business. He was soon called back to the company's home office, and his replacement spent a year undoing the damage he left in his wake.

How do you weed out people like the man who failed in Korea? The companies that manage expats successfully use a variety of tools to assess cultural sensitivity, from casual observation to formal testing. Interestingly, however, almost all evaluate people early in their careers in order to eliminate some from the potential pool of expats and help others build cross-cultural skills.

Although the companies differ in how they conduct their assessments, our research shows that they seek the following similar characteristics in their expats:

A drive to communicate. Most expats will try to communicate with local people in their new country, but people who end up being successful in their jobs are those that don't give up after early attempts either fail or embarrass them. To identify such people, the most effective companies in our research scanned their ranks for employees who were both enthusiastic and extroverted in conversation, and not afraid to try out their fractured French or talk with someone whose English was weak.

Broad-based sociability. The tendency for many people posted overseas is to stick with a small circle of fellow expats. By contrast, successful global managers establish social ties to the local residents, from shopkeepers to government officials. There is no better source for insights into a local market and no better way to adjust to strange surroundings.

Cultural flexibility. It is human nature to gravitate toward the familiar – that's why many Americans overseas find themselves eating lunch at McDonald's. But the expats who add the most value to their companies – by staying for the duration and being open to local market trends – are those who willingly experiment with different customs. In India, such people eat dal and chapatis for lunch; in Brazil, they follow the fortunes of the local jai alai team.

Cosmopolitan orientation. Expats with a cosmopolitan mind-set intuitively understand that different cultural norms have value and meaning to those who practice them. Companies that send the right people abroad have identified individuals who respect diverse viewpoints; they live and let live.

A collaborative negotiation style. When expats negotiate with foreigners, the potential for conflict is much higher than it is when they are dealing with compatriots. Different cultures can hold radically different expectations about the way negotiations should be conducted. Thus a collaborative negotiation style, which can be important enough in business at home, becomes absolutely critical abroad.

Consider the approach taken by the vice chairman of Huntsman Corporation, a private chemicals company based in Salt Lake City with sales of

$4.75 billion. Over the last five years, Jon Huntsman, Jr., has developed an informal but highly successful method for assessing cultural aptitudes in his employees. He regularly asks managers that he thinks have global leadership potential to accompany him on international trips, even if immediate business needs don't justify the expense. During such trips, he takes the managers to local restaurants, shopping areas, and side streets and observes their behavior. Do they approach the strange and unusual sights, sounds, smells, and tastes with curiosity or do they look for the nearest Pizza Hut? Do they try to communicate with local shopkeepers or do they hustle back to the Hilton?

Huntsman also observes how managers act among foreigners at home. In social settings, he watches to see if they seek out the foreign guests or talk only with people they already know. During negotiations with foreigners, he gauges his managers' ability to take a collaborative rather than a combative approach.

Although time-consuming and sometimes costly, Huntsman's approach to screening potential expats is actually remarkably efficient. He is able to assess candidates before the pressures of an impending international problem make a quick decision necessary. Consequently, he makes fewer expensive mistakes when choosing whom to send abroad.

Other companies, such as LG Group, a $70-billion Korean conglomerate, take a more formal approach to assessing candidates for foreign assignments. Early in their careers, candidates complete a survey of about 100 questions designed to rate their preparation for global assignments and their cross-cultural skills. Afterward, LG employees and their managers discuss how specific training courses or future on-the-job experiences could help them enhance their strengths and overcome their weaknesses. From this discussion, a personalized development plan and timetable are generated. Because LG's potential expats are given time to develop their skills, about 97 percent of them succeed in meeting the company's expectations when they are eventually sent on international assignments.

The surveys used by LG were purchased from an outside company and cost from $300 to $500 per person. Other organizations develop them in-house, with the help of their training or HR departments. In either case, the survey questions generally ask people not to evaluate their own characteristics but to describe their past behavior. For example, they might be asked when they had last eaten a meal from a cuisine that was unfamiliar to them.

A third approach to identifying potential expats is used by Colgate-Palmolive, which has about 70 percent of its sales outside the United States and decades of international experience. To fill its entry-level marketing positions, the company recruits students from universities or business schools who can demonstrate an ability to handle cross-cultural situations. They may have already worked or lived abroad and will at the very least have traveled extensively; they will often be able to speak a foreign language. In this way, Colgate-Palmolive leverages the investment that other companies have made in an employee's first experience abroad.

Colgate-Palmolive takes a similarly cautious approach once such promising young people are on staff. Instead of sending them on long assignments abroad, it sends them on a series of training stints lasting 6 to 18 months. These assignments do not come with the costly benefits that are provided to high-level expats, such as allowances for housing and a car. This strategy means the company can provide young managers with a broad range of overseas experience. One manager hired in the United States, for example, spent time in the Czech Republic and the Baltic states and recently became country manager in Ukraine – all before celebrating his thirtieth birthday.

Companies face a trade-off between the accuracy and the cost of expat assessment. Although Colgate-Palmolive's approach is probably the most accurate way to assess an individual's potential to succeed on international assignments, it comes with a substantial price tag. That approach is probably most appropriate for a multinational that needs a large cadre of global managers. For companies with lesser workforce requirements, the less costly approaches of Huntsman and LG may make more sense. In any case, the key to success is having a systematic way of assessing the cross-cultural aptitudes of people you may want to send abroad.

FINISHING THE RIGHT WAY

Virtually every effective company we studied took the matter of repatriation seriously. Most companies, however, do not. Consider the findings of our research: about one-third of the expats we surveyed were still filling temporary assignments three months after coming home. More than three-quarters felt that their permanent position upon returning home was a demotion from their posting abroad, and 61 percent said that they lacked opportunities to put their foreign experience to work. No wonder the average turnover rate of returning professionals reaches 25 percent. We know of one company that over a two-year period lost all the managers it sent on international assignments within a year of their return – 25 people in all. It might just as well have written a check for $50 million and tossed it to the winds.

The story of a senior engineer from a European electronics company is typical. The man was sent to Saudi Arabia on a four-year assignment, at a cost to his employers of about $4 million. During those four years, he learned fluent Arabic, gained new technical skills, and made friends with important business-people in the Saudi community. But upon returning home the man was shocked to find himself frequently scolded that "the way things were done in Saudi Arabia has nothing to do with the way we do things at headquarters". Worse, he was kept waiting almost nine months for a permanent assignment which, when it came, gave him less authority than he had had abroad. Not surprisingly, the engineer left to join a direct competitor a few months later and ended up using the knowledge and skills he had acquired in Saudi Arabia against his former employer.

International assignments end badly for several reasons. First, although employers give little thought to their return, expats believe that a successful overseas assignment is an achievement that deserves recognition. They want to put their new skills and knowledge to use and are often disappointed both by the blasé attitude at headquarters toward their return and by their new jobs. That disappointment can be particularly strong for senior expats who have gotten used to the independence of running a foreign operation. As one UK expatriate recently observed, "If you have been the orchestra conductor overseas, it is very difficult to accept a position as second fiddle back home".

Changes in and out of the office can also make homecoming difficult. The company may have reshuffled its top management, reorganized its reporting structure, or even reshaped its culture. Old mentors may have moved on, leaving the returning employee to deal with new decision makers and power brokers. Things change in people's personal lives, too. Friends may have moved away, figuratively or literally. Children may find it hard to settle back into school or relate to old playmates.

The effective companies in our research used straightforward processes to solve these problems. At Monsanto, for example, the head office starts thinking about the next assignments for returning expats three to six months before they will return. As a first step, an HR officer and a line manager who is senior to the expat – both with international experience – assess the skills that the expat has gained during her experience overseas. They also review potential job openings within Monsanto. At the same time, the expat herself writes a report that includes a self-assessment and describes career goals. The three then meet and decide which of the available jobs best fits the expat's capabilities and the organization's needs.

In the six years since it introduced the system, Monsanto has dramatically reduced the turnover rate of its returning expatriates. And because returning employees participate in the process they feel valued and treated fairly – even if they don't get their job of first choice.

Along with finding their returning expats suitable jobs, effective companies also prepare them for changes in their personal and professional landscapes. For example, the oil and gas company Unocal offers all expats and their families a daylong debriefing program upon their return. The program focuses on common repatriation difficulties, from communicating with colleagues who have not worked abroad to helping children fit in again with their peers. The participants watch videos of past expats and their families discussing their experiences. That sets the stage for a live discussion. In many cases, participants end up sharing tips for coping with repatriation, such as keeping a journal. The journal is useful, many returning expats say, because it helps them examine the sources of their frustrations and anxieties, which in turn helps them think about what they might do to deal with them better.

Although participants find repatriation programs useful, it is seldom cost effective for a company to provide them in-house unless its volume of international assignments is heavy. Most companies that offer such programs outsource them to professional training companies or form consortiums with other companies to share the costs. Effective companies have realized that the money they spend on these programs is a small price to pay for retaining people with global insight and experience.

Companies that manage their expats successfully follow the three practices that make the assignments work from beginning to end. They focus on creating knowledge and developing global leadership skills; they make sure that candidates have cross-cultural skills to match their technical abilities; and they prepare people to make the transition back to their home offices.

Given the poor record that most companies have when it comes to managing expats, it's probably no surprise that we often encounter organizations in which none of the three practices are at work. Some companies, however, are committed to one or two of the practices, and so the question arises: Do you have to follow all three to see a payback on your expat investment? The answer, our research would suggest, is yes. The practices not only reinforce one another, they also cover the entire expat experience, from assignment to return home.

Consider the dividends reaped by Honda of America Manufacturing, perhaps one of the best examples of a company that implements all three practices. Honda starts expat assignments with clear strategic objectives such as the development of a new car model or improved supplier relations. Assignees then complete a survey to identify personal strengths and weaknesses related to the upcoming assignment. Six months before an expat is scheduled to return home, the company initiates an active matchmaking process to locate a suitable job for that person; a debriefing interview is conducted upon repatriation to capture lessons learned from the assignment.

As a result of Honda's integrated approach, nearly all of its expats consistently perform at or above expectations, and the turnover rate for returning employees is less than 5 percent. Most important, its expats consistently attain the key strategic objectives established at the beginning of each assignment.

Companies like Honda, GE, and Nokia have learned how to reap the full value of international assignments. Their CEOs share a conviction that sustained global growth rests on the shoulders of key individuals, particularly those with international experience. As a result, those companies are poised to capture tomorrow's global market opportunities by making their international assignments – the largest single investments in executive development that they will make – financially successful today.

Nancy J. Adler

COMPETITIVE FRONTIERS:
WOMEN MANAGING ACROSS BORDERS

It doesn't make any difference if you are blue, green, purple, or a frog, if you have the best product at the best price, they'll buy.

American woman manager based in Hong Kong

ABOUT THE SINGLE MOST uncontroversial, incontrovertible statement to make about women in international management is that there are very few of them. The evidence is both subjective and objective [1, p. 58]. As an executive in a global firm, would you hire a woman for an international management position? Would you send her abroad as an expatriate manager? Would she succeed? Would hiring her increase or decrease your firm's competitiveness?

GLOBAL COMPETITION

Business today increasingly competes on a worldwide basis. Few firms have the luxury of competing primarily within their own domestic market. While some firms use country-specific multidomestic strategies, and thus compete in independent domestic markets, a much greater number have embraced globally integrated strategies structured around worldwide lines of business [13]. As global competition continues to intensify, firms are evolving transnational strategies. Such strategies simultaneously require the local responsiveness demanded by multidomestic strategies, the worldwide integration demanded by global strategies, along with an increased emphasis on organizational learning and innovation [14]. These business dynamics lead to:

Transnational networks of firms and divisions within firms, including an increasingly complex web of strategic alliances. Transnational firms . . . are less hierarchically structured than firms operating in the previous phases. Power is no longer centered in a single headquarters that is . . . dominated by any one national culture. As a consequence, both structural and cultural dominance are minimized, with cross-cultural interaction no longer following any pre-defined "passport hierarchy".[3, p. 56]

These organizational changes are affecting the number and role of women managers.

WOMEN AND TRANSNATIONAL CORPORATIONS

Given the increasing importance of transnational corporations, it is encouraging that their impact on women in management, to date, has been primarily positive. Transnational corporations include women in ways that domestic, multidomestic, and multinational firms do not. First, the extremely competitive business environment forces transnational firms to select the very best people available. The opportunity cost of prejudice – of rejecting women and limiting selection to men – is much higher than in previous economic environments. As *Fortune* succinctly stated, "The best reason for believing that more women will be in charge before long is that in a ferociously competitive global economy, no company can afford to waste valuable brainpower simply because it's wearing a skirt" [15, p. 56]. This competitive advantage is heightened by a growing worldwide education differential favouring women.

Second, whereas domestic and multidomestic companies hire primarily local nationals, and therefore must closely adhere to local norms on hiring – or not hiring – female managers, transnational corporations are not similarly limited. Because the corporate culture of transnational firms is not coincident with the local culture of any particular country, transnationals have greater flexibility in defining selection and promotion criteria that best fit the firm's needs rather than those which most closely mimic the historic patterns of a particular country. Said simply, transnationals can and do hire local women managers even in countries in which the local companies rarely do so.

US-based transnational corporations, for example, have often hired local female managers when local firms would not. This dynamic has been particularly pronounced in Japan where foreign corporations have had difficulty attracting top ranked male applicants (see [16, 17]). American firms have led the way in hiring excellent Japanese women, while Japanese firms are still extremely reticent to hire them (see [18]). Interestingly, while still hiring fewer women than most American firms, Japanese multinationals operating in the United States hire more female managers in their American affiliates than they do in their home country operations [19].

By hiring women, transnationals act as role models for firms in many countries which have not seriously considered promoting significant numbers of women into managerial positions. The greater the number of expatriates involved in foreign affiliates, the less likely they are to follow local human resource practices – including being less likely to restrict the number of female managers [19]. The firm's transnational character allows it organizational freedoms and imposes competitive demands not present in domestic or multidomestic environments.

Third, transnational corporations have begun to send women abroad as expatriate managers [8]. Because transnationals use expatriates and local managers, they can benefit from the greater flexibility that many cultures afford foreign women. As will be described, most countries do not hold foreign women to the same professionally limiting roles that restrict local women (see [4, 10]). The outstanding success of these female expatriate managers in all geographies – Africa, the Americas, Asia, Europe, and the Middle East – is encouraging firms both to continue sending women abroad [4,20] and to begin to promote more local women into management [10].

Fourth, whereas domestic, multidomestic, and multinational firms have been characterized by structural hierarchies, transnationals are increasingly characterized by networks of equals. Recent research suggests that women work particularly well in such networks:

> Women . . . are countering the values of the hierarchy with those of the web [21, p. 52] . . . when describing their roles in their organizations, women usually refer . . . to themselves as being in the middle of things . . . Inseparable from their sense of themselves as being in the middle . . . [is] women's notion of being connected to those around them. . . . [21, pp. 45–6]

Not surprisingly, transnational firms see women managers as bringing needed collaborative and participative skills to the workplace [22].

Fifth, leading management scholars have identified innovation as a key factor in global competitiveness (among others, see [14, 23, 24]). An inherent source of innovation is well-managed diversity, including gender diversity [25]. Women bring diversity to transnational corporations which have heretofore been primarily male.

Transnational corporations thus include more women than their predecessors could (or would) and benefit organizationally from their professional contributions in new ways. They benefit both from women's increased representation at all levels of the organization as well as from their unique ways of contributing to the organization that complement those of men.

FUNDAMENTAL ASSUMPTIONS: DIFFERENT APPROACHES

Given women's current scarcity in the managerial ranks, transnational firms can use two approaches to leverage the potential of female managers: they can increase the number of female managers and executives and they can encourage their unique contribution. Unfortunately, many of their predecessors – domestic, multidomestic, and multinational firms – adopted neither approach; or limited themselves by focusing on only one of the two approaches.

As shown in Table 1 firms have traditionally made one of two fundamentally different assumptions about the ideal role of women in management. Although generally implicit, the first reflects an equity approach based on assumed similarity, while the second defines a complementary contribution approach based on assumed difference. The first focuses on increasing the representation of women managers; the second on increasing their utilization at all levels of the organization.

The first, the equity approach, based on assumed similarity, has been used most pervasively in the United States. In this approach, firms assume that women are identical, as professionals, to men, and therefore equally capable of contributing in ways similar to those of men. From this equity perspective, the primary question is one of entry into and representation within management. Is the firm

Table 1. Two approaches to women in management

Assumptions	Equity approach	Complementary contribution approach
Fundamental assumptions	Similarity	Difference
Men's and women's contributions	Identical	Complementary
Fairness based on	Equity	Valuing difference
Strategic goal	Equal access	Recognizing and valuing difference
Assessment	Quantitative	Qualitative
Measured by	Statistical proportion of women at each hierarchical level	Assessing women's contribution to organization's goals
Process	Counting women	Assessing women's contribution
Measuring of effectiveness:		
Women's contribution	Identical to men's	Complementary to men's
Norms	Identical for men and women	Unique to men and women
Based on	Historical "male" norms	Women's own contribution
Referent	Men	Women
Acculturation process	Assimilation	Synergy
Expected behaviour	Standardized	Differentiated
Based on	Male norms	Female norms
Essence	"Dress for success" business suit	Elegant, feminine attire
Example	United States: "The melting pot"	France: "Vive la différence!"

Source: [11, pp. 3–32].

hiring and promoting sufficient numbers of female managers? Primary change strategies include affirmative action programmes, equal rights legislation, and structural changes designed to avoid tokenism and to train women in managerial skills traditionally neglected during their formal education and informal socialization.

Given the equity approach's emphasis on equal entry into and equal representation within the male-dominated world of management, the equity approach's implicit goal for female managers is assimilation. Firms expected women to think, dress, and act like the men who had traditionally held the aspired-to management positions. Understandably, firms measured effectiveness against male norms: Could she do what he had been doing as well as he had been doing it? Or, according to *Fortune* [22, p. 58], "If you can't join 'em, beat 'em . . . the way to overcome [discrimination] is to . . . start outdoing men at their own game". The potential for women to make unique, but equally valuable, contributions to organizations remained outside the logic of the equity approach and therefore largely unrealized.

In contrast, the second approach, the complementary contribution approach, is based on the assumption of difference, not similarity. While originally used to describe Swedish managers [26], it has been pervasive throughout Europe and Japan, and evident in most other areas of the world. In the complementary contribution approach, firms assume women and men differ and therefore are capable of making different, but equally valuable, contributions to the organization (see [27–34]). Unlike in the equity approach, the goal is not assumed to be equal statistical representation, but rather equivalent recognition of and benefit from women's and men's differing patterns and styles of contribution at all levels of the organization.

From this second perspective, change strategies focus first on identifying the unique contributions of female and male managers; second, on creating enabling conditions to encourage and reward both types of contribution; and third, on creating synergy – combining women's and men's contributions to form more innovative and powerful organizational solutions to business challenges. Under this second set of assumptions, firms expect female managers to think, to dress, and to act like women. Female managers' thinking and behaviour, though similar in many ways to that of their male colleagues, is seen to differ in important respects.

Progress, as measured by the equity approach, is quantitative – a statistical accounting of the proportion of female managers in the organization by rank, salary, and status. As measured by the complementary contribution approach, progress is qualitative – an assessment of the organization's track record in encouraging and rewarding women and men for making unique contributions and for building organizationally effective combinations of those contributions; that is, for increasing innovation and organizational learning.

Interestingly, each approach has tended to be labelled as heresy when viewed through the eyes of the other. From the perspective of the equity approach, viewing women (or any other distinct group) as different was seen as tantamount to judging them as inferior (see [29]). Recognizing differences among female and male managers was implicitly equated with prejudice [25]. From this point of view, only one best way to manage exists, and equity demands that women be given equal access to that one way. By contrast, the complementary contribution approach posits that there are many equally valid, yet different, ways to manage. The best approach, based on recognizing, valuing, and combining differences, is synergistic. From this second perspective, not to see a female manager's uniqueness is to negate her identity and, consequently, to negate the potential for her unique contribution to the organization.

To predict what women's roles in management will be in the 1990s and the twenty-first century, it is important to understand the underlying assumptions that firms make in each country about the role of women in management. To what extent is difference viewed as heresy, versus as a potential resource? To what extent is uniqueness seen as a constraint rather than as a valuable asset? Unlike their predecessors, transnational firms view female managers' increased representation and potentially unique contribution as complementary sources of competitive advantage rather than as either–or solutions, or, even more limiting, as societal constraints.

UNEXPECTED SUCCESS: WOMEN MANAGERS ACROSS BORDERS

Cross-border business is fundamental to transnational firms. Unlike their previous approaches, such firms define managerial roles transnationally, with expatriate assignments forming a central component. Given the historical scarcity of local women managers in most countries, firms have questioned if women can function successfully in cross-border managerial assignments. They have believed that the relative absence of local women managers formed a basis for accurately predicting the potential for success, or lack thereof, of expatriate women.

Given the importance of these questions to future business success, a multi-part study was conducted on the role of women as expatriate managers. The research revealed the story of a noun, *woman*, that appears to have become mixed up with an adjective, *foreign*, when predicting expatriate managers' success. It revealed a set of assumptions that managers and executives make about how foreigners would treat expatriate women, based on their beliefs about how foreign firms treat their own local women. The problem with the story is that the assumptions proved to be false. Moreover, because the assumptions fail to reflect reality accurately, they are inadvertently causing executives to make decisions that are neither effective nor equitable.

The first part of the study sought to determine the proportion of women being selected for expatriate positions. Major North American multinational firms (686) were surveyed. They reported sending over 13,338 expatriate managers abroad, of whom 402, or 3 per cent, were women. Thus, North American firms send 32 times as many male as female expatriate managers abroad (see [8, 9]). In comparison with this 3 per cent in international management, women held 37 per cent of domestic US management positions, 12 times as many as they held abroad [35].

Although the 3 per cent represents significantly fewer women working as expatriate managers than the proportion holding domestic management positions, this should not be viewed strictly as a poor showing, but rather as the beginning of a new trend. The vast majority of women who had ever held expatriate management positions were sent so recently that they are currently still working abroad.

Given transnationals' needs for the best qualified managers — whether female or male — the second, third, and fourth parts of the study sought to explain why so few women hold international management positions. Each part addressed one of the three most commonly held "myths" about women in international management:

(1)   Women do not want to be international managers.
(2)   Companies refuse to send women abroad.
(3)   Foreigners' prejudice against women renders them ineffective, even when interested in foreign assignments and successful in being sent.

These beliefs were labelled "myths" because, although widely held by both men and women, their accuracy had never been tested.

Myth 1: Women do not want to be international managers

Is the problem that women are less interested than men in pursuing international careers? The study tested this myth by surveying more than 1,000 graduating MBAs from seven top management schools in the United States, Canada, and Europe [5, 7]. The results revealed an overwhelming case of no significant difference: female and male MBAs display equal interest, or disinterest, in pursuing international careers. More than four out of five MBAs — both women and men — want an international assignment at some time during their career. Both female and male MBAs, however, agree that firms offer fewer opportunities to women than to men, and significantly fewer opportunities to women pursuing international careers than to those pursuing domestic careers.

Although there may have been a difference in the past, women and men today are equally interested in international management, including expatriate assignments. The first myth — that women do not want to be international managers — is, in fact, a myth.

Myth 2: Companies refuse to send women abroad

If the problem is not women's lack of interest, is it that companies refuse to select women for international assignments? To test if the myth of corporate resistance was true, human resource vice-presidents and managers from 60 of the largest North American multinationals were surveyed (see [6]). Over half of the companies reported that they hesitate to send women abroad. Almost four times as many reported being reluctant to select women for international assignments as for domestic management positions. When asked why they hesitate, almost three-quarters reported believing that foreigners were so prejudiced against women that the female managers could not succeed even if sent. Similarly, 70 per cent believed that dual-career issues were insurmountable. In addition, some human resource executives expressed concern about the women's physical safety, the hazards involved in travelling in underdeveloped countries, and, especially in the case of single women, the isolation and loneliness.

Many of the women who succeeded in being sent abroad as expatriate managers report having confronted some form of corporate resistance before being sent abroad. For example:

> *Malaysia*. Management assumed that women didn't have the physical stamina to survive in the tropics. They claimed I couldn't hack it [in Malaysia].

> *Japan and Korea*. Everyone was more or less curious if it would work. My American boss tried to advise me, "Don't be upset if it's difficult in Japan and Korea". The American male manager in Tokyo was also hesitant. Finally the Chinese boss in Hong Kong said, "We have to try!" Then they sent me.

A few women experienced severe resistance from their companies to sending any female managers abroad. Their firms seemed to offer them an expatriate position only after all potential male candidates had turned it down. For example:

> *Thailand*. Every advance in responsibility is because the Americans had no choice. I've never been chosen over someone else.

> *Japan*. They never would have considered me. But then the financial manager in Tokyo had a heart attack, and they had to send someone. So they sent me, on a month's notice, as a temporary until they could find a man to fill the permanent position. It worked out, and I stayed.

Although most of the women are sent in the same capacity as their male expatriate colleagues, some companies demonstrate their hesitation by offering temporary or travel assignments rather than regular expatriate positions. For instance:

> *Hong Kong*. After offering me the job, they hesitated: "Could a woman work with the Chinese?" So my job was defined as temporary, a one-year position to train a Chinese man to replace me. I succeeded and became permanent.

These findings concur with those of 100 top line managers in *Fortune* 500 firms; the majority of whom believe that women face overwhelming resistance when seeking managerial positions in international divisions of US firms [36]. Similarly, 80 per cent of US firms report believing that women would face disadvantages if sent abroad [20]. Thus, the second myth is, in fact, true: firms are hesitant, if not outright resistant, to sending female managers abroad.

Myth 3: Foreigners' "prejudice" against female expatriate managers

Is it true that foreigners are so prejudiced against women that they could not succeed as international managers? Would sending a female manager abroad be neither fair to the woman nor effective for the company? Is the treatment of local women the best predictor of expatriate women's potential to succeed? The fundamental question was, and remains: is the historic discrimination against local women worldwide a valid basis for predicting expatriate women's success as international managers?

To investigate this third myth – that foreigners' prejudice against women renders them ineffective as international managers, over 100 women managers from major North American firms who were on expatriate assignments around the world were surveyed. Fifty-two were interviewed while in Asia or after having returned from Asia to North America [4, 10]. Since most of the women held regional responsibility, their experience represents multiple countries rather than just their country of foreign residence.

Who are the female expatriate managers? The women were very well educated and quite internationally experienced. Almost all held graduate degrees, the MBA being the most common. Over three-quarters had had extensive international interests and experience prior to their present company sending them abroad. On average, the women spoke two or three languages, with some fluently speaking as many as six. In addition, they had excellent social skills. Nearly two-thirds were single and only three had children.

Firms using transnational strategies sent more women than did those using other strategies, with financial institutions leading all other industries. On average, the expatriate assignments lasted two-and-a-half years, with a range from six months to six years. The women supervised up to 25 subordinates, with the average falling just below five. Their titles and levels within their firms varied: some held very junior positions – assistant account manager – while others held quite senior positions, including one regional vice-president. In no firm did a female expatriate hold her company's number one position in the region or in any country.

The women were considerably younger than the typical male expatriate. Their ages ranged from 23 to 41 years, with the average age just under 30. This reflects the relatively high proportion of women sent by financial institutions – an industry that sends fairly junior managers on international assignments – and the relatively low proportion sent by manufacturing firms, which select quite senior managers for expatriate positions (such as country or regional director).

The decision to go. For most firms, the female expatriates were "firsts": only 10 per cent followed another woman into her international position. Of the

90 per cent who were "firsts", almost a quarter represented the first female manager the firm had ever sent abroad. Others were the first women sent to the region, the first sent to the particular country, or the first to fill the specific expatriate position. Clearly, neither the women nor the companies had the luxury of role models or of following previously established patterns. Except for several major financial institutions, both the women and the companies found themselves experimenting, in hope of uncertain success.

Most women described themselves as needing to encourage their companies to consider the possibility of assigning international positions to women in general and to themselves in particular. In more than four out of five cases, the woman initially suggested the idea of an international assignment to her boss and company. For only six women did the company first suggest the assignment.

Since most firms had never considered sending a female manager abroad, the women used a number of strategies to introduce the idea and to position their careers internationally. Many explored the possibility of an international assignment during their original job interview and eliminated companies from consideration which were totally against the idea. Other women informally introduced the idea to their boss and continued to mention it at appropriate moments until the company ultimately decided to offer her an expatriate position. A few women formally applied for a number of international assignments prior to actually being selected and sent.

Many women attempted to be in the right place at the right time. For example, one woman who predicted that Hong Kong would be her firm's next major business centre arranged to assume responsibility for the Hong Kong desk in New York, leaving the rest of Asia to a male colleague. The strategy paid off: within a year, the company elevated its Hong Kong operations to a regional centre and sent her to Asia as their first female expatriate manager.

Most women claimed that their companies had failed to recognize the possibility of selecting women for international assignments, rather than having thoroughly considered the idea and then having rejected it. For the majority of the women, the obstacle appeared to be the company's naïvety, not malice. For many women, the most difficult hurdle in their international career involved being sent abroad in the first place, not – as most had anticipated – gaining the respect of foreigners and succeeding once sent.

Did it work? The impact of being female. Almost all of the female expatriate managers (97 per cent) reported that their international assignments were successful. This success rate is considerably higher than that reported for North American male expatriates. While the women's assessments are subjective, objective indicators support that most assignments, in fact, succeeded. For example, the majority of the firms – after experimenting with their first female expatriate manager – decided to send more women abroad. In addition, most companies promoted the women on the basis of their foreign performance and/ or offered them other international assignments following completion of the first one.

Advantages. Given the third myth, the women would have been expected to experience a series of difficulties caused by their being female and, perhaps, to create a corresponding set of solutions designed to overcome each difficulty.

This was not the case. Almost half of the expatriates (42 per cent) reported that being female served as more of an advantage than a disadvantage; 16 per cent found it to be both positive and negative; 22 per cent saw it as being either irrelevant or neutral; and only 20 per cent found it to be primarily negative.

The women reported numerous professional advantages to being female. Most frequently, they described the advantage of being highly visible. Foreign clients were curious about them, wanted to meet them, and remembered them after the first encounter. The women therefore found it easier for them than for their male colleagues to gain access to foreign clients' time and attention. The women gave examples of this high visibility, accessibility, and memorability, such as:

> *Japan.* It's the visibility as an expat, and even more as a woman. I stick in their minds. I know I've obtained more business than my two male colleagues . . . [My clients] are extra interested in me.

> *India and Pakistan.* In India and Pakistan, being a woman helps in marketing and client contact. I got in to see customers because they had never seen a female banker before . . . Having a female banker adds value to the client.

Again contrary to the third myth, the female managers discovered a number of advantages based on their interpersonal skills, including that the local men could talk more easily about a wider range of topics with them than with their male counterparts. For example:

> *Indonesia.* I often take advantage of being a woman. I'm more supportive than my male colleagues . . . [Clients] relax and talk more. And 50 per cent of my effectiveness is based on volunteered information.

> *Korea.* Women are better at treating men sensitively, and they just like you. One of my Korean clients told me, "I really enjoyed . . . working with you".

Many women also described the high social status accorded local women and found that such status was not denied them as foreign women. The women often received special treatment which their male counterparts did not receive. Clearly, it was always salient that they were women, but being a woman was not antithetical to succeeding as a manager.

> *Hong Kong.* Single female expats travel easier and are treated better. Never hassled. No safety issues. Local offices take better care of you. They meet you, take you through customs . . . It's the combination of treating you like a lady and a professional.

> *Japan.* It's an advantage that attracts attention. They are interested in meeting a *gaijin*, a foreign woman. Women attract more clients. On

calls to clients, they elevate me, give me more rank. If anything, the problem, for men and women, is youth, not gender.

In addition, most of the women described benefiting from a "halo effect". The majority of the women's foreign colleagues and clients had never met or previously worked with a female expatriate manager. Similarly, the local community was highly aware of how unusual it was for North American multinationals to send female managers abroad. Hence, the local managers assumed that the women would not have been sent unless they were "the best", and therefore expected them to be "very, very good".

> *Indonesia*. It's easier being a woman here than in any place in the world, including New York City . . . I never get the comments I got in New York, like "What is a nice woman like you doing in this job?"

> *Japan*. They assumed I must be good if I was sent. They became friends.

Some women found being female to have no impact whatsoever on their professional life. Many of these women worked primarily with the Chinese:

> *Hong Kong*. There are many expat and foreign women in top positions here. If you are good at what you do, they acccept you. One Chinese woman told me, "Americans are always watching you. One mistake and you are done. Chinese take a while to accept you and then stop testing you".

> *Asia*. There's no difference. They respect professionalism . . . including in Japan. There is no problem in Asia.

Disadvantages. The women also experienced a number of disadvantages in being female expatriate managers. Interestingly enough, the majority of the disadvantages involved the women's relationship with their home companies, not with their foreign colleagues and clients. As noted earlier, a major problem involved the women's difficulty in obtaining an international position in the first place.

Another problem involved home companies initially limiting the duration of the women's assignments to six months or a year, rather than offering the more standard two to three years. While temporary assignments may appear to offer companies a logically cautious strategy, in reality they create an unfortunate self-fulfilling prophecy. When the home company is not convinced that a woman can succeed (and therefore offers her a temporary rather than a permanent position), it communicates the company's lack of confidence to foreign colleagues and clients as a lack of commitment. The foreigners then mirror the home company's behaviour by also failing to take the woman manager seriously. Assignments become very difficult, or can fail altogether, when companies demonstrate a lack of initial confidence and commitment. As one expatriate woman working in Indonesia described, "It is very important to clients that I am permanent. It increases trust, and that is critical."

A subsequent problem involved the home company limiting the woman's professional opportunities and job scope once she was abroad. More than half of the female expatriates experienced difficulties in persuading their home companies to give them latitude equivalent to that given to their male counterparts, especially initially. For example, some companies, out of supposed concern for the woman's safety, limited her travel (and thus the regional scope of her responsibility), thus excluding very remote, rural, and underdeveloped areas. Other companies, as mentioned previously, initially limited the duration of the woman's assignment to six months or a year, rather than the more standard two to three years. For example:

Japan. My problem is overwhelmingly with Americans. They identify it as a male market . . . geisha girls . . .

Thailand (petroleum company). The Ameicans wouldn't let me on the drilling rigs, because they said there were no accommodations for a woman. Everyone blames it on something else. They gave me different work. They had me on the sidelines, not planning and communicating with drilling people. It's the expat Americans, not the Thais, who'll go to someone else before they come to me.

A few companies limited the women to working only internally with company employees, rather than externally with clients. These companies often implicitly assumed that their own employees were somehow less prejudiced than were outsiders. In reality, the women often found the opposite to be true. They faced more problems from the home country nationals within their own organizations than externally from local clients and colleagues. As one woman described:

Hong Kong. It was somewhat difficult internally. They feel threatened, hesitant to do what I say, resentful. They assume I don't have the credibility a man would have. Perhaps it's harder internally than externally, because client relationships are one-on-one and internally it's more of a group; or perhaps it's harder because they have to live with it longer internally; or perhaps it's because they fear that I'm setting a precedent or because they fear criticism from their peers.

Managing foreign clients' and colleagues' initial expectations was one area that proved difficult for many women. Some found initial meetings to be "tricky", especially when a male colleague from their own company was present. Since most local managers had never previously met a North American expatriate woman who held a managerial position, there was considerable ambiguity as to who she was, her status, her level of expertise, authority, and responsibility, and therefore the appropriate form of address and demeanour towards her.

People's Republic of China. I speak Chinese, which is a plus. But they'd talk to the men, not to me. They'd assume that I, as a woman, had no

> authority. The Chinese want to deal with top, top level people, and there is always a man at a higher level.

> *Asia.* It took extra time to establish credibility with the Japanese and Chinese. One Japanese manager said to me, "When I first met you, I thought you would not be any good because you were a woman."

Since most of the North American women whom local managers had ever met previously were expatriates' wives or secretaries, they naturally assumed that the new woman was not a manager. Hence, they often directed initial conversations to male colleagues, not to the newly arrived female manager. Senior male colleagues, particularly those from the head office, became very important in redirecting the focus of early discussions back towards the women. When this was done, old patterns were quickly broken and smooth ongoing work relationships were established. When the pattern was ignored or poorly managed, the challenges to credibility, authority, and responsibility became chronic and undermined the women's effectiveness.

As mentioned earlier, many women described the most difficult aspect of the foreign assignment as getting sent abroad in the first place. Overcoming resistance from the North American home company frequently proved more challenging than gaining local clients' and colleagues' respect and acceptance. In most cases, assumptions about foreigners' prejudice against female expatriate managers appear to have been exaggerated: the anticipated prejudice and the reality did not match. It appears that foreigners are not as prejudiced as many North American managers had assumed.

THE GAIJIN SYNDROME

One pattern is particularly clear: first and foremost, foreigners are seen as foreigners. Like their male colleagues, female expatriates are seen as foreigners, not as local people. A woman who is a foreigner (a *gaijin*) is not expected to act like the local women. Therefore, the societal and cultural rules, governing the behaviour of local women, which limit their access to managerial positions and responsibility do not apply to foreign women. Although women are considered the "culture bearers" in all societies, foreign women are not expected to assume the cultural roles that societies have traditionally reserved for their own women. As one female expatriate in Japan described:

> The Japanese are very smart: they can tell that I am not Japanese, and they do not expect me to act as a Japanese woman. They will allow and condone behaviour in foreign women that would be absolutely unacceptable in their own women.

Similarly a Tokyo-based personnel vice-president for a major international bank explained [37, pp. 1; 27]:

Being a foreigner is so weird to the Japanese that the marginal impact of being a woman is nothing. If I were a Japanese woman, I couldn't be doing what I'm doing here. But they know perfectly well that I'm not.

Many of the female expatriates related similar examples of their unique status as "foreign women" rather than as "women" *per se*. For example:

Japan and Korea. Japan and Korea are the hardest, but they know that I'm an American woman, and they don't expect me to be like a Japanese or Korean woman. It's possible to be effective even in Japan and Korea if you send a senior woman with at least three or four years of experience, especially if she's fluent in Japanese.

Pakistan. Will I have problems? No! There is a double standard between expats and local women. The Pakistanis test you, but you enter as a respected person.

Japan. I don't think the Japanese could work for a Japanese woman . . . but they just block it out for foreigners.

Hong Kong. Hong Kong is very cosmopolitan. I'm seen as an expat, not as an Asian, even though I am an Asian American.

CONCLUSION

It seems that we have confused an adjective, *foreign*, with a noun, *woman*, in predicting foreigners' reactions to expatriate women. We expected the most salient characteristic of a female expatriate manager to be that she is a woman and predicted her success based on the success of the local women in each country. In fact, the most salient characteristic is that expatriates are foreign, and the best predictor of their success is the success of other foreigners (in this case, other North Americans) in the particular country. Local managers see female expatriates as foreigners who happen to be women, not as women who happen to be foreigners. The difference is crucial. Given the uncertainty involved in sending women managers to all areas of the world, our assumptions about the greater salience of gender (female/male) over nationality (foreign/local) have caused us to make false predictions concerning women's potential to succeed as executives and managers in foreign countries.

The third myth – that foreigners' prejudice precludes women's effectiveness as international managers – is, in fact, a myth. Of the three myths, only the second myth proved to be true. The first myth proved false: Women *are* interested in working internationally. The third myth proved false: Women do succeed internationally, once sent. However, the second myth proved to be true: Companies are hesitant, if not completely unwilling, to send women managers abroad. Given that the problem is caused primarily by the home companies' assumptions and decisions, the solutions are also largely within their control.

RECOMMENDATIONS

In considering women managers for international assignments, both the companies and the women need to approach the decision and the assignment in a number of new ways.

Recommendations to companies:

(1) *Do not assume that it will not work.* Do not assume that foreigners will treat expatriate female managers the same way they treat their own local women. Our assumptions about the salience of gender over nationality have led to totally inaccurate predictions. Therefore, do not confuse adjectives with nouns; do not use the success or failure of local women to predict that of female foreigners.

(2) *Do not confuse the role of a spouse with that of a manager.* Although the single most common reason for male expatriates' failure and early return from international assignments is the dissatisfaction of their wives, this does not mean that women cannot cope in a foreign environment. The role of the spouse (whether male or female) is much more ambiguous and, consequently, the cross-cultural adjustment is much more demanding for the spouse than for the employee [25]. Wives (female spouses) have had trouble adjusting, but their situation is not analogous to that of female managers, and therefore is not predictive.

(3) *Do not assume that a woman will not want to go abroad.* Ask her. Although both single and married women need to balance private- and professional-life considerations, many are very interested in taking international assignments. Moreover, the proportion of women interested in working abroad is identical to that of men, and can be predicted to increase over the coming decade.

(4) *Offer flexible benefits packages.* Given that most expatriate benefits packages have been designed to meet the needs of traditional families (employed husband, non-employed wife, and children), companies should be prepared to modify their benefits packages to meet the needs of managers who are single (female or male) and dual-career couples. Such modifications might include increased lead time in announcing assignments, executive search services for the partner in dual-career couples, and payment for "staying connected" – including telephone and airfare expenses – for couples who choose some form of commuting rather than both simultaneously relocating abroad.

(5) *Give women every opportunity to succeed.* Accord her full status at the outset – not that of a temporary or experimental expatriate – with the appropriate title to communicate the home office's commitment to her. Do not be surprised if local colleagues and clients initially direct their comments to

male managers rather than to the new female expatriate during their first meeting with her. However, do not accept such behaviour: redirect discussion, where appropriate, to the woman. Such behaviour from foreign colleagues should not be interpreted as prejudice, but rather as a reaction to a new, ambiguous, and unexpected situation.

Recommendations to female expatriate managers:

The female expatriates had a number of suggestions for the women managers who will follow in their footsteps.

(1) *Assume naïvety, not malice.* Realize that sending women abroad is new, perceived as risky, and still fairly poorly understood. In most cases, companies and foreign managers are operating on the basis of untested assumptions, many of which are faulty, not on the basis of prejudice. The most successful approach is to be gently persistent in "educating" the company to be open to the possibility of sending a woman abroad and granting her the status and support usually accorded to male peers in similar situations.

(2) *Be excellent.* Given that expatriating women is perceived as risky, no woman will be sent abroad if she is not seen as technically and professionally excellent. In addition, beyond being extremely well qualified, arrange to be in the right place at the right time.

(3) *Address private life issues directly.* For single women, the issue of loneliness, and for married women, the issue of managing a dual-career relationship, must be addressed. Contact with other expatriate women has proved helpful in both situations. For dual-career couples, most women considered it critical that they had discussed the possibility of an international assignment with their husband long before it became a reality, and that they had developed options that would work for them as a couple. For most couples, this meant creating alternatives that had never, or rarely, been tried in the particular company. Realize that expatriate status inadvertently helps to solve some of the role overload problems experienced by women who are managers, wives, and mothers. Since most expatriate managers can afford household help while on expatriate assignment, but not in their home country, they are able to reduce substantially the demands on their time. As one American expatriate manager in Hong Kong described, "It would be impossible for me to do what I'm doing here if I was still in the United States. There just wouldn't be enough time!"

Global competition is, and will continue to be, intense in the 1990s. Transnational corporations, faced with the most intense global competition, may well continue to lead in hiring and promoting women into significant international management positions. Can they risk not choosing the best person just because her gender does not fit the traditional managerial profile? Needs for competitive advantage, not an all-consuming social conscience, may answer the question, if not in fact define it. Successful companies will select both women and men to manage their cross-border operations. The options of limiting international management to one gender has become an archaic "luxury" that no company can afford. The only remaining question is how quickly and effectively each company will increase the number and use of women in their worldwide managerial workforce.

ACKNOWLEDGMENT

I would like to thank the Social Sciences and Humanities Research Council of Canada for its generous support of the research reported here. I owe special thanks to Dr Homa Mahmoudi for her help, creativity, and professional insight in helping to conduct the Asian interviews.

This article is based on Dr Adler's recent work on transnationals [2, 3] and her research on female expatriate managers [4–10]. The equity and complementary contribution approaches were originally presented in Adler [11] and Adler and Izraeli's first book, *Women in Management Worldwide* [12].

NOTES

1   Caulkin, S., "Women in Management", *Management Today*, September 1977, pp. 58–63.
2   Adler, N. J., "Competitive Frontiers: Women Managers in the Triad", *International Studies of Management and Organization*, Vol. 23 No. 2, 1993, pp. 3–23.
3   Adler, N. J. and Bartholomew, S., "Managing Globally Competent People", *Academy of Management Executive*, Vol. 6 No. 3, 1992, pp. 52–65.
4   Adler, N. J., "Pacific Basin Managers: A Gaijin, Not a Woman", *Human Resource Management*, Vol. 26 No. 2, 1987, pp. 169–91.
5   Adler, N. J., "Do MBAs Want International Careers?", *International Journal of Intercultural Relations*, Vol. 10 No. 3, 1986, pp. 277–300.
6   Adler, N. J., "Expecting International Success: Female Managers Overseas", *Columbia Journal of World Business*, Vol. 19 No. 3, 1984, pp. 79–85.
7   Adler, N. J., "Women Do Not Want International Careers: and Other Myths about International Management", *Organizational Dynamics*, Vol. 13 No. 2, 1984, pp. 66–79.
8   Adler, N. J., "Women in International Management: Where Are They?", *California Management Review*, Vol. 26 No. 4, 1984, pp. 78–89.
9   Adler, N. J., "Women as Androgynous Managers: A Conceptualization of the Potential for American Women in International Management", *International Journal of Intercultural Relations*, Vol. 3 No. 4, 1979, pp. 407–35.
10   Jelinek, M. and Adler, N. J., "Women: World-class Managers for Global Competition", *Academy of Management Executive*, Vol. 2 No. 1, 1988, pp. 11–19.
11   Adler, N. J., "Women in Management Worldwide" *International Studies of Management and Organization*, Vol. XVI Nos. 3–4, 1986–7, pp. 3–32.
12   Adler, N. J. and Izraeli, D. N. (eds), *Women in Management Worldwide*, M. E. Sharpe, Armonk, New York, NY, 1988.
13   Adler, N. J. and Ghadar, F., "Strategic Human Resource Management: A Global Perspective", in Pieper, R. (ed.), *Human Resource Management in International Comparison*, de Gruyter, Berlin, 1990, pp. 235–60.
14   Bartlett, C. A. and Ghoshal, S., *Managing across Borders: The Transnational Solution*, Harvard Business School Press, Boston, Mass. 1989.
15   Fisher, A.B., "When Will Women Get to the Top?", *Fortune*, 21 September 1992, pp. 44–56.
16   Lansing, P. and Ready, K, "Hiring Women Managers in Japan: an Alternative for Foreign Employers", *California Management Review*, Vol. 30 No. 3, 1988, pp. 112–27.

17 Steinhoff, P. G. and Tanaka, K., "Women Managers in Japan", in Adler, N. J. and Izraeli, D. N. (eds), *Women in Management Worldwide*, M. E. Sharpe, Armonk, New York, NY, 1988, pp. 103–21.

18 Steinhoff, P. G. and Tanaka, K., "Women Managers in Japan", in Adler, N. J. and Izraeli, D. N., *Competitive Frontiers: Women Managers in a Global Economy*, Blackwell, Cambridge, Mass/Oxford, 1993.

19 Rosenzweig, P. M. and Nohria, N., "Human Resource Management in MNC Affiliates: Internal Consistency or Local Isomorphism", working paper, Harvard Business School, Boston, Mass. 1992.

20 Moran, Stahl and Boyer Inc., *Status of American Female Expatriate Employees: Survey Results*, International Division, Boulder, Colo. 1988.

21 Helgesen, S., *The Female Advantage: Women's Ways of Leadership*, Doubleday, New York, 1990.

22 Perry, N. J., "If You Can't Join 'Em, Beat 'Em", *Fortune*, 21 September 1992, pp. 58–9.

23 Porter, M., *The Competitive Advantage of Nations*, The Free Press, New York, 1990.

24 Hammond, V. and Holton, V., "The Scenario for Women Managers in Britain in the 1990s", *Competitive Frontiers: Women Managers in a Global Economy*, Blackwell, Cambridge, Mass. 1993.

25 Adler, N. J., *International Dimensions of Organizational Behavior*, 2nd edn, PWS-Kent Publishing, Boston, Mass. 1991.

26 Gunilla Masreliez Steen originally presented the two approaches in a working paper, "Male and Female Culture: a View from Sweden", 1987, and at the International Federation of Training and Development Organizations conference.

27 Aptheker, B., *Tapestries of Life: Women's Work, Women's Consciousness, and the Meaning of Daily Experience*, University of Massachusetts Press, Amherst, Mass., 1989.

28 Calvert, L. M. and Ramsey, V. J., "Bringing Women's Voice to Research on Women in Management: a Feminist Perspective", *Journal of Management Inquiry*, Vol. 1 No. 1, 1992, pp. 79–68.

29 Fossan, J., "Women in Organization", *Implementing Strategies and Achieving Change*, Seminar Research Report, Aspen Institute, Berlin, 1989.

30 Gilligan, C., *In a Different Voice*, Harvard University Press, Cambridge, Mass. 1982.

31 Korabik, K., "Is the Ideal Manager Masculine? The Contribution of Femininity to Managerial Effectiveness", Annual Academy of Management Meetings, Anaheim, Calif. August 1988.

32 Loden, M., *Feminine Leadership or How to Succeed in Business without Being One of the Boys*, Times Books, New York, 1987.

33 Miller, J. B., *Toward a New Psychology of Women*, Beacon, Boston, Mass. 1976.

34 Miller, J. B., *Women and Power*, working paper, Wellesley College, Stone Center for Development Services and Studies, Wellesley, Mass. 1982.

35 *Yearbook of Labor Statistics*, International Labor Office, Geneva, 1987.

36 Thal, N. and Cateora, P., "Opportunities for Women in International Business", *Business Horizons*, Vol. 22 No. 6, 1979, pp. 21–7.

37 Morgenthaler, E., "Women of the World: More US Firms Put Females in Key Posts in Foreign Countries", *Wall Street Journal*, 16 March 1978, pp. 1–17.

FURTHER READING

Antal, A. B. and Izraeli, D. N., "Woman Managers from a Global Perspective: Women Managers in their International Homelands and as Expatriates", in Fagenson, E. (ed.), *Women in Management: Trends, Issues and Challenges in Management Diversity, Women and Work*, Vol. 4, Sage, Newbury Park, Calif. 1993.

Yearbook of Labor Statistics, International Labor Office, Geneva, 1986.

Yearbook of Labor Statistics, International Labor Office, Geneva, 1991.

Christophe Falcoz and Sylvie Roussillon

CAREER MANAGEMENT OF HIGHFLIERS AT ALCATEL

ALCATEL-ALSTHOM

Alcatel is a quintessentially French company. Its corporate offices have always been in Paris, and for years all of its main subsidiaries were French. Until October 1995, most of its top managers were also French. In many ways, Alcatel provides a perfect case study of the French methods of managing highfliers.

Recently, however, Alcatel has diversified and established subsidiaries in several different countries. A large number of non-French executives now work for the corporation, and these executives come from widely differing cultural, organizational, and national backgrounds. At the same time, following a decade of steady growth during the 1980s, major technological and market shifts have forced the Group and its subsidiaries to undergo radical restructuring and rationalization. Current business conditions require new areas of specialization and competency in managers – skills that are sometimes lacking in the top managers who led the firm so successfully until 1992, when it achieved a record profit of 7 billion francs (about $1.4 billion). These recent challenges have raised crucial questions about how best to identify high-potential employees and prepare them to assume top management positions.

Alcatel-Alsthom is France's third largest employer, after the Postal Service and the national water company (La Générale des Eaux). There are about 45,000 managers in Alcatel, 23 percent of the approximately 104,000 employees. *It's the second largest French exporter*, with more than 110 billion francs in profits earned abroad in 1994. The Group's profits rank 44th internationally, 21st in Europe, and 4th in France, after Elf-Aquitaine, EDB, and Renault. Alcatel's main activity is telecommunications. In 1994, 67.3 percent of Alcatel's business was in

Table 1. Alcatel's profit and employees

Total 1994	France	Rest of Europe	Rest of World
Total Profit: 336 million	27.6%	39.4%	33%
Employees: 197,000	41.2%	45.5%	13.3%

telecommunications, while only 17.2 percent of its business was for GEC-Alsthom (energy and transportation), 9.2 percent for Cegelec (electrical engineering), 2.4 percent for SAFT (accumulators) and 3.9 percent for services and miscellaneous.

As Table 1 shows, the Group maintains a strong Franco-European character. But it's important to note that Alcatel ranks as one of the top three international telecommunications equipment groups, next to AT&T and Motorola. Alcatel is unquestionably a leader in this industry, with dominant market shares in most European countries and a significant reputation in technology.

CHALLENGES FACING ALCATEL

Technological transformations in the industry

Ever since the telecommunications environment began to destabilize in the 1980s, the international telecommunications equipment market has been mushrooming. Technological innovations, American and European deregulation, and a growing split between the private and public sectors have all affected the industry, which grew at a rate of about 3.6 percent per year between 1989 and 1995. In 1995, the industry achieved about $545.5 billion in international profits related to goods and services.

The technological revolutions in the telecommunications industry require that competitors cope with new market patterns and new competitive challenges. One major industry change is the merging of the formerly separate fields of data processing, telecommunications, and electronics. In fact, with the development of digital networks, the distinction that used to exist between vocal communication and data transmission is rapidly disappearing.[1] The number of computer engineers hired by Alcatel – several hundred per year over the last five years – and the growing importance of such subsidiaries as Alcatel TITN Answare are a clear indication of the new alliance between data processing and telecommunications.

New technology and services for information transmission – including cables, satellites, optical fibers, telephone lines, digital networks, and Hertz transmission equipment – have also been important elements of change in the industry. So has the field of micro-electronics. Telephone networks can now be used as virtual computer networks, interconnected with powerful mainframes using software that greatly enhances the performance of telephone exchanges. Miniaturization of electronic components has reduced production costs. At the same time, the ever-increasing demand for efficient data exchange between international firms and their markets has greatly increased global demand for information processing within the telecommunications industry. The growing, relatively new market for cellular telephones – which were originally only convenience products – is a perfect example of this development. The cellular telephone industry has grown beyond its traditional markets and has become extremely competitive. Alcatel has not done well in this area, however; its international market share was only 10 percent in 1995, which represented only 4.5 percent of its profits.

The push for standardization, combined with the increasingly rapid spread of basic technologies, creates new concerns for firms like Alcatel. Alcatel, which has never been strictly regulated – nor shielded against competition by protectionist legislation – now faces new competitors. Computer firms like IBM, integrated circuit and semi-conductor manufacturers, and even software firms like Intel and Microsoft have all entered the market with competitive low-cost products. Alcatel, with its higher labor and overhead costs, is suddenly at a disadvantage.

Given these new market conditions, investment in research and development has become critical to survival. Yet innovation is complex and expensive. Nor can it be done in isolation from other research efforts within the industry. Alcatel has signed a number of technology transfer and standardization agreements to avoid this isolation, and also to help it stay abreast of unexpected changes in international standards.

The most important consequence of all these developments is that an industry that once relied on technological superiority alone must now become an industry able to supply "custom-built" solutions for increasingly demanding customers. The integration of data processing and telecommunications, the growing importance of customer services and marketing, the need for flexibility and rapid reaction to increasingly specific demands, and the push for new innovations done in cooperation with competitors, have all become real challenges. Engineering logic once reigned supreme in this industry, but new challenges now require a revolution in corporate mentality.

Foreign subsidiaries

Because of a virtually uninterrupted series of takeovers and mergers, the Group has become a kind of shifting jigsaw puzzle that includes about 200 companies and holdings in France and about 700 abroad. As a result, Alcatel faces several difficult challenges. It must integrate the different centers of the Group and establish a common corporate culture, while at the same time accommodating the unique national cultures of foreign customers, where most of the growth is now occurring. In the process, the company must help its managers to develop the skills required for these new market conditions – as well as the skills needed to cope with the changing environment within the more mature markets.

The management style of the head office is not management by formal authority, but rather by informal influence. Teamwork is important, and is used to arrive at compromises acceptable to the subsidiary managers. However, that management style hasn't been very effective in achieving integration between foreign subsidiaries, which are closely tied to their own national cultures and to the markets within those cultures.

A couple of examples illustrate the difficulties and risks of isolating the subsidiaries within the Group. In one case, Alcatel SEL, the German subsidiary that Alcatel acquired from ITT, changed its domestic strategies and performed badly for two years. Even though Alcatel normally allows its subsidiaries a large degree of autonomy, in this case general management requested that SEL change its strategy. SEL managers resisted. In response, Alcatel dramatically changed its approach, and fired most of the managers at SEL.

Isolation also hurts research and development. For instance, at one time five subsidiaries were conducting very similar research on ATM terminals; all five, in fact, were developing new state-of-the-art technologies. When this type of duplication has occurred, subsidiaries have often resisted abandoning their research projects in favor of another subsidiary in another country. This leaves the final decision to the head office – a decision that is made more difficult when each subsidiary points out the national specificity of its market.

A similar situation arose during lengthy negotiations to make subsidiary names uniform. CIT, for example, was changed to CIT-Alcatel and finally to Alcatel CIT. A similar process occurred with Alcatel SEL. In each case, a difficult process proved how strongly each company was attached to its own history and background.

The unification of brands and names took place after the Group was renamed Alcatel-Alsthom from CGE on January 1, 1991. The purpose of this name unification was to make the structure of the Group more clear to its customers and to help the subsidiaries understand that, though they were often in competition with each other in the global market, they had to speak with the same voice. But "home-town thinking" – a national subsidiary + a national market + a national culture + a unique history – is dying a hard death. In 1995, the head office resorted to shuffling groups of products around the subsidiaries in an attempt to make their product-activity matrix less dependent on local fiefdoms. But the strategy wasn't particularly effective.

The autonomy so dear to the subsidiaries plainly poses a couple of questions related to issues of coordination and subsidiary independence: how far can the parent company intervene in the choice of local managers? And how much horizontal cooperation can exist between managers in different subsidiaries?

ALCATEL'S HIPO SELECTION METHODS

All of these challenges mean that the selection and training of top managers has become more critical to the company's success than ever before. New methods of HIPO selection are gaining ground within the Group, especially among the foreign subsidiaries. As Alcatel has consciously allowed each business unit to maintain its autonomy and national characteristics, a diversity of models has emerged. This decentralization of power has been a key element in the history of Alcatel's high-potential management policy.

At the same time, traditional models are still very much in use. For the last 25 years, Alcatel groomed its high-potential employees in traditionally French ways. During that time, neither the selection criteria nor the profiles of the managers themselves changed much. This is most clearly seen in the criteria used to select the CEO and other top-echelon officers.

The competitive examination model

The succession of men who have led the Group shows clearly the importance that the French place on a limited number of professional schools. These highly competitive French schools aren't business schools but are schools of engineering and public administration. In the case of Alcatel, a degree from a single university – Polytechnique[2] – has become a crucial qualification for reaching the highest echelon.

Besides having the correct degree, top managers at Alcatel, which is a private corporation, have usually spent a lengthy period working for the national government. This period of service seems to be an important springboard to high management positions in large French corporations – which is not surprising, given the close connection between government and business in France. The careers of top Alcatel managers from 1965 to 1995 as illustrated in Table 2 demonstrate this phenomenon. We call this process for selecting future leaders the "Competitive Examination Model".

For example, in 1982 G. Pebereau became CEO of Alcatel. At the time, Pebereau's career was one of the most impressive among top French business leaders. He entered Polytechnique University at the age of 19; upon graduating five years later as an engineer, he worked for the Ministry of Public Works (Ponts et Chaussées), then went on to become head of several government departments. Pebereau left government service at the age of 37 to join the former Alcatel (CGE) as Deputy Director General of CIT.

Here, he worked to reposition the group around its most profitable activities. He sold a subsidiary to Saint-Gobain and purchased 44 percent of Framathome. In 1983 he helped acquire a share worth 10 billion francs in Alsthom, held at that time by

Table 2. Education and public service of Alcatel CEOs

CEO from/to	Diploma	Public service
1965–70	Polytechnique, Ecole Supérieur D'Electricité	Mayor, Senator, Minister
1970–82	Polytechnique	Head of Public Works Ministry
1982–86	Polytechnique	Head of Public Works Ministry, Ministry for Equipment
1986–95	Polytechnique	Finance Ministry, Paris Airports Administration
1995–present	Polytechnique	

Thomson CSF. This first real step in the process of takeover was facilitated by the personal relationship between the CEOs of the two firms. And, true to French tradition, the takeover was helped along by government participation. At the time, the CEO of Thomson was himself a Polytechnique graduate and a member of the Ponts et Chaussées. The resulting cooperation between CIT and Thomson, which came to an end in 1990, resulted in differentiated activities within the French electronics industry: CGE focused on telecommunications equipment and Thomson on hi-fi, household appliances, electronics for national defense, and data processing.

The takeover by Alcatel of ITT's telecommunications business in Europe helped it achieve its present size, doubled its profits, and made it an international force. The credit for this ITT merger doesn't go to Pebereau, however, but to P. Suard, his successor. Suard spent two years at the Finance Ministry, from 1966 to 1968, then five years at the Paris Airports Administration. He joined CGE in 1973 and three years later took over Câbles de Lyon, a subsidiary that was struggling at the time. There Suard gained a reputation of being a shrewd financier, capable of carrying the company through the most difficult of economic recoveries.

From 1984 onward, Pebereau, impressed by this young man from Savoy, took him on to help complete the merger agreement with ITT. In 1986, at about the time Alcatel was becoming privatized, Suard was appointed CEO of CGE – by the French Minister for the Economy, Finance and Privatizations. The appointment of a CEO by a government minister is just one more unusual aspect of French capitalism, demonstrating the fact that in France there is a strong link between top government officials, politicians in office, and the heads of both public and private companies. These political/business connections mean that changes in capital ownership, either public or private, have little effect on the criteria used in the selection of CEOs, or in the scrutiny given them during the selection process.

The current CEO of Alcatel replaced Suard when he encountered legal problems. S. Tchuruk came directly from the oil industry, after a long career there. Tchuruk had joined Mobil Corporation in 1964, where he remained for 15 years, becoming Director of Strategic Planning, Director of Human Resources and then finally CEO of Mobil Benelux. He then spent six years with the group Rhône-Poulenc, becoming CEO in 1983. Three years later, the government appointed him chairman of the board of Orkem (formerly CDF-Chimie). And in 1990, Tchuruk became President and CEO of Total, the government-sponsored French oil company.

The only common strand in the careers of Tchuruk and his predecessors is the fact that they all graduated from Polytechnique. In fact, Tchuruk spent his whole career in the business world, outside the realm of the political/administrative elite. Still, Tchuruk is a member of the same old-boy network. The way this network functions is typical of the Competitive Examinations Model, in which success in an informal "test" leads to membership in an influential group. And the group works to help its members succeed.

In this case, the test is simple, even if recruiters don't acknowledge it: you must have the "correct" alma mater. Besides Polytechnique, two other universities are strongly represented among Alcatel's top echelon. About 140 Polytechnique graduates hold highly responsible positions at Alcatel, 60 top executives are graduates of HEC (France's leading business school), and 14 went to ENA (France's elite public administration school). Alcatel isn't alone in its preferences. Some 56 percent of the CEOs of the 200 leading French corporations are graduates of one of these three schools.[3]

At Alcatel, the presence of so many engineers among top management has had a strong influence on the corporate culture and market approach. Alcatel is a company that emphasizes production and research and development, probably because Polytechnique graduates have steered the company in that direction. However, the need to develop other areas, such as marketing, has become a major challenge for Alcatel. As we shall see, Alcatel's new models for managing highfliers should significantly help the Group meet these challenges.

The feudal model

Besides the technical and engineering culture and the importance of certain elite schools in the French parent company, a third dynamic shapes Alcatel's traditional management development strategies: the "Feudal Model". In this model, informal co-opting mechanisms structure the organization at the highest levels, and networking within subsidiaries is an important step in attaining high management positions.

When legal action was brought against P. Suard[4] the crisis resulted in a redefinition of management teams within Alcatel and several of its subsidiaries. The new teams were homogenous and very loyal to one another. Around the beginning of 1995, a select executive committee of nine was set up under the chairmanship of Suard; five of these had already sat on the management committee in 1991. To these were added the President-CEOs of Cegelec, SAFT and GEC-Alsthom and the financial director of Alcatel-Alsthom.

At the time, only two members of the 19-member general management team at Alcatel were not French. Among that group were eight graduates of Polytechnique, two from ENA, and one from HEC. Most of these managers had responsibilities both at the Alcatel-Alsthom corporate office and at the Alcatel subsidiary office. Seven of the 19 managers had been members of the Câbles de Lyon, where P. Suard was president from 1976 to 1986. Five of these former Câbles de Lyon cronies were also on the board of directors. Suard had built up a virtual fiefdom.

It's important to note that the human resources manager of Alcatel is not a member of these two committees, nor is the director of communications. None of the top 19 managers has any specific background in marketing, commercial development or production. Where there is an obvious need to serve and satisfy the customer, no one within the inner circles has a working knowledge of how to accomplish this.[5]

Titles and job descriptions often have little to do with true influence and power within the company. There seems to be little connection between the formal hierarchical structure and the relationships that exist within the informal decision-making bodies. Anyone seeking to climb to the top must decipher, by interpreting situational and personal cues, the true power structure. In most cases, of course, they must also learn to work within this informal power network.

The professional model

A different model for identifying highfliers exists within the Group's subsidiaries and can be illustrated by a look at Alcatel Bell (Alcatel Belgium). Alcatel Bell is one of the companies acquired from ITT in 1987.

In Belgium, an "executive" is defined differently than in France. Within Alcatel Bell, an executive is anyone who manages people below the level of engineer and/or who is responsible for several important projects. Executives are mostly university graduates in the humanities or various specializations, and usually have five years of experience.

The pay scale is an important tool used in identifying who among these executives are highfliers. First, each new recruit is formally assessed by his/her immediate superior. The written assessment is used to plan salary increases. If the immediate supervisor predicts four salary increases over the next five years, and that the person will reach a level of grade twelve or higher (on a scale of 1–20) before age 50, the person is identified as a highflier.

In each department, a certain number of these individuals are selected by the Human Resources Department and given a career counseling session. After further interviews with HR and immediate superiors, each department develops a shortlist of ten or so candidates for further development. These candidates are then sent to an external development and assessment center. Some of them may then be referred to the central Human Resources Management Department and to the central Management Committee for training at the parent company, for example in the PACE program. Those who have not been shortlisted may be offered other support positions.

In this "Professional Model", a diploma from a certain elite school isn't the main criterion for success. Instead, the company carefully defines the characteristics of a good executive, and gives the candidate several years of experience. A person makes his or her career within a single division, developing necessary areas of expertise as he/she climbs the ladder rung by rung.

In contrast to the French subsidiaries, Alcatel Bell identifies and develops highfliers with the help of external specialists. Alcatel Bell is also careful to avoid creating perceptual imbalance between the treatment given to highfliers and non-highfliers. The management techniques used for HIPO employees are the same – although modified – as those used for all employees.

Within the entire Alcatel Group, several similar models are in use. Other foreign subsidiaries, particularly in Germany and the United States, use different forms of the Professional Model. But since Alcatel is a French firm managed by the French, it's inevitable that the Competitive Examination Model described earlier is dominant throughout the firm in selecting top managers. In addition, the mosaic-like, expansionist structure of the firm makes it a theater of hidden power struggles.

NOTES

1   Commutation and transmission are now carried out digitally by using a computer coding system that has replaced the old analogue technique.
2   Polytechnique, called "X", is the most prestigious of the French engineering schools and is under the Ministry of Defense. The top graduates go to public ministries: Bureau of Mines (15 per year), Public Works (12 per year), Telecommunications (2 per year), Armament (1 per year).
3   Other engineering schools are strongly represented in Alcatel-Alsthom, but the graduates tend mostly to be employed in a specialization close to that taught at their school. For example, a hundred or so come from ESTP and are essentially in Cegelec and Alsthom, about 50 from the Ecole Nationale Superieure de l'Aéronautique et de l'Espace are with Alcatel Espace, 80 are from les Ecoles des Mines, and involved in specialized engineering, and so on.
4   P. Suard was taken to court on a charge of political and financial corruption.
5   A marketing department was created at Alcatel's head office in January of 1995.

REFERENCES

Alpha, the Alcatel-Alsthom company magazine
Bauer, M. and Bertin-Mourot, B. (1987). "Les 200: comment devient-on grand patron?" in *L'Epreuve des Faits* (Paris: Seuil), 123–45
Bourdieu, P. (1987). "Variations et invariants: éléments pour une histoire structurale du champ des grandes écoles", *Actes de la Reserche en Science Sociale*, 3–30
CANAL TEL, the Alcatel Business Systems Division Magazine
Cohen, E. and Bauer, M. (1985). *Les Grandes Maneuvres Industrielles* (Paris: P. Belfond Publisher), 181–203
EUROSTAF (1991), "l'industrie mondiale des telecommunications: enjeux economiques, stratégies industrielles, performance financière" (for further information on telecommunications industry)
Gallard, P. and Constanty, H. (October 7, 1994). "Alcatel: le chamion est nu", *Le Nouvel Economiste*, no. 966
Jolinet, J. P. (1990). "Le retour de Thomson dans les télécoms civilies", *L'Usine Nouvelle*, no. 2251, vol. 18.1
Lettre de l'IDATE (October 1995), no. 5, "Réseaux et Télécoms" (for information on the telecommunications industry)
Nexon, M. (September 26–October 9, 1995). "Radiotéléphone: trois hommes pour un réseau", *L'Expansion*, no. 483
Nexon, M. and Fortin, D. (November, 1995). "Reconstruive Alcatel", *L'Expansion*, no. 512, 10–22

William H. Roof and Barbara Bakhtari

RECRUITING A MANAGER FOR BRB, ISRAEL

BRB Inc., a multinational electronics corporation, plans to establish a new subsidiary in Israel. The firm's base is in Los Angeles, California, with a second overseas head-quarters in England. The US office staffs and operates six North American divisions and three South American subsidiaries. The UK office is responsible for operations in Europe and Asia. The Israeli venture is the company's first business thrust in the turbulent Middle East.

During the past 10 years, BRB's phenomenal growth resulted largely from its ability to enter the market with new, technically advanced products ahead of the competition. The technology mainly responsible for BRB's recent growth is a special type of radar signal processing. With Fourier transforms, BRB's small, lightweight, and inexpensive radar systems outperform the competitions' larger systems in range, resolution, and price. It is this type of lightweight, portable radar technology that has enormous potential for Israel during conflicts with the Arab States.

BRB's human resource functions in the United States and Europe each boast a vice president. John Conners is the Vice President of Human Resources in the United States, and Francis O'Leary is the Vice President of Human Resources in the United Kingdom. Paul Lizfeld, the CEO of BRB, contacted the two vice presidents and told them to recruit a general manager for the Israeli operation. "I don't care who finds him, but he better be right for the job. I cannot afford to replace him in six months. Is that clear!" Lizfeld told them to look independently and then coordinate together to select the right person. They knew that their jobs could be in jeopardy with this task.

The two human resource operations were independent, and each was managed individually. Recruiting processes differed between US and UK operations. Each had different organizational structures and corporate cultures. The only link between the two was Lizfeld's strong micromanagement style, which emphasized cost control.

US OPERATIONS

John Conners has worked for BRB for the past 20 years. He started with a degree in engineering and worked in the engineering department. After earning his MBA in human resource management from UCLA, he transferred to the human resource department. Management felt that someone with an engineering background could hire the best technical employees for BRB. With BRB's high turnover rate, they felt that someone who could relate to the technical side of the business could better attract and screen the right people for the organization. BRB promoted Conners to vice president three years ago, after he hired the staffs for the subsidiaries in Peru and Brazil. Except for the general managers, they were all correct fits. Conners felt that the problem with the general managers was an inability to work with Lizfeld.

John Conners looked at many different strategies to determine how to begin recuiting for the Israeli position. He wanted to be sure he found the right person for the job. The first step in choosing the ideal candidate was to determine the selection criteria.

Conners defined the task in Israel to include control and management of BRB's Israeli operations. The GM must work with the Israeli government both directly and indirectly. The political unrest in Israel also requires the GM to conduct sensitive transactions with the Israeli government. This person would also work directly with Lizfeld, taking direction from him and reporting regularly to him.

As with many countries in the Middle East, Israel was in turmoil. Conners actually knew very little about the Israeli culture, but decided to ask different associates who had past dealings with Israel. He knew that the threat of war constantly hung over Israel. The country was also suffering from high inflation rates and troubled economics. Lately, he also learned that the country had become divided over certain political and cultural issues. The person accepting this job needed nerves of steel and extraordinary patience.

Conners decided the selection criteria that would be important for the candidate included technical skill, cultural empathy, a strong sense of politics, language ability, organizational abilities, and an adaptive and supportive family. He also felt that the GM would have to have the following characteristics: persuasiveness, ability to make decisions, resourcefulness, flexibility, and adaptability to new challenges. Now all he needed to do was find a person who had all these attributes.

He decided to begin his search for candidates within the organization. He knew this route had both advantages and disadvantages. Since BRB was still in the beginning stages of internationalization in Israel, a "home country" presence might prove to be very helpful. Lizfeld would appreciate this. The disadvantages would be many. It might be very difficult to find someone willing to relocate in Israel. The increased cost of living and the political unrest make it a tough package to sell. Conners knew of the "Israeli mentality". He also knew he would have to take care in sending someone who might either overpower the Israelis or break under their aggressive business style. Conners knew that Lizfeld wanted to have the home country atmosphere in Israel and planned to be very active in the management of Israeli operations.

The second option Conners had was to recruit from outside the company. The ideal candidate would have both domestic and international experience. Conners could recruit either by contacting an employment agency or by placing an ad in the *Wall Street Journal*. He thought he could find a person with the right qualifications, but he also knew it would be difficult to find someone Lizfeld liked outside the company. Conners had hired two managers for the South American offices, and Lizfeld had driven them over the edge within six months. Conners knew that he had to be extra careful. One more "unqualified" candidate might put his own job on the line.

Conners found three potential candidates for the Israeli position. One candidate, Joel Goldberg, was a recommendation from the headhunter Conners had commissioned. Goldberg had thirty-five years of electronics and radar experience. He had been CEO of Radar Developments Incorporated, a major electronics corporation in New York. Goldberg had taken control of Radar Developments Incorporated in 1981. By 1986, the company had tripled sales and increased profits fivefold. Goldberg had the technical knowledge to perform the job. He also had the necessary individual characteristics Conners felt would be important for this position. Goldberg had studied in Israel on a kibbutz for two years after college, spoke fluent Hebrew, and was a practicing Jew. He wanted to retire in Israel in a few years. Conners worried that Goldberg would not stay with the company long enough to establish a solid organization. Goldberg also liked running his own show, and that created a potential problem with Lizfeld.

The next candidate was Robert Kyle, Vice President of BRB's radar electronics department. Kyle had been with BRB for more than twenty years and headed two other international divisions for BRB in Japan and Canada. Kyle was familiar with the international process and the BRB corporate culture. Lizfeld had given him excellent reviews in the other two international positions. He had strong management skills and was highly respected both within the organization and in the industry. Kyle received his PhD from MIT in electrical engineering and his MBA from Dartmouth. He had the technical expertise and was familiar with the company and its procedures. Conners was afraid of Kyle's cultural acceptance in Israel since he did not speak the language and was not familiar with Israeli attitudes. He could require Kyle to participate in extensive cultural training, but Conners still had some reservations about sending a gentile to head operations in Israel.

The last candidate was Rochelle Cohen, an Israeli who relocated to the United States in 1982. She originally relocated to assist the head of the electronics division of Yassar Aircraft, an Israeli company that opened its first international office in 1978. Cohen did very well and brought Israeli thoroughness and assertiveness to the US operations. She now wanted to move back to Israel to be with her family. Additionally, her fiancé recently relocated in Israel, and she wanted to return to marry and raise a family. Cohen had experience in the international circuit, having worked in the United States, United Kingdom, and Israel, but Conners was still worried about hiring her. Although she had the political knowledge and the proper connections in the Israeli government, the problems were her young age, lack of technical expertise, and sex.

Conners contacted O'Leary to see what progress he had made. Knowing the consequences that would come from this decision, Conners realized it was going to be a difficult one to make.

UK OPERATIONS

Francis O'Leary reflected on his past eight years with BRB. His rise from the strife-torn east side of Belfast to BRB's corporate vice president for human resources was extraordinary. While most Irish business careers in large English firms peak at middle management, O'Leary's actually began at that point. He proved his capabilities through hard work, constant study, and an astute ability to judge the character and substance of people on first sight. His task of finding a suitable general manager for the new division in Israel offered a challenge he readily accepted.

O'Leary excelled at recruiting and hiring innovative employees who brought technical ideas with them to BRB. The management structure at BRB in England did not support internal growth of technology and innovation, so new ideas and technological advances were not rewarded with commensurate fiscal incentives. As such, turnover of experienced innovators forced O'Leary to recruit and hire innovation on a "rotating stock" basis. It was this success in hiring innovators that broke him from the shackles of middle management and thrust him to the top of the corporation. Four years ago, through a well-planned and well-executed recruiting program, O'Leary hired Rani Gilboa, a young Israeli engineer and former Israeli army officer. For Gilboa, the need for lightweight, inexpensive battlefield systems drove a desire to approach the problem from a new aspect: signal processing. After graduate study in this field, Gilboa sought and found a company that would support his concepts. That company was BRB. Gilboa's subsequent contributions to BRB's profits secured his and O'Leary's positions atop their respective disciplines within the firm.

Since that time, O'Leary had other successes hiring innovators from Israel. This stemmed largely from his tireless self-study of Israeli culture. With a feel for the Israeli people rivaling that of an "insider", O'Leary enjoyed success in pirating established innovators from Israeli firms. Now, he faced the task of recruiting and hiring a general manager for the newly established electronics division near Haifa.

Selecting the right manager would be more difficult than expected. With his knowledge of the Israeli culture, O'Leary knew intuitively that an Israeli should head the new division. Acceptance by the division's employees, ability to speak Hebrew, spousal support, and knowledge of Israeli government regulations and tax structures were vital to the success of the new division. Unfortunately, BRB's CEO preferred home country presence in the new division and directed O'Leary to recruit with that as the top priority. After O'Leary presented a strong case, however, the CEO agreed to review all candidates. Another potential problem arose when Lizfeld, the CEO, announced a hands-on management style with plans to participate actively in the management of the Israeli division. To O'Leary, this meant that Western values, along with the current innovative recruiting strategy practiced in England, would extend to Israel as well.

Until recently, O'Leary's recruiting for management positions concentrated on internal promotions. A known performer from within was a better bet than an outsider. When current employees could not meet the job requirements, O'Leary typically turned to newspapers as his primary source of candidates, The recent emergence of reputable executive placement services in England gave him an additional sourcing tool. At times, O'Leary had turned to social contacts, job centers, and the internal labor market as candidate sources, but the percentages of good leads from these were comparatively low.

After months of reading résumés, introductory letters, and job applications, three candidates emerged for the position in Israel. It was now up to O'Leary to decide the candidate he would recommend to Lizfeld.

Michael Flack worked for BRB for more than nineteen years. After graduating from Cambridge College with a degree in general engineering, Flack joined the company as a mechanical engineer. Initially, he worked in the mechanical design group of the radar division. After five years, BRB promoted Flack to engineering section manager. While in this position, he enjoyed various successes in radar miniaturization design. During his eleventh year, BRB again promoted Flack to department head in the manufacturing engineering group. Emphasis in this position shifted from design to production. During his seventeenth year, he became director of engineering design, where he was responsible for managing forty-three engineers' efforts in new-product design.

Flack had no international experience, and he was a reputed "tinkerer". He liked to spend time in the labs designing mechanical components along with his engineers. This generated tremendous esprit within his department but often resulted in inattention to his administrative responsibilities.

Rani Gilboa thought his friend Yair Shafrir was perfect for the position. Shafrir was currently vice-president of engineering at Elta Electronics in Israel. Elta is one of Israel's top radar firms, with several products proven in actual combat during the last Arab–Israeli conflict. Shafrir received his degree in electrical engineering from the University of Jerusalem. He had spent his professional career in Israel, usually changing companies to accept promotions. He had been with four companies since graduating from the university nineteen years ago. Shafrir was a strong-willed, organized individual who took pride in his record of technical management accomplishments. He had been able to complete projects on schedule and within budget over 70 percent of the time, a rare feat for an Israeli company. This record resulted mainly from the force of his personal leadership and strength of will. With his entire career spent in Israeli companies, O'Leary had little doubt that Shafrir could manage BRB's new electronics division. Culturally, he was perfect for the job. O'Leary had concerns, however, about Paul Lizfeld's injection of Western culture through his active management plan. The obstinate Shafrir, with no international business experience, might resent the interference.

A well-placed advertisement in the London *Times'* employment section drew a number of responses. One of the three final candidates responded to the ad about four weeks after it appeared in *The Times*.

Harold Michaelson was an English citizen of Jewish faith. Michaelson's family fled Poland in 1938 when Harold's father insisted that the "Nazi madman" would never attack England, especially after Prime Minister Chamberlain's successful visit to Munich. Harold was born to the newly naturalized couple in 1940. Later, he attended college in the United States, where he earned both bachelor's and master's degrees in electrical engineering at Georgia Tech. After graduating, Harold spent two years with General Electric until his father's illness forced him to return to England. He accepted an engineering position with Marconi, and he has remained with that company. Shortly after his return, his father died. Michaelson continued to take care of his mother for the next year. Mrs. Michaelson had always dreamed of living in the Jewish homeland – a dream not shared by her husband. One year after his death, she joined her sister's family in Haifa. Harold had readily accepted a position with Marconi in Israel to work on the new Israeli defense fighter LAVI. Unfortunately, cancellation of the LAVI program also canceled his chances to work in Israel for Marconi. At the time of the interview, Harold was vice president of engineering for Marconi's air radio division. He was also the youngest vice president in the corporation. His background in engineering and administrative functions, coupled with his ability to speak Hebrew, made Harold a strong candidate for the position. During the interview, he mentioned his mother's failing health and her refusal to leave Israel. He intended, if selected, to take care of her there. O'Leary wondered if that was Harold's main reason for wanting to live in Israel. Would he still want to live and work there if he lost his mother? O'Leary was anxious to discuss his candidates with John Conners.

J. Stewart Black

FRED BAILEY: AN INNOCENT ABROAD*

Fred gazed out the window of his 24th floor office at the tranquil beauty of the
Imperial Palace amidst the hustle and bustle of downtown Tokyo. It had only been
six months ago that Fred had arrived with his wife and two children for this three
year assignment as the director of Kline & Associates' Tokyo office. Kline & Associates
was a multinational consulting firm with offices in nine countries worldwide. Fred
was now trying to decide if he should simply pack up and tell the home office that
he was coming home or whether he should try to somehow convince his wife and
himself that they should stay and try to finish the assignment. Given how excited Fred
thought they all were about the assignment to begin with, it was a mystery to him
as to how things had gotten to this point. As he watched the swans glide across the
water in the moat that surrounds the Imperial Palace, Fred reflected back on the
past seven months.

Seven months ago, the managing partner, Dave Steiner, of the main office in
Boston asked Fred to lunch to discuss "business". To Fred's surprise, the "business"
was not the major project that he and his team had just successfully finished, but
was instead a very big promotion and career move. Fred was offered the position of
managing director of the firm's relatively new Tokyo office which had a staff of 30,
including seven Americans. Most of the Americans in the Tokyo office were either
associate consultants or research analysts. Fred would be in charge of the whole
office and would report to a senior partner (located in Boston) who was over the
Asian region. It was implied to Fred that if this assignment went as well as his past, it
would be the last step before becoming a partner in the firm.

How could Fred go back now? Certainly going back early would be the kiss of
death for his career in Kline. But Jenny was not in a mood to discuss things. As far as

she was concerned, there was nothing to discuss. She hated Japan. She felt the company and Fred had oversold the country and how "well they would be looked after". Fred worked 80+ hours a week because of all the after hours socializing that he had to do with clients. He was never home and "had no idea what life was really like in Japan". Jenny had given Fred an ultimatum: either they packed up together or she went home alone. That things had escalated this far just didn't seem possible to Fred. What was he supposed to do? Sacrifice everything he had worked for over the years? His Harvard MBA would no doubt get him another job, but he had a real future at Kline if he could just hit even a double in this assignment. But if he walked away from the plate now, his career was over. On the other hand, he loved his wife and children and did not want to lose them. What had gone wrong?

FRED AND JENNY

Fred and Jenny met during their last year in college in a senior seminar class on business ethics. Fred was instantly attracted to Jenny's warm smile and flair for fashion. Jenny recognized in Fred ambition and a kind heart. The two started dating only a week after the class started.

Jenny came from a well to do family in Connecticut. Her father was a senior executive with a major firm headquartered in New York. She had majored in fashion merchandising as a way of combining her interest and talent for fashion and her father's advice about studying something practical.

Fred was the oldest of six children and was the first to go to college. His father was a construction worker and his mother a beautician. Fred had worked hard in high school and graduated second in his class. Even with a partial scholarship, and loans, tuition help from his parents put a real financial burden on them. Fred was determined to take advantage of the opportunity he was being given and make his parents proud.

Fred and Jenny were married on a warm June afternoon. Although skeptical at first, Jenny's parents gradually came to recognize in Fred what Jenny saw from the beginning. Fred was bright and determined but his humble background sparked in him a genuine interest in others that put them at ease whenever Fred was around.

Before and after getting married, Fred and Jenny talked at length about careers and family. Fred wanted to go back and get his MBA after a couple of years of work. He had landed a great job with American Express after graduation and hoped with two years experience in a name brand company, his stellar college grades, and good GMAT scores he could get into a top MBA program. Jenny wanted to be a buyer for a major store like Saks Fifth Avenue and later have her own shop. They both wanted children but thought they would wait until Fred finished his MBA before starting a family. At that point, Jenny would take a few years off and then start her own small clothing store once the kids were in school. They both thought that owning her own shop would give Jenny the flexibility and time to spend with their children that she wanted.

Everything had gone according to plan up until the offer to go to Japan.

THE OFFER

Fred joined Kline right after graduating from Harvard. He had a couple of other offers, but including expected performance bonuses, the job at Kline paid 20 percent more than any of the others. Fred took it and immediately was put on the San Francisco team of one of the hardest charging young consultants at Kline.

Rick Savage was one year away from the magical "up or out" decision concerning partnership. This decision typically happened about the seventh year of employment for typical MBA hires. Rick had been given a very high profile assignment with Kline's largest client. Success here would guarantee a partnership. Fred felt his life must be charmed to have landed on Rick's team out of the gate.

That first project and nearly every other project Fred had been part of were successes in his first three years at Kline. In his fourth year, he was given a major assignment and led a team of 7 consultants and associates. Fred had just completed this 10-month assignment when Dave asked him to lunch.

Fred was stunned by the Tokyo offer. The Tokyo office was opened in part to serve major US clients' operations in Japan. From the same base, Kline would begin to develop relationships with Japanese firms. Once the relationships were formed, Kline would be able to service the Japanese multinational's American operations from their established offices in seven major cities in the US. The strategic significance of the office and the offer did not escape Fred.

Fred's predecessor in Japan had opened the office a year ago. George Woodward was a partner with a mixed reputation. George had friends at the very top of Kline, but he also had enemies all along the way. Fred wasn't sure why George had been suddenly transferred to the UK. Because the transfer to England was taking place "right away", Dave told Fred that he and his family had about three weeks to get prepared for the move.

When Fred told his wife about the unbelievable opportunity, he was shocked at her less than enthusiastic response. Jenny thought that it would be rather difficult to have the children live and go to school in a foreign country for three years, especially when Christine, the youngest, would be starting first grade next year. Besides, now that the kids were in school, Jenny wanted to open her own clothing store.

Fred explained that the career opportunity was just too good to pass up and that the company's overseas package would make living in Japan terrific. The company would pay all the expenses to move whatever the Baileys wanted to take with them. The company had a very nice house in an expensive district of Tokyo that would be provided rent free. Additionally, the company would rent their house in Boston during their absence. The firm would provide a car and driver, education expenses for the children to attend private schools, and a cost of living adjustment and overseas compensation that would nearly double Fred's gross annual salary. After two days of consideration and discussion, Fred told Mr. Steiner he would accept the assignment.

PREPARING FOR THE MOVE

Between getting things at the office transferred to Bob Newcome, who was being promoted to Fred's position, and the logistic hassles of getting furniture and the like ready to be moved, neither Fred nor his family had much time to really find out much about Japan, other than what was in the encyclopedia.

Kline handled many of the logistical and relocation details internally. Unfortunately, a number of things went wrong. For example, when the packers came, they were totally unprepared for the fact that some of the Baileys' stuff was going into storage and some was being shipped to Japan. On a "look see visit" a week after Fred had accepted the assignment, Jenny saw the house in Japan where they were to live and instantly knew that not even a third of their belongings would fit. In fact, none of the antiques would fit through the door, let alone in the house.

FRED'S EARLY EXPERIENCES

When the Baileys arrived in Japan, they were greeted at the airport by one of the young Japanese associate consultants and the senior American expatriate. Fred and his family were quite tired from the long trip and the two hour ride back to Tokyo was a rather quiet one. After a few days of just settling in, Fred spent his first full day at the office.

Fred's first order of business was to have a general meeting with all the employees of associate consultant rank and higher. Although Fred didn't really notice it at the time, all the Japanese staff sat together and all the Americans sat together. After Fred introduced himself and his general ideas about the potential and future directions of the Tokyo office, he called on a few individuals to get their ideas about how things for which they were responsible would likely fit into his overall plan.

From the Americans, Fred got a mixture of opinions with specific reasons about why certain things might or might not fit well. From the Japanese, he got very vague answers. When Fred pushed to get more specific information, he was surprised to find that a couple of Japanese simply made a sucking sound as they breathed and said that it was "difficult to say". Fred sensed the meeting was not meeting his objectives, and so he thanked everyone for coming and said he looked forward to their all working together to make the Tokyo office the fastest growing office in the company.

After they had been in Japan about a month, Fred's wife complained to him about the difficulty she had getting certain products like maple syrup, peanut butter, and quality beef. She said that when she could get it at one of the specialty stores, it cost three and four times what it would cost in the States. She also complained that the washer and dryer were much too small and so she had to spend extra money by sending things out to be cleaned. On top of all that, unless she went to the American Club in downtown Tokyo, she never had anyone to talk to. After all, Fred was gone 10 to 16 hours a day. Unfortunately, at the time Fred was preoccupied, thinking about his upcoming meeting between his firm and a significant prospective client – a top 100 Japanese multinational company.

The next day, along with the lead American consultant for the potential contract, Ralph Webster, and one of the Japanese associate consultants, Kenichi Kurokawa, who spoke perfect English, Fred met with a team from the Japanese firm. The Japanese team consisted of four members – the VP of administration, the director of international personnel, and two staff specialists. After shaking hands and a few awkward bows, the Japanese offered to exchange business cards. Fred's staff had prepared his cards in advance with Japanese on one side and English on the other. Fred handed his cards to each Japanese with the English side up.

After the card exchange, Fred said that he knew the Japanese gentlemen were busy and he didn't want to waste their time so he would get right to the point. Fred then had Ralph Webster lay out Kline's proposal for the project and what the project would cost. After the presentation, Fred asked the Japanese what their reaction to the proposal was. The Japanese did not respond immediately and so Fred launched into his summary version of the proposal thinking that the translation might have been insufficient. But again, the Japanese had only the vaguest of responses to his direct questions.

The recollection of the frustration of that meeting was enough to shake Fred back to reality. The reality was that in the five months since the first meeting little progress had been made and the contract between the firms was yet to be signed. "I can never seem to get a direct response from Japanese," he thought to himself. This feeling of frustration led him to remember a related incident that happened about a month after his first meeting with this client.

Fred had decided that the reason not much progress was being made with the client was that Fred and his group just didn't know enough about the client to package the proposal in a way that was appealing to the client. Consequently, he called in the senior American associated with the proposal, Ralph Webster, and asked him to develop a report on the client so the proposal could be re-evaluated and changed where necessary. Jointly, they decided that one of the more promising Japanese research associates, Tashiro Watanabe, would be the best person to take the lead on this report.

To impress upon Tashiro the importance of this task and the great potential they saw in him, they decided to have the young Japanese associate meet with both Fred and Ralph. In the meeting Fred had Ralph lay out the nature and importance of the task, at which point Fred leaned forward in his chair and said, "You can see that this is an important assignment and that we are placing a lot of confidence in you by giving you this assignment. We need the report this time next week so that we can revise and re-present our proposal. What do you think?" After a somewhat pregnant pause, the Japanese responded somewhat hesitantly, "I'm not sure what to say." At that point Fred smiled, got up from his chair and walked over to the young Japanese associate, extended his hand, and said, "Hey, there's nothing to say. We're just giving you the opportunity you deserve."

The day before the report was due, Fred asked Ralph how the report was coming. Ralph said that since he had heard nothing from Tashiro that he assumed everything was under control, but that he would double check. Ralph later ran into one of the American research associates, John Maynard. Ralph knew that John was hired because of his language ability in Japanese and that unlike any of the other Americans, John often went out after work with some of the Japanese research associates, including Tashiro. So, Ralph asked John if he knew how Tashiro was coming on the report. John then recounted that last night at the office Tashiro had asked if Americans sometimes fired employees for being late with reports. John had sensed that this was more than a hypothetical question and asked Tashiro why he wanted to know. Tashiro did not respond immediately and since it was 8:30 in the evening, John suggested they go out for a drink. At first Tashiro resisted, but then John assured him that they would grab a drink at a nearby bar and come right back.

At the bar John got Tashiro to open up. Tashiro explained the nature of the report that he had been requested to produce. Tashiro continued to explain that even though he had worked long into the night every night to complete the report that it was just impossible and that he had doubted from the beginning whether he could complete the report in a week.

At this point Ralph asked John, "Why the hell didn't Tashiro say something in the first place?" Ralph didn't wait to hear whether John had an answer to his question or not. He headed straight to Tashiro's desk.

The incident just got worse from that point. Ralph chewed Tashiro out and then went to Fred explaining that the report would not be ready and that Tashiro didn't think it could be from the start. "Then why didn't he say something?" Fred asked. No one had any answers and the whole thing just left everyone more suspect and uncomfortable with each other than ever.

There were other incidents, big and small, that had made especially the last two months frustrating, but Fred was too tired to remember them all. To Fred it seemed that working with Japanese both inside and outside the firm was like working with people from another planet. Fred felt he just couldn't communicate with them, and he could never figure out what they were thinking. It drove him crazy.

JENNY'S EARLY EXPERIENCES

Jenny's life in Japan was equally frustrating. Jenny was determined at first to make an adventure of living in Japan. During the first week, she went down to the local grocery store to buy some food and basic household supplies. However, not being able to read the labels had its drawbacks. She had mistakenly bought a bluish colored bathroom cleaning liquid believing it was mouthwash and only discovered the mistake after "swishing", "gargling", and nearly choking to death on the stuff.

After about a month, Jenny tried to take the Tokyo subway system from her house to the American Club. What was supposed to be a 15 minute ride turned into a four hour ordeal. Jenny missed her stop but didn't discover it for several more. Then, when she did, she got off the train, only to discover she had no idea how to get to the other side of the tracks and head back the opposite way. She exited the station and tried to ask how to get to the other side. Finally, someone in broken English pointed out some stairs that led to a tunnel that went under the tracks to the other side.

However, arriving there, she found that she had no idea how much a ticket would cost to the stop she wanted and she had no change on her, only yen bills.

At this point she was so frustrated and broke into tears as she saw little grade school kids buy tickets and go through the turnstile. She saw a pay phone and tried to call Fred with the prepaid phone card she had been given. After a couple of times of the phone spitting the card back out, she realized she was inserting it in upside down. When she finally got through to Fred, she was crying and he seemed irritated at being called out of a meeting because she was lost on the subway system.

After a brief discussion, Fred and Jenny reasoned that she should take the escalator up out of the subway and hail a taxi. Fortunately, the Japanese taxi driver understood "American Club please" and Jenny arrived just as the group Jenny was supposed to meet was breaking up.

Two in the group were more than sympathetic to Jenny's ordeal and could not say enough about the "stupid" things they encountered in "this most backward of all developed countries". As part of this cathartic complaint session, Jenny related her "mouthwash" incident. After they all had a good laugh, one of the women told Jenny about National Azabu, a small but American grocery store. "At least there you can get decent food," she said.

THE BOMBSHELL

For Jenny, these incidents were only the tip of the iceberg. She wanted to go home, and yesterday was not soon enough. Even though the kids seemed to be doing OK, she was tired of Japan – tired of being stared at, of people trying to touch her hair, of not understanding anybody or being understood, of not being able to find what she wanted at the store, of not being able to drive and read the road signs, of not having anything to watch on TV, of not being involved in anything. She wanted to go home and she could not think of any reason why they shouldn't. After all, she reasoned they owed nothing to the company because the company had led them to believe this was just another assignment, like the two years they spent in San Francisco, and it was anything but that!

Fred tried to reason with her, but the more he countered, the more determined she became. Suddenly she dropped the bombshell on him: either they could go home together or he could stay here alone.

THE DECISION

Fred looked out the window once more, wishing that somehow everything could be fixed, or turned back or something. What had gone wrong? Why was Jenny being so unreasonable? Did he dare call Dave and explain the situation? Dave was very old fashioned and had once made a derogatory comment about a promising young consultant whose future looked dimmer and dimmer because he "couldn't control his complaining wife".

Looking down again, Fred could see traffic backed up down the street and around the corner. Though the traffic lights changed, the cars and trucks didn't seem to be moving. Fortunately, in the ground below, one of the world's most advanced, efficient, and clean subway systems moved hundreds of thousands of people about the city and to their homes.

NOTE

*   This case was written by Professor J. Stewart Black as a basis for class discussion rather than to illustrate either effective or ineffective handling of an administrative situation. Revised 12/12/96.

PART 3

Training, performance management, appraisal and compensation issues for global managers

Marja Tahvanainen

EXPATRIATE PERFORMANCE MANAGEMENT: THE CASE OF NOKIA TELECOMMUNICATIONS

INTRODUCTION

TODAY'S COMPANIES NO LONGER succeed by frequent introduction of new products or use of first-class technology alone. Companies have realized that they must also seek sustaining competitive advantage from the effective management of human resources. Unlike new production technology, for example, the success that comes from managing people effectively is often transparent with regard to its source (Pucik, 1992; Gratton, 1997; Beer, 1997).

Traditionally, performance appraisal has been used as a guide for employee performance. Lately, it has been supplanted in more and more companies with performance management (PM), a more comprehensive human resource management process. Through goal setting, performance appraisal and feedback, continuous training and development efforts, and performance-related pay, PM can help companies incorporate strategy into individual employee efforts and turn employees' potential into the desired results (Delery and Doty, 1996; Sparrow and Hiltrop, 1994). Other benefits of PM are that it can assist in motivating employees for good performance and can strengthen their commitment to the organization. Furthermore, it can assist in other organizational processes that are important to a company's long-term success, such as organizational learning, knowledge management, change management, and succession management. Thus, good performance management provides a company with the basis for managing its business today and preparing for its future through the performance of its people (Williams, 1991).

Effective performance management becomes particularly relevant to expatriate employees who are critical to multinational corporations' (MNCs) strategy formulation and implementation (Black, Gregersen, Mendenhall, and Stroh, 1998; Dowling, Welch, and Schuler, 1999). For example, expatriates can establish a company or a company function in a foreign location and can provide a foreign unit with the knowledge that the parent company considers necessary for the foreign unit to function effectively. Other rationales for sending expatriates are to serve as key contacts for coordination and to act in a control function between the parent company and subsidiaries (Edström and Galbraith, 1977; Torbiörn, 1982; Ondrack, 1985; Borg, 1987; Black et al., 1998).

Since expatriates can play a central role in the global success of companies and their use is expensive (Harvey, 1996), it seems critical to manage expatriate PM effectively; yet the research literature in this area is scarce. For domestic employees, studies are available regarding all elements of a PM system, namely goal setting, performance appraisal, training and development, and performance-related pay. For expatriates, similar studies are practically nonexistent. For example, it is not well known whether performance goals should be set by the sending company unit or the receiving unit for an engineer leaving from France to work in the United States. How should the engineer's training and development matters be dealt with while s/he is on assignment? What if the receiving unit uses a different performance management system than the sending unit? Whose system should then be used to manage the engineer's performance? Essentially, the research completed to date in an international setting is limited to one segment of PM, namely performance appraisal (Mendenhall and Oddou, 1991; Schuler and Florkowski, 1994; Gregersen, Hite, and Black, 1996). Yet, expatriate goal setting, training and development, and performance-related pay, for example, are areas in need of much more research.

In response to this need, I present several key findings from a case study on performance management practices at Nokia Telecommunications (NTC). The study addresses previously neglected areas of expatriate PM in an attempt to increase our understanding of this increasingly key international HRM topic. To accomplish this objective, I explore several aspects of the following research question: How is the performance of expatriates managed in different types of international assignments?

RESEARCH APPROACH

Due to the process nature of PM as well as the lack of rigorous theoretical models, a qualitative case study approach was deemed an appropriate method for exploring expatriate PM (Yin, 1994; Eisenhardt, 1989). For that purpose, Nokia Telecommunications, a Finnish-based MNC operating in the telecommunications industry, was selected as the case company. In the Finnish context, Nokia has extensive experience sending and receiving people on foreign assignments (15 years), and it has more expatriates on assignment (about 1,200) than any other company based in Finland. It could, therefore, be expected that NTC would have numerous established practices for managing expatriate performance.

Primarily, I collected data through 81 semistructured interviews. The inter-viewees consisted of company expatriates (mainly Finnish) who worked in different positions and different situations, line managers who had experience of sending expatriates on foreign assignments, local employees working outside Finland, and human resource personnel. The aim in collecting data from different types of employees who understood expatriate PM was to get a holistic understanding of the process. The interviews were conducted in NTC units in Finland, Thailand, China, the United Kingdom, and the United States. To cross-check and complement the interview data, I also assessed an extensive amount of internal company documents on expatriate PM.

These data were analyzed at several stages: (1) after the interviews in Finland, (2) after each data collection trip abroad, and, finally, (3) when all the data necessary for reaching a saturation point were collected. These analyses produced five groups of expatriates. While PM practices for members in a particular group were similar, clear differences in PM existed between groups. My search to explain the differences among these groups produced, in turn, several contingency factors for expatriate PM. These factors were identified by noticing variations in expatriate PM and then asking why such differences occurred. To answer the why question, potential contingency factors emerged. The relevance of the factors thus identified was then compared to other expatriate situations at NTC. This process continued until convergence occurred for the major contingency factors for expatriate PM.

RESULTS OF THE RESEARCH

Expatriate performance management practices at NTC

Although Nokia Telecommunications has a global, standardized PM system in place, meaning that all employees' performance is managed (to a great extent) similarly, my analysis revealed a reality that strayed from this unity – especially given that five groups of expatriates emerged at NTC. These groups were defined primarily by the nature of their job and included the following categories:

1. top managers
2. middle managers
3. business establishers
4. customer project employees
5. R&D project personnel

For each of these expatriate groups, it was common PM practice that all expatriates knew what was expected of them, how well they were performing, and that they received the opportunity to develop new competencies in order to meet the requirements of present and future job assignments.

Some differences in the PM among the expatriate groups were also clear. These differences revolved around: (1) whether and how performance goals were set, who set them, and what type of goals they were; (2) how expatriates' performance was evaluated and who conducted the evaluation; (3) whether training and development plans were agreed upon with expatriates; (4) whether expatriates had the opportunity to attend training while on assignment; and (5) what type and how clear the linkage was between expatriate performance and pay. The following section reviews the typical PM characteristics of each expatriate group.

Top manager expatriates

Top manager expatriates occupied highly independent senior positions overseas, and their performance was managed distantly; they commonly formulated their own performance goals. One interviewee explained, "My boss and I agreed on key result areas that were important, then it was my task to set more specific goals and milestones." Because of the wide scope of their jobs, these inter-viewees' performance management goals were fairly broad. For instance, one goal that was derived from a Finnish expatriate's key result area, Project Management Improvement, was "managing future projects more in line with each project management handbook".

Most of the top managers' performance goals were concrete – defined in their incentive scheme. To illustrate, a goal such as "profitability" was specified in the incentive scheme by assigning a target level of operating profit. Linkages between performance goals and incentive objectives were very clear for the expatriates in this group. In fact, expatriates in this group generally perceived incentive objectives as their major goals.

Top manager expatriates' superiors were located in a country other than the expatriates – either at corporate headquarters or regional headquarters. For example, two superiors of the country manager in Italy were both located in Finland. As a result, top manager expatriates' performance was evaluated by a supervisor located in another country – a situation suggested as prone to evaluation bias (Gregersen et al., 1996; Oddou and Mendenhall, 1991). The interviewees did not find this a major problem, yet sometimes they wished that their manager had been more geographically proximate to discuss puzzling issues in the foreign location.

In PM discussions with their managers, expatriates at high organizational levels cover developmental and longer-term matters (i.e., career planning); however, their managers rarely initiated discussions about top manager expatri-ates' training needs. Instead, these expatriates generally knew when additional training was necessary and had no trouble communicating those needs to their managers.

Middle manager expatriates

In addition to having superiors co-located in the host country, some middle manager expatriates reported to one or more superiors back at headquarters in

Finland. Performance goals for the middle manager expatriates, however, were agreed upon in the host country as a joint effort between the employee and the superior. Middle managers' performance goals varied from fairly specific to very specific, for example, ranging from "achieve targeted market share and results" to "collect accounts receivable in 60 days or less". Qualitative, yet quantitatively measurable, goals also were included; for example, "employee satisfaction" was measured through a yearly opinion survey.

When middle manager expatriates' performance had been evaluated formally, the evaluation was done in general by the host country manager. If the expatriate also had a manager in the home country, the local manager discussed the expatriate's performance with the home country manager prior to evaluation. Most of the ongoing performance feedback was given by the host country manager, and expatriates in this group generally felt it was satisfactory.

Each expatriate in this group worked under an incentive scheme. Unlike top manager expatriates, the linkage between the PM goals and incentive objectives was not always clear, since most middle managers' incentive goals were referred to as "next higher level goals", for example, "net sales of the department" in which the person worked. As a result, it was not always easy to identify the linkage between the expatriate's personal performance and the achievement of incentive objectives. Nevertheless, the host country manager determined the size of financial rewards for middle manager expatriates, and together they developed the training and long-term development plans for the expatriates. If desired and needed, middle manager expatriates could take training courses while on assignment.

Business establisher expatriates

Business establisher expatriates were generally profit- and loss-responsible for starting up new businesses in foreign countries. These start-ups might be greenfield sites or turnkey operations, or they might be marketing operations in a new geographical area. A common characteristic of business establisher PM was that s/he worked with only a few performance goals. For example, a manager sent to China was given one performance objective: to establish a production line that produced mobile phone base stations. Another business establisher said of the only performance goal that he received before embarking on his assignment, "Before leaving for my international assignment, my boss in Finland was very clear about what I was supposed to accomplish during the assignment: acquire customers – period."

Some business establishers had primary managers in the home country, while those who were sent to establish a specialized function in a host location (e.g., finance, accounting, marketing, human resources) generally had a primary superior co-located in the host country. Most business establishers did not have time to participate in training activities, although training plans had been agreed upon in earlier superior–subordinate PM discussions. Furthermore, most business establishers operated in the context of an incentive system, but the linkage between focused performance goals and incentive objectives was frequently unclear.

Customer project expatriates

Most customer project expatriates work on intensive projects for current customers that can last from a few months to several years. Expatriates are employed for all three project phases: (1) network planning, (2) implementation, and (3) operation and maintenance. Depending on the phase of a project, and the size and scope of it, the number of employees working for any one customer project varies. The largest number of employees, including expatriates, are needed during the implementation phase.

Unlike the expatriates in the three previous groups, customer project expatriates did not enter the assignment with agreed-upon, job-related performance goals. Instead, depending on the local manager and the nature of the project, expatriates received information about performance expectations through day-to-day relationships with the project manager, project team members, and/or other project stakeholders. When customer project expatriates failed to get information about their performance expectations informally, however, they had to rely on a formal job description. It should be pointed out that most customer project expatriates put little trust in the value of formally agreed-upon performance goals. As one Finnish expatriate with extensive customer project experience explained:

> It is very difficult to set specific personal goals for expatriates working on customer projects. In fact, it's not even necessary. Instead, we put a goal on the wall that the network has to be operating by such and such a date. It's usually much clearer that way.

Paralleling this relatively vague goal setting practice, performance evaluation, formal and informal, was practically nonexistent for customer project expatriates. Except for one interviewee, customer project expatriates felt that they did not receive sufficient ongoing feedback. Thus, it appeared that a structured and formal goal setting and performance evaluation tradition did not prevail in "customer focused" projects. In other words, it appeared that job-related performance goals and performance evaluation were not covered in PM discussions with customer project expatriates.

Customer project expatriates, however, did engage in PM discussions that focused on training and development issues. These discussions were held with their home-based administrative manager, not the on-site project manager in the foreign country. These discussions took place in between foreign project assignments or during holiday breaks in the home country. The expatriates' development plans were discussed in these PM meetings, as well as suitable training courses for reaching personal development objectives. As the projects are often hectic in nature, project expatriates could rarely take educational courses while on assignment, and usually ended up taking them in between assignments.

Finally, because of the informal goal setting and evaluation approach with expatriates in customer projects, a strict linkage between performance and pay did not exist. Instead, the prevailing practice was for project expatriates to get a yearly bonus that was related not only to on-the-job performance, but also to the large number of extra hours that project expatriates typically put into completing a project.

Research and development project expatriates

Research and development (R&D) projects are similar to customer projects, yet are also different. From a performance management perspective, one important difference is that R&D employees are physically proximal to their managers, whereas customer projects might be conducted at several sites, located hundreds of kilometers apart. As a consequence, in R&D projects, the delivery of ongoing feedback and daily PM tasks are easier to complete. Another important difference is that, unlike customer projects, R&D projects are internal to the company. Thus, there is less direct connection to the customer, and as a result, the uncertainty faced by R&D project expatriates is lower so R&D projects are usually well planned and job tasks determined in detail. Naturally though, the specificity of R&D jobs varies. For example, a mechanical engineer's job is less structured than a system engineer's or system designer's job.

Unlike expatriates working on customer projects, R&D project expatriates engaged in PM discussions that covered the standard three topics of goal setting, performance evaluation, and development. Performance goals set in PM discussions for R&D expatriates remained fairly vague and at the operative level. For example, one expatriate faced the broad goal of learning everything about a new generation telecommunications product. Typically, communication of specific performance goals happened in weekly or bi-weekly project meetings. Along with task information received in project meetings, job descriptions generally conveyed a rough level of what was expected from R&D expatriates. Like customer project expatriates, R&D expatriates at the operational level did not desire more specific PM goals; they generally regarded their jobs as so clear that more specific goals were unnecessary. For R&D expatriates operating at a high hierarchical level, however, goals agreed upon in PM discussions tended to be more specific. This specification was done most often through a separate PM form, including key result areas and deadlines.

In general, R&D expatriates received a sufficient amount of ongoing performance feedback. They were physically proximate to superiors, and in project meetings, past project performance was reviewed regularly – although not always at the individual level. In one-on-one PM discussions, specific personal level feedback was given and received.

Developmental matters were also covered in PM discussions with R&D expatriates, yet it was very rare that they actually engaged in any training during the international assignment. There were several reasons for this: (1) expatriates' lack of knowledge as to available training courses in host locations; (2) superiors' inability to guide R&D expatriates' development since expatriates often had more job experience than local managers; (3) an R&D expatriate's job during the assignment was seen as personal development; and (4) unless training was arranged in the downtime phase of a project, expatriates were not allowed to participate in it. Finally, R&D expatriates were entitled to pay bonuses based on either attaining project milestones or at the discretion of a superivising manager.

Summary of expatriate performance management practices

To highlight the differences among expatriate groups, Table 1 summarizes the key characteristics of PM for the five types of expatriates studied at Nokia Telecommunications. As the table shows, differences between the groups focus primarily on the location of the manager who agrees to expatriate performance goals and then evaluates their performance; the type of goals set; the possibility of taking training courses while on assignment; and the type and clarity of linkage between performance and pay.

MANAGERIAL IMPLICATIONS

This article illustrates how expatriate performance management occurs in a large MNC – Nokia Telecommunications. This case study manifests the criticality of contingency factors when managing expatriate performance. The Nokia Telecommunications case underlines this point by demonstrating that despite the company's standard performance management system intended for global use, expatriate performance was managed differently in at least five categories of expatriate assignments. One managerial implication of this result is that when developing an expatriate PM system, a company should pay attention to specific situations and plan accordingly. Essentially, off-the-shelf solutions may not produce the desired improvements in expatriate and company performance.

Another managerial implication of this study is that companies may need to provide several PM tools for superiors' and subordinates' use. While standardizing the objectives of a performance management process seems attractive (for example, all employees know what is expected from their performance, understand how they are currently performing, and receive consistent training and development), allowing diversity in the means and tools to achieve these objectives may be quite useful. In fact, the development of alternative PM tools – modified from a standardized global set – may result in a more effective implementation of performance management worldwide as it would likely formalize prevailing PM situations, unify the different existing PM practices, and provide appropriate tools for managing the differing expatriate experiences. On the basis of the interviews conducted at NTC, at least two types of PM approaches could be useful: one for managing managerial and professional expatriate performance and the other for customer and R&D project expatriate performance.

Furthermore, interview data suggested the importance of a well-understood relationship between the incentive system and performance management system.

Table 1. Summary of the key performance management characteristics in five types of expatriate groups at Nokia Telecommunications

	Top manager	Middle manager	Business establisher	Customer project	R&D project
Goal setting	• To a great extent self-developed goals that are agreed with manager(s) located in another country (at the HQ or area HQ) • Emphasis on clear, financial goals	• The manager in a host location sets the goals, yet many expatriates also have a manager at HQ • Goals vary from fairly specific to very specific	• Goals are agreed upon with the primary manager, located either in the host or the home country • Relatively few, broad goals	• No formal, work-related goal setting	• The manager in the host location sets the goals • Goals vary from vague to specific
Performance evaluation	• By the manager(s) located in another country	• When actually done, performed by a manager in the host location • Satisfactory amount of ongoing performance feedback for most	• By the primary manager(s) • Satisfactory amount of ongoing performance feedback for some	• Formal evaluation rather nonexistent; if it happens, it is done by a host country manager • Insufficient amount of ongoing feedback	• By a manager in the host location • Satisfactory amount of ongoing performance feedback
Training and development	• Expectation that the expatriate raises the issue	• Discussed and agreed with the host location manager • Expatriates engaged in training while on assignment	• Discussed and agreed with the primary manager • Expatriates had no time to engage in training while on assignment	• Discussed and agreed with an administrative manager in the home country • Expatriates had no time to engage in training while on assignment	• Discussed and agreed with a host country manager • Expatriates had no time to engage in training while on assignment
Performance-related pay	• Clear linkage between performance and incentives	• All worked under an an incentive scheme, yet the linkage between performance and pay was often unclear	• Most worked under an incentive scheme, yet the linkage between performance and pay was often unclear	• Entitled to yearly bonuses that were not linked strictly to individual performance	• Some expatriates entitled to bonuses that were linked only in part to individual performance

It seems that integrating these two systems so that a part of incentive objectives clearly stem from PM goals would prove beneficial, as then the systems would strengthen and complement each other.

Regardless of the effectiveness or availability of PM tools, expatriate PM success depends largely on the manager and expatriate in question: how well they both understand, internalize, and accept PM, and how skillful they are in its implementation (Latham and Wexley, 1982; Carson, Cardy, and Dobbins, 1991; Lindholm, Tahvanainen and Björkman, 1999). To this end, appropriate PM training should be available for all expatriates, including their superiors.

RESEARCH IMPLICATIONS

As this study examined expatriate performance management in a Finnish company that is large, highly internationalized, and uses hundreds of expatriates, future research could benefit by focusing on expatriate PM issues in smaller and less internationalized companies having fewer expatriates. Prior PM research and the findings of this study indicate that in such companies, expatriate performance management processes may well differ.

Replication of this case study in non-Finnish MNCs could provide further understanding, for example, about the effect of national culture on expatriate PM. This study did not address this issue directly because it studied expatriates who were mostly Finns in a Finnish company with largely Finnish superiors. As a result, cultural differences between superiors and subordinates were relatively small, and cultural differences in PM did not surface as much as they might have if superiors and subordinates had been from vastly different cultures (Hofstede, 1984; Trompenaars, 1993).

To conclude, this study scratched the surface of the complexity of expatriate performance management. Future studies should explore factors such as organizational structure, the managerial style and skills of the manager and expatriate, top management support for PM, and the maturity of operations in the host country. Clearly, at the domestic, international, and global levels, numerous intriguing questions for research and practice merit further inquiry.

REFERENCES

Beer, M. (1997). The transformation of the human resource function: Resolving the tension between a traditional administrative and a new strategic role. Human Resource Management, 36(1), 49–56.

Black, J. S., Gregersen, H. B., Mendenhall, M., and Stroh, L. (1998). Globalizing people through international assignments. Boston, Mass.: Addison-Wesley.

Borg, M. (1987). International transfers of managers in multinational corporations: Transfer patterns and organizational control. Published doctoral dissertation, University of Uppsala, Department of Business Administration. Uppsala: Reproc, HSC.

Carson, K. P., Cardy, R. L., and Dobbins, G. H. (1991). Performance appraisal as effective management or deadly management disease: Two initial empirical investigations. Group and Organization Studies, 16(2), 143–59.

Delery, J. E., and Doty, D. H. (1996). Modes of theorizing in strategic human resource management: Tests of universalistic, contingency, and configurational performance predictions. Academy of Management Journal, 39(4), 802–35.

Dowling, P. J., Welch, D. E., and Schuler, R. S. (1999). International human resource management: Managing people in a multinational context. Cincinnati, Ohio: South-Western College Publishing.

Edström, A., and Galbraith, J. (1977). Alternative policies for international transfers of managers. Management International Review, 17(2), 11–22.

Eisenhardt, K. (1989). Building theories from case study research. Academy of Management Review, 14(4), 532–50.

Gratton, L. (1997). Tomorrow people. People Management, July, 22–7.

Gregersen, H. B., Hite, J. M., and Black, J. S. (1996). Expatriate performance appraisal in U.S multinational firms. Journal of International Business Studies, Fall, 711–38.

Harvey, M. (1996). A planning perspective. The Columbia Journal of World Business, 102–18.

Hofstede, G. (1984). Culture's consequences: International differences in work-related values. Thousand Oaks, Calif.: Sage Publications, Inc.

Latham, G. P., and Wexley, K. N. (1982). Increasing productivity through performance appraisal. Boston, Mass.: Addison-Wesley.

Lindholm, N., Tahvanainen, M., and Björkman, I. (1999). Performance appraisal of host country employees: Western MNCs in China. In C. Brewster and H. Harris (eds.), International HRM: Contemporary issues in Europe (pp. 143–59). London: Routledge.

Mendenhall, M., and Oddou, G. (1991). Readings and cases in international human resource management. Boston, Mass.: PWS-Kent Publishing Company.

Oddou, G., and Mendenhall, M. (1991). Expatriate appraisal: Problems and solutions. In Mendenhall M. and Oddou, G. (eds.), Readings and cases in international human resource management (pp. 364–74). Boston, Mass.: PWS-KENT Publishing Company.

Ondrack, D. (1985). International transfers of managers in North American and European MNEs. Journal of International Business Studies, 16(3), 1–19.

Pucik, V. (1992). Globalization and human resource management. In V. Pucik, N. M. Tichy, and C. K. Barnett (eds.), Globalizing management: Creating and leading the competitive organization (pp. 61–81). New York: John Wiley & Sons, Inc.

Schuler, R. S., and Florkowski, G. W. (1994). Research in international human resource management. In B. J. Punnett and O. Shenkar (eds.), Handbook of international management research, London: Blackwell Publishers.

Sparrow, P., and Hiltrop, J.-M. (1994). European human resource management in transition. Hertfordshire: Prentice-Hall International (UK) Limited.

Torbiörn, I. (1982). Living abroad: Personal adjustment and personnel policy in the overseas setting. New York: John Wiley & Sons, Inc.

Trompenaars, F. (1993). Riding the waves of culture: Understanding cultural diversity in business. London: Nicholas Brealey Publishing.

Williams, S. (1991). Strategy and objectives. In F. Neale (ed.), The handbook of performance management (pp. 7–24). Exeter: Short Run Press Ltd.

Yin, R. (1994). Case study research: design and methods. (2nd edn). Beverly Hills, Calif.: Sage Publications.

Soo Min Toh and Angelo S. DeNisi

A LOCAL PERSPECTIVE TO EXPATRIATE SUCCESS

A LOCAL PERSPECTIVE TO EXPATRIATE SUCCESS

WITH INCREASING FOREIGN REVENUES, multinational companies' (MNCs) need for expatriate assignments shows little signs of slowing down. Maintaining an expatriate is a costly and often complicated process – and if the expatriate fails in his or her assignment, the expatriate exercise becomes even more costly for all involved. Losses and damages resulting from expatriate failure include loss of business and productivity, damage to other employees and relationships with customers, suppliers, and host government officials, as well as the financial and emotional costs borne by the expatriate and his or her family.[1] Given these potential costs, it is imperative that expatriate assignments are managed effectively.

A recent survey released by the US National Foreign Trade Council reported failure to adjust to the foreign cultural environment as a key reason for expatriate failure.[2] MNCs' records for providing sufficient pre-departure training for expatriates and their families have been poor. Expatriates often complain that they are not well prepared for the challenges they face on the assignments. Selection practices have also frequently been criticized for emphasizing technical competence and neglecting critical success factors such as relational skills and cross-cultural competence. Therefore, in addition to providing attractive expatriate packages, many MNCs have worked to improve training and orientation programs for expatriates, and to fine-tune the selection criteria to better match identified critical success factors.

Clearly, the onus for completion of a successful assignment has been primarily on the expatriate, as well as the parent company, whose responsibility has been to engage in various activities that are deemed to facilitate the adjustment of expatriates. Whereas these efforts have been met with measured success, many MNCs have overlooked the potential of yet another important avenue to facilitate adjustment. This potential lies in the local or host country staff with whom the expatriates work closely while on assignment. Traditionally, local employees were the expatriate's subordinates, but they are increasingly the coworkers and supervisors of expatriate assignees as well. As we will discuss in the present paper, local staff could be the expatriate's best on-site trainers as expatriates wade in possibly treacherous cultural waters. In the same vein, local staff could also seriously jeopardize the expatriate's ability to carry out his or her assignment by engaging in various counterproductive behaviors at work. Yet, with few exceptions, multinationals overlook the socializing potential of local staff in aiding expatriates in their adjustment and are not cognizant of how the very practices meant to ensure the success of expatriates can also inadvertently lead to their failure.

Given the potential importance of local staff to any multinational, the present paper has three main objectives. First, we identify the HR practices in MNCs that may adversely affect the organizations' effectiveness. Certain types of expatriate HR practices, especially ethnocentric ones, can be perceived as inequitable by local staff and create unforeseen (and unwanted) effects on the local staff's work attitudes and behaviors. Lowered commitment and job satisfaction, as well as counterproductive work behaviors such as absenteeism and turnover, are potential outcomes of ethnocentric HR practices, and can ultimately hurt the effectiveness of the multinational. Second, we demonstrate how violating equity between local and expatriate employees is detrimental to expatriate adjustment. The fates of the two groups of employees are often inextricably linked – the expatriates cannot be successful if their host country counterparts are not. In fact, it seems obvious that expatriates will find it much more difficult to succeed in their assignments without the support of local staff. Unfortunately, ethnocentric HR practices do not create the conditions that would cause such support to be forthcoming. Last, we propose several alternative interventions adopted by companies that have been relatively successful at managing expatriate assignments, which multinationals should consider as means to motivate and retain local staff as well as to better harness the important socializing potential that local staff can offer to expatriates. Hence, our recommendations for the design of HR practices consider their larger effects on all employees in the organization and not merely on any particular subset of employees in the organization. Throughout, we highlight real-life issues faced by multinationals, provide real-life solutions adopted around the globe, and report relevant findings of organizational research.

LOCAL EMPLOYEES ARE IMPORTANT TOO

A critical factor often considered by MNCs when making decisions about where to locate overseas subsidiaries is the availability of qualified local workers. MNCs depend on a qualified local workforce to be effective and this dependence amplifies significantly if it is the MNC's aim to completely localize its overseas subsidiaries. Siemens AG, for example, locates itself worldwide and relies heavily on local workers to achieve its goals – in the US alone it employs over 60,000 Americans, and hires more than 20,000 personnel in China. New research also suggests that local managers can offer more control to the MNC than expatriates can in situations where cultural asymmetries between the headquarters country and the host country are high and the operating environment is risky.[3] Furthermore, if the market that the MNC enters is one where its existing personnel have little relevant knowledge or expertise to effectively run the local subsidiary, local human capital would be especially useful because the local managers speak the local business language and also understand the country's culture and political system better than most expatriates sent to perform the job. Local staff are thus often better equipped than expatriates to penetrate the target market. The experience of MNCs in China, for example, has demonstrated that capable local managers and professionals are indispensable for the success of MNCs because expatriates continue to flounder in unfamiliar territory. Hence, there is little dispute that capable local employees are strategic assets to a MNC.

It is also in host countries like China that we find much discontent among local staff and resentment towards expatriates because often inept expatriates are ostensibly treated as superior relative to the locals in terms of their compensation, benefits, and developmental opportunities.[4] This is especially so when expatriates do not have a clear advantage over the local employees in terms of work qualifications, expertise, or experience. Local staff may feel that they are treated like second-class citizens when working alongside expatriates in their own country, and may resent that fact. They may also perceive expatriates as being sent to be "watchdogs" for headquarters instead of value-added resources. Clearly, this mistrust of and dissatisfaction with the expatriate and the multinational set the stage for a whole host of negative consequences for the multinational, such as lowered productivity and effectiveness and higher rates of turnover and absenteeism. When resentment is high, more extreme counterproductive work behaviors may also ensue, such as theft and sabotage. It is clear that multinationals truly cannot afford to be insensitive to the feelings and opinions of the local staff in their organization.

However, local staff have yet another important part to play. It lies in their potential significance as a valuable socializing agent and facilitator of the expatriate's role in the host unit organization. Most of us are probably able to recall that time when we first started a new job: adjusting to the new environment, new responsibilities, and new relationships were probably made easier if we had received some guidance and support from someone in the early transition stages of our job. This person (or persons) probably had more experience and greater knowledge of the job and environment we were entering into than we did. This person was also often someone holding a similar or higher post than us, who had been in the organization longer than us, and had sufficient history with the organization to understand how things worked or how best to get things done. Organizational research corroborates these experiences by showing very clearly that the stresses related to starting a new job can be assuaged by supportive relationships within the work organization (e.g., coworker, supervisor, mentor).

Hence, many organizations apply this principle by adopting mentoring and buddy systems to orient new employees in domestic operations, and the effects have often been very positive. For example, Sun Microsystems Inc. in Palo Alto, California, pairs newcomers with more experienced "Sun Visors", while the New York office of PriceWaterhouseCoopers uses a buddy system, as well as more senior coaches, to supplement their formal training and orientation programs. In some companies, peers and designated mentors are also put through training programs to become effective coaches, and hiring managers attend workshops on getting ready for new employees joining the unit. A US-based company, National City Corp., uses a similar training program where managers are trained to communicate effectively and create supportive environments, and reports that the training is highly successful. Specifically, they report decreased turnover and absenteeism rates and higher productivity, which resulted in annual savings of over a million dollars after implementing the program.[5]

The same principles could and should be applied more widely to the context of the host unit organization where an expatriate assignee needs to learn the ropes of being a new member of the host subsidiary despite possibly having had experience in the parent company. He or she must also quickly become proficient in the performances of his or her job, while at the same time adapting to the unfamiliar surroundings and culture. MNCs like SAS Institute and Intel recognize the importance of expatriates gaining the cooperation of their local counterparts, loyalty from their subordinates, and the trust of their supervisors. Instead of placing the onus solely on the expatriate to develop effective working relationships and strong bonds with the local staff, these organizations adopt buddy systems where local peers act as ad hoc trainers for the expatriate. They also encourage and prepare the receiving managers and local teammates of the expatriate to ensure that the newcomer expatriates are assimilated quickly. Intel, for example, trains managers who are about to receive an expatriate. The training emphasizes ways to integrate and work with groups of people of other cultural backgrounds. With this training, local managers are better equipped to interact with expatriates and are less likely to find expatriates forbidding. Faced with more approachable local counterparts, expatriates are less likely to be isolated by the local staff, and have greater opportunities to learn from them and develop effective work relationships with them.

We will return later to other steps MNCs can employ to help insure that local employees contribute more fully. Before we do, however, we need to address how local staff can contribute to the adjustment and success of expatriates through the informational support, cooperation, and emotional support they provide to those expatriates.

Informational support

Expatriates face substantial uncertainty regarding their new role in the organization when they first arrive in their new location. They must figure out how things work and what the best way is to approach problems that they may encounter.

Any information the expatriates gain regarding the new job, the organization, and the larger cultural environment will help them learn what to expect, how to interpret various stimuli they encounter day-to-day, and what the appropriate behavior is in a given situation. In most situations, expatriates need to have a working knowledge and good understanding of the cultural mores of the organization and the national context in order to be effective. This need is especially critical when the job is novel and challenging for the expatriate, when the culture of the organization and the country is unfamiliar, or when sources of information which the expatriate relied upon in his or her home country are not readily available.

Informational support is also important if the expatriates are sent to host subsidiaries to acquire knowledge and gain cultural competence. Such assignments are increasingly popular as MNCs recognize the importance of gaining international experience among their employees. For example, ABB (Asea Brown Boveri) rotates about 500 managers around the world to different countries every few years to develop a cadre of managers with a global outlook.[6] Similarly, expatriates who are sent to the host location to set up "greenfield" operations will also need to acquire rich local knowledge in order to find sources for raw material, human resources, potential business associates, and potential customers. This necessity has been encountered by many companies that have tried to set up shop in China and found it to be a culturally challenging environment and impossible without local "guanxi", because these social networks are also very rich informational networks. The expatriates may be left out of important decisions and information if they are unable to penetrate existing informational networks.[7]

Of course, the local employees at the host organization would have these different types of information. By virtue of being born and raised in the host country and having been members of the host organization longer than the expatriate, local staff possess the additional experience and understanding of the culture and the organization, and also have developed the necessary network of relationships that could facilitate the conduct of many of the expatriates' tasks. The local staff's advantage is even greater in new markets for the multinational where expatriates are likely to be treading in unfamiliar political, economic, and social waters. If local staff are willing to share their intimate local knowledge with the expatriates, expatriates can set up shop in the host country or learn what they were sent to learn much more successfully. Local staff also possess critical information regarding the cultural mores of the workplace.[8] For example, many Western managers in Beijing report the Chinese culture as being quite incomprehensible and they have great difficulty operating effectively in the Chinese context. Sharing insights about the cultural norms and idiosyncrasies with fledgling expatriates will help them better establish the necessary networks within the organization and facilitate their adjustment to the new organizational and national culture. Knowing what is culturally acceptable and appropriate behavior is also critical for expatriates to avoid offending local coworkers, subordinates, and supervisors. As in the case of a *Fortune* 100 company, it was reported that its expatriates across 19 worldwide locations demonstrated greater adjustment to their work and social interactions when they had access to on-site host country mentors.[9] Clearly, the informational support from local staff is integral to an expatriate's ability to succeed.

Paradoxically, informational support from local staff most critical to the successful experience of the expatriate is also likely to be more difficult to gain. Many local staff have traditionally expected to learn from expatriates, because the expatriates are often viewed to be the experts with specialized knowledge, sent to the host unit to lead local staff rather than to learn from them. When these expectations are coupled with the fact that expatriates often earn much more than the local staff, the local employees may feel resentful. This resentment may be expressed by shutting out expatriates from informational networks since they may feel that doing so, and helping expatriates out, are not really part of their job requirement. As a result, the expatriates and the organization lose a valuable source of country and organizational information. Thus, it is important that the practices of the multinational do not breed resentment, but encourage the sharing of information between local staff and expatriates.

Cooperation

Expatriates sent to lead subsidiaries in various capacities will find gaining the local staff's cooperation indispensable to the performance of their job. Without the following of local subordinates and the cooperation of other local managers – neither of which expatriates should erroneously take for granted – expatriates may find their leadership role seriously frustrated and undermined. Those sent to manage local employees quickly lose credibility if they appear to have little local understanding or lack endorsement from other local staff managers. Also, if expatriates do not become part of the social network, decisions may be made without the full input and acceptance of the local employees. With the increased use of teams, expatriates who are not well integrated and accepted by their local staff colleagues are less likely to perform the job well or be satisfied with work relationships within the team. In the case of expatriates sent to transfer knowledge and expertise to local staff and train future local managers, these expatriates will not be successful if local staff are not receptive to their presence in the host organization and are unwilling to learn from them.

Poor expatriate–local relations may also lead to other counterproductive work behaviors ranging from tardiness and absenteeism to more extreme behaviors such as insubordination, withholding of vital information, and even sabotage. For example, local American executives admit that they would continue to produce data with errors because they are not willing to work around the clock to make it error free no matter what their Japanese bosses say; and local Chinese managers deliberately exclude the expatriate manager whom they view as an outsider in the making of major decisions.[10] A top manager from a Swedish–Swiss MNC recounts how Singaporean employees deliberately did not alert an expatriate manager of a bad decision because the expatriate simply "should know better". These problems could have been avoided if expatriates had been able to gain the local staff's cooperation or if the organization had ways in which to encourage and reward cooperation.

Emotional support

Whereas the importance of the spouse's emotional and moral support has been recognized in research and practice, the role of local staff as a source of emotional support for expatriates has not been widely regarded as important. However, research in newcomer adjustment finds unequivocal evidence for the importance of supportive work relationships as well. Emotional support helps a person to believe that he or she is cared for, esteemed, valued, and belongs to a network of communication and mutual obligation.[11] It includes the friendships that provide emotional reassurance, or instrumental aid in dealing with stressful situations. No doubt, being a newcomer in a new organization or a newcomer in a foreign country can be a highly stressful experience. But with the support of others in the organization, the newcomer can better make the transition to the new job and situation. We see evidence of this in a group of expatriates in Hong Kong, where expatriates' level of adjustment was significantly higher when support was available from their local coworkers than if such support was not available.[12]

According to existing research, even if actual support is not needed or sought after, the mere knowledge of the existence and availability of such support for the newcomer can be quite reassuring, and in turn can reduce the level of stress experienced by the individual. Thus, although the expatriate may never encounter the need to confide in local staff, just knowing that local staff are available and willing confidants alleviates some of the stress the expatriate faces. Furthermore, having supportive relationships in the organization can create a stronger sense of belonging for expatriates. Expatriates feel like they "fit in" with their local colleagues better and thus enjoy greater levels of work satisfaction and commitment to the host organization. The lack of such support could, on the other hand, hinder the expatriate's adjustment. Expatriates in US and Europe based multinationals reported lower levels of commitment and adjustment when they felt that they were being ostracized by their local colleagues.[13] The lack of deep friendships is especially disappointing for expatriates of more relationship-oriented cultures. For example, Korean expatriates in the US find their American counterparts friendly on a superficial level, but quite unwilling to develop stronger relationships. This often results in hurt feelings, disappointment, and a sense of isolation. The expatriates, in turn, become reluctant to socialize with the native-born Americans because they feel that they do not understand them and therefore seek solace through the friendships with the other expatriates.[14] The distancing of expatriate groups ultimately hurts the overall adjustment of expatriates, and also negatively affects their job performance and their ability and willingness to learn from their local counterparts.

However, just as is the case with informational support and cooperation, providing care and support to another employee is not usually specified in one's job description. Forming supportive relationships or friendships with the expatriates they work with is not required by local staff's jobs and would have to occur on their own initiative. Given suitable circumstances, local staff may be willing to go out of their way to support expatriates and help socialize them during their time of transition along the dimensions discussed. Unfortunately, several conditions are prevalent in multinational organizations that could cause local staff to be unwilling socializing agents. We discuss these factors next, and highlight how HR policies can inadvertently discourage the socializing role of local staff.

HR PRACTICES THAT DISCOURAGE THE SOCIALIZING ROLE OF LOCAL EMPLOYEES

What would determine whether local staff chose to exhibit or withhold critical socializing behaviors? Empathy is a critical driving force for an employee's decision to help a fellow coworker.[15] Employees who like and care about their coworker are more likely to provide help on their own accord, whenever help is needed by the coworker. Employees in cohesive work groups, or groups with enhanced positive relationships among members, are more likely to spontaneously help out than employees in less cohesive groups. Similarly, local staff who empathize and have positive feelings towards their expatriate coworkers will be more willing to help expatriates in the course of their work if expatriates appear to need it.

Many HR practices adopted by MNCs have the potential to indirectly hurt the establishment of cohesiveness and rapport between expatriates and local staff. Ethnocentric HR practices that favor the expatriate over local staff, whether intentionally or unintentionally, send a message to local staff that they are less valued than the expatriates. As a result, local staff are less likely to feel friendly or supportive towards expatriates who receive favorable treatment for reasons that may not always seem obvious or acceptable. The inequitable treatment also draws clear lines between local staff and expatriates, creating an intergroup mentality where local staff view expatriates as "outsiders" and expatriates remain in their exclusive expatriate cliques. The clear differentials could reinforce us-versus-them stereotypes, increase friction and frustration, and could create further misunderstandings and conflict.[16] All of these factors would make it unlikely that local staff will feel empathetic towards their expatriate counterparts or go out of their way to help them out when needed. These differentiating HR practices, which we will discuss, include compensation, selection and promotion, and training.

Compensation

A potentially long-standing sore point between expatriates and local staff has been the way both parties are compensated relative to each other. Many multinational organizations seek to minimize expatriate failure by providing expatriates with enough incentives to take on and remain on the assignment until the task is completed. When expatriates are transferred to the host country organization, they expect that the relocation will not be disadvantageous to them in any way, and may in fact be beneficial to their future with the company. According to the 1997–98 North American Survey of International Assignment

Policies and Practices published by Organization Resources Counselors Inc. (ORC), the most popular approach to compensating expatriates is still the "balance-sheet approach". The balance sheet approach sets salary according to the base pay and benefits of their home country, plus various allowances (e.g., cost-of-living, housing standard, hardship) and tax equalization. With the inclusion of the various allowances and benefits, the relocation usually results in a financial gain for expatriates, especially if the relocation involves moving to a host location with a higher cost of living.

Even though the balance sheet approach has several advantages, it is particularly problematic for maintaining internal equity among local staff and expatriates in the host unit organization. Expatriates who come from a country of higher standards of living are likely to have a base pay that is much higher than that of the local staff, in addition to the various allowances and incentives awarded to the expatriates for taking on the assignment. When expatriates are moved to a destination with a high cost of living such as Tokyo or London, MNCs usually make significant adjustments to the expatriates' total compensation package to allow the expatriate to maintain a standard of living comparable to that which they would have enjoyed in their home country.

Few companies attempt to replicate local peers' pay in the assignment location, and expatriates are often lavishly rewarded with various perks that are not available to the locals. Consequently, it is not unusual to find cases of differentiation where a local manager's total compensation forms only a fraction of the expatriate's pay package.[17] For example, expatriates of a German chemical company in China are paid an average of $300,000 a year, including salary, housing, education of children and other benefits, but the local managers are paid only 10–20 percent as much.[18] Such significant wage discrepancies will not be viewed as justified by the local staff if they do not view the expatriates as being more qualified and deserving of higher pay. These discrepancies can lead to strained relationships between the two groups of employees, making it unlikely that the local staff will go out of their way to help out an expatriate who may be having difficulties adjusting to the new job and environment. Worse, these discrepancies can result in resentment, leading the local staff to be unwilling to cooperate with the expatriate on any aspect of the assignment, and potentially frustrating the expatriate's efforts to be successful. Thus, the very compensation practices often put in place to help ensure expatriate success may actually jeopardize it instead.

Selection, promotion, and training

Ethnocentric HR practices can also be found in selection, promotion, and training. In many MNCs, the staffing of top positions in overseas units continues to be reserved for individuals from the parent country company. This is especially true when headquarters believes that having a parent country expatriate at the helm has some strategic value. Frequently, for control purposes, parent companies prefer their own nationals to hold those positions whether or not they are necessarily the best-qualified persons for the job. It becomes frustrating for local staff when they view expatriates getting choice positions while a similarly qualified local gets passed over. Singaporean managers, for example, often report being disadvantaged when competing against parent company expatriates for opportunities in training and promotion.[19] Local managers in Japanese corporations' overseas subsidiaries recognize that they would have to be exceptional to be selected over a Japanese manager for a high level post. Such ethnocentric practices often come at the expense of the promotion and development of capable local staff, further perpetuating the large wage discrepancies between local staff and expatriates and creating resentment among them.[20] Feeling like they have little future in an organization that treats them as second-class citizens, local staff display little loyalty towards the host organization and are more likely to leave when better job opportunities arise elsewhere.

SO WHAT HAS CHANGED?

The HR practices we have described have generally been in place for quite some time, yet they have not always resulted in the negative consequences we are suggesting in this article.[21] The reason for this is that many aspects of globalization have changed, but the HR practices have not changed accordingly. One thing that has changed is the relative competence of expatriates versus local staff.

The basis for much of the global economy has its roots in colonialism. From the earliest days of colonization, the home country was significantly more developed and had superior resources relative to the overseas host (colony) destinations. This easily led to the practice whereby managers from Western multinationals were sent to Asia, South America, and other locations to fill needs in foreign operations that could not be satisfied with local labor, and provide a source of much desired control over the foreign operations. Local staff would have been unlikely to view themselves as comparable to expatriates because of the vast differences in backgrounds, qualifications, and experience. Thus, local staff were more accepting of expatriates being managers and of the privileges they enjoyed.[22] They may also have already been quite satisfied with the relatively favorable remuneration they received compared to their previous job or their present alternatives. One study found that Chinese managers felt fairly treated by their organization because they perceived themselves to be better off compared to other locals in the same company or in other international joint ventures, even though they were worse off than the expatriates in their organization.[23] We also find this situation outside multinational organizations – in universities, for example, among professors and trainers who are sent to places such as Asia to team-teach courses where they receive much higher salaries than their local counterparts.[24]

The new reality, however, presents quite a different scenario. Popular host countries in the Asia Pacific region, such as China, India, Malaysia, and Singapore are no longer merely sources of cheap labor, but the homes of some of the most competitive workforces in the world with high work aspirations.[25] The gap between the parent and host countries in terms of level of economic development has narrowed and the local staff are often trained in many of the same institutions as the expatriates. They are increasingly similar to expatriates in qualifications, and thus are more often coworkers, rather than merely subordinates, of expatriates. These locals are progressively more fluent in English, are trained in the West or in Western managerial ideology, and on top of that have an advantage over expatriates with their intimate understanding of the local culture and practices.[26] They are also less likely to encounter the adjustment and commitment issues faced by expatriates. Accordingly, their perceptions and expectations of how they should be treated by the organization change. Many Russian managers feel that they are generally better educated and cultured than their Western peers and expect to be treated similarly to the expatriates. As a result, the acute pay discrepancies that traditionally occur are now quite unacceptable in far more situations than before.

In addition, international assignments are increasingly treated by MNCs as a key developmental activity for their personnel and future executives. Expatriates are posted overseas to gain international experience and learn new processes that are unique to the host organization.[27] This could be a form of on-the-job training for expatriate managers as they learn how to operate effectively in a different environment. Thus, these expatriates are sent to learn from the local staff. When local staff perceive expatriates as not possessing any unique or specialized skill above what they themselves possess, or may in fact know more about the task than the expatriates and end up being the person the expatriate has to lean on to perform the expatriate's job, the large wage discrepancies between them quickly become objectionable.[28] In other words, if expatriates are viewed to be less qualified than the local staff in the organization, the extra privileges awarded to them will be viewed by the local staff as unfair and unacceptable.

Interestingly, despite the changes that have been occurring, we find that cultural differences sometimes mitigate the problems we highlight in this article, i.e., the reaction to inequity is not universal. Cultures differ in their sensitivity to inequity. Fairness is defined differently by people of different cultures. Some cultures, such as many Asian and Latin cultures, prefer rewards to be allocated based on seniority or need, rather than equity.[29] The importance and value placed on various forms of rewards also differs. Monetary rewards are often not necessarily the most valued. Thus, salary differences, per se, may not be as important to local staff as significant differences in status or other benefits such as housing, medical, and transportation. In certain economies, such as that of Russia, where commodities are often more valuable than money, differentials in salaries are likely to be less undesirable and offensive than differentials in prized commodities. In collective societies, harmony may take precedence over pay equity. We often find that the assumed "same job same pay" mentality is not prevalent among local staff in the organizations of various host countries. As such, local staff's reactions to compensation differentials and differences in treatment and opportunities vary according to the cultural values that they hold and the problems that we suggest to result from differential treatment are not necessarily universal.

WHAT CAN ORGANIZATIONS DO?

Thus far, we have described a situation where expatriates need the help and support of local staff, but where multinational HR policies may be working to reduce the willingness of the local staff to do so. Although there may be exceptions, as noted above, any such unwillingness on the part of local staff will certainly be unacceptable in the long run. But, even in cases where local staff are sensitive to pay differentials, there are some steps a multinational firm could take to minimize this problem. Specifically, we propose seven recommendations for MNCs to consider (see Table 1): (1) change existing compensation practices; (2) select expatriates more carefully; (3) use transparent procedures to determine

Table 1. How to improve expatriate–local relations

At the headquarters of the organization:

1. *Change Existing Compensation Policies* – Pay expatriates salaries more in line with local employees. But, in order to do this, the organization should:
   a. Develop better plans for repatriation to assure expatriates that they will get comparable jobs upon return.
   b. If overseas assignments are truly valued as a developmental activity, include procedures so that they can be rewarded.
   – In the end, the real question is "Will managers still accept expatriate assignments?" If the answer is "no", then the organization must consider alternatives.
2. *Select More Carefully* – Ensure that expatriates are qualified to perform the jobs expected of them at a level consistent with the pay they will receive. But this will require the organization to:
   a. Make sure that expatriate managers have social as well as technical skills needed.
   b. See if there are local employees who are equally qualified. If so, are they paid comparably?
   c. Communicate performance expectations and criteria for success clearly to the expatriate.
   – There will be fewer problems if host country nationals can see clear evidence that the expatriate is "worth" what he or she is paid.
3. *Use Transparent Pay and Promotion Policies* – Develop pay policies that are viewed as fair and that are clear to all involved. But this requires the organization to:
   a. Actually develop pay policies that can stand scrutiny by local employees as well as by home country employees.
   b. Communicate pay policies as well as the basis for expatriate compensation rates (clear statement of hardships and barriers to overcome).
   – If host country nationals come to see that the fact that they are paid less than expatriates is based on fair procedures, they will be less resentful.

At the host country site:

4. *Emphasize Favorable Referents* – Identify alternative referent persons for host country national comparisons instead of the expatriate manager. But this requires that the organization should:
   a. Determine that such reasonable comparison others exist and make them public.
   b. Work to make expatriates less salient as referents.
   – If host country nationals can be convinced to compare their pay (and treatment) to other employees in their country, instead of expatriates, they will be more satisfied with their conditions.

5. *Breed Organizational Identification* – Build a single organizational identity instead of allowing an "us vs. them" mentality to develop. But, for this to happen, the organization must:
   a. Develop a superordinate corporate identity strong enough to overcome identification based on nationality.
   b. Insure that host country nationals have access to various organizational "symbols" such as a company car or parking spaces.
   c. Increase the number and frequency of experiences that expatriates and host country nationals share.
   d. Develop common goals for host country nationals and expatriates to work towards.
   – If host country nationals develop a strong corporate identity they will work harder towards company goals and be less concerned about comparisons within the company.
6. *Prepare Local Staff* – The local employees should be trained and oriented to deal with the incoming expatriates in much the same way as expatriates are often trained to deal with locals. But this would require the company to:
   a. Spend resources on training and orientation for employees who usually do not receive such attention.
   – The entire expatriate assignment process requires adjustment and consideration on the part of everyone involved, and if local employees could be trained to know more about the culture of incoming expatriates, this would make the process easier.
7. *Use and Reward Local Mentors* – Identifying mentoring expatriates as part of the local employee's job and then rewarding such behavior will make it more likely to occur. But this would require the company to:
   a. Recognize the important role local staff play in the success of expatriates.
   b. Recognize that, normally, local staff behavior aimed at helping expatriates adjust is exhibited on a purely voluntary basis.
   c. Actually reward local staff for behaviors that help expatriates succeed.
   – This lies at the heart of our arguments about the importance of local employees. They are critical to expatriate success, but this fact must be recognized by organizations and encouraged as well as rewarded.

---

pay and promotion; (4) emphasize favorable comparative referents; (5) breed organizational identification; (6) prepare local staff; and (7) use and reward local staff buddies or mentors. We will discuss each of these in greater detail.

Change existing expatriate compensation practices

As noted, many multinational firms have adopted HR practices that serve to differentiate expatriates from local staff which are often inequitable from the perspective of the local staff. Clearly, if a firm minimizes the differential treatment between expatriates and local staff, the perceptions of inequity are likely to diminish. However, less than generous incentives for expatriates may deter employees from taking on overseas assignments, and thus expatriate packages are quite resistant to change. Many of the large MNCs, such as the traditional manufacturing enterprises, have become too large, complex, and entrenched in their existing practices to effect changes to compensation policies easily. Thus, even though the benefits of a more flexible approach are widely recognized, a 2000 PriceWaterhouseCoopers survey of 270 European multinational organizations reported that only 7 percent of the companies surveyed adopted such an approach. Furthermore, expatriates still tend to expect favorable compensation packages for their relocation. For example, expatriate managers of 49 Taiwanese multinationals reported that the compensation package was the most important factor in deciding whether or not to relocate internationally.[30] Without favorable remuneration, organizations will have trouble finding enough interested employees to take on overseas postings.

In time, change should become easier as expatriates come to view overseas assignment as a valuable part of their portfolio and become willing parties to the assignment even without lavish compensation packages. However, many expatriates still have concerns over their career progression while they are away on assignment, as well as having a suitable job and promising career upon repatriation.[31] The truth of the matter is, most multinationals do not guarantee a job upon return and do not counsel repatriates when they come home.[32] Hence, we find that employees sometimes view overseas assignments as a career graveyard, and that organizations are forced to provide attractive incentives to convince employees to accept long-term overseas assignments. If, however, MNCs develop better strategies for managing the careers of expatriates, including specific plans for repatriation prior to the assignment, expatriates may be more willing to forgo lavish compensation packages and view assignments as a benefit by itself.

More companies have also turned to paying expatriates at host country levels (localization) or adopting more flexible approaches for compensating their employees in order to reduce their wage bills and lower pay discrepancies between expatriates and locals.[33] Many companies, such as Nokia Asia Pacific, localize their expatriate employees after a certain number of years in the host country whereby the employee takes on the same pay package as would a local employee. Companies like Deloitte & Touche, National Semiconductor, and Towers Perrin have also started on paying for performance programs, varying compensation packages based on assignment length and type, and using more sophisticated measures to calculate cost-of-living differences.[34] As a result, discrepancies between expatriates and local staff may be reduced. Also, more and more multinational companies are using short-term assignments and extended business trips, as opposed to long-term expatriate assignments, thus avoiding the need to pay excessive benefits and adjustments to the expatriate. We see this trend as being quite positive, and as having the potential to truly reduce resentment among the local staff.

Yet we recognize that there is only so much an organization can do to adjust these HR policies, especially in the short run, since most organizations must still somehow induce managers to accept overseas assignments, or at least assure them that they will not suffer as a result of those assignments. Eventually, salary localization policies and increased reliance upon short-term assignments may make it easier to adopt HR practices that treat expatriates and local staff the same. Expatriates sent overseas for developmental reasons should not necessarily expect a significant pay adjustment since the stint is usually short-term and potentially beneficial for the employee. For now, though, expatriate HR practices, especially in the area of compensation, will probably continue to favor expatriates over local staff. As such, MNCs must turn to other means to overcome the negative effects of internally inequitable expatriate compensation packages.

Select more carefully

One alternative to changing compensation practices in order to reduce problems caused by perceived inequity is to ensure that the expatriates MNCs send overseas are in fact suitably qualified to perform the job in question and deserving of any higher pay they receive. As noted, expatriates encounter resentment if they are viewed as overpaid by local staff (i.e., being equally or under qualified for the position they hold in the host unit, but at the same time being paid more than a local holding the same position). If expatriates demonstrate competence worthy of higher pay, local staff will be less dissatisfied. Many experts suggest that it is important to select expatriates who not only have the technical knowledge, but also the social and cultural skills needed to be effective in a different culture. Expatriates equipped with good communication skills will be able to integrate themselves better into the new culture and work more effectively with local staff. The European division of ICI, a British chemicals company, selects individuals who are good at getting along with colleagues at home because this is usually a good predictor of how much effort they will put in building understanding and trust with local staff.[35] Thus, adopting selection techniques that take into consideration these "soft skills", and prepare expatriates adequately for the assignment and all the challenges that it entails is a highly pertinent measure that MNCs could take.

At the same time, MNCs should make the criteria and procedures for selecting candidates to hold high level positions in the host unit as clear as possible. Unambiguously stated criteria and procedures could reduce perceptions of nepotism. Seeking and utilizing input from local staff in making assignment decisions can be helpful for selecting the appropriate candidate, and could increase the legitimacy of the expatriate assignee in the local staff's eyes. Where suitable, other qualified local staff should also be allowed to compete for promotions alongside expatriates. This creates opportunities for local staff to gain desirable jobs within the organization and debunk any views of favoritism in the organization. Local staff who do compete for the promotion should be kept informed throughout the process. Transparency of the selection and promotion procedures is especially important if the local employee is not selected because local staff might feel that they have been unfairly rejected. In such instances, it is especially imperative that management treats the rejected applicant with much sensitivity and dignity to avoid hurt feelings or misunderstandings.

Use transparent procedures to determine pay

In addition to using open and rigorous selection procedures, MNCs should also ensure that the procedures used to determine pay packages for expatriates and local staff be transparent and fair. If local staff view the procedures used to arrive at the pay packages (and selection, promotion, and training decisions) as legitimate, receive reasonable explanations and justifications for the discrepancies, and feel that their concerns and needs are treated with care and sensitivity by the organization, their dissatisfaction with any inequity may be reduced.[36] Local staff often do not realize the challenges faced and sacrifices made by expatriates. To that effect, multinational organizations should be proactive in explaining the purpose of sending expatriates and establishing and communicating clear and fair procedures to local staff. If reward discrepancies have to persist, then it is imperative that organizations make an extra effort to be sensitive to the reactions of the local staff and also to treat them with the necessary dignity and respect.

Emphasize favorable comparative referents

Organizations can also reduce the negative perceptions held by local staff by emphasizing the ways in which local staff are better off compared to other groups of employees. As mentioned earlier, one study found that locals in a Hong Kong joint venture were not disturbed by having lower wages than expatriates because they were cognizant of how much better off they were compared to other Chinese employed by local firms. Often, even though local staff feel disadvantaged relative to the expatriates in their organization, they may still regard their higher wages, greater autonomy, and better opportunities for career development as very attractive aspects of being employed by a MNC. Furthermore, if expatriates are a less prominent comparative referent in local staff's minds, and local staff are satisfied with other aspects of their jobs, local staff react less negatively to the inequity between themselves and the expatriates. MNCs can redirect local staff's attention away from expatriates by publishing statistics that emphasize the advantages these employees have in terms of their pay packages, investments in training and development, and other employee benefits relative to employees of other local organizations or other industry competitors. In general, MNCs have access to a large pool of resources to make more investments in their human resources, which are not matched by local enterprises. Clearly, some careful impression management goes a long way in helping multinational organizations avoid the negative consequences we have suggested.

Breed organizational identification

Us-versus-them perceptions by local staff can be minimized by emphasizing the corporate identity to local staff so that expatriates are viewed less as outsiders, but fellow members of the larger, more inclusive organizational group. This process is known as "recategorization", where enhancing the prominence of an overarching identity reduces the prominence of a lower level group identity. In the case of the host unit, emphasizing organizational identity over national identity may reduce the local staff's likelihood of viewing an expatriate in the organization as someone they are competing against for organizational rewards.[37] Emphasizing the superordinate identity has another advantage of raising organizational commitment, and drawing attention away from contentious tendencies within the organization to focus on extra-organizational referents, such as the organization's competitors. In other words, intergroup comparisons can be diverted to occur across organizations (e.g., industry competitors), rather than within the organization between the local staff and the expatriates. As far as possible, organizations should minimize referring to expatriates as a separate group from local staff. Distinctions in day-to-day operations should be avoided and expatriates integrated to the local unit as much as possible so that they are perceptibly less different from the local staff. Organizational symbols, such as office space, parking spaces, common cafeterias, and informal socializing grounds act as subtle yet strong signals to local staff about how much distinction the organization makes between the two groups, and thus should be minimized.

Organizational identification can also be developed by putting both local staff and expatriates together in orientation and training programs. The shared experiences help develop a sense of cohesiveness. Examples of this type of socialization include McDonald's policy of having all restaurant managers attend Hamburger University, or joint training exercises for NATO military units. In each case, the process builds a strong corporate identity that could transcend other types of group identities (e.g., nationality) by putting employees through similar socialization experiences.

Increasing the interactions between expatriates and local staff as well as emphasizing common work goals can also breed organizational identification and minimize the perception of expatriates as outsiders. By having more frequent interactions with their expatriate colleagues, local staff have more opportunities to learn about each expatriate personally and develop more accurate understanding of the expatriates with whom they work. In this way, pre-existing stereotypes may be refuted and the locals can come to view expatriates more as "one of us" rather than "one of them". Organizing expatriates and local staff in teams, working together to achieve common objectives, can help local staff and expatriates be more attuned to a common fate shared between them. When local staff perceive themselves and the expatriates to be working towards the same overarching goal(s), the prominence of the national boundaries may diminish and the perception of expatriates as part of the organization may heighten. As local staff begin to view expatriates as part of their ingroup, they will also be more likely to support and cooperate with them.

Prepare local staff

MNCs should also provide both expatriates and local staff adequate training in cross-cultural communication and understanding. Being able to communicate effectively with each other is a key step in developing supportive relationships. Local staff, as well as the expatriates, need to be equipped with the necessary knowledge and skills to interact and work effectively with foreign nationals. Research suggests that large cross-cultural differences pose significant obstacles to the effective transfer of knowledge between locals and expatriates.[38] Thus, when Tellabs acquired Helsinki-based Martis Oy, all foreign executives underwent training on conducting business meetings, developing supervisory–subordinate relationships, and communicating effectively. Many Finnish engineers were also sent to headquarters to learn how to interface with their American colleagues and other employees.[39]

People make assumptions about an individual's intelligence, competence, and even social class based on how the individual speaks and carries him or herself. Cultural sensitivity training will help avoid misunderstandings, educate both local staff and expatriates on the appropriate behaviors, and dispel whatever negative stereotypes and assumptions they have about each other. In an experimental study of American host country managers confronted with Japanese managers, it was found that the extent to which the American managers' expectations of the Japanese managers' behaviors were met influenced subsequent intentions to trust them and to associate with them.[40] The researchers concluded that it is important to equip receiving local managers with realistic expectations of foreign managerial behavior in order for more positive relationships to be developed between them.

Some MNCs make the mistake of not carrying out cultural training based on the fact that the host country and the expatriates share the same language. However, even if expatriates and local staff speak the same language, misunderstandings can still occur. The director of an international provider of international assignment support programs recounts how a Texan in the UK came across to her British colleagues as arrogant and vulgar because she talked too loud and slowly, and was prematurely familiar with her colleagues both verbally and in her body language.[41] As a result, she was unable to fit in with her work group. It is important that organizations do not overlook the significance of preparing both the expatriates and the local staff for cross-cultural encounters at work.

Use and reward local buddies or mentors

As noted before, there is often no formal requirement or reward for local staff to facilitate the adjustment of expatriates and thus helping expatriates out or being cooperative needs to stem from their own initiative. To avoid leaving such behaviors to chance, MNCs could provide formal incentives to local staff for displaying cooperative and supportive behaviors towards expatriates. MNCs could pair up expatriates with local staff for a period of time and reward local staff involved in socializing newcomer expatriates, or for participating in some sort of buddy program that facilitates the expatriate's entry to the host unit. In this way, local staff's socializing behaviors are formalized and rewarded, and the help that expatriates need from local staff is better ensured. MNCs should also make efforts to involve local staff in the planning and facilitation of an expatriate's transition. This not only boosts local staff morale but also improves the chances of expatriate success.[42] Getting the local staff involved in the process also increases the transparency of the policies surrounding expatriation and the local staff who themselves are interested in developing their international experience could gain from being in continuous contact with incoming expatriates. This informational exchange greatly benefits both parties.

To ensure that information is shared with expatriates, SAS Institute's regional headquarters in Heidelberg, Germany, assigns insider buddies to expatriate newcomers to help the newcomer to be self-sufficient and reach high levels of productivity as quickly as possible. These buddies are volunteers with no explicit or formal obligations. They help listen and answer simple questions expatriates may have, offer simple advice, and help point expatriates in the right direction on work and non-work matters. Similarly, at Korean multinational semiconductor manufacturer Samsung's Texas computer memory chip factory, each incoming expatriate is paired with an American counterpart upon arriving at Austin. These "buddies" help the Korean expatriates with work and with their downtime. The locals take the Korean workers on nights out, lunch meetings, and weekend trips.[43] With the help of local staff who are willing to share information with expatriates, the expatriates enjoy greater success in their efforts to adjust to their work demands and cultural challenges.[44]

THE LOCAL PERSPECTIVE

In this paper we have discussed how HR practices designed to help and encourage expatriates can produce negative reactions by the local staff. We believe that this possibility has been largely overlooked because multinationals have tended to focus more on the expatriates than on the locals. We also believe, however, that the changing competitive landscape, the development of human capital in local markets, and the importance of cooperation and teamwork in a global economy, all point to a need to increase the attention paid to the local workforce. No global organization can hope to be truly competitive unless it fully utilizes its entire workforce. Furthermore, as we have pointed out in this paper, local staff are important, not only in their own right as potentially productive members of the organization, but also as a source of support and help for expatriate managers sent to their country.

What does this mean? It means that multinational organizations must pay attention to and gather information on the attitudes, goals and feelings of the local staff. It also means that organizations need to develop programs to increase the motivation and commitment of those local employees. Many managers of MNCs view local staff as dispensable – perhaps more so now than before. Local staff are still likely to believe that the multinational pays better and treats employees better than the alternatives, and would still be motivated and committed to the organization. However, we believe that a local perspective means that the MNC will no longer take those things for granted. Instead, the MNC will recognize that the local staff have alternatives in third-party countries, or with other MNCs, and that the organization needs to work at motivation and commitment of the local staff. Of course, this perspective would also require the MNC to consider the impact upon local staff of any proposed policy, and weigh this impact when deciding whether or not to implement these programs. We believe it is critical that MNCs adopt such a perspective in order to be successful in the future.

CONCLUSIONS

The present paper represents a call for attention to be paid to local staff. We began by pointing out how, although local staff employees are increasingly well-trained and well-educated, many HR policies for expatriates still favor expatriates over local staff, and so do not recognize these accomplishments. We also discuss how local staff could compare their outcomes to those of the expatriates and how this could result in local staff believing they are being treated unfairly. These beliefs could then result in those local employees withholding advice and support which, while not required as part of the local employee's job, are important for the ultimate success of the expatriate.

But, as we also note, a number of global companies are coming to recognize the importance of local staff, and are implementing programs designed to improve commitment and perceptions of fairness by those local employees. We also suggest a number of other interventions and programs which might help local staff feel appreciated, fairly treated, and committed to the larger organization. Several of these suggestions mirror those implemented by some more innovative multinationals, and we discuss these examples as well.

Therefore, we end by reiterating the message that local staff is important and must be recognized as such by MNCs. We believe that many organizations are coming to recognize this and act accordingly, but we also believe that there is much more that can be done. We believe that it is increasingly clear that the effective management of local staff will be a key component of effective competition in the coming years.

ACKNOWLEDGMENTS

We thank the Editor Bob Ford, Jim Wilkerson, Sonia Chainini, and the two anonymous reviewers for their input.

NOTES

1   Vatikiotis, M., Clifford, M., and McBeth, J. 1994. The lure of Asia. *Far Eastern Economic Review*, 157(5): 32–4.
2   Cited from Swaak, R. A. 1995. Expatriate failures: too many, too much cost, too little planning. *Compensation and Benefits Review*, 27(6): 47–55. Over 90 percent of the respondents cited failure to adjust as the key reason for expatriate failure.
3   Volkmar, J. A. 2003. Context and control in foreign subsidiaries: making a case for the host country national manager. *Journal of Leadership and Organizational Studies*, 10(1): 93–105.
4   Li, L., and Kleiner, B. H. 2001. Expatriate–local relationships and organizational effectiveness: a study of multinational companies in China. *Management Research News*, 24(3/4): 49–55.

5   Hammers, M. 2003. Quashing quick quits. *Workforce*, 82(5): 50.

6   Deresky, H. 2002. *Global management: Strategic and interpersonal*. Upper Saddle River, NJ. Prentice-Hall.

7   Bjorkman, I., and Schaap, A. 1994. Outsiders in the Middle Kingdom: expatriate managers in Chinese–Western joint ventures. *European Management Journal*, 12(2): 147–53.

8   Black, J. S., Mendenhall, M., and Oddou, G. 1991. Toward a comprehensive model of international adjustment: an integration of multiple theoretical perspectives. *Academy of Management Review*, 16(2): 291–317.

9   Feldman, D. C. and Bolino, M. C. 1999. The impact of on-site mentoring on expatriate socialization: a structural equation modeling approach. *International Journal of Human Resource Management*, 10(1): 54–71.

10 Li and Kleiner, op. cit.; Bjorkman and Schaap, op. cit.

11 Fisher, C. D. 1985. Social support and adjustment to work: a longitudinal study. *Journal of Management*, 11(3): 39–53; Kirmeyer, S. L. and Lin, T. R. 1987. Social support: its relationship to observed communication with peers and superiors. *Academy of Management Journal*, 30(1): 138–51.

12 Aryee, S., and Stone, R. J. 1996. Work experiences, work adjustment and psychological well-being of expatriate employees in Hong Kong. *International Journal of Human Resource Management*, 7(1): 150–62.

13 Florkowski, G. W., and Fogel, D. S. 1999. Expatriate adjustment and commitment: the role of host-unit treatment. *International Journal of Human Resource Management*, 10(5): 783–807.

14 Solomon, C. M. 1997. Destination USA. *Workforce*, April: 18–22.

15 Barr, S. H., and Pawar, B. S. 1995. Organizational citizenship behavior: domain specifications for three middle range theories. *Academy of Management Best Paper Proceedings*, 302–6.

16 Schneider, S. C. and Barsoux, J.-L. 2003. *Managing across Cultures*. 2nd edn. Essex. Prentice-Hall.

17 For more on expatriate pay policies, how they are developed and what they mean for pay differentials, see Beamish, P. 1998. Equity joint ventures in China: compensation and motivation. *Ivey Business Quarterly*, 63(1): 67–8; Dowling, P., Welch, D. E., and Schuler, R. S. 1999. *International Human Resource Management; Managing People in a Multinational Context*. Cincinnati, South-Western College; Hodgetts, R. M., and Luthans, F. 1993. U.S. multinationals' expatriate compensation strategies. *Compensation & Benefits Review*, 25(1): 57–62; Peters, S. 1994. Expatriates' pay exceeds nationals' in Central and Eastern Europe. *Personnel Journal*, 73(5): 19–20.

18 Hagerty, B. 1997. Executive pay (A special report) – Asian Scramble: Multinationals in China hope lucrative compensation packages can attract the local executives they desperately need. *Wall Street Journal*, 10 April, R12.

19 Hailey, J. 1996. The expatriate myth: cross-cultural perceptions of expatriate managers. *The International Executive*, 38(2): 255–71.

20 Further discussions of multinational policies regarding opportunities for local staff versus expatriates can be found in Geringer, J. M., and Hebert, L. 1989. Control and performance of international joint ventures. *Journal of International Business Studies*, 20(2): 235–54; Hamill, J., and Hunt, G. 1996. Joint ventures in Hungary: criteria for success. In Arch G. Woodside and Robert E. Pitts (eds.) *Creating and Managing International Joint Ventures*, 77–106. Westport, Conn.: Quorum Books; and Shenkar, O., and Zeira, Y. 1987. Human resources management in international joint ventures: directions for research. *Academy of Management Review*, 12(3): 546–57.

21 Leung, K., Smith, P. B., Wang, Z., and Sun, H. 1996. Job satisfaction in joint ventures hotels in China: an organizational justice analysis. *Journal of International Business Studies*, 27(5): 947–62.

22 Hailey, op. cit.

23 Chen, C. C., Choi, J., and Chi, S. C. 2002. Making justice sense of local–expatriate compensation disparity: mitigation by local referents, ideological explanations, and interpersonal sensitivity in China–foreign joint ventures. *Academy of Management Journal*, 45(4): 807.

24   Bates, R. A. 2001. Equity, respect, and responsibility: an international perspective. *Advances in Developing Human Resources*, 3(1): 11–25.

25   For example, Delisle, P., and Chin, S. 1997. Remunerating employees in China – the complicated task faced by foreign firms. *Benefits & Compensation International*, 24(2): 16–20.

26   Hailey, op. cit.; Vatikiotis et al., op. cit.

27   For example, Carpenter, M. A., Sanders, W. G., and Gregersen, H. B. 2001. Bundling human capital with organizational context: the impact of international assignment experience on multinational firm performance and CEO pay. *Academy of Management Journal*, 44(3): 493–511; Hailey, op. cit.; Solomon, C. M. 1995. Global compensation: learn the ABCs. *Personnel Journal*, 74(7): 70–5; Torbiorn, I. 1994. Operative and strategic use of expatriates in new organizations and market structures. *International Studies of Management and Organizations*, 24(3): 5–17.

28   Semeneko, I. 2002. Study: expat managers ethical but big headed. *Moscow Times*; Hailey, op. cit., 263.

29   Clearly, the relationship between culture and fairness models is more complicated than we can discuss here. More extensive treatments of the relationship between fairness models and nationality are provided by Kim, K. I., Park, H.-J., and Suzuki, N. 1990. Reward allocations in the United States, Japan, and Korea: a comparison of individualistic and collectivistic cultures. *Academy of Management Journal*, 33(1): 188–98; and Mueller and Clarke, op. cit. A more detailed discussion of culture and sensitivity to differential outcomes is provided by Chen, C. C. 1995. New trends in rewards allocation preferences: a Sino-US comparison. *Academy of Management Journal*, 38(2): 408–28; Chen, C. C., Meindl, J. R., and Hui, H. 1998. Deciding on equity or parity: a test of situational, cultural and individual factors. *Journal of Organizational Behavior*, 19(2): 115–29; Chen, Y., Brockner, J., and Katz, T. 1998. Toward an explanation of cultural differences in in-group favoritism: the role of individual versus collective primacy. *Journal of Personality and Social Psychology*, 75(6): 1490–1502. Several other authors have addressed cultural differences in the importance attached to inputs versus outcomes for deciding upon fairness. These include Beamish, op. cit.; Huo, Y. P. and Steers, R. M. 1993. Cultural influences on the design of incentive systems: the case of East Asia. *Asia Pacific Journal of Management*, 10(1): 71–85; Leung et al., op. cit.

30   Huang, L.-Y. 2003. Attitudes toward the management of international assignments – a comparative study. *Journal of American Academy of Business*, 3(2): 336–44.

31   Yan, A. M., Zhu, G., and Hall, D. T. 2002. International assignments for career building: a model of agency relationships and psychological contracts. *Academy of Management Review*, 27(3): 373–91.

32   GMAC Global Relocation Services. 2002. *Global relocation trends 2002 survey report.* February 2002.

33   Milkovich, G. T., and Bloom, M. 1998. Rethinking international compensation. *Compensation and Benefits Review*, 30(1): 15–23.

34   Mervosh, E. M. 1997. Managing expatriate compensation. *Industry Week*, 246(14): 13–16; and Barton, R., and Bishko, M. 1998. Global mobility strategy. *HR Focus*, 75(3): S7–S9.

35   Schneider and Barsoux, op. cit.

36   Chen, et al., op. cit.; Kickul, J., Lester, S. W., and Finkl, J. 2002. Promise breaking during radical organizational change: Do justice interventions make a difference? *Journal of Organizational Behavior*, 23(4): 469–88.

37   Toh, S. M., and DeNisi, A. S. 2003. Host country national (HCN) reactions to expatriate pay policies: a proposed model and some implications. *Academy of Management Review*, 28(4): 606–21.

38   Bhagat, R. S., Kedia, B. L., Harveston, P. D., and Triandis, H. C. 2002. Cultural variations in the cross-border transfer of organizational knowledge: an integrative framework. *Academy of Management Review*, 27(2): 204–21.

39   Solomon, C. 1995. Learning to manage host-country nationals. *Workforce*, 74(3): 60–7.

40   Thomas, D. C., and Ravlin, E. C. 1995. Responses of employees to cultural adaptation by a foreign manager. *Journal of Applied Psychology*, 80(1): 133–46.

41   Melles, R. 2003. "They speak the same language so I'll be ok." Not so fast. *Canadian HR Reporter*, September, 23, 11–12.

42   Ashamalla and Crocitto, op. cit.

43   Gallaga, O. M. 1997. Welcome to Austin: Samsung helps new employees feel at home. *Austin American Statesman*, 6 August, D1.

44   Aryee, S., and Stone, R. J. 1996. Work experiences, work adjustment and psychological well-being of expatriate employees in Hong Kong. *International Journal of Human Resource Management*, 7(1); 150–62.

Gary R. Oddou and Mark E. Mendenhall

EXPATRIATE PERFORMANCE APPRAISAL: PROBLEMS AND SOLUTIONS

FOR MORE AND MORE companies, gaining a competitive edge increasingly means making decisions that reflect an acute understanding of the global marketplace – how other countries utilize and view marketing strategies, accounting and financial systems, labor laws, leadership, communication, negotiation and decision-making styles. Gaining a knowledge of these components is most directly accomplished by sending managers to work in an overseas subsidiary and utilizing them on reentry.

Our research shows clearly that expatriates develop valuable managerial skills abroad that can be extremely useful to their development as effective senior managers. Based on current research on expatriates, including our own surveying and interviewing of more than 150 of them, probably the most significant skills expatriates develop as a result of their overseas assignments include the following:

- Being able to manage a workforce with cultural and subcultural differences
- Being able to plan for, and conceptualize, the dynamics of a complex, multinational environment
- Being more open-minded about alternative methods for solving problems
- Being more flexible in dealing with people and systems
- Understanding the interdependencies among the firm's domestic and foreign operations

These skills are the natural outgrowth of the increased autonomy and potential impact expatriates experience in their international assignment. In fact, in our study, 67 percent reported having more independence, and they also indicated they had more potential impact on the operation's performance than in their domestic position. With increased decision-making responsibilities in a foreign environment, expatriates are subjected to a fairly intense working environment in which they must learn the ropes quickly.

The skills expatriate managers gain are obviously crucial to effectively managing any business operation, particularly at the international and multi-national level. Nightmares abound in the business press of the inept decisions sometimes made by top management due to ignorance of cross-cultural differences in business practices. The ability to plan and conceptualize based on the complex interdependencies of a global market environment with significant cultural differences is required of top management in MNCs.

In short, expatriates can become a very valuable human resource for firms with international or multinational operations. However, one of the most serious stumbling blocks to expatriates' career paths is the lack of recognition of the value of expatriation and the informality with which firms accurately evaluate their expatriates' overseas performance. Although the attributes expatriates gain overseas can and do translate into concrete advantages for their firms, a quick glance at the skills previously listed indicates intangibles that are often difficult to measure and usually are not measured – or are measured inaccurately – by present performance evaluation methods. Hence, it is critical to more closely examine this potential stumbling block to expatriates' careers and to make specific recommendations to improve the process and accuracy of such reviews.

APPRAISING THE EXPATRIATE'S PERFORMANCE

Several problems are inherent to appraising an expatriate's performance. First, an examination of those who evaluate an expatriate's job performance is relevant. Those evaluators include the host national management and often the home office management.

Host national management's perceptions of actual job performance

That local management evaluates the expatriate is probably necessary; however, such a process sometimes is problematic. Local management typically evaluates the expatriate's performance from its own cultural frame of reference and set of expectations. For example, one American expatriate manager we talked to used participative decision making in India but was thought of by local workers as rather incompetent because of the Indian notion that managers, partly owing to their social class level, are seen as the experts. Therefore, a manager should not have to ask subordinates for ideas. Being seen as incompetent negatively affected local management's review of this expatriate's performance, and he was denied a promotion on return to the United States. Local management's appraisal is not the only potential problem, however. In fact, based on our research with expatriates, local management's evaluation is usually perceived as being more accurate than that of the home office.

Home office management's perceptions of actual job performance

Because the home office management is geographically distanced from the expatriate, it is often not fully aware of what is happening overseas. As a result, for middle and upper management, home office management will often use a different set of variables than those used by local management. Typically, more visible performance criteria are used to measure the expatriate's success (for example, profits, market share, productivity levels). Such measures ignore other, less visible variables that in reality drastically affect the company's performance. Local events such as strikes, devaluation of the currency, political instability, and runaway inflation are examples of phenomena that are beyond the control of the expatriate and are sometimes "invisible" to the home office.

One expatriate executive told us that in Chile he had almost singlehandedly stopped a strike that would have shut down their factory completely for months and worsened relations between the Chileans and the parent company in the United States. In a land where strikes are commonplace, such an accomplishment was quite a coup, especially for an American. The numerous mettings and talks with labor representatives, government officials, and local management required an acute understanding of their culture and a sensitivity beyond the ability of most people. However, because of exchange rate fluctuations with its primary trading partners in South America, the demand for their ore temporarily decreased by 30 percent during the expatriate's tenure. Rather than applauding the efforts this expatriate executive made to avert a strike and recognizing the superb negotiation skills he demonstrated, the home office saw the expatriate as being only somewhat better than a mediocre performer. In other words, because for home office management the most visible criterion of the expatriate's performance was somewhat negative (sales figures), it was assumed that he had not performed adequately. And though the expatriate's boss knew a strike had been averted, the bottom-line concern for sales dollars overshadowed any other significant accomplishments.

The expatriate manager must walk a tightrope. He must deal with a new cultural work group, learn the ins and outs of the new business environment, possibly determine how to work with a foreign boss, find out what foreign management expects of him, and so on. He must also understand the rules of the game on the home front. It is difficult, and sometimes impossible, to please both. Attempting to please both can result in a temporarily, or permanently, railroaded career. So it was with an individual who was considered a "high potential" in a semiconductor firm. He was sent to an overseas operation without the proper product knowledge preparation and barely kept his head above water because of the difficulties of cracking a nearly impossible market. On returning to the United States, he was physically and mentally exhausted from the battle. He sought a much less challenging position and got it because top management then believed they had overestimated his potential. In fact, top management never did understand what the expatriate was up against in the foreign market.

In fact, expatriates frequently indicate that headquarters does not really understand their experience – neither the difficulty of it nor the value of it. One study found that one-third of the expatriates felt that corporate headquarters did not understand the expatriate's experience at all. In a 1981 Korn/Ferry survey, 69 percent of the managers reported they felt isolated from domestic operations and their US managers. It is clear from others' and our own research that most US senior management does not understand the value of an international assignment or try to utilize the expatriate's skills gained abroad when they return to the home office. The underlying problem seems to be top management's ethnocentricity.

Management ethnocentricity

Two of the most significant aspects of management's inability to understand the expatriate's experience, value it, and thereby more accurately measure his or her performance are (1) the communication gap between the expatriate and the home office and (2) the lack of domestic management's international experience.

The communication gap. Being physically separated by thousands of miles and in different time zones poses distinct problems of communication. Not only does the expatriate have difficulty talking directly with his manager, but usually both the US manager and the expatriate executive have plenty of other responsibilities to attend to. Fixing the day-to-day problems tends to take precedence over other concerns, such as maintaining contact with one's boss (or subordinate) in order to be kept up to date on organizational changes or simply to inform him or her of what one is doing. Most of the expatriates in our research indicated they had very irregular contact with their home office and that often it was not with their immediate superior. Rarely did the boss initiate direct contact with the expatriate more than once or twice a year.

The lack of international experience. The old Indian expression "To walk a mile in another man's moccasins" has direct meaning here. How can one understand what another person's overseas managerial experience is like – its difficulties, challenges, stresses, and the like – without having lived and worked overseas oneself? According to one study, more than two-thirds of upper management in corporations today have never had an international assignment. If they have not lived or worked overseas, and if the expatriate and US manager are not communicating regularly about the assignment, the US manager cannot evaluate the expatriate's performance appropriately.

Of course, how the US manager and foreign manager perceive the expatriate's performance will depend partly on the expatriate's actual performance and partly on the managers' *perceptions* of the expatriate's performance. Up to now, we have discussed the managers' perceptions of the expatriate's performance.

Let's now turn our attention to what usually composes the expatriate's *actual* performance to better understand why evaluating it is problematic.

Actual job performance

As repeatedly mentioned by the expatriates in our study and in other research, the primary factors relating to the expatriate's actual job performance include his or her technical job know-how, personal adjustment to the culture, and various environmental factors.

Technical job know-how. As with all jobs, one's success overseas partly depends on one's expertise in the technical area of the job. Our research indicates that approximately 95 percent of the expatriates believe that technical competency is crucial to successful job performance. Although common sense supports this notion, research shows that technical competence is not sufficient in itself for successful job performance. For example, an engineer who is an expert in his or her field and who tends to ignore cultural variables that are important to job performance will likely be ineffective. He or she might be less flexible with local personnel, policies, and practices because of his or her reliance on technical know-how or because of differences in cultural views. As a result, the host nationals might become alienated by the expatriate's style and become quite resistant to his or her objectives and strategies. A less experienced engineer, with less technical competence, might be more willing to defer to the host country's employees and their procedures and customs. A shade of humility is always more likely to breed flexibility, and in the long run, the less experienced engineer might develop the trust of the foreign employees and might well be more effective than the experienced engineer.

We have been given numerous examples by expatriates, in fact, where this has been the case. One expatriate who represented a large construction firm was sent to a worksite in India. The expatriate was an expert in his field and operated in the same fashion as he did in the United States. He unintentionally ignored local work customs and became an object of hatred and distrust. The project was delayed for more than six months because of his behavior.

Adjustment to a new culture. Just as important as the expatriate's technical expertise is his or her ability to adapt to the foreign environment, enabling him or her to deal with the indigenous people. Nearly every expatriate in our survey felt understanding the foreign culture, having an ability to communicate with the foreign nationals, and being able to reduce stress were as – if not more – important to successful job performance than was technical competence. Regardless of how much an expatriate knows, if he or she is unable to communicate with and understand the host nationals, the work will not get done.

An expatriate's adjustment overseas is also related to at least two personal variables: (1) one's marital and family status (that is, whether accompanied by a spouse and children) and (2) the executive's own personal and the family's predisposition to acculturation. Research clearly indicates that expatriates who have their family abroad are often less successful because of the stress on the family of being in a foreign environment. The stress on the spouse negatively affects the employee's concentration and job performance. With an increasing number of dual-career couples being affected by expatriation, the problems are even keener. A number of expatriates reported that their formerly career-positioned spouse suffered from depression most of the time they were overseas. Moving from experiencing the dynamics of a challenging career to having no business-world activity and being unable to communicate the most basic needs is a grueling transition for many career-oriented spouses.

Company variables affecting cultural and work adjustment also come into play. The thoroughness of the company's expatriate selection method and the type and degree of cross-cultural training will affect expatriate adjustment and performance. In other words, if the firm is not selective about the personality of the expatriate or does not appropriately prepare the employee and dependents, the firm may be building in failure before the manager ever leaves the United States.

All these factors influence the expatriate's learning curve in a foreign business environment. More time is thus required to learn the ins and outs of the job than for the expatriate's domestic counterpart who might have just taken a comparable position stateside. In fact, most expatriates say it takes three to six months to even begin to perform at the same level as in the domestic operation. Hence, *performance evaluations at the company's normal time interval may be too early to accurately and fairly reflect the expatriate's performance.*

A SUMMARY OF FACTORS AFFECTING EXPATRIATION PERFORMANCE

In summary, an expatriate's performance is based on overseas adjustment, his or her technical know-how, and various relevant environmental factors. Actual performance, however, is evaluated in terms of perceived performance, which is based on a set of fairly complex variables usually below the evaluator's level of awareness. Much of the perceived performance concerns perceptions of the expatriate and his or her situation. Depending on whether the manager assessing the expatriate's performance has had personal overseas experience or is otherwise sensitive to problems associated with overseas work, the performance appraisal will be more or less valid. *The bottom line for the expatriate is that the performance appraisal will influence the promotion potential and type of position the expatriate receives on returning to the United States.* Because expatriates generally return from their experience with valuable managerial skills, especially for firms pursuing an international or global market path, it behooves organizations to carefully review their process of appraising expatriates and the evaluation criteria themselves.

GUIDELINES ON HOW TO APPRAISE AN EXPATRIATE'S PERFORMANCE

Human resource personnel: giving guidelines for performance evaluation

Human resources departments can do a couple of things to help guide the evaluator's perspective on the evaluation.

A basic breakdown of the difficulty level of the assignment should be done to properly evaluate the expatriate's performance. For example, working in Japan is generally considered more difficult than working in England or English-speaking Canada. The learning curve in Japan will take longer because of the very different ways business is conducted, the language barrier that exists, and the isolation that most Americans feel within the Japanese culture. Major variables such as the following should be considered when determining the difficulty level of the assignment:

- Operational language used in the firm
- Cultural "distance", based often on the region of the world (for example, Western Europe, Middle East, Asia)
- Stability of the factors affecting the expatriate's performance (for example, labor force, exchange rate)

Many foreigners speak English, but their proficiency does not always allow them to speak effectively or comfortably, so they rely on their native language when possible. In addition, they usually do not speak English among themselves because it is not natural. In Germany, for example, one expatriate said that while relying on English allowed a minimum level of work to be performed, the fact that he did not speak German limited his effectiveness. Secretaries, for example, had very limited English-speaking skills. German workers rarely spoke English together and therefore unknowingly excluded the expatriate from casual and often work-related conversations. And outside work he had to spend three to four times the amount of time to accomplish the same things that he did easily in the United States. Most of the problem was because he could not speak good enough German, and many of the Germans could not speak good enough English.

Although sharing the same language facilitates effective communication, it is only the surface level of communication. More deep-rooted, cultural-based phenomena can more seriously affect an expatriate's performance.

Countries or regions where the company sends expatriates can be fairly easily divided into categories such as these: (1) somewhat more difficult than the United States, (2) more difficult than the United States, and (3) much more difficult than the United States. Plenty of information is available to help evaluate the difficulty level of assignments. The US State Department and military branches have these types of ratings. In addition, feedback from a firm's own expatriates can help build the picture of the varying level of assignment difficulty.

Rather than having the manager try to subjectively build the difficulty level of the assignment into his or her performance appraisal, human resources could have a built-in, numerical difficulty factor that is multiplied times the quantity obtained by the normal evaluation process (for example, somewhat more difficult = $\times$ 1.2; more difficult = $\times$ 1.4; much more difficult = $\times$ 1.6).

Evaluator: trying to objectify the evaluation

Several things can be done to try to make the evaluator's estimation more objective.

1. Most expatriates agree that it makes more sense to weight the evaluation based more on the on-site manager's appraisal than the home-site manager's notions of the employee's performance. This is the individual who has been actually working with the expatriate and who has more information to use in the evaluation. Having the on-site manager evaluate the expatriate is especially valid when the on-site manager is of the same nationality as the expatriate. This helps avoid culturally biased interpretations of the expatriate's performance.

2. In reality, however, currently the home-site manager usually performs the actual written performance evaluation after the on-site manager has given some input. When this is the case, a former expatriate from the same location should be involved in the appraisal process. This should occur particularly with evaluation dimensions where the manager is trying to evaluate the individual against criteria with which he or she is unfamiliar relative to the overseas site. For example, in South America the dynamics of the workplace can be considerably different from those of the United States. Where stability characterizes the United States, instability often characterizes much of Latin America. Labor unrest, political upheavals, different labor laws, and other elements all serve to modify the actual effects a supervisor can have on the productivity of the labor force in a company in Latin America. A manager who has not personally experienced these frustrations will not be able to evaluate an expatriate's productivity accurately. In short, if production is down while the expatriate is the supervisor, the American boss tends to believe it is because the supervisor was not effective.

3. On the other hand, when it is a foreign, on-site manager who is making the written, formal evaluation, expatriates agree that the home-site manager should be consulted before the on-site manager completes a formal terminal evaluation. This makes sense because consulting the home-site manager can balance an otherwise hostile evaluation caused by an intercultural misunderstanding.

    One expatriate we interviewed related this experience. In France, women are legally allowed to take six months off for having a baby. They are paid during that time but are not supposed to do any work related to their job. This expatriate had two of the three secretaries take maternity leave. Because they were going to be coming back, they were not replaced with temporary help. The same amount of work, however, still existed. The American expatriate asked them to do some work at home, not really understanding the legalities of such a request. The French women could be fired from their jobs for doing work at home. One of the women agreed to do it because she felt sorry for him. When the American's French boss found out one of these two secretaries was helping he became very angry and intolerant of the American's actions. As a result, the American felt he was given a lower performance evaluation than he deserved. When the American asked his former boss to intercede and help the French boss understand his reasoning, the French boss modified the performance evalution to something more reasonable to the American expatriate. The French manager had assumed the American should have been aware of French laws governing maternity leave.

Performance criteria

Here again, special consideration needs to be given to the expatriate's experience. Expatriates are not only performing a specific function, as they would in their domestic operation, they are also broadening their understanding of their firm's total operations and the inherent interdependencies thereof. As a result, two recommendations are suggested.

1. Modify the normal performance criteria of the evaluation sheet for that particular position to fit the overseas position and site characteristics.

Using the Latin American example referred to before might serve to illustrate this point. In most US firms, maintaining positive management–labor relations is not a primary performance evaluation criterion. Stabilizing the workforce is not highly valued because the workforce is already usually a stable entity. Instead, productivity in terms of number of units produced is a highly valued outcome. As such, motivating the workforce to work faster and harder is important. In Chile, however, the workforce is not so stable as it is in the United States. Stability is related to constant production – not necessarily to increasing production – and a stable production amount can be crucial to maintaining marketshare. In this case, if an expatriate is able to maintain positive management–labor relations such that the workforce goes on strike only two times instead of twenty-five times, the expatriate should be rewarded commensurately. In other words, while the expatriate's US counterpart might be rated primarily on increases in production, the expatriate in Chile should be rated on stability of production.

How can such modifications in the normal performance criteria be determined? Ideally, returned expatriates who worked at the same site or in the same country should be involved in developing the appropriate criteria or ranking of the performance criteria or both. Only they have first-hand experience of what the possibilities and constraints are like at that site. This developmental cycle should occur approximately every five years, depending on the stability of the site – its culture, personnel, and business cycles. Reevaluating the criteria and their prioritization periodically will make sure the performance evaluation criteria remain current with the reality of the overseas situation. If expatriate availability is a problem, outside consultants who specialize in international human resource management issues can be hired to help create country-specific performance evaluation forms and criteria.

2.   Include an expatriate's insights as part of the evaluation.

"Soft" criteria are difficult to measure and therefore legally difficult to support. Nevertheless, every attempt should be made to give the expatriate credit for relevant insights into the interdependencies of the domestic and foreign operations. For example, if an expatriate learns that the reason the firm's plant in India needs supplies by certain dates is to accommodate cultural norms – or even local laws – such information can be invaluable. Previously, no one at the domestic site understood why the plant in India always seemed to have such odd or erratic demands about delivery dates. And no one in India bothered to think that their US supplier didn't operate the same way. If delivering supplies by specific dates asked for by their India colleagues ensures smoother production or increased sales and profits for the Indian operation, and if the expatriate is a critical link in the communication gap between the United States and India, the expatriate should be given credit for such insights. This should be reflected in his or her performance review.

To obtain this kind of information, either human resource or operational personnel should formally have a debriefing session with the expatriate on his or her return. It should be in an informal interview format so that specific and open-ended questions can be asked. Questions specific to the technical nature of the expatriate's work that relate to the firm's interdependencies should be asked. General questions concerning observations about the relationship between the two operations should also be included.

There is another, even more effective way this aspect of performance review can be handled. At regular intervals, say, every three to six months, the expatriate could be questioned by human resource or operational personnel in the domestic site about how the two operations might better work together. Doing it this way helps maximize the possibility of noting all relevant insights.

CONCLUSION

With the marketplace becoming increasingly global, the firms that carefully select and manage their internationally assigned personnel will reap the benefits. Today, there is about a 20 percent turnover rate for expatriates when they return. Such a turnover rate is mostly due to firms not managing their expatriates' careers well. Firms are not prepared to appropriately reassign expatriates on their reentry. This obviously indicates that firms do not value the expatriate's experience. This further carries over into the lack of emphasis on appropriately evaluating an expatriate's performance. Appropriately evaluating an expatriate's performance is an issue of both fairness to the expatriate and competitive advantage to the firm. With the valuable experience and insights that expatriates gain, retaining them and effectively positioning them in a firm will mean the firm's business strategy will be increasingly guided by those who understand the companies' worldwide operations and markets.

J. Stewart Black and
Mark E. Mendenhall

A PRACTICAL BUT THEORY-BASED
FRAMEWORK FOR SELECTING
CROSS-CULTURAL TRAINING METHODS

> Global citizenship is no longer just a nice phrase in the lexicon of rosy
> futurologists. It is every bit as real and concrete as measurable
> changes in GNP or trade flows. (Ohmae, 1989, p. 154)

THERE IS LITTLE DEBATE that for executives in large multinational
corporations (MNCs) today globalization is a daily reality. Yet most of those
executives have not been specifically educated, trained, or groomed to deal with
the complexities that are inherent in the globalization of business markets. Peter
Vaill (1989) likens the ever-changing, dynamic business world of the 1990s to
"permanent white water".

> Most managers are taught to think of themselves as paddling their
> canoes on calm, still lakes. . . . They're led to believe that they should
> be pretty much able to go where they want, when they want, using
> means that are under their control. . . . But it has been my experience
> that they never get out of the rapids! (Vaill, 1989, p. 2)

How does one begin to learn to navigate the permanent white water of the
international business environment? Vaill asserts that we are in a revolution
of the total business situation: executives cannot count on the predictability of
markets, technologies, competitors, legislators, employees, governments, etc.
(Vaill, 1989). In this destabilized and international context, multinational
corporations and their executives face several significant challenges (Sundaram,
1990) and the new skills to successfully meet these challenges. One of the first
issues that an MNC faces is that because it operates in multiple countries, it must

deal with multiple sources of sovereign authority. This involves working with different laws and legal systems, or in some cases the lack of systematic legal structures and processes. Executives in positions at headquarters or in foreign subsidiaries must have the skills to understand the impact of various laws, tariffs, taxes, enforcement practices, overarching legal systems, and be able to work with host government officials in enacting and maintaining reasonable legislation across a wide variety of countries and cultures.

Second, MNCs must also operate in different markets with different cultures, histories, values, social systems, languages, etc., which often require not only product diversification but intra-product differentiation by country. This requires executives who have a "sensitivity to local conditions" (Doz and Prahalad, 1986) and who can understand, work with, and direct, people from various cultures.

Third, different "countries offer different strategic opportunities for MNCs. . . . Differences in size, resource endowment, economic development, political regime, national development and industrial policies . . . play roles in differentiating the opportunities offered to MNCs by individual countries" (Doz and Prahalad, 1986, p. 56). This requires executives who can analyze these country endowments and form strategy that balances local demands and global priorities. Thus, the current and future business environment demands executives who can work effectively across national and cultural boundaries or can, in Ohmae's words (1989), manage "in a borderless world".

American executives will not pick up such skills in the US educational system, in their normal life experience, or in their typical working career. For most US MNCs, an international assignment is not even an important criterion in the succession planning process (Tung, 1988).

Despite the need for cross-cultural skills and the shortage of managers who possess these skills, most human resource decision makers do nothing in terms of cross-cultural training for employees in general or even specifically for selected employees embarking on international assignments (Baker and Ivancevich, 1971; Black, 1988; Runzheimer, 1984; Tung, 1981). For example, 70 percent of US expatriates and 90 percent of their families are sent overseas without any cross-cultural training (Baker and Ivancevich, 1971; Black, 1988; Black and Stephens, 1989; Runzheimer, 1984; Tung, 1981).

This is significant given that studies have found between 16 and 40 percent of all expatriate managers sent on foreign assignments return before they are supposed to, due to poor performance or the inability of the employee and/or the family to effectively adjust to the foreign environment (Baker and Ivancevich, 1971; Black, 1988; Dunbar and Ehrlich, 1986; Tung, 1981). Other studies have found that negotiations between businesspeople of different cultures often fail because of problems related to cross-cultural differences (Black, 1987; Graham, 1985; Tung, 1984). The costs of failed cross-cultural encounters are high; for example, studies have estimated the cost of a failed expatriate assignment to be $50,000 to $150,000 (Copeland and Griggs, 1985; Harris and Moran, 1979; Misa and Fabricatore, 1979). For a firm with hundreds of expatriate employees worldwide, the costs can easily reach into the tens of millions of dollars per year. In fact, Copeland and Griggs (1985) have estimated that the direct costs of failed expatriate assignments for US corporations is over $2 billion a year, and this does not include unmeasured losses such as damaged corporate reputations or lost business opportunities. In addition, Lanier (1979) estimates that as high as 50 percent of American expatriates who do not return early are none the less ineffective in their overseas jobs, or what she terms "brownouts". Given that the average compensation package for a US expatriate is $200,000–$250,000 (Black, 1988; Copeland and Griggs, 1985), the costs of brownouts are staggering.

Cross-cultural training (CCT) has long been advocated as a means of facilitating effective cross-cultural interactions (Brislin, 1981; Landis and Brislin, 1983; Bouchner, 1982; Harris and Moran, 1979; Mendenhall, Dunbar, and Oddou, 1987; Tung, 1981). However, its use in American business organizations is not widespread. Various reasons have been cited by business organizations for the low use of cross-cultural training; the most prevalent being that such training is not thought to be necessary or effective, and thus, top management sees no need for it (Baker and Ivancevich, 1971; Mendenhall and Oddou, 1985; Runzheimer, 1984; Schwind, 1985; Tung, 1981; Zeira, 1975). However, the fundamental reason behind the lack of training seems to lie in the same assumption that causes American corporations to look only at domestic track record and to ignore cross-cultural related skills when selecting expatriate candidates. The assumption is that good management is good management, and therefore, an effective manager in New York or Los Angeles will do fine in Hong Kong or Tokyo (Miller, 1973). Consequently, based on this assumption, it is logical for HR decision makers to conclude that CCT would not be needed or justified.

An extensive review of the cross-cultural training literature, however, suggests that HR managers are mistaken in their assumption that good management is good management worldwide. Their belief that a firm can simply select employees who have been successful in the US for overseas assignments and that cross-cultural training is not necessary or effective jeopardizes a firm's competitive advantage. Harvey (1982) argued that domestic track record is not a good predictor of whether or not an expatriate will return early from an overseas assignment. A simple example can illustrate the reason for this finding. Generally in the US, setting clear, realistic, and difficult goals with specific time lines and then rewarding individuals who achieve the goals on time would be considered a good management practice (see Locke and Latham, 1984 for a detailed review). People will be motivated if they believe they know what is expected, believe they can achieve the goal, and believe they will be rewarded for their efforts. However, in Japan such goal specificity would be contrary to cultural norms and the rewarding of an individual for personal achievement can often result in decreased motivation on the part of the rewarded individual, because he/she would not want to stand out from or above the group (Mendenhall and Oddou, 1986a). This is a work-related norm that would be counter-intuitive to an American expatriate manager with no training regarding Japanese culture or management practices.

A review of the CCT literature and its effectiveness also strongly indicates that American managers are mistaken in their belief that CCT is not necessary or effective. In a recent review of the empirical literature, Black and Mendenhall

(1990) examined the effectiveness of CCT relative to three outcomes: (1) cross-cultural skill development, (2) cross-cultural adjustment, and (3) job performance:

- Of the 10 studies that examined the relationship between CCT and self-confidence concerning one's ability to function effectively in cross-cultural situations, 9 found a positive relationship.
- Nineteen out of nineteen studies found a positive relationship between CCT and increased cross-cultural relational skills.
- Sixteen out of sixteen studies found a positive relationship between CCT and more accurate cross-cultural perceptions.
- Nine out of nine studies found a positive relationship between CCT and cross-cultural adjustment.
- Eleven out of 15 studies found a positive relationship between CCT and job performance in the cross-cultural situation.

However, the review also found that most of the empirical work was not founded on a theoretical framework per se, and that the literature lacked a systematic approach to the study of CCT effectiveness. *It is possible that the lack of a systematic stream of research has allowed the belief that CCT is not effective to persist.* Additionally, the lack of a theoretical framework has left managers with little means of deciding who would benefit most from training, or what training method would be most effective, or how to best design such training programs. Perhaps until managers are presented with a systematic yet practical means of addressing these questions, they will continue to resist the prescriptions from academics (or consultants) that CCT is necessary and effective.

The purpose of this article is to begin to shed some light on a framework for CCT that would be both theoretically sound and useful in practice. Recently, scholars have argued that Social Learning Theory (SLT) provides a solid theoretical basis for understanding cross-cultural learning, training, and adjustment (Black and Mendenhall, 1990; Church, 1982; David, 1976). This article explores the utility of SLT as a framework for systematically examining four important questions:

(1) how can the level of training rigor of specific cross-cultural training methods be determined;
(2) who would benefit most from cross-cultural training;
(3) what CCT methods are most appropriate in specific situations; and
(4) what level of CCT rigor is needed for maximum positive results?

A brief review of past typologies and frameworks of CCT is followed by a discussion of the major components of SLT. Finally, we outline a new framework of cross-cultural training based on SLT and practical implications are explored.

REVIEW OF PAST FRAMEWORKS

Most of the writing in the cross-cultural training literature has focused on the discussion of different methods of training and general classifications of these methodologies, while less attention has been focused on the development of frameworks that would determine which training methods to utilize or the important contingency factors to consider in such determinations. The first part of this section summarizes a generally accepted typology of CCT methods, and the second part reviews two recent frameworks that try to help managers determine appropriate methods for their organizations.

Landis and Brislin (1983) have proposed a typology of methods based on a broad review of the cross-cultural training literature. Their classification scheme is summarized in Table 1.

Given the fragmented state of the literature, the development of the foregoing classification scheme was an important step in improving an understanding of the area. However, managers responsible for training within corporations were often left in a quandary as to which of the methodologies were more or less rigorous, effective, and appropriate for specific training situations. Recent research attempts to facilitate making some of these determinations.

Table 1. Fundamental cross-cultural training methodologies

Information or Fact-Oriented Training: Trainees are presented with various facts about the country in which they are about to live via lectures, videotapes and reading materials.

Attributions Training: The attribution approach focuses on explanations of behavior from the point of view of the native. The goal is to learn the cognitive standards by which the host-nationals process behavioral input so that the trainee can understand why the host-nationals behave as they do and adapt his/her own behavior to match the standards of behavior in the host country.

Cultural Awareness Training: The aim is to study the values, attitudes, and behaviors that are common in one's own culture, so that the trainee better understands how culture impacts his/her own behavior. Once this is understood, it is assumed that he/she can better understand how culture affects human behavior in other countries.

Cognitive-Behavior Modification: The focus here is to assist trainees in linking what they find to be rewarding and punishing in their own subcultures (work, family, religion, etc.), and then to examine the reward/punishment structure in the host culture. Through an examination of the differences and similarities, strategies are developed to assist the trainee to obtain rewards – and avoid punishments – in the host culture.

Experimental Learning: The goal of this approach is to involve the trainees as active participants, to introduce the nature of life in another culture by actively experiencing that culture via field trips, complex role-plays and cultural simulations.

Interaction Training: Here trainees interact with natives or returned expatriates in order to become more comfortable with host-nationals and to learn from the first-hand experience of the returned expatriates. The methods utilized can range from in-depth role plays to casual, informal discussions.

Source: Adapted from Landis and Brislin (1983).

Tung's framework of training method selection

Tung (1981) presented a contingency framework for choosing an appropriate CCT method and its level of rigor. She argued for two determining factors: the degree of interaction required in the host culture and the similarity between the individual's native culture and the new culture. Related training elements involved the content and rigor of the training. Essentially, Tung proposed:

1. If the expected interaction between the individual and members of the target or host culture was low, and the degree of dissimilarity between the individual's native culture and the host culture was low, then the content of the training should focus on task and job related issues as opposed to culture related issues, and the level of rigor necessary for effective training should be relatively low.
2. If there was a high level of expected interaction with host nationals and a large dissimilarity between the cultures, then the content of the training should focus on the new culture and on cross-cultural skill development, as well as on the new task, and the level of rigor of such training should be moderate to high.

While this framework does specify some criteria (i.e., degree of expected interaction and cultural similarity) for choosing CCT methods, the conclusions that users can draw from it are rather general. Essentially, the framework suggests that the user emphasize task issues by utilizing training methods with relatively low levels of rigor and to emphasize culture learning, skill development, and task issues by utilizing a relatively high level of rigor. However, the framework does not help managers determine which specific training methods to use. In addition, the framework does not define what training "rigor" is, and therefore, does not help determine which specific training methods are more or less rigorous.

Mendenhall and Oddou's framework for selecting training methods

Mendenhall and Oddou's (1986b) more recent framework moves beyond Tung's and provides more specificity. Like Tung's, it acknowledges that the degree of expected interaction and similarity between the native and host cultures is important in determining the cross-cultural training method. In addition, it proposes three key elements related to training:

1. Training methods.
2. Low, medium, and high levels of training rigor.
3. Duration of the training relative to degree of interaction and culture novelty.

Mendenhall and Oddou's (1986b) framework is a significant improvement over the more general one offered by Tung (1982). It provides a grouping of specific methods by low, medium, and high levels of rigor and also discusses the duration of training relative to interaction and culture similarity. Despite these important improvements, the framework does not explain how the level of rigor of a specific CCT method or group of methods was determined. It tells us little about the training and learning processes, and therefore, why the particular determinations are made. The content of the training all seems to be "cultural" in nature and little integration of the individual's new job-related tasks and the new host culture is made. Finally, while both frameworks make intuitive sense, their theoretical grounding is never made explicit. Thus, lacking empirical data to support them, it is difficult to evaluate their soundness for use and success in the real world.

THE NEED FOR A THEORETICAL FRAMEWORK

Despite the plethora of work advocating the use of cross-cultural training in organizations, both empirical research and conceptual work have been almost totally devoid of a theoretical framework (Adler, 1986; Black and Mendenhall, 1990; Roberts and Boyacigiller, 1982; Schollhammer, 1975). Bochner states cross-cultural "research cannot be said to have been conducted with a great deal of theoretical sophistication. The tendency has been to use lengthy and diffuse questionnaires and/or interviews that generate masses of unrelated information" (1982, p. 16). A previous review of the empirical literature in cross-cultural training indicates that, in general, cross-cultural training seems to have a positive impact on skill development, adjustment, and performance (Black and Mendenhall, 1990); however, the lack of a theoretical framework leaves essentially unanswered questions like why cross-cultural training is effective and which situations are best served by what specific training methods. The purpose of this next section is to examine social learning theory (SLT) as a theoretical framework that would begin to shed light on these questions.

Social learning theory

The potential of SLT to facilitate an understanding of the theoretical relationship between cross-cultural training and cross-cultural performance is significant (Church, 1982; David, 1976). Before discussing the particular relevance of SLT to cross-cultural training and its effectiveness, it is perhaps useful to briefly summarize the main points of the theory.

SLT, as described by one of its leading proponents (Bandura, 1977), argues that learning takes place both (1) by the effect reinforcement has on behavior and (2) by imitating or modeling the behavior of others and symbolically or vicariously making associations between behavior and consequence without direct, actual experience. As described by Bandura, SLT has four central elements: attention, retention, reproduction, and incentives (see Figure 1).

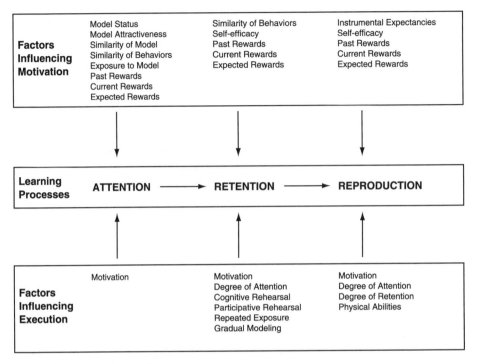

Figure 1. Social learning theory process

Attention. Before someone or something can be modeled, it must be noticed by the learner. Several factors have been found to influence the attention process of the subject/observer, including: (1) the status of the model; (2) the attractiveness of the model; (3) the similarity of the model; (4) the repeated availability of the model; and (5) past reinforcement for paying attention to the model (either actual or vicarious rewards).

Retention. Retention is the process by which the modeled behavior becomes encoded as a memory by the observer. Two representational systems are involved. The imaginal system is utilized during exposure to the framework. During exposure images are associated on the basis of physical contiguity. These images are stored as "cognitive maps" which can later guide the observer in imitation. The second system is the verbal system. It represents the coded information in abbreviated verbal systems and groups similar patterns of behavior into larger integrated units. It should be noted that both the repeated modeling of a behavior and the repeated cognitive rehearsal of the modeled behavior serve to solidify the retention process.

Reproduction. The third major component of the modeling process involves the translation of the symbolic representations of the modeled stimuli into overt actions. As individuals try to imitate the modeled behavior, they check their performance against their memory of what was modeled. Actual reproduction of the modeled behavior, of course, can be inhibited by physical differences between the model and the person imitating the model, how well the model is observed, and how well the modeled behavior is retained.

Incentives and the Motivational Processes. The fourth major component of SLT involves the influences of incentives on the motivational processes of modeling behavior. Incentives have three primary sources. Incentives can come from the direct external environment, from vicarious association, and from the individual him- or herself. In turn, each of these different sources of incentives can affect several aspects of the learning process. Incentives can affect which models are observed and how much attention is paid to observed models. Incentives can influence the degree to which the modeled behavior is retained and rehearsed. Also, incentives can influence which learned behaviors are emitted. *It is important to note that Bandura (1977) argued on the basis of empirical work that incentives play a much larger role in influencing what behavior is emitted as opposed to what behavior is learned.* He concluded that individuals learn numerous behaviors which are not usually emitted because they are not positively rewarded. However, if the reward structure is changed the behaviors are performed.

Expectancies. In relation to the motivational processes of learning, Bandura (1977) distinguishes between two types of expectancies. The first type of expectations Bandura calls "efficacy expectations". The individual's self-efficacy is the degree to which the individual believes he or she can successfully execute a particular behavior. This expectation is similar to the "effort to performance" expectancy proposed by Vroom (1964). In his review of the literature, Bandura (1977) found that higher levels of self-efficacy led individuals to persist at imitating modeled behavior longer and to be more willing to try to imitate novel behavior. The sources for increasing self-efficacy, in order of importance, include past experience ("I've done it or something like it before"), vicarious experience ("other people have done it"), and verbal persuasion ("people say I can do it").

In addition to efficacy expectations, Bandura (1977) argues that outcome expectations influence the modeling process. Outcome expectations are people's beliefs that the execution of certain behaviors will lead to desired outcomes. These expectations are similar to the "expectancy-of-performance-to-outcome" (instrumentality expectancies) proposed by Vroom (1964). Bandura concluded that in addition to the modeling processes of attention, retention, and reproduction, (1) incentives influence what people learn and (2) incentives, efficacy, and outcome expectancies influence what learned behaviors are emitted.

Important Empirical Findings. Although a number of empirical findings are reviewed by Bandura (1977), several are important to summarize because of the insight they provide about fundamental elements in the learning process. The first finding is that gradual modeling is more effective than "one-shot" modeling, especially if the modeled behaviors are novel to the observer. Gradual modeling involves providing successive approximations of the final behavior to be modeled. This modeling process is more effective than modeling only the final behavior for several reasons: (1) observers pay more attention to models and modeled behaviors which are more familiar; (2) observers can more easily retain models which are more similar to cognitive maps already possessed; (3) observers have higher expectations of efficacy and outcome of behaviors

which are more familiar; and (4) observers are more likely to be able to reproduce more familiar behaviors.

Second, Bandura argues that individuals can learn completely through
symbolic modeling, that is just by watching and rehearsing mentally. This symbolic learning process can be facilitated by the other variables discussed
(attractiveness of the model, similarity of the model, etc.) and by having multiple
models. Also, Bandura found that participative modeling is generally more
effective than symbolic processes alone. Participative reproduction simply means
that the observer actually practices (as opposed to only cognitive rehearsals) the
modeled behavior. The external, and especially the internal, feedback processes
serve to refine the observer's ability to reproduce the modeled behavior at a later
time in the appropriate situation.

SOCIAL LEARNING THEORY AND CROSS-CULTURAL TRAINING

SLT provides a theoretical framework for systematically examining the level of
rigor that specific CCT methods generally contain and for determining the
appropriate cross-cultural training approach for specific training cases and
situations. Based on the central variable of "modeling process" in SLT, the first
part of this section explores a means of ranking specific cross-cultural training
methods by the degree of rigor generally contained in the methods and examining two other factors that are related to the total rigor a training program might
have. The second part of this section examines how SLT processes can provide
a heuristic framework for deciding which CCT methods would be appropriate
in specific situations. Throughout the second part of this section, we examine the
practical implications of the framework through case illustrations.

SLT and CCT rigor

As was mentioned earlier, many of the past attempts to provide a means of
choosing CCT methods have included the concept of training rigor but have not
attempted to define what the term meant. Within the framework of SLT, rigor
is essentially the degree of cognitive involvement of the learner or trainee. The
modeling processes in SLT provide a useful means of not only defining rigor
but also in determining the relative degree of rigor that specific training
methods generally have. Within SLT there are basically two modeling processes
– symbolic and participative.

Symbolic modeling simply involves observing modeled behaviors. However,
this observation can have two forms. The first form consists of the learner or
trainee hearing about the behavior and then translating those verbal messages
into imagined images. Thus, the learner or trainee observes the behaviors in his
or her mind. Cross-cultural training methods that generally exhibit this type
of modeling process include verbal factual briefings, lectures, and books. The
second form of symbolic modeling involves the trainee actually seeing visually

the behavior being modeled. In this case the trainee both sees and retains a cognitive image of the behavior and is more cognitively involved than when the symbolic modeling process only involves translating verbal messages into cognitive images. Specific CCT methods that generally exhibit this type of modeling include films, role modeling, demonstrations, and nonparticipative language training.

Participative modeling essentially means that in addition to observing the modeled behavior, the trainee also participates in modeling the behavior. This participation can take two forms. The first form involves "verbal" participation. In other words, the trainee participates in modeling the behavior by describing verbally what he or she would do. Cross-cultural training methods that generally exhibit this type of participative modeling include case studies and culture assimilations. The second form of participative modeling involves more physical participation in modeling the behaviors being learned. Cross-cultural training methods that generally require this type of participative modeling include role plays, interactive language training, field trips, and interactive simulations. Trainees are more cognitively involved when they must physically as opposed to only verbally participate in modeling the behaviors being taught.

Rehearsal increases the level of cognitive involvement during symbolic or participative modeling and has two basic forms. *Cognitive rehearsal* involves the mental rehearsal or practices of the modeled behavior (e.g., practicing eating with chopsticks in one's mind). *Behavioral rehearsal* involves actual physical practice of the modeled behavior. Because behavioral rehearsal involves both mental and physical processes, it is more cognitively engaging than cognitive rehearsal alone, and therefore, is more rigorous. By definition, symbolic modeling can only utilize cognitive rehearsal, while participative modeling can utilize either cognitive or behavioral rehearsal or both. Thus, the rigor of any specific CCT method could be enhanced through cognitive or behavioral rehearsal.

By examining the modeling and rehearsal processes involved, the relative rigor of a specific CCT method can be approximated. Figure 2 provides an illustration of the relative ranking in terms of rigor for a set of specific and common CCT methods.

The duration and intensity of any CCT program is a function of the total hours of training and the time frame within which the training is conducted. *Thus, all other things being equal, a training program that involved a total of 25 training hours over five days would be less rigorous than a program that involved 100 total hours over three weeks.*

In general, the SLT literature and the CCT literature provide evidence to strongly suggest that the more rigorous the training the more effectively the trainee will be able to actually and appropriately execute the learned behaviors (Bandura, 1977; Black and Mendenhall, 1990; Tung, 1981). The basic explanation for this relationship is that rigor (i.e., cognitive involvement) increases the level of attention and retention, thereby improving reproduction proficiency.

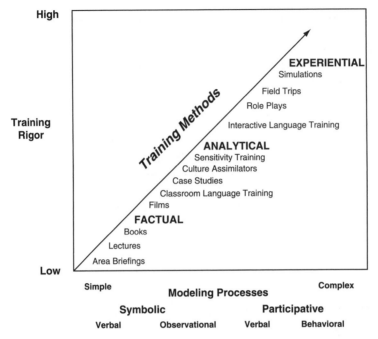

Figure 2. Modeling processes, rigor, and training methods

Important situational factors

In addition to providing a means of determining the general level of rigor of specific CCT methods, SLT also provides a framework for identifying situational factors that are important to consider in choosing appropriate CCT methods in specific situations. The contextual factors that are relevant to CCT are briefly discussed below.

Culture Novelty. Based on SLT and the arguments just made, the more novel the host culture is, the more difficult it will be for the individual to attend to and retain the various models of appropriate behavior (in both training and actual situations). More assistance through rigorous training is needed in order to learn the new behaviors appropriate in a highly foreign culture.

An important practical question is: "How does one determine the degree of novelty in the host culture?" Once this question is answered, then the HR decision maker can begin to determine the appropriate levels of CCT rigor and corresponding specific CCT methods. While definitive decision rules are perhaps impossible to create, past cross-cultural research presents some rough guidelines (Haire, Ghiselli, and Porter, 1966; England and Lee, 1974; Hofstede, 1980).

Hofstede (1980) presents perhaps the most comprehensive yet simple means of estimating cultural novelty. He examined native employees in a US multi-national firm in 48 countries along four different scales (power distance, uncertainty avoidance, individualism, masculinity). A rough estimate of culture novelty can be obtained by calculating the absolute difference in scores on each one of the four scales between the employees of the target country and the American employees and then summing these differences. The larger the final number, the greater the culture novelty relative to the American culture. Torbiorn's work (1982) also gives insight into the degree of cultural novelty. He found that for Scandinavians, the most difficult regions of the world in which to live and work were: (1) Africa, (2) Middle East, (3) Far East, (4) South America, (5) Eastern Bloc, (6) Europe, (7) North America, and (8) Australia and New Zealand.

In addition to using Hofstede's (1980) results, one might estimate culture novelty by simply assessing whether the language of the host culture is different from that of the individual's home culture and whether learning the language will be a necessity for living and working in the host country. For example, even though Cantonese Chinese is the most common language of use in Hong Kong, English is still an official language and one can survive without Chinese language skills; however, survival would be more difficult without Spanish language skills in a country such as Chile (Kepler, Kepler, Gaither, and Gaither, 1983).

The next step in assessing the novelty of the target country and culture is to examine the previous experience of the specific individual candidate. Social learning theory would argue that the more experience the individual has had with a specific culture, even if that experience was in the distant past, the more the individual is able to recall and utilize those past experiences in coping with the present situation in the host culture. It should be mentioned that both the duration and intensity of the past experience serve to deepen what was retained from the experience and to facilitate later recall (Bandura, 1977). Thus, all things being equal, the Indonesian culture would be less novel for the candidate who lived there before than the candidate who had not. Likewise, all other things being equal, the candidate who had frequent and involved interactions with Indonesians during a three year stay would find the culture less novel in a later visit than an individual who had infrequent and superficial interactions with Indonesians during a similar three year stay. Thus, both the "quantity" and "quality" of an individual's previous experience must be examined. In addition, there is some empirical support that suggests that previous international experience, even if it is not in the host country's culture, reduces the novelty of the culture (Black, 1988). Based on SLT, one would expect that (1) a candidate with previous experience in a country or region similar to the host country and culture would perceive less culture novelty, have an easier adjustment, and need less training than a candidate with previous experience in a totally different country or region, and (2) a candidate with frequent and involved previous interactions would need less training than a candidate with infrequent and super-ficial interactions. The following simple equation represents the basic assessment process: Net Culture Novelty = Objective Culture Novelty − (the Quality + Quantity of an Individual's Previous Experience).

Degree of Interaction. The second situational factor in determining the degree of CCT rigor needed is the degree of expected interaction between the individual and members of the host culture. Interaction intensity can be viewed in three ways.

1. Frequency. One can assess the degree of interaction through the relative frequency of interaction expected between the individual and members of the host culture.

2. Importance. One can assess the degree through the importance of the interactions. If one expects relatively few and mostly trivial interactions between the individual and members of the host culture, then the individual's ability to reproduce appropriate behaviors in the host culture is less important. Therefore, the individual's attention and retention needs and the individual's need to get help to enhance attention, retention, and reproduction through rigorous training would be correspondingly low on importance. If, on the other hand, one expects many and primarily important interactions between the individual and members of the host culture, then the individual's ability to reproduce appropriate behaviors is more important (and therefore, so would be the individual's need in getting help to enhance that ability).

3. Nature. Specific aspects of the nature of the interactions with host country nationals include the following:
    (1) how familiar or novel the interaction is;
    (2) the directionality of the interaction (one-way vs. two-way);
    (3) the type of interactions (routine vs. unique);
    (4) the form of the interactions (face-to-face vs. other forms like mail);
    (5) the total duration of the cross-cultural interaction (e.g., 1 vs. 5 years); and
    (6) the format of interaction (formal vs. informal).

Based on the communication literature (Jablin, Putnam, Roberts, and Porter, 1987), one would expect that novel, two-way, unique, face-to-face, long-term, and informal cross-cultural interactions would be more difficult than the opposite. The following equation represents the basic assessment of degree of interaction: Degree of Interaction = (Frequency of Interactions with Host Nationals) × (Importance of Interactions) × (Nature of Interactions).

Job Novelty. The third important situational factor involves the novelty of the new job and its related tasks. Based on precisely the same theoretical arguments that were presented concerning culture novelty, the more novel the tasks of the new job in the new culture, the more assistance the individual will need through rigorous training to produce the desired and necessary behaviors to be effective in the new job. Some scholars may reason that it is difficult to separate culture novelty from job novelty, arguing that if the culture is novel then to some degree the job will also be novel. Although culture novelty and job novelty are not independent of each other, there is both logical and empirical basis for separating the two issues.

1. If there is little interaction between elements of the new culture and the job, and if the new job is very similar to the previous job, then it is quite possible to have a situation involving a novel culture but a non-novel job.

2. Likewise, it is possible to have a situation in which the new job is very different from the previous job, but the host culture is similar to the

individual's home culture. Recent empirical evidence suggests that individuals in international assignments adjust differentially to the culture and the job (Black, 1988; Black and Stephens, 1989), which suggests that while the novelty of the new job and culture can be linked they are not necessarily intertwined.

The question the HR decision maker must ask is, "How novel is the new job and its tasks and responsibilities?" Although it is perhaps impossible to draw a definitive line between what would and would not be a novel job, Stewart's (1982) framework of job characteristics provides a useful means of determining where "job novelties" might occur. First, the HR decision maker should try to determine if the new *job demands* are similar to or different from those of previous jobs held by the candidate.

- Are performance standards the same?
- Is the degree of personal involvement required in the work unit the same?
- Are the types of tasks to be done similar?
- Are the bureaucratic procedures that must be followed similar?

Next the HR decision maker must determine how similar the new *job constraints* are.

- Are resource limitations the same?
- Are the legal restrictions similar?
- Are the technological limitations familiar?

Finally, the HR decision maker must determine the novelty of the new *job choices*.

- Is the freedom to decide how work gets done the same?
- Is the discretion about what work gets done similar?
- Is the freedom to decide who does which tasks the same?
- Are the choices about what work gets delegated similar?

If the HR decision maker examines the three job characteristics proposed by Stewart (1982), he or she should be able to make a rough estimate of the extent to which the new job is novel relative to a specific candidate. According to SLT, the more novel the new responsibilities and tasks, the more help the individual will need through rigorous training to learn and execute the desired and necessary behaviors.

The family and CCT

The previous discussion has been presented with singular attention to the HR decision maker's consideration of the employee. However, research provides strong evidence to suggest that the candidate's family, especially the spouse, is also an important concern (Black, 1988; Black and Stephens, 1989; Harvey, 1985; Tung, 1981).

Culture Novelty. Determining the extent of family training needed begins with an assessment of culture novelty. There are two important qualifications. First, the final assessment of the host country's culture novelty must be made relative to the family's previous experience. Second, children under the age of about 13 may need much less preparation than older children because they seem to have less difficulty adjusting to foreign cultures (Tung, 1984). Finally, spouses must be given nearly equal consideration as that of the candidate because their adjustment or lack of it can be a critical determinant of the candidate's success or failure in the foreign culture (Black, 1988; Black and Stephens, 1989; Tung, 1981).

Degree of Interaction. The spouse should also be considered in determining the level of CCT rigor needed to prepare him/her for functioning effectively as an "interactor" in the foreign culture. The degree of expected interaction can be assessed in much the same manner as was suggested for the candidate (i.e., frequency and intensity). However, there are some important differences between candidates and spouses. First, most spouses do not work in the host culture even if they worked before the foreign assignment (Stephens and Black, 1991). Second, even if spouses are not required to interact with host country nationals, lack of the ability to interact can lead to feelings of isolation and loneliness, which in turn can be the primary cause of inadequate adjustment to the host culture and an early or premature return on the part of the entire family (Harvey, 1985; Tung, 1984; 1988). Consequently, even if required degree of interaction between the spouse and host country nationals is low, the spouse will be better adjusted if he or she has the ability to interact effectively (Black and Stephens, 1989). Thus, it may be important to facilitate this ability through rigorous CCT even if the required degree of interaction does not seem to merit it.

Integrating culture novelty, interaction, job novelty, and CCT rigor

The theoretical reasoning behind the integration of culture novelty, interaction, and job novelty is relatively straightforward. The greater the culture novelty, required interaction, and job novelty, the greater the need for rigorous CCT. However, each of these three conditions is not "created equally". *Research shows that it is more difficult to adjust to the culture and to interacting with host country nationals than to the job* (Black, 1988; Black and Stephens, 1989). This can be represented pictorially through a three-dimensional cube with a line running through the cube diagonally from the front left corner to the back right corner (see Figure 3).

The vertical axis represents the dimension of job novelty, ranging from low to high novelty. The bottom horizontal axis represents the dimension of interaction, ranging from low to high required interaction. The top horizontal axis represents relative culture novelty, ranging from low to high novelty. The

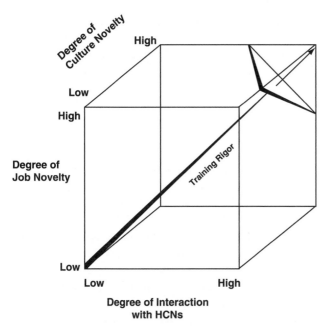

Figure 3. Integration of cross-cultural training rigor and main contingency factors

diagonal line, which runs from the front left corner to the back right corner represents training methods and rigor, ranging from low to high rigor. Thus, a point can be plotted in the three-dimensional space by estimating the culture novelty, degree of required interaction, and job novelty of a specific impending cross-cultural assignment. The intersection of the plotted point and the diagonal line, and therefore the determination of the requisite level of rigor, can be determined by imagining a plane at a right angle to, and traveling on the same diagonal as the CCT rigor line. When the plane intersects the point plotted based on estimates relative to each of the three dimensions, it also intersects with a point on the diagonal line representing CCT rigor. That intersection provides a rough estimation of the CCT rigor required.

The plane is placed at a right angle because research has demonstrated that adjusting to a novel job in the work situation of an overseas assignment is easier than adjusting to the general culture or interacting with host nationals (Black, 1988; Black and Stephens, 1989). Thus, even in the case of a highly novel job but low culture novelty and low required interaction with host nationals, the highest level of CCT rigor is not required. By contrast, even if the level of job novelty is moderate, a high level of culture novelty and required interaction necessitates a high level of CCT rigor.

The content of the training would, of course, be a direct function of the three dimensions discussed. If the assessment indicates that there will be a high level of job novelty, then the CCT program should include content relative to the new behaviors that need to be learned to effectively perform the job. If there is a high degree of interaction required, then the CCT program should include in its content such topics as cross-cultural communication, interpersonal skills, perception, ethnocentricity, etc. If there is a high degree of culture novelty, then topics such as the host country's values, religious systems, political systems, social customs, business practices, etc. should be included. The relative emphasis of the content would be a direct reflection of the relative low or high scores on each of the three dimensions.

Two case illustrations

Case 1. Wave, as one of the market leaders in the computer software industry, had just sealed a joint venture pact with one of Japan's largest designers and manufacturers of computers, Nippon Kankei. Wave, a Seattle-based company, agreed to send six Americans to work in Tokyo with 15 of Nippon Kankei's best "high potential" software designers. The purpose of this effort was to train the Japanese designers in state of the art software design while working on software applications for Nippon Kankei's products. Also, Nippon Kankei, through its distribution network, would market any products created by the joint venture research and development team to other computer manufacturers, distributors, and retailers as well. Wave would retain the copyright and share significantly in profits generated by the joint venture.

Wave retained complete managerial and creative control of the R & D team. The Project Manager was to be designated by Wave, John Selby was selected, and agreed to go. John had vast experience in all aspects of the industry and had overseen four projects in the US from the idea to the final product. The other five designers had limited managerial experience – they were pure designers. Nippon Kankei's management hoped that by rubbing shoulders and working jointly with these American designers their own staff would get "up to speed" in software design.

All of the married designers agreed to relocate to Japan after feeling that their families' financial position and standard of living would not suffer because of the move. No one indicated any reluctance on the part of his spouse concerning the three-year assignment; however, there were rumors that at least three of the wives were "less than thrilled" about disrupting their children's education and creating a new life in Japan.

What practical guidance concerning the cross-cultural training of this team of expatriates who are about to be sent to Japan can the framework we have discussed provide? The first step is to assess the culture novelty of the host country to which the team is being sent.

Generalizing Hofstede's (1980) research of Japanese who worked for an American multinational corporation (MNC) to those Japanese who will be working with Wave's people in the joint venture, we find the following:

(1)   Japanese have a much higher power distance (the degree workers accept power difference between managers and subordinates) of about 20 index points;

(2)   Americans are much more risk taking (53 index points on uncertainty avoidance);

(3)   Americans are much more individual and less group-oriented than the Japanese (45 index points); and

(4)   Japanese accept traditional sex roles and have a higher work ethic than Americans (35 point differential).

Hofstede's results suggest that not only does Japan have a culture quite different from American culture, but it is one of the most different. The main language of Japan is also different. But, to what degree will the expatriates from Wave need to speak Japanese? The ability of the Japanese assigned to the joint venture to read English is quite high, but their speaking and listening comprehension skills are marginal. Also, the American expatriates are likely to find it difficult to function effectively without Japanese language ability outside the workplace.

Next, Wave must assess the previous experience of the candidates. Unfortunately, though many had vacationed a time or two overseas, none of the candidates has lived or worked either in Japan or outside the US. Thus, their previous experience would not reduce the culture novelty or the need for CCT. Based on all this information, it seems clear that the level of "culture novelty" that the Wave expatriates will experience will be quite high.

At first the degree of required interaction with Japanese workers for the American software designers would be fairly low, but would be much higher for John Selby, the project manager. However, the group-oriented nature of Japanese work organizations and the practice of consensus decision making increases the likelihood that all of Wave's expatriates will be interacting frequently with the Japanese. Additionally, the interactions are likely to be face-to-face, two-way, informal, and both routine and unique in nature over several years. Thus, while the degree of required interaction is likely to be higher for John Selby, it is still likely to be high for the other expatriates as well.

For Wave, on the surface it does not appear that the job novelty for the group of expatriates is very high. John Selby has managed four "start-up" projects before and all the designers have had considerable experience in new product design. There are no new technical skills needed by the designers, and coming up with programs for new hardware systems is what they do for a living. Upon closer examination of the job demands, it seems that there is a high potential that performance standards, the tasks concerning training or working with Japanese, the way in which decisions get made, and the bureaucratic procedures that must be followed will be different compared to their old jobs back in Seattle. Wave must also consider the novelty of job constraints. There is a high probability that resource limitations (e.g., communicating with colleagues and experts back at Wave), budgets, and legal restrictions, are significantly different in Japan compared to Seattle. Finally, Wave needs to examine the novelty of job choices or discretion. Will the American designers be free to decide how to get work done (e.g., working hours) as they were in Seattle? Will John Selby be able to assign tasks and manage the team the same way he did back home? It is quite likely that all the members of the Wave team will need to make adjustments in order to work effectively with the Japanese. Wave's answers to these questions suggest that job choice novelty will be moderately high as well.

While there may be limits to Wave's budget, if it can, spouses should be included in the CCT program. This is because the novelty of the culture is high and the ability to interact with shopkeepers, neighbors, banks, etc. greatly facilitates the spouse's ability to adjust to the new culture. As mentioned earlier the spouse's adjustment is important because of its significance for expatriate adjustment (Black, 1988; Black and Stephens, 1989).

Thus, based on Figure 3, Wave needs to design or purchase a CCT program of fairly high rigor. The program should include some elements of symbolic modeling (both symbolic and observational) such as lectures, articles, books, and films on Japanese culture and business. But the CCT program should also include training methods that involve participative modeling as well. Specific methods might include case studies, culture assimilator exercises, interactive language study, role plays, and perhaps a pre-move visit to Japan. Additionally, the content of the training should include job, business, and general culture issues given the novelty of both task and culture. Obviously, a training program that includes all of these specific training methods will take time to execute. A reasonable estimate is that at least 60 hours of training will be needed. If time and scheduling constraints prevent all the training from occurring before departure to Japan, some follow-up training might be useful once the expatriates were settled in Japan.

Case 2. An academic association of management educators, primarily university and college business professors, were planning to hold a joint conference in Japan with Japanese business and business education leaders. The American professors were asked to submit professional papers on a wide range of business topics and 60 were selected to participate in the international conference. The conference organizers decided to provide some type of CCT for the selected participants.

The designers of the training program had to first determine the culture novelty of Japan relative to the US. As has already been described, the work by Hofstede suggests that Japan is one of the most novel countries in relationship to America. However, the previous international experience of the selected participants in general or specifically in Japan were not known. Because participation in the training session could not be required, it was assumed that those who had the least amount of previous experience with Japan would be most likely to attend the training session. This, in fact, turned out to be the case. Thus, the degree of culture novelty was high.

Next, the degree of interaction with host nationals had to be assessed. The design of the conference was such that there would be a mixture of formal, one-way interaction and informal, two-way interaction. The conference was scheduled to last only four days, so the duration of the interaction would be quite short but would involve frequent interactions during the four days. Although one of the purposes of the conference was to create better ties between the American and Japanese business scholars, the importance of the interactions was considered moderate. Also, the degree that the American scholars would need to know and utilize Japanese was small. It was expected that the Japanese participants would have a reasonable command of English, since the entire program was to be conducted in English with very few sessions providing translators. Thus, the overall degree of interaction between Americans and Japanese was expected to be low to moderate.

Finally, the job novelty for the American scholars had to be assessed. At first glance, job novelty would seem quite low. In terms of presenting and listening to papers at an academic conference, this conference design looked quite similar to programs held in the US. However, the demands of presenting research results to a culturally mixed audience (Japanese and Americans) were somewhat different from those of presenting to a homogeneous audience of American scholars. Overall, however, the job novelty for the American scholars was considered to be low to moderate.

Based on these assessments, Figure 3 would suggest the use of moderately rigorous training methods. Figure 2 indicates that moderate levels of training rigor consist of primarily symbolic modeling processes. Consequently, the training program was scheduled for a single day and included symbolic verbal modeling via:

(1)   short lectures on specific aspects of Japan and Japanese culture that the American professors would likely encounter in their four-day stay,
(2)   a short video on the specific location of the conference, and
(3)   classroom language training focused on simple Japanese greetings and phrases.

The training program also included some symbolic observational modeling via (1) demonstrations of such things as greetings and the exchanging of business cards, and (2) role plays to benefit the training participants on presenting (*a*) to a culturally mixed audience and (*b*) using a translator.

Although the preceding example of a group preparing for an academic conference may seem somewhat unrelated to business, it is actually representative of a number of short-term overseas business situations. For example, industrial trade shows, troubleshooting trips, technology transfers, or negotiations often involve (1) short-term stays in a foreign country, (2) low to moderate interaction intensity, and (3) tasks that seem familiar. In these cases, just as in the academic conference case illustration, the model presented would suggest that low to moderate levels of cross-cultural training rigor would be appropriate preparation (see Figure 2). Additionally, the content of the training should focus on those specific elements of the tasks that would be somewhat altered because of the culture in which the tasks would be carried out.

CONCLUSIONS

A variety of implications can be derived from a SLT-based approach to CCT. The first three implications are related specifically to international or expatriate assignments. The next two implications are related to broader issues of good global development practices.

CCT is a necessity not a luxury

It is very clear from the research literature that the vast majority of senior executives do not support CCT programs for their employees who must work with foreign business people. The research literature is equally clear that American expatriates who work with foreigners without the benefit of CCT are less effective than those who have been trained. With so much at stake, from the success of business negotiations to the effective operation of overseas subsidiaries or joint ventures, there seems to be little reason not to invest time and money into training people who must work internationally. The training costs are small compared to the potential costs of early returns or business losses due to the lack of cross-cultural competency. As with any training intervention, unless top management support exists, the potential of a successful CCT program is low. HRM staff generally do not try to push through programs that are not sanctioned from on high; American senior executives need to start blessing the utilization of CCT programs – it's as simple as that.

It's a family affair

Of the few firms in the US that do offer CCT to their expatriates, few offer such training to their spouses or other family members, despite the fact that research has demonstrated the impact of spouse and family adjustment on premature expatriate returns. A simple way to counteract this problem is to send spouses to the training sessions and to give them the same CCT the employee receives. While large portions of the training may be business-related, much of it is applicable to the non-working spouse, because cultural values and norms that affect business behavior also affect social behavior outside of the workplace. Also, understanding the work challenges may assist the spouse in offering support to the employee during the assignment. A more substantial effort would be to tailor a program that deals with the specific daily and cultural challenges that the spouse will face overseas. In some aspects, the spouse faces more challenges than does the employee. While the employee has his/her job and people at work, the spouse often has an empty house, no friends, and isolation with which to contend. Although much of the focus of this paper has centered on the employee and determining appropriate CCT methods for the employee, we have argued that these same assessment processes could be used to determine when it would be more or less critical to provide CCT for the spouse as well.

Avoid "dog and pony" shows

Since many firms do not have the in-house expertise to design CCT programs, the use of external consultants and trainers is common. The lack of internal CCT expertise means that the ability of the HR staff to evaluate the quality and suitability of external CCT programs may be less than desired. The framework presented in this article provides HR decision makers with at least a rough template by which they can evaluate the quality, rigor, and appropriateness of training programs offered by consultants or universities. The decision maker could use the framework to evaluate consultants' bids or university programs in a more analytical fashion by comparing the training methodology to the various methods described earlier. Next, by examining the various dimensions discussed, the decision maker could determine if he/she were buying more than was needed or whether the proposed training program would be inadequate and not sufficiently rigorous to meet the trainees' needs in order to be more effective in their cross-cultural assignments.

CCT is not just for expatriates

Throughout this article much of the focus has been on expatriate employees; however, CCT is necessary for repatriated employees, for employees who go on short-term assignments, for good succession planning, and for general managerial development.

Repatriation. Just as the framework can be a guide for selecting or designing CCT for expatriates being sent overseas, it can also be used for selecting or designing training programs for employees returning to their home country after an international assignment. Although many managers would think that "coming home" would be "no big deal", Adler (1986) found that for most managers, returning to the US was more difficult than adjusting to the foreign country.

Short-term Assignments. In addition to CCT for employees embarking on or returning from long-term international assignments, our framework and theory suggest that employees sent on short-term assignments need CCT as well. The content of the training may need to be more focused and topic-specific than for those headed for 2–4 year assignments (as illustrated in the case of the American professors going to Japan for a four-day conference), but it is still necessary. Companies often send managers overseas for important tasks that take a relatively shorter period of time, yet fail to train these individuals as well. Sending someone to Korea to "explore business opportunities" or "work through the details of a joint venture agreement" requires cross-cultural knowledge and skills. For example, Graham (1985) has demonstrated that Americans who do not understand Japanese negotiation tactics and their underlying values often utilize negotiation tactics and strategies that are counter-productive. The framework outlined in this article regarding CCT methodology provides a means of determining the level of CCT rigor that is needed and specific appropriate methods.

Succession Planning. The lack of CCT for international assignments can have a rather significant impact on succession planning for American firms. Consider the following scenario. USA MNC, Inc. does not provide CCT before international assignments. As a consequence many good employees fail in their international assignment because they were not adequately prepared. Also, the firm does not provide CCT for returning expatriates or managers sent on short-term assignments. Some of these employees also fail because of inadequate preparation. Other bright employees notice this. Not wanting the same fate to befall them, the best and the brightest decline to accept international assignments. These best and brightest, who lack any in-depth international experience then continue to move to the top of the firm. Once they make it to the top, one has to wonder how capable they will be at dealing with foreign competitors, with global markets, with international suppliers, with multicultural workforces, and so on.

In the introduction we cited scholars who argue that corporations need to develop managers with the new skills, such as global visioning skills, multicultural relation skills, and so on, to effectively lead firms in the 1990s and into the 21st century. Consequently, developing these skills is a critical element of succession planning. At a macro level, the framework presented suggests that if managers in the future must deal with cultures different from their own, must tackle tasks quite novel from those in which they currently engage, and must be proficient in interacting with people from other cultures, then they must receive over the course of their career and development quite rigorous cross-cultural training. Thus, the framework can provide guidance concerning the level of CCT rigor and specific training methods, such as culture assimilators, necessary for a specific international assignment, but it can also suggest the level of CCT rigor and training methods, such as international assignments, needed to prepare individuals for general positions and responsibilities in the future.

Ethics and CCT

In addition to the "utilitarian" functions that CCT may serve, firms may want to consider the issue from a social responsibility or ethical perspective. The military trains its soldiers before sending them into battle, churches educate and train their missionaries before sending them out to proselytize, and governments train secret agents before they go under "deep" cover; but US firms send employees overseas cold. Such a "sink-or-swim" approach would seem irresponsible and unreasonable to the military, clergy, or government, why then does it seem logical to the industrial sector? One must wonder if it is ethical to uproot an individual or family, send them across the Pacific or Atlantic Oceans, and expect them to make their way skillfully through an alien business and social culture on their own. Perhaps American executives reason that the extraordinary compensation packages expatriates receive make the exchange a fair and ethical one.

Living and working overseas involves adjustments and stress of a high magnitude. Placing individuals in such conditions without giving them the tools to manage these conditions seems not only economically costly to the firm, and personally costly to the individuals, but simply wrong. It is understandable because most Americans making decisions on international assignments have not lived and worked overseas (Miller, 1973) and thus are simply ignorant of the challenges, stresses, and difficulties expatriates face; however, at the bottom line, ignorance is not held to be justifiable for failure domestically – why then should it be a justification for failure regarding international assignments? If US firms are to successfully compete in what is becoming a global battleground, they must provide their soldiers with the weapons and ammunition necessary to wage effective and victorious campaigns.

REFERENCES

Alder, N. (1986). *International dimensions of organizational behavior*. Boston, Mass.: Kent Publishing.

Baker, J. C., and Ivancevich, J. M. (1971). The assignment of American executives abroad: systematic, haphazard, or chaotic? *California Management Review, 13*, 39–44.

Bandura, A. (1977). *Social learning theory*. Englewood Cliffs, NJ: Prentice-Hall.

Black, J. S. (1987). Japanese/American negotiations: the Japanese perspective. *Business and Economic Review, 6*(1), 27–30.

Black, J. S. (1988). Work role transitions: a study of American expatriate managers in Japan. *Journal of International Business Studies, 19*, 277–94.

Black, J. S., and Mendenhall, M. (1990). Cross-culture training effectiveness: a review and theoretical framework for future research. *Academy of Management Review, 15*, 113–36.

Black, J. S., and Stephens, G. K. (1989). The influence of the spouse on American expatriate adjustment and intent to stay in Pacific Rim assignments. *Journal of Management, 15*, 529–44.

Bochner, S. (1982). *Culture in contact: studies in cross-cultural interaction*. Elmsford, NY: Pergamon Press.

Brein, M., and David, K. H. (1971). Intercultural communication and adjustment of the sojourner. *Psychology Bulletin, 76*, 215–30.

Brislin, R. W. (1981). *Cross-cultural encounters*. Elmsford, NY: Pergamon Press.

Church, A. T. (1982). Sojourn adjustment. *Psychological Bulletin, 91*, 540–71.

Copeland, L., and Griggs, L. (1985). *Going international*. New York: Random House.

David, K. H. (1976). The use of social learning in preventing intercultural adjustment problems. In P. Pedersen, W. J. Lonner, and J. Draguns (eds.), *Counseling across cultures*. Honolulu: University of Hawaii Press.

Doz, Y., and Prahalad, C. K. (1986). Controlled variety: a challenge for human resource management in the MNC. *Human Resource Management, 25*(1), 55–71.

Dunbar, E., and Ehrlich, M. (1986). *International practices, selection, training, and managing the international staff: a survey report*. The Project on International Human Resource. Columbia University-Teachers College.

Early, P. C. (1987). Intercultural training for managers: a comparison of documentary and interpersonal methods. *Academy of Management Journal, 30*, 685–98.

England, G., and Lee, R. (1974). The relationship between managerial values and managerial success in the U.S., Japan, India, and Australia. *Journal of Applied Psychology, 59*, 411–19.

Graham, J. (1985). The influence of culture on the process of business negotiations: an exploritory study. *Journal of International Business Studies*, Spring, 81–95.

Gudykunst, W. B., Hammer, M. R., and Wiseman, R. L. (1977). An analysis of an integrated approach to cross-cultural training. *International Journal of Intercultural Relations, 1*, 99–110.

Haire, M., Ghiselli, E. E., and Porter, L. W. (1966). *Managerial thinking: an international study*. New York: Wiley.

Harris, P., and Moran, R. T. (1979). *Managing cultural differences*. Houston, Tex.: Gulf.

Harvey, M. C. (1982). The other side of the foreign assignment: dealing with repatriation problems. *Columbia Journal of World Business*, Spring, 53–9.

Harvey, M. C. (1985). The executive family: an overlooked variable in international assignments. *Columbia Journal of World Business*, Spring, 84–92.

Hofstede, G. (1980). *Culture's consequences: international differences in work related values*. Beverly Hills, Calif.: Sage.

Jablin, F. M., Putnam, L. L., Roberts, K. H., and Porter, L. W. (1987). *Handbook of organizational communication*. Beverly Hills, Calif.: Sage.

Kepler, J. Z., Kepler, P. J., Gaither, O. D., and Gaither, M. C. (1983). *Americans abroad*. New York: Praeger.

Landis, D., and Brislin, R. (1983). *Handbook on intercultural training* (Vol. 1). Elmsford, NY: Pergamon Press.

Lanier, A. R. (1979). Selection and preparation for overseas transfers. *Personnel Journal, 58*, 160–3.

Latham, G. (1988). Human resource training and development. *Annual Review of Psychology, 39*, 545–82.

Locke, E., and Latham, G. (1984). *Goal setting: a motivational technique that works*. Englewood Cliffs, NJ: Prentice-Hall.

Mendenhall, M., and Oddou, G. (1985). The dimensions of expatriate acculturation. *Academy of Management Review, 10*, 39–47.

Mendenhall, M., and Oddou, G. (1986a). The cognitive, psychological, and social contexts of Japanese management. *Asia Pacific Journal of Management, 4*(1), 24–37.

Mendenhall, M., and Oddou, G. (1986b). Acculturation profiles of expatriate managers: implications for cross-cultural training programs. *Columbia Journal of World Business, 21*, 73–9.

Mendenhall, M., Dunbar, E., and Oddou, G. (1987). Expatriate selection, training, and career-pathing: a review and critique. *Human Resource Management, 26*, 331–45.

Miller, E. (1973). The international selection decision: a study of managerial behavior in the selection decision process. *Academy of Management Journal, 16*, 234–52.

Misa, K. F., and Fabricatore, J. M. (1979). Return on investment of overseas personnel. *Financial Executive*, April, 42–6.

Ohmae, K. (1989). Managing in a borderless world. *Harvard Business Review*, May–June, 152–61.

Roberts, K. H., and Boyacigiller, N. (1982). *Issues in cross national management research: the state of the art*. Paper presented at the National Meeting of the Academy of Management, New York.

Runzheimer Executive Report. (1984). Expatriation/repatriation survey. No. 31. Rochester, Wis.

Schollhammer, H. (1975). Current research on international and comparative management issues. *Management International Review, 15*, 29–45.

Schwind, H. F. (1985). The state of the art in cross-cultural management training. In R. Doktor (ed.), *International Human Resource Development Annual* (Vol. 1, pp. 7–15). Alexandria, Va: ASTD.

Stephens, G. K., and Black, J. S. (1991). The impact of the spouse's career orientation on managers during international transfers. *Journal of Management Studies 28*(4), 417–28.

Stewart, R. (1982). *Choices for managers*. Englewood Cliffs, NJ: Prentice-Hall.

Sundaram, A. (1990). *Unique aspects of MNCs: a top-down perspective*. Working paper series, Amos Tuck School of Business Administration, Dartmouth College.

Torbiorn, I. (1982). *Living abroad*. New York: Wiley.

Tung, R. (1981). Selecting and training of personnel for overseas assignments. *Columbia Journal of World Business, 16*, 68–78.

Tung, R. (1984). *Key to Japan's economic strength: human power*. Lexington, Mass.: Lexington Books.

Tung, R. (1988). *The new expatriates*. Cambridge, Mass.: Ballinger.

Vaill, P. (1989). *Managing as a performing art: new ideas for a world of chaotic change*. San Francisco, Calif.: Jossey-Bass.

Vroom, V. (1964). *Work and motivation*. New York: Wiley.

Zeira, Y. (1975). Overlooked personnel problems in multinational corporations. *Columbia Journal of World Business, 10*(2), 96–103.

Evalde Mutabazi and C. Brooklyn Derr

SOCOMETAL: REWARDING AFRICAN WORKERS

It was a most unusual meeting at a local café in Dakar. Diop, a young Senegalese engineer who was educated at one of Frances's elite engineering *grandes écoles* in Lyon, was meeting with N'Diaye, a model factory worker to whom other workers from his tribe often turned when there were personal or professional difficulties. N'Diaye was a chief's son, but he didn't belong to the union and he was not an official representative of any group within the factory.

Socometal is a metal container and can company. While multinational, this particular plant is a joint venture wherein 52 percent is owned by the French parent company and 48 percent is Senegalese. Over the last twenty years Socometal has grown in size from 150 to 800 employees and it has returns of about 400 million FCFA (African francs) or $144 million. The firm is often held up as a model in terms of its Africanization of management policies, whereby most managers are now West African with only 8–10 top managers coming from France.

During the meeting N'Diaye asked Diop if he would accept an agreement to pay each worker for two extra hours in exchange for a 30 percent increase in daily production levels. If so, N'Diaye would be the guarantor for this target production level that would enable the company to meet the order in the shortest time period. "If you accept my offer," he said with a smile, "we could even produce more. We are at 12,000 [units] a day, but we've never been confronted with this situation. I would never have made this proposal to Mr. Bernard but, if you agree today, I will see that the 20,000 [unit] level is reached as of tomorrow evening. I'll ask each worker to find ways of going faster, to communicate this to the others and to help each other if they have problems . . ."

Mr. Olivier Bernard, a graduate of Ecole Centrale in Paris (one of France's more prestigious engineering schools), was the French production manager, and Diop was the assistant production manager. Mr. Bernard was about 40 and had not succeeded at climbing the hierarchal ladder in the parent company. Some report that this was due to his tendency to be arrogant, uncommunicative and negative. His family lived in a very nice neighborhood in Marseille, and it was his practice to come to Dakar, precisely organize the work using various flowcharts, tell Diop exactly what was expected by a certain date and then return to France for periods of two to six weeks. This time he maintained that he had contracted a virus and needed to return for medical treatment.

Shortly before Mr. Bernard fell ill, Socometal agreed to a contract requiring them to reach in short time a volume of production never before achieved. Mr. Bernard, after having done a quick calculation, declared, "We'll never get that from our workers – c'est impossible!" After organizing as best he could, he left for Marseille.

Diop pondered what N'Diaye had proposed, and then he sought the opinions of influential people in different departments. Some of the French and Italian expatriates told him they were sure that the workers would not do overtime, but most agreed it was worth a try. Two days after his meeting with N'Diaye, Diop felt confident enough to take the risk. The next morning N'Diaye and Diop met in front of the factory and Diop gave his agreement on the condition that the 30 percent rise in daily production levels be reached that evening. He and the management would take a final decision on a wage increase only after assessing the results and on evaluating the ability of the workers to maintain this level of production in the long run.

The reasons given by the French and Italian expatriates for why the Senegalese would not perform overtime or speed up their productivity are interesting. One older French logistics manager said, "Africans aren't lazy but they work to live, and once they have enough they refuse to do more. It won't make any sense to them to work harder or longer for more pay." And the Italian human resource manager exclaimed, "We already tried two years ago to get them to do more faster. We threatened to fire anyone caught going too slow or missing more than one day's work per month, and we told them they would all get bonuses if they reached the production target. We had the sense that they were laughing behind our backs and doing just enough to keep their jobs while maintaining the same production levels."

Four days after their first negotiation, the contract between Diop and N'Diaye went into action. Throughout the day N'Diaye gave his job on the line to two of his colleagues in order to have enough time and energy to mobilize all the workers. The workers found the agreement an excellent initiative. "This will be a chance to earn a bit more money, but especially to show them [the French management] that we're more capable than they think," declared one of the Senegalese foremen. From its first day of application the formula worked wonders. Working only one extra hour per day, every work unit produced 8 percent more than was forecast by Diop and N'Diaye. Over the next two months, the daily production level oscillated between 18,000 and 22,000 units per day – between 38 and 43 percent more than the previous daily production. It was at this production level, never experienced during the history of the company, that Mr. Bernard found things when he returned from his illness.

"I", said Diop, "was very happy to see the workers so proud of their results, so satisfied with their pay raise and finally really involved in their work. . . . In view of some expatriates' attitudes it was a veritable miracle. . . . But, instead of rejoicing, Mr. Bernard reproached me for giving two hours' pay to the workers, who were only really doing one hour more than usual. 'By making this absurd decision,' he said, 'you have put the management in danger of losing its authority over the workers. You have acted against house rules. . . . You have created a precedent too costly for our business. Now, we must stop this ridiculous operation as quickly as possible. We must apply work regulations. . . .' And he slammed the door in my face before I had the time to say anything. After all, he has more power than me in this company, which is financed 52 percent by French people. Nevertheless, I thought I would go to see the managing director and explain myself and present my arguments. I owed this action to N'Diaye and his workers, who had trusted me, and I didn't care if it made Bernard any angrier."

In the meantime the workers decided to maintain the new production level in order to honor their word to N'Diaye and Diop. A foreman and friend of N'Diaye stated, "At least he knows how to listen and speak to us like men."

The foreman indicated, however, that they might return to the former production level if Bernard dealt with them as he did before.

CASE DISCUSSION QUESTIONS

1. What are the underlying cultural assumptions for Mr. Bernard and how are these different from the basic assumptions of N'Diaye and Diop?
2. What would you do if you were Bernard's boss, the managing director?
3. In what ways is a reward system a cultural phenomenon? How might you design an effective reward system for Senegal?

Günter K. Stahl and
Mark E. Mendenhall

ANDREAS WEBER'S REWARD FOR SUCCESS IN AN INTERNATIONAL ASSIGNMENT: A RETURN TO AN UNCERTAIN FUTURE

Andreas Weber's mind would not stop racing. Normally, an intense run in the evening had the effect of dissipating his worries, but tonight this did not work. The further he jogged along his standard route on the banks of the Hudson River, the more he could not get out of his mind the letter he knew he must write tomorrow. "How had it all come to this?" he wondered. This thought triggered his memory back seven years, to the initial event that had set in motion the process that led to his current trouble.

ANDREAS' DECISION TO PURSUE AN INTERNATIONAL CAREER

Andreas remembered the occasion clearly. Herr Görner, the managing director, had walked into his office at the Frankfurt headquarters of his bank, and offered him the chance to participate in a company-wide international leadership development program. Herr Görner explained that the program involved an international assignment with the intention of fostering the professional development of young, aspiring managers. After their overseas assignments, the trainees would constitute a pool of internationally experienced young managers with the potential for senior management positions at corporate headquarters. Andreas accepted the offer on the spot, with pride. He had worked very hard since joining the bank and felt that his efforts had finally paid off.

The program started with a one-week seminar at a leading business school in the United States. The CEO had flown in from Frankfurt, demonstrating the commitment of top management to this program. In his speech to the participants, the CEO stressed that the major challenge and "number one" priority for the bank in the future was globalization. He made it clear that international experience was a key value and a prerequisite for promotion into the ranks of senior management. Andreas felt confident that he had made the right decision in accepting the offer and in pursuing an international career.

Shortly after the program started, an unexpected vacancy opened up in the bank's New York branch, and Andreas was asked if he was interested. He discussed the prospect of a three-year assignment to New York with his wife, Lina. The offer looked very attractive from all angles, and they quickly agreed that Andreas should accept it. Two months later, he was transferred to New York.

ASSIGNMENT NEW YORK: THE FIRST YEAR

Andreas remembered the day of his arrival as if it were yesterday. He arrived at JFK Airport early in the afternoon. Since his only contact point about the job assignment was corporate HR in Frankfurt, he assumed that they had made all the necessary arrangements with the New York office for his arrival. However, no one came to the airport to pick him up. He took a taxi and went directly to the New York branch of the bank. When he arrived, he was not sure where he should go. He had not been informed about whom he should contact after his arrival, so he went straight to the office of the head of the corporate finance department where he was supposed to work. When he entered the office and told the secretary that he was the new manager from Germany, she looked at her notebook, shook her head, and told him that they were not expecting anybody. Confused, Andreas rushed to the HR department and soon found that several misunderstandings had occurred. First, it was not the corporate finance department but the credit department that had requested his transfer. Second, contrary to what he was told in Frankfurt, there was only a non-management position vacant. They were looking for a credit analyst, basically the same job that he had done in Germany.

Andreas shook his head in reaction to the memory: "There I stood, in what was supposed to be my new office, with three pieces of luggage on the desk, and wondering whether I should stay or take the next plane home!"

Why he decided to stay in New York, he could never quite figure out. In retrospect it was probably just a split-second decision to make the best of the situation. The whirl of images of the next two months flashed across his memory: rushed days and nights trying to learn the ropes of a new office with new procedures, looking for a place to live, meeting new people, and exploring new places. Then a clear memory interrupted the collage of memories of those first two months – Lina's arrival. Lina, his wife, and their three-year-old daughter, Anne-Marie, followed Andreas to New York two months after his arrival. They moved into a small house on the outskirts of New York. Lina knew New York pretty well, as she had worked there for a couple of months as an intern at a reinsurance company. She arrived excited to rediscover her favorite restaurants, art galleries and museums.

Except for occasional attacks of homesickness, Lina was satisfied with her new life. The week after they had moved into their new house, they received a dinner invitation from a young married couple next door. To their surprise, their American neighbors quickly embraced the Webers. Since Lina was not able to get a work permit, she joined her new acquaintance in doing volunteer work at a local art museum. Anne-Marie spent every second afternoon at a local kindergarten, which gave Lina plenty of time to pursue her own interests. At the end of their first year in the United States, a second daughter, Elena, was born. By then, the Webers had already made several more new friends, both Americans and other expatriates. When the Webers stepped off the plane at JFK after their first home leave to Germany, it felt more like they were coming home than returning to a temporary assignment.

ANDREAS' FAST-TRACK CAREER AS AN EXPATRIATE

Professionally, things had gone extremely well during this time period. The New York branch of the bank had been right at the start of a boom-phase that lasted for several years. Throughout the boom, the bank's staff increased significantly. After eight months of working in the back office, Andreas was promoted to supervisor of a group of credit analysts. Then, one year after his first promotion, a position opened up at the senior management level. The deputy head of the rapidly expanding corporate finance department – a German expatriate – had unexpectedly left for a job at one of their American competitors, and the bank had to fill his position with a manager who spoke fluent German, was familiar with the finance departments of a number of German and other European companies, and was instantly available. Andreas was asked if he was willing to extend his foreign service contract for another three years and accept the position as deputy head of the corporate finance department. After discussing it with Lina, Andreas accepted.

In the fifth year of his assignment, Andreas made another step upward in his career. His boss retired, and Andreas was promoted to head of the corporate finance department. He was now one of five managing directors in the branch. When Andreas signed his new contract, it was agreed that he would stay with the New York branch of the bank for another three years and would then return to the bank's German headquarters.

These were warm memories, memories that somewhat buffered the intensity of Andreas' frustration and anger over his current situation. But, as he continued running, the warmth of the past dissipated into the turmoil of the present.

"It all started with that promotion," he muttered to himself. As head of the corporate finance department, Andreas' professional and private lives had unexpectedly changed. He was now responsible for a huge area – his business activities no longer concentrated on North American subsidiaries of foreign-based companies, but included their headquarters in Europe and East Asia. In the first six months of his new job, Andreas had traveled almost 100,000 miles, mainly on business flights to Europe. His extensive traveling was hard on Lina. She felt alone, and was concerned about their children's education. Their eldest daughter, Anne-Marie, was now nine years old and had spent most of her life outside of Germany. Lina was also concerned about her missing out on a German high school education. Anne-Marie's German language skills had gradually deteriorated over the last two years, and that troubled Lina as well. Their second daughter, Elena, was attending kindergarten and, except for the yearly home leave, she had no contact with other German children. Elena's German was quite poor. In fact, both Anne-Marie and Elena considered themselves Americans.

Lina also started to be more and more discontented with her life as a housewife. Obtaining a work permit in the United States remained impossible, and it was not easy for her to find new volunteer activities to quench her interests. To make things worse, Lina's father fell ill and died in that same year, leaving her mother alone. Andreas remembered the long conversations he had had with Lina during this period of time, many of which were by telephone from hotel rooms in faraway places. When he was home, they spoke often in the quiet of their living room, and on long walks – Andreas lost count of the multitude of times they had talked as they walked through the same park he was now running through.

ANDREAS' DILEMMA: STAYING IN NEW YORK OR RETURNING HOME TO AN UNCERTAIN FUTURE

"It was an extremely difficult situation," Andreas remembered, "not so much for the children, but for Lina and me. . . . From a professional standpoint, my assignment to New York was the best thing that could ever happen to me: I worked in the financial center of the world; I loved my job, the freedom of being away from the bureaucracy at corporate headquarters, the opportunities to travel; I became a member of the senior management team at a very young age – impossible if I stayed in Germany. Personally, we were also happy: our children felt at home in New York; we were quickly embraced by our neighbors and the expatriate community; we had many friends. . . . The question we continually wrestled with was: 'Does it make sense to give all these up for a return to an uncertain future in Germany?' In principle, the answer would clearly have been: 'No.' But, on a long-term basis, moving back to Germany appeared to be the best solution for our children. After all, we felt responsible for their future."

After several weeks of consideration and discussion, Lina and Andreas decided to move back to Germany. This was about a year ago. Immediately after the decision was made, Andreas contacted the bank's corporate headquarters and informed the human resource executive in charge of international assignments about his decision. Three weeks later, Andreas received a short letter from him, stating that there were currently no positions available in Germany at his level. Part of the problem, Andreas was told, was due to the current economic downturn in Europe, but since several new branches were due to be opened in the eastern part of Germany over the course of the next year, he was told that chances were good that the company would be able to find him a suitable return assignment within the next six months. Since then, Andreas had had several meetings with executives at corporate headquarters, as well as with managers of domestic branches of the bank, but he still had not been offered any reentry position.

Lina gradually became discouraged. She had told her mother that they were coming home immediately after they made their decision to return to Germany, but eight months had passed, and her mother kept asking when they were coming. Andreas' parents were persistent in their queries as well. Finally, last week, Andreas received a telephone call from the corporate HR department, in which he was informed that they had found what they called a "challenging" return assignment. They offered him the position of deputy head of a medium-sized branch of the bank in the eastern part of Germany. Andreas was told that a letter explaining the details of the position offer had already been sent.

THE OFFER

The memory of opening that letter and reading it, and the resulting emotions of anger, betrayal, disbelief, and frustration, all came back to him. He stopped running, and sat down on a park bench alongside the jogging trail. "Not only will I earn little more than half the salary that I currently make in New York, I will not be able to use the skills and experiences that I gained during my overseas assignment, I will be out of touch with all the important decisions being made at headquarters, and on top of that I will be posted to this God-forsaken place!" he thought bitterly.

With all the frustrations and anger welling up in his chest, Andreas thought cynically, "The bank's promotion policy – if there ever was any rational policy – is to punish those who are really committed to the organization. They assign you to one of those programs for highfliers and send you abroad, but there is no career planning whatsoever. If there just happens to be a job vacant when you return, you are lucky. If not, they let you wait and wait and wait, until you finally accept the most ridiculous job offer. ... Their slogan that international experience is a key value and a prerequisite for promotion into the ranks of senior management is garbage! If you look at the actual promotion and career development practices in this organization, it becomes clear it's only lip service ... and lies! ... In this bank, the better you perform overseas, the more you get screwed when you come back."

He began to wonder if he should accept the offer. Perhaps they should just stay in New York and make their home here. But then images of Lina, Lina's mother, Anne-Marie, Elena, and his parents, and all of their combined needs enveloped him.

Leaning back on the park bench, he blankly stared down the path that would lead out of the park and into the street, and then home.

This case was prepared by Günter K. Stahl, Associate Professor of Organizational Behavior at INSEAD, and Mark E. Mendenhall, J. Burton Frierson Professor of Leadership at the University of Tennessee. It is intended to be used as a basis for class discussion rather than to illustrate either effective or ineffective handling of an administrative situation.

Martin Hilb

COMPUTEX CORPORATION

Goteborg, May 30, 1985

Mr. Peter Jones
Vice President – Europe
Computex Corporation
San Francisco
USA

The writers of this letter are the headcount of the Sales Department of Computex Sweden, AS, except for the Sales Manager.

We have decided to bring to your attention a problem which unsolved probably will lead to a situation where the majority among us will leave the company within a rather short period of time. None of us want to be in this situation, and we are approaching you purely as an attempt to save the team for the benefit of ourselves as well as Computex Corporation.

We consider ourselves an experienced, professional, and sales-oriented group of people. Computex Corporation is a company which we are proud to work for. The majority among us have been employed for several years. Consequently, a great number of key customers in different areas of Sweden see us as representatives of Computex Corporation. It is correct to say that the many excellent contacts we have made have been established over years; many of them are friends of ours.

These traits give a very short background because we have never met you. What kind of problem forces us to such a serious step as to contact you?

Problems arise as a result of character traits and behavior of our General Manager, Mr. Miller.

Firstly, we are more and more convinced that we are tools that he is utilizing in order to "climb the ladder". In meetings with us individually, or as a group, he gives visions about the future, how he values us, how he wants to delegate and involve us in business, the importance of cooperation and communication, etc. When it comes to the point, these phrases turn out to be only words.

Mr. Miller loses his temper almost daily, and his outbursts and reactions are not equivalent to the possible error. His mood and views can change almost from hour to hour. This fact causes a situation where we feel uncertain when facing him and consequently are reluctant to do so. Regarding human relationships, his behavior is not acceptable, especially for a manager.

The extent of the experience of this varies within the group due to our location. Some of us are seldom in the office.

Secondly, we have experienced clearly that he has various means of suppressing and discouraging people within the organization.

The new "victim" now is our Sales Manager, Mr. Johansson. Because he is our boss, it is obvious that we regret such a situation, which to a considerable extent influences our working conditions.

There are also other victims among us. It is indeed very difficult to carry through what is stated in our job descriptions.

We feel terribly sorry and wonder how it can be possible for one person almost to ruin a whole organization.

If this group consisted of people less mature, many of us would have left Computex Corporation already. So far only one has left the company due to the above reasons.

From September 1, two new Sales Representatives are joining the company. We regret very much that new employees get their first contact with the company under the present circumstances. An immediate action is therefore required.

It is not our objective to get rid of Mr. Miller as General Manager. Without going into details, we are thankful for what he has done to the company from a business point of view. If he could control his mood, show some respect for his colleagues, keep words, and stick to plans, we believe that we can succeed under his leadership.

We are fully aware of the seriousness of contacting you, and we have been in doubt whether or not to contact you directly before talking to Mr. Miller.

After serious discussions and considerations, we have reached the conclusion that a problem of this nature unfortunately cannot be solved without some sort of action from the superior. If possible, direct confrontation must be avoided. It can only make things worse.

We are hoping for a positive solution.

Six of your Sales Representatives in Sweden

Peter Jones let out a long sigh as he gazed over the letter from Sweden. "What do I do now?" he thought, and began to reflect on the problem. He wondered who was right and who was wrong in this squabble, and he questioned whether he would ever get all the information necessary to make a wise decision. He didn't know much about the Swedes, and was unsure whether this was strictly a work problem or a "cross-cultural" problem. "How can I tease those two issues apart?" he asked himself, as he locked his office and made his way down the hallway to the elevator.

As Peter pulled out of the parking garage and onto the street, he began to devise a plan to deal with the problem. "This will be a test of my conflict management skills," he thought, "no doubt about it!" As he merged into the freeway traffic from the on-ramp and began his commute home, he began to wish that he had never sent Miller to Sweden in the first place. "But would Gonzalez or Harris have done any better? Would I have done any better?" Few answers seemed to come to him as he plodded along in the bumper-to-bumper traffic on Interstate 440.

PART 4

Challenges and trends in IHRM: employee relations, mergers and acquisitions and international joint ventures, global virtual teams and ethics

Cases:
- **Joyce S. Osland and Pedro Ferreira**
  ANATOMY OF A PARAGUAYAN STRIKE

- **Ngo Minh Hang**
  THE CASE OF ABB TRANSFORMER IN VIETNAM

- **Joseph J. DiStefano**
  JOHANNES VAN DEN BOSCH SENDS AN EMAIL

Ruth V. Aguilera and John C. Dencker

THE ROLE OF HUMAN RESOURCE MANAGEMENT IN CROSS-BORDER MERGERS AND ACQUISITIONS

INTRODUCTION

MERGERS AND ACQUISITIONS (M&As) have become the dominant mode of growth for firms seeking competitive advantage in an increasingly complex and global business economy (Adler, 1997). Nevertheless, M&As are beset by numerous problems (Newburry and Zeira, 1997), with 50 per cent of domestic acquisitions – and 70 per cent of cross-border acquisitions – failing to produce intended results (Capron, 1999). Scholars have examined these problems in terms of strategic market entry choice (Hennart and Park, 1993), market valuations (Jensen and Ruback, 1983), value creation (Haspeslagh and Jemison, 1991) and firm performance (Galbraith and Stiles, 1984; Chatterjee, 1986; Blackburn and Lang, 1989), finding that difficulties in M&As trace to a lack of a compelling strategic rationale, unrealistic expectations of possible synergies and paying too much for acquired firms. However, although financial and strategic studies have significantly increased our knowledge of M&As, this research is incomplete, in large measure due to a failure to account for personnel issues.

Frequent calls within the human resource management field and international business, to study the human side of international M&As, have generated studies exploring the role of HRM in M&As, such as studies of personnel issues surrounding M&As that focus on top management turnover following an acquisition (Walsh, 1988; Krug and Hegarty, 2001). However, most of the existing research within the HRM field relies on anecdotal evidence of personnel issues in M&As, resulting in little systematic theory (Hunt and Downing, 1990; Buono and Bowditch, 1989; Marks and Mirvis, 1998) that focuses on domestic M&As. In part, this lack of attention with regard to HRM in M&As stems from the marginal role that CEOs have designated to the HRM function in M&As, particularly in the early stages of the M&A process. Perhaps reflecting the sometimes low relative standing of the personnel function within the firm, the M&A literature has focused primarily on financial due diligence and strategic issues in the merger process, with HRM being an afterthought that becomes relevant only in the integration stage of an M&A when the merger is implemented.

The failure to account for personnel issues is somewhat surprising since HRM has the potential to play an important role in M&A integration, for example, by managing personnel conflict, reinforcing the new HRM system and corporate culture and providing leadership and communication to reduce turnover. Yet, the literature does not tackle from a theoretical point of view how HRM systems and practices create value by helping to realize potential postmerger synergies. We argue that the strategic literature provides a useful starting point, since the role of HRM in an M&A will be conditional upon the strategic rationale chosen by the merging firms. In particular, HRM strategies in the integration stage of an M&A should be tightly aligned to the undertaken M&A strategy in a manner that enhances the likelihood of successful M&A outcomes. For example, staffing decisions will differ depending on whether the M&A strategy requires the elimination of redundancies or, conversely, the preservation of human capital and knowledge. We examine the fit between M&A strategy and HR strategy by looking at the effects of organizational resources, processes and values in the M&A integration stage.

An additional difficulty for HRM in merger integration is that realizing synergies is often much easier in domestic M&As than in cross-border M&As. In particular, given difficulties in managing fit among various HRM practices in individual firms (Wright and Snell, 1998), integrating HRM systems from different national and organizational contexts is likely to create a myriad of uncertainties. In principle, we would agree that the uniqueness of national environments makes the role of HRM in cross-border M&As differ significantly from M&As occurring within countries. Without claiming a convergence argument, we acknowledge that differences between firms in the international arena are largely a matter of degree, as pointed out by Sparrow et al. (1994). That is, even though evidence indicates that many HRM practices in cross-border M&As tend to converge on a single best model – making the role of HRM more predictable – it also demonstrates that other practices implemented in the integration stage retain the country-specific characteristics of one of the merging firms (Child et al., 2001; Faulkner et al., 2002). As Child and colleagues note, the issue of integration "involves considering not just 'how much?' but also 'on the basis of which practice?' " (2001: 17).

In effect, M&A integration is especially difficult in cross-border M&As due to the embeddedness of firms undergoing acquisitions in their respective national contexts. Thus, in order to understand the role that HRM plays in contributing to the success of cross-border M&As, it is important to consider not only the fit between M&A strategy and HRM strategy, but also the contingencies at the national level in the merger process. By so doing, we can obtain an assessment of "the 'fit' between environmental conditions and the structure and strategies that firms put in place" (Child et al., 2003: 244).

National contexts have been categorized along many dimensions, such as legal (La Porta *et al.*, 1998), cultural (Hofstede, 1980), financial (Zysman, 1983), employment systems (Marsden, 1999), economic organization and control (Whitley, 1999) or corporate governance regimes (Aguilera and Jackson, 2003). Following Hall and Soskice (2001), we divide countries into two broad categories that encompass most economic and social aspects of firm life. We propose that, when the two merging firms belong to the same country group, HRM strategic fit will be different than when the two merging firms belong to two different country groups.

In sum, we suggest that it is incumbent to further understand not only the "what" and "how" of acquisition strategy – such as the role the HRM function plays – but also "which" HRM elements lead to expected outcomes for cross-border merged firms. This paper is a theoretical attempt to get at these issues. We begin by analysing strategic rationales for different types of M&As, examining the fit between M&A strategies and HRM strategies. We then consider how personnel issues are contingent upon the embeddedness of mergers within the broader institutional context. Based on these contingencies and strategies, we specify broad roles of HRM in the integration stage of a cross-border M&A as they relate to organizational resources, processes and values when a merger takes place within as well as across national groups. Finally, because the HRM practices that we discuss do not exhaust all possible types, we conclude by discussing the validity of our framework in other contexts.

STRATEGIC FIT BETWEEN M&As AND HRM

The strategic HRM literature posits the importance of aligning a firm's HRM strategy to its business strategy (Fombrun *et al.*, 1984; Schuler and Jackson, 1987). Based on Chandler's (1962) notion that organizational structure follows an organization's strategy, Fombrun and colleagues (1984) emphasize that there is a tight fit between strategy, structure and HRM, with strategy being the dominant force. Schuler and Jackson (1987) confirm this strategic fit notion, showing that firms that differed in their strategies would use the same HRM practices in different ways and that firms that changed strategies were likely to change their HRM practices. Similarly, Sanz-Valle and colleagues (1999) find a link between some HRM practices and business strategy in a study of Spanish companies.

We argue that, for merging firms to integrate successfully, they need to align their HRM strategy to their M&A strategy. Thus, it is important to have a clear understanding of M&A strategies to be able to specify the role that HRM should play. Moreover, in order to consider the fit between M&A and HRM strategies, and to help make sense of HRM challenges in the different types of M&As, we rely on three conceptual tools: resources, processes and values (Bower, 2001). *Resources* are defined as tangible assets, such as money and people, and intangible assets, such as brands and relationships. In the context of HRM in M&As, decisions about resources involve staffing and retention issues, with termination decisions being particularly important. *Processes* refer to activities that firms use to convert the resources into valuable goods and services. For example, in our case, these would be training and development programmes as well as appraisal and rewards systems. Finally, *values* are the way in which employees think about what they do and why they do it. Values shape employees' priorities and decision-making.

Below, we analyse key issues in the strategic literature with regard to M&As in light of recent research by Bower (2001) and on M&A strategies. We identify the fit between this M&A typology and HRM strategies and practices by using the resources, processes and values framework.

Strategies for M&As

Firms can undertake a number of common M&A strategies in order to obtain competitive advantage. For example, scholars have profitably used the Federal Trade Commission (FTC) typology of M&As developed in the 1970s – namely horizontal, vertical, product extension, market extension and unrelated M&As (Federal Trade Commission, 1975) – to study the M&A process (Buono and Bowditch, 1989). However, the merger climate of the 1990s has led to the creation of new forms of M&A strategies that are not adequately captured in the FTC framework. Thus, in this article we refer to Bower's (2001) recent strategic M&A typology, which was established by a group of scholars who conducted an extensive yearlong study of firms involved in M&As. This typology captures effectively the nature of cross-border M&As that were occurring during the 1990s, and it allows us to provide the necessary theoretical link between business and HRM strategies through considering decisions of firms involved in this transaction process.

Bower (2001) proposes five distinct M&A strategies: (1) the overcapacity M&A; (2) the geographic roll-up M&A; (3) the product or market extension M&A; (4) the M&A as R&D; and (5) the industry convergence M&A. We discuss each of them in turn, highlighting the potential general HRM implications in terms of resources, processes and values.

An *overcapacity M&A* occurs when an acquiring company seeks to eliminate excess capacity to create a more efficient corporation. In effect, the acquiring company's strategic goal is to achieve economies of scale in order to gain market share, doing so in part by eliminating human resources. This type of M&A often arises in oligopolistic industries characterized by excess capacity and involves firms of similar size. For example, there have been a number of overcapacity M&As in the petroleum sector (e.g. British Petroleum's acquisition of Amoco) and the automobile sector (e.g. Daimler's acquisition of Chrysler). An important concern in this type of M&A is that, although processes and values of the merging entities are frequently similar, relative status differences stemming from a merger of near equals can create problems in M&A integration.

A *geographic roll-up M&A* takes place when companies seek to expand geographically, often with operating units remaining at the local level. In many instances, large companies acquire smaller companies that they try to keep intact and therefore these firms tend to retain local managers. These types of M&As are common in the banking sector, as exemplified by Banc One's acquisitions of several regional banks. Although these M&As are similar to overcapacity M&As in that both involve consolidation of businesses, they differ significantly in that geographic roll-up M&As are more likely to occur at an earlier point in an industry's life-cycle. Strategically, roll-ups "are designed to achieve economies of scale and scope and are associated with the building of industry giants" (Bower, 2001: 98), while overcapacity M&As seek to reduce capacity and duplication. Although in geographic roll-up M&As human resources are less disposable, the processes and values of the merging entities are likely to differ more than in the overcapacity M&A. Nevertheless, since the size of the acquirer tends to be greater than that of the acquired firm, conflict stemming from status differences is possibly not as prevalent as in the overcapacity M&A.

A *product* or *market extension M&A* involves expanding product lines or expanding geographically across borders. This type of M&A occurs when the acquiring and acquired companies are functionally related in production and/or distribution but sell products that do not compete directly with one another, or when a company seeks to diversify geographically, such as when two companies manufacture the same product, yet sell it in different markets (Buono and Bowditch, 1989: 63). In effect, in this type of M&A, firms seek to achieve long-term strategic goals by investing in less saturated markets – often doing so to obtain economies of scale necessary for global competition (Weston *et al.*, 2001: 350). The likelihood of success of product or market extension M&As depends on the relative size of the merging firms and the experience of the acquired firm in M&As. For example, large firms such as GE acquire many relatively small firms, thereby increasing their chances of subsequent successful mergers.

Similarly to in the geographic roll-up M&A, human resources in product or market extension M&As frequently remain unchanged in the new entity. However, in product or market extension mergers, some firms have difficulties in changing the processes and values of acquired firms, particularly in cross-border M&As. For example, Marks & Spencer experienced geographical distribution problems when it acquired the Canadian firm Peoples Department Stores (Bower, 2001). By contrast, when GE acquired the Italian engine producer Nuovo Pignone in 1992, it introduced its systems only sequentially over time (Bower, 2001). What GE felt was most crucial in the short term was for Nuovo Pignone's managers to use GE's resources to develop their business.

An *M&A as a substitute for R&D* occurs when acquisitions are used as a means of gaining access to new R&D knowledge or technological capabilities by acquiring innovative firms rather than producing the knowledge in-house (Granstrand and Sjolander, 1990). Acquiring firms in this type of M&A tend to be larger than the acquired firm, and sometimes have significant practical merger experience, as in the case of Microsoft and Cisco Systems.

In an M&A as a substitute for R&D, the retention of human resources and knowledge is a paramount goal. Processes and values of the newly formed entity will, however, probably need to be changed, a complex proposition since the entrepreneurial employees often feel their values are constrained by the more bureaucratic structure of the acquiring firm. The success of this type of cross-border M&A will therefore depend on the acquired firm's integration capabilities and the acquiring firm's learning capacity. Integration issues will, however, be industry contingent. For example, the product development cycle is often much shorter in information technology (IT) firms than in pharmaceutical firms, indicating the need for more rapid integration in M&As in the IT industry.

An *industry convergence M&A* involves creating a new industry from existing industries whose boundaries are eroding. An example of this type of M&A is the Viacom acquisition of Paramount and Blockbuster. Although this type of merger will probably increase in the future, it is rare and not yet fully understood, making it difficult to analyse. In addition, acquired companies in this type of merger are typically given wide berth, perhaps to a greater extent than in the M&As as a substitute for R&D, with integration driven by a need to create value rather than a desire to create a symmetrical organization.

In sum, the brief discussion above demonstrates that each M&A strategy would involve different HRM strategies. In the next section, we include another layer of complexity by bringing in the influence of the national context.

THE ENVIRONMENTAL CONTEXT OF CROSS-BORDER M&As

Contingency theory suggests that firm strategies and structures will be dependent upon environmental conditions, the more varied the environment the more differentiated the structure (Lawrence and Lorsch, 1967). As certain parts of an organization are more open to environmental influences, the effect of the broader context on organizational structure will vary within organizations. For example, Schuler and Jackson (1987) argue that managerial practices need to be aligned with environmental demands so that desired work behaviours arise, and Schuler (2001) shows how this notion can be effectively implemented in international joint ventures.

In effect, organizations are embedded in national and supra-national environments that can provide a source of competitive advantage for, as well as act as a constraint on, cross-border M&As. For example, environments influence business practices through legal systems such as the case of the European Commission, which objected to the $37 million marriage between two American telephone companies, MCI and WorldCom. The result is that organizations do not operate in a vacuum; rather, they are located within certain national boundaries. The key therefore is to discern when and how the national environment influences cross-border M&As.

The notion of embeddedness suggests that environmental characteristics such as institutions or culture influence organizational strategies and structures. National culture is often reflected in a country's organizational and managerial practices, such as individual performance awards, team-oriented, short-term results and decentralized and informal organizational structures (Schneider, 1989). Countries perceived to be similar or compatible along national cultural dimensions and business styles tend to engage in a higher rate of business partnerships among themselves (Cartwright and Cooper, 1993). Firms that engage in cross-border M&As therefore need to be aware of the possible consequences of national cultural differences, as is suggested by cross-cultural managerial studies showing that behaviours such as individualism and openness to foreign cultures differ across national boundaries (Adler *et al.*, 1986) and might influence cross-border M&As (Gertsen *et al.*, 1998).

National cultures are part of a broader institutional environment that also influences how much room for transformation merging firms have. National institutional effects include but are not limited to: the country characteristics of the state; the financial system; education and training systems; labour–management relations (Berger and Dore, 1996; Hollingsworth and Boyer, 1997; Whitley and Kristensen, 1997). All of these nationally embedded institutional settings will differ across countries, providing country-specific firm capabilities and performance profiles (Porter, 1990; Sorge, 1991; Whitley, 1999). Consequently, when two firms belonging to two different countries merge, we should expect some influence from the national environment, although the contingent environmental effects will depend on how different these two countries are along a number of important dimensions. At an abstract level, nations can be divided into two types based on the institutions characterizing their financial and labour market systems: liberal market economies (LME) and co-ordinated market economies (CME) (Hall and Soskice, 2001; Gospel and Pendleton, 2003).

LME countries are distinguished by competitive market arrangements, with supply and demand forces having a large impact on organizational outcomes and processes. In terms of financial systems, LMEs often are seen as "shareholder value" nations, with performance measured by market value, returns evaluated on a short-term basis and the state rarely intervening in the economy. In effect, in these nations, the market for corporate governance focuses on current earnings, with regulatory regimes being tolerant of M&As. Hall and Soskice (2001) note that, among OECD nations, the following countries can be classified as LMEs: Britain, the US, Australia, Canada, New Zealand and Ireland.

In contrast to LMEs, CMEs – such as Germany, Japan, Switzerland and the Benelux and Scandinavian countries – are characterized by non-market relationships (Hall and Soskice, 2001). In these "stakeholder capitalism" national models, employees, suppliers, customers and financial institutions are part of the context within which the overall firm is judged. The market for corporate governance is such that firms are not entirely dependent on publicly available financial data or current returns. Thus, firms can be more long-term oriented and the network of relationships among stakeholders will restrict M&As in a number of ways.

A recent example highlighting the differences in corporate governance between LMEs and CMEs is the successful hostile takeover bid of Mannesmann (German) by Vodafone (English) in 1999. Vodafone not only had to deal with codetermination, but also with an entirely different ownership structure influenced by banks, opaque accounting and disclosure rules, a two-tiered board structure with a strong orientation towards consensus decision-making, different company laws, a German corporate culture with a strong orientation towards production and engineering, and a relatively weak "equity culture" (Hopner and Jackson, 2001).

Adjustments to the national institutional environment are also salient in the HRM field. For instance, HRM practices in CMEs "include more restricted employer autonomy, difficult hiring and firing decisions, lower geographic and professional employee mobility, and a stronger link between type of education and career progression" (Sparrow et al., 1994: 286). In CMEs, firms are obligated to protect employee rights, collective bargaining tends to be co-ordinated, minority shareholders are poorly protected in favour of large owners and corporate returns tend to be measured on a long-term basis. For instance, in German industrial organization, work councils police collective bargaining agreements and training policies inside the companies and have a legal right to intervene in work reorganization (Casper and Hancké, 1999). In addition, German workers tend to have flexible portable skills learned through the vocational training system. By contrast, in LMEs, industrial relations are characterized primarily by open labour market relationships, with firms having the freedom to hire and fire employees almost at will and collective bargaining being uncoordinated and taking place at the firm level. Training and education in LMEs frequently occurs in schools and universities, with skills acquired by employees being relatively general, in part because investment in firm-specific skills can be lost due to poaching.

In the next section, we examine how M&A strategies determine the role of the HRM function for merged entities in these two main national groups: liberal market economies (LME) and co-ordinated market economies (CME). Although the countries we examine do not exhaust all possible types, firms within these market economies have undertaken the majority of large cross-border M&As in the industrialized world. Perhaps as a result, evidence on HRM practices and policies that are enacted during the M&A process are most prevalent for countries in these two economic types (Larsson and Finkelstein, 1999; Birkinshaw and Bresman, 2000; Child et al., 2001; Faulkner et al., 2002).

THE ROLE OF HRM IN CROSS-BORDER M&As

Before conducting our analysis, we briefly review the nature of the merger process. The literature has dissected the M&A process into three main stages: pre-announcement; pre-merger; and integration. The pre-announcement stage involves due diligence. Issues discussed among potential merging firms in this stage are M&A strategy and the financial structure of the deal. The pre-merger stage occurs between the announcement of the merger and its closing date and includes planning for the integration, such as communicating expected roles in the newly formed entity. The integration stage implies the physical integration of the various elements of the M&A following the closing date, including personnel.

In theory, HRM can have an influence on the success of M&As in each stage of the process. For example, during the pre-merger stages, HRM tends to focus on ensuring legal compliance, such as with regard to equal opportunity and collective bargaining agreements (Mirvis and Marks, 1992). HRM can also begin the planning process following deal announcement, for instance by managing retention agreements and assessing compensation differences between the potentially merging entities. Nevertheless, evidence and practice indicate that the main role in which HR can influence M&As is in the integration stage, when M&A practices and policies are implemented. As Child and colleagues (2001) state, the attention "to human resources is particularly important following an acquisition, the more so if cultural differences are involved". As noted, these differences will affect many of the firm practices and policies, often due to variation in the nature of integration across countries. In the following section, we examine the role of HR in the integration phase of cross-border M&As.

Integration stage

An important consideration for HRM in implementing M&As is the level and speed of integration. Two key dimensions identified by Haspeslagh and Jemison (1991) are important in this regard: the need for strategic interdependence or fit and the need for structural autonomy. Based on these two dimensions, they created a four-fold typology of the degree of integration, which also depends on the size of the acquiring firm relative to the acquired firm. With respect to cross-border M&As, Child and colleagues (2001) find differing levels of integration across countries, ranging from no integration, to partial integration, to full integration. For example, they demonstrate that firms in the US and the UK integrate their subsidiaries to a greater extent than do firms in Japan, Germany and France. Similar cross-country variation may be found in terms of integration speed, as Empson (2000) argues that gradual integration is important for success in mergers between professional service firms.

We examine the role of HRM in the integration phase of cross-border M&As through the lens of the resources, processes and values framework. This framework encompasses HRM practices and policies, such as Poole's (1990) culture, organizational structure, performance management, resources and communication and corporate responsibility categories and Pucik's (1988) HR planning, staffing, training and development, appraisal and rewards and organizational design and control dimensions. As the number of HRM practices involved in an M&A can be endless, we pay particular attention to staffing and retention when we refer to *resources*, to training and development, appraisal and reward, as well as other HRM systems and practices when we refer to *processes*, and to national and organizational culture at work when we refer to *values*. In addition, we focus on the following M&A strategies: overcapacity M&As, product or market extension M&As and M&A as R&D. We do not discuss the geographic roll-up M&A because these mergers rarely take place across borders, and we do not discuss the industry convergence M&A as it is relatively new and occurs infrequently. For comparative purposes, we begin our analysis of each M&A strategy within the same country group (i.e. CME–CME or LME–LME) and continue with a discussion of M&A strategy between firms belonging to different national groups (i.e. CME–LME or LME–CME). This systematic comparison of the three M&A strategies, as exemplified in Table 1, allows us to draw sharp comparisons of how national contexts influence cross-border M&As.

Table 1. HR resources, processes and values in cross-border mergers and acquisitions in different market economies

| HR | M&A strategy | | |
	Overcapacity	Product or market extension	M&A as R&D
Resources	• Staffing reduction limited by CME regulations and institutions • Relative ease of lay-offs encourages greater incidence of CME–LME M&As relative to LME–CME	• Expect few lay-offs and focus on retention	• Retention as overriding goal • Hold on to talent and embedded knowledge • Retention dependent on ability to change processes

Processes	• Process differences exacerbated in cross-border M&A
	• Pay for performance use increases, but varies according to market system of acquiring firm
	• Use of training systems increases
	• Use of teams increases
		• Processes can be transformed slowly if acquiring firm is experienced and much larger than acquired firm
		• Experience varies by country, with LME firms integrating more than CME firms
		• Increased training, especially when acquiring firm is in CME
			• Need for assimilation requires change of all processes
			• Speed of assimilation varies by
			  a) industry
			  b) nationality of acquiring firm
			• Limits on use of contingent pay
			• Integration varies by industry

Values	• Values differences create host of problems • Merger of equals exacerbates conflict over control	• Values differences can be minimized through slow assimilation • Communication important • LME firms more likely to reproduce their values than CME firms	• Values less different in high-technology sector • Universal codified knowledge

Overcapacity M&As

Resources. In overcapacity M&As, large-scale lay-offs are inevitable. Thus, the HRM function will have to decide quickly upon a downsizing strategy, with planning and staffing duties – such as outplacement programmes – critical to the success of the merger. The focus on human resources is not, however, solely on downsizing, as retention issues might also play a key role. For example, Walsh (1988) and Buono and Bowditch (1989) argue that top management turnover will be higher in related mergers (e.g. overcapacity M&As) than in unrelated ones because management is familiar with the acquired firm's business in related mergers.

Downsizing in overcapacity M&As will also be contingent on the countries involved in the M&A, with LMEs having fewer institutional constraints on lay-offs than CMEs – although some variation exists in the use of lay-offs within market economies. For example, within LMEs, firms in the US tend to have a more short-term focus with respect to recruitment and termination than do UK firms (Child *et al.*, 2001). However, in the case of M&As involving countries from two different market economies, acquiring firms will be more constrained when the acquired firm is in a CME, in large part because of legal protection offered in these countries to employees, but also due to a long-term view of employment relations among actors in these labour markets.

Processes. In domestic overcapacity M&As, there is often little change made to HRM processes. For example, Child *et al.* (2001: 89) show that, in mergers between UK firms, the acquiring firm made relatively few changes to their practices relative to changes made by foreign firms that purchased UK firms. Similarly, when firms belong to the same market economy type, they will also experience little transformation in processes. Thus, UK firms were found to be closely related to US firms in the nature of their HRM systems, such as the use of pay for performance systems, as well as other practices and management styles (Child *et al.*, 2001: 178). These similarities stem in part from common values held by firms that are located in the same country type.

When an M&A occurs across market economies, strategic fit issues become more complex, as exemplified in the well-known example of a CME firm purchasing an LME firm – the Daimler–Chrysler M&A. This merger shows similar characteristics to domestic overcapacity M&As in that it was a merger of near equals, with conflict arising over numerous issues, including HRM. For example, Daimler-Benz paid executives much less than did Chrysler, making it necessary to adjust the various performance systems. This issue also highlights the contingency of transformation processes on the nationality of the acquiring firm, with firms in LMEs more likely to change processes in acquired firms than firms in CMEs. In the Daimler–Chrysler M&A, Daimler executives felt that it would be impossible to raise the pay of German executives to the level received by the American executives, in no small part because of pressures that would arise from German works councils. Nevertheless, there is some evidence of convergence among other practices – particularly in terms of increased use of teams and training systems – for LME firms in cross-border M&As, as Child and colleagues (2001) find in the case of Japanese and German CME firms that acquired firms in the UK.

Values. Bower (2001) notes that overcapacity M&As are predominantly mergers of near equals, with slight differences in values creating conflict and therefore difficulties in integrating the merging firms. In particular, overcapacity M&As can be difficult to accomplish because of the entrenched processes and values of the firms in the industries in which overcapacity is common. For example, problems may occur in this type of merger strategy because the "loser" in this situation may make things difficult for the acquiring firm.

The Daimler–Chrysler merger highlights how national differences across market economies can exacerbate conflict stemming from a merger of near equals. For example, typical of large German firms, Daimler was a bureaucratic organization that relied heavily on rules and procedures to manage employees. By contrast, Chrysler had a more decentralized decision-making apparatus and was more flexible. Thus, in addition to national culture differences (e.g. having wine with lunch), variation in ways of managing and organizational values created problems in the human dimension of this merger (Vlasic and Stertz, 2000). Obviously, in M&As, plans may change as the merger process unfolds. However, as seems to be evident in the Daimler–Chrysler merger, top managers at Daimler Benz knew from the beginning that they would eventually possess all top positions in the merged entity, but neglected to make this known until a few years into the merger. As a result, a number of key executives have left the firm, highlighting the important role that both trust and communication play in the merger process, particularly in M&As across market economies.

Product or market extension M&As

Resources. In terms of human resources, HRM strategies in product or market extension M&As often involve lay-offs, although the focus will be primarily on retention. That is, lay-offs will not be the overriding goal of acquiring firms since there tends to be little overlap between firms due to the strategic intent of the merger, which involves purchasing new product lines or expanding into new markets.

As in overcapacity M&As, there is some variation across countries in the extent of lay-offs in product or market extension M&As. For example, within LMEs, firms tend to be more short-term oriented towards resources, with US firms that acquired UK firms more likely to reduce staff than in acquisitions across market economies (Child *et al.*, 2001). By contrast, Child and colleagues show that when CME firms purchase LME firms, they take a *laissez-faire* attitude, with German and Japanese firms tending to leave the UK acquisitions as they were, reflecting the CME long-term orientation to staffing and, to a certain extent, cultural traits. Although there is less empirical evidence for the case of acquisitions of CME firms by LME firms, there is perhaps a discernible trend towards retention of human resources. For example, GE often takes a long-term focus when it undertakes cross-border M&As, in part as a response to past negative experiences. The protection offered to employees in CMEs also plays a role in this regard.

Processes. There is more variation in processes across firms in product or market extension M&As than in overcapacity M&As, thus suggesting the need for altering business and HRM systems and practices. That is, although the products among merging firms do not overlap, processes related to the manufacture and distribution of these products may necessitate some changes in other systems. For example, advertising and distribution processes in Quaker Oats were unsuited for Snapple's product line (Bower, 2001), with these systems being changed in an attempt to make the merger work. This tendency to integrate processes held for M&As within LMEs, with US firms transforming a number of HRM practices in UK firms, for example, by reducing the number of managerial hierarchical levels and by increasing the use of job rotation (Child *et al.*, 2001).

In general, the desire for process transformation will reflect the market economy of the acquiring firm, with LMEs much more likely to integrate an acquired company fully relative to CMEs. As noted, the literature shows that Japanese and German firms were more likely to bring acquired UK firms into the fold only slowly, if at all, although they were more likely to increase the use of training than acquiring firms from LMEs. For example, Child and colleagues (2001) illustrate how a German pharmaceutical firm obtained a new product line by acquiring a UK firm. The UK firm retained autonomy over many decisions and practices, but the German firm did set up a training programme in the UK firm.

Obviously, the long-term focus by CME acquiring firms reflects country-specific characteristics, but it may also stem from a lack of experience on the part of acquiring firms, as was the case for a number of Japanese acquisitions of UK firms in the Child study. Similarly, acquisitions of CME firms by LME firms involve less integration than acquisitions of LME firms by other LME firms. For example, GE takes a more gradual approach to transforming processes in acquisitions of CME firms than they do in domestic acquisitions.

Values. Bower notes that organizational values tend to differ more for firms engaged in product or market extension M&As compared to firms engaged in overcapacity M&As. However, conflict over resources and processes may be relatively lower in product or market extension M&As, especially when the acquiring firm is larger than the acquired firm. For instance, although Japanese firms are known for their collective-oriented values, empirical evidence indicates that they are unlikely to force those values on acquired firms, taking instead a subtle or soft approach to integration (Child *et al.*, 2001). With respect to acquisitions of CME firms by LME firms, the GE case illustrates the desire on the part of large, experienced firms to refrain from imposing values on the acquired firm, and instead bringing processes in line with the GE way slowly over time. Conversely, US firms were more likely to reproduce their values in acquisitions of other LME firms.

M&A as a substitute for R&D

Resources. In an M&A as a substitute for R&D, a critical component of the HRM function is to retain valued employees. In this type of M&A strategy, acquiring firms will purchase a company in order to obtain knowledge that is held by employees of the acquired firm. The HRM function's crucial role will therefore be to hold on to human and social capital. Retention can be a challenge though, since employees in acquired firms often receive a large remuneration from their stock sale, as was the case in many M&As in IT firms recently.

When the M&A as a substitute for R&D involves firms from different market economy types, the focus in terms of resources will be on employee retention to much the same extent as in domestic M&As of this type. For example, a German manufacturing firm that acquired an entrepreneurial UK firm retained the entrepreneur (Child et al., 2001). Similarly, three Swedish CME firms made a concerted effort to retain employees in acquisitions of US and UK R&D firms, with retention percentages ranging from 90 to 100 per cent of acquired employees (Birkinshaw and Bresman, 2000). This finding was also true for firms in LMEs that acquired CME firms. For example, in Microsoft's purchase of the Japanese firm TITUS, Microsoft strongly supported the management team they acquired, with a similar outcome in Cisco Systems's acquisition of the Israeli firm Pentacom.

Processes. A key factor in obtaining a successful M&A as a substitute for R&D is that HRM will be called on to set up systems to facilitate the transfer of knowledge from the acquired firm to the acquiring firm. Specifically, the HRM function should enable the lines of communication and develop learning processes. In addition, Bower (2001) notes that the M&A as a substitute for R&D allows little time for slow assimilation, because the terrain in R&D shifts rather quickly, particularly in IT-related M&As. Thus, HRM may need to bring the new systems online quickly. One firm that does an exceptional job in assimilating new employees is Cisco Systems. As Child et al. (2001: 3) point out, in the merger between Cisco and Cerent Corporation, Cisco utilized a transition team that "mapped" Cerent employees into jobs at Cisco, and communicated this information to these employees. Although integration is costly for Cisco Systems, it prefers to acquire knowledge through M&As if the development cycle is longer than six months.

It is important to note that the speed of assimilation will be industry specific as well as specific to the country of the acquiring firm. For example, the development cycle in pharmaceutical firms is normally slower than it is in IT firms, as is the case in acquisitions of LME firms by CME firms. Specifically, CME firms that engaged in cross-border M&As with LME firms as a substitute for R&D tend to leave the processes in the acquired company as they were. A risk in this hands-off acquisition style with respect to an M&A as a substitute for R&D is that the acquiring firm may lose out on potential synergies, as was the case for a Japanese firm that bought a UK pharmaceutical firm (Child et al., 2001). In effect, in this instance the M&A strategy may be inconsistent with country-specific characteristics, although it is possible that difficulties resulted from a lack of experience on the part of the Japanese acquirer. For example, two German firms also took a hands-off approach in their M&As as a substitute for R&D (Child *et al.*, 2001), yet were more successful than the Japanese acquisition was. By contrast, the tendency among US firms – such as Microsoft and Cisco Systems – is to assimilate the acquired firm, even if the firm is in a CME. These firms will, however, make exceptions to a full integration policy. For example, Cisco Systems is willing to pursue a hands-off policy with respect to certain practices if the systems of the acquired firm are superior to those of Cisco.

Values. Assimilation in an M&A as a substitute for R&D can be challenging since the acquiring firm is likely to be more bureaucratic than the acquired firm, and because the values of the merging firms, while similar, can create negative effects. For example, Bower (2001) notes that smaller, entrepreneurial firms will probably feel constrained once acquired, no matter how much attention is paid to integration. Nevertheless, in general, firms involved in an M&A as a substitute for R&D may hold similar values irrespective of the countries in which the firms are headquartered, particularly in IT firms. This similarity in values reflects the importance of knowledge and ideas in the production process, to the extent that industry values reduce problems resulting from differences in country-specific values.

DISCUSSION AND CONCLUSION

In this paper we develop a strategic fit framework to examine the strategies and contingencies of cross-border M&As. We do so by aligning the role of HRM cross-border M&As – in terms of resources, processes and values – to the M&A strategy that firms adopt, conditional on country-specific characteristics of acquiring and acquired firms. Confirmation of the usefulness of our framework comes from a variety of broad empirical studies.

Although we have supported our discussions of strategic fit and contextual contingencies with existing robust empirical studies, there are always exceptions to the rule and variations within countries (Whitley, 1999) and country types. In particular, although at a broad level practices such as pay-for-performance systems are common across market economy types, at a more refined level there are non-trivial differences that HRM has to manage. For example, Campbell (1999) notes that the compensation systems in the BP Amoco merger – which involved two firms in LMEs – had to be redesigned because they differed significantly. He also notes that other HRM processes were altered, such as the creation of a new job structure framework. Thus, even firms in countries within the same market economic type will experience some degree of localization in HRM practices and policies and therefore may need to adjust the role of HRM accordingly.

The M&As examined in this paper are representative of the majority of the largest mergers occurring in recent decades in the industrialized world, yet do not exhaust all such M&As. For example, large M&As are fairly common in what Hall and Soskice (2001) call Mediterranean market economies (MMEs), such as

France, Spain and Italy. MMEs can be seen as a hybrid between CMEs and LMEs, with financial policies being similar to those in LMEs and labour market policies similar to those in CMEs. Although we do not consider the MME case here, our strategic fit framework can adequately capture it. Hence, possibly reflecting the hybrid nature of MMEs, it has been shown that French firms tend to engage in partial integration of LME firms, with French managers having a colonial attitude in their acquisitions of UK firms (Child *et al.*, 2001).

Our framework demonstrates that convergence among certain HRM practices to a best practice model was consistent with the strategic intent of the merger. However, further research is needed to consider why a number of other practices retained specific country characteristics and, perhaps more importantly, the effect that these unique factors had on the performance of an M&A. Our framework also sheds light on problems created in M&As, such as when certain types of M&A strategies are incompatible with country preferences for the degree and speed of merger integration. In addition, there are other contingencies, such as experience and size differences between acquiring and acquired firms, that would be interesting to consider further. For example, as firms in CMEs gain more experience in conducting M&As, it is an open question whether they will begin to assert their values and processes to a greater extent, stay on the same course or converge to LME systems.

REFERENCES

Adler, N. (1997) *International Dimensions of Organizational Behavior*. Cincinnati, Ohio: South-Western College Publishing.

Adler, N., Doktor, R. and Redding, S. (1986) "From the Atlantic to the Pacific Century: Cross-Cultural Management Reviewed", *Journal of Management*, 12: 295–318.

Aguilera, R. V. and Jackson, G. (2003) "The Cross-National Diversity of Corporate Governance: Dimensions and Determinants", *Academy of Management Review*, 28: 447–65.

Berger, S. and Dore, R. (eds) (1996) *National Diversity and Global Capitalism*. Ithaca, NY: Cornell University Press.

Birkinshaw, J. and Bresman, H. (2000) "Managing the Post-Acquisition Integration Process: How the Human Integration and Task Integration Processes Interact to Foster Value Creation", *Journal of Management Studies*, 37: 395–425.

Blackburn, V. and Lang, J. (1989) "Toward a Market/Ownership Constrained Theory of Merger Behavior", *Journal of Management*, 15: 77–88.

Bower, J. L. (2001) "Not all M&As Are Alike and That Matters", *Harvard Business Review*, Reprint R0103F.

Buono, A. F. and Bowditch, J. L. (1989) *The Human Side of Mergers and Acquisitions*. San Francisco, Calif.: Jossey-Bass.

Campbell, J. (1999) "Partner Presentation", University of Illinois Center for Human Resource Management, Fall 1999, Partner Roundtable, Oak Brook, Illinois.

Capron, L. (1999) "The Long Term Performance of Horizontal Acquisitions", *Strategic Management Journal*, 20: 987–1018.

Cartwright, S. and Cooper, C. (1993) "The Role of Cultural Compatibility in Successful Organizational Marriage", *Academy of Management Executive*, 7: 57–70.

Casper, S. and Hancké, R. (1999) "Global Quality Norms within National Production Regimes: ISO 9000 Standards in the French and German Car Industries", *Organization Studies*, 20: 961–85.

Chandler, A. (1962) *Strategy and Structure*. Cambridge, Mass.: MIT Press.

Chatterjee, S. (1986) "Types of Synergy and Economic Value: The Impact of Acquisitions on Merging and Rival Firms", *Strategic Management Journal*, 7: 199–239.

Child, J., Chung, L. and Davies, H. (2003) "The Performance of Cross-Border Units in China: A Test of Natural Selection, Strategic Choice and Contingency Theories", *Journal of International Business Studies*, 34: 242–54.

Child, J., Faulkner, D. and Pitkethly, R. (2001) *The Management of International Acquisitions*. New York: Oxford University Press.

Empson, L. (2000) "Merging Professional Service Firms", *Business Strategy Review*, 11: 39–46.

Faulkner, D., Pitkethly, R. and Child, J. (2002) "International Mergers and Acquisitions in the UK 1985–94: A Comparison of National HRM Practices", *International Journal of Human Resource Management*, 13: 106–22.

Federal Trade Commission, Bureau of Economics (1975) *Statistical Report on Mergers and Acquisitions*. Washington, DC: US Government Printing Office.

Fombrun, C., Tichy, N. and Devanna, M. (1984) *Strategic Human Resource Management*. New York: Wiley.

Galbraith, C. and Stiles, C. (1984) "Merger Strategies as a Response to Bilateral Market Power", *Academy of Management Journal*, 27: 66–72.

Gertsen, M., Soderberg, A. and Torp, J. (eds) (1998) *Cultural Dimensions of International Mergers and Acquisitions*, Berlin: Walter de Gruyter.

Gospel, A. and Pendleton, P. (2003) "Finance, Corporate Governance, and the Management of Labour: A Conceptual and Comparative Analysis", *British Journal of Industrial Relations*, 41: 557–82.

Granstrand, O. and Sjolander, S. (1990) "The Acquisition of Technology and Small Firms by Large Firms", *Journal of Economic Behavior and Organization*, 13: 367–86.

Hall, P. and Soskice, D. (2001) "Introduction". In Hall, P. and Soskice, D. (eds) *Varieties of Capitalism: The Institutional Foundations of Comparative Advantage*. New York: Oxford University Press.

Haspeslagh, P. and Jemison, D. (1991) *Managing Acquisitions: Creating Value through Corporate Renewal*. New York: The Free Press.

Hennart, J. F. and Park, Y. R. (1993) "Greenfield versus Acquisition: The Strategy of Japanese Investors in the United States", *Management Science*, 39: 483–97.

Hofstede, G. (1980) *Culture's Consequences: International Differences in Work-related Values*. Beverly Hills, Calif.: Sage.

Hollingsworth, J. and Boyer, R. (eds) (1997) *Contemporary Capitalism: The Embeddedness of Institutions*. Cambridge: Cambridge University Press.

Hopner, M. and Jackson, G. (2001) "Political Economy of Takeovers in Germany: The Case of Mannesmann and its Implications for Institutional Change", Working Paper of the Max Planck Institute for the Study of Societies, Cologne.

Hunt, J. and Downing, S. (1990) "Mergers, Acquisitions and Human Resource Management", *International Journal of Human Resource Management*, 1: 195–209.

Jensen, M. C. and Ruback, R. (1983) "The Market for Corporate Control: The Scientific Evidence", *Journal of Financial Economics*, 11: 5–50.

Krug, J. and Hegarty, W. (1997) "Postacquisition Turnover among US Top Management Teams: An Analysis of the Effects of Foreign vs. Domestic Acquisitions of US Targets", *Strategic Management Journal*, 18: 667–75.

La Porta, R., Lopez-de-Silanes, F., Shleifer, A. and Vishny, R. W. (1998) "Law and Finance", *Journal of Political Economy*, 106: 1113–55.

Larsson, R. and Finkelstein, S. (1999) "Integrating Strategic, Organizational, and Human Resource Perspectives on Mergers and Acquisitions: A Case Survey of Synergy Realization", *Organization Science*, 10: 1–26.

Lawrence, P. and Lorsch, J. (1967) *Organization and Environment*. Boston, Mass.: Harvard Business School Press.

Marks, M. and Mirvis, P. (1998) *Joining Forces: Making One Plus One Equal Three in Mergers, Acquisitions, and Alliances*. San Francisco, Calif.: Jossey-Bass.

Marsden, D. (1999) *A Theory of Employment Systems: Micro-foundations of Societal Diversity*. Oxford: Oxford University Press.

Mirvis, P. and Marks, M. (1992) *Managing the Merger: Making it Work*. Englewood Cliffs, NJ: Prentice-Hall.

Newburry, W. and Zeira, Y. (1997) "Generic Differences between Equity International Joint Ventures (EIJVS), International Acquisitions (IAs) and International Greenfield Investments (IGIs): Implications for Parent Companies", *Journal of World Business*, 32: 87–102.

Poole, M. (1990) "Human Resource Management in an International Perspective", *International Journal of Human Resource Management*, 1: 1–15.

Porter, M. (1990) *The Competitive Advantage of Nations*. New York: The Free Press.

Pucik, V. (1988) "Strategic Alliances, Organizational Learning, and Competitive Advantage: The HRM Agenda", *Human Resource Management*, 27: 77–93.

Sanz-Valle, R., Sabater-Sanchez, R. and Aragon-Sanchez, A. (1999) "Human Resource Management and Business Strategy Links: An Empirical Study", *International Journal of Human Resource Management*, 10: 655–71.

Schneider, S. (1989) "Strategy Formulation: The Impact of National Culture", *Organization Studies*, 10: 149–68.

Schuler, R. (2001) "Human Resource Issues and Activities in International Joint Ventures", *International Journal of Human Resource Management*, 12: 1–52.

Schuler, R. and Jackson, S. (1987) "Linking Competitive Strategy and Human Resource Management Practices", *Academy of Management Executive*, 3: 207–19.

Sorge, A. (1991) "Strategical Fit and Societal Effect: Interpreting Cross-National Comparisons of Technology, Organization and Human Resources," *Organization Studies*, 12: 161–90.

Sparrow, P., Schuler, R. and Jackson, S. (1994) "Convergence or Divergence: Human Resource Practices and Policies for Competitive Advantage Worldwide", *International Journal of Human Resource Management*, 5: 267–99.

Vlasic, B. and Stertz, B. (2000) *How Daimler–Benz Drove off with Chrysler*. New York: Morrow.

Walsh, J. P. (1988) "Top Management Turnover Following Mergers and Acquisitions", *Strategic Management Journal*, 9: 173–83.

Weston, J., Chung, K. and Siu, J. (2001) *Takeovers, Restructuring, and Corporate Governance*, 3rd edn. Upper Saddle River, NJ: Prentice-Hall.

Whitley, R. (1999) *Divergent Capitalisms: The Social Structuring and Change of Business Systems*. Oxford: Oxford University Press.

Whitley, R. and Kristensen, P. (eds) (1997) *Governance at Work: The Social Regulation of Economic Relations*. Oxford: Oxford University Press.

Wright, P. M. and Snell, S. A. (1998) "Toward a Unifying Framework for Exploring Fit and Flexibility in Strategic Human Resource Management", *Academy of Management Review*, 23: 756–72.

Zysman, J. (1983) *Governments, Markets, and Growth: Financial Systems and the Politics of Industrial Change*. Ithaca, NY: Cornell University Press.

Tom O'Neill

WEAVING WAGES, INDEBTEDNESS, AND REMITTANCES IN THE NEPALESE CARPET INDUSTRY

IN DECEMBER 1998, POLICE raided a ramshackle carpet factory in Chabahil, a periurban community northeast of Kathmandu, Nepal. Inside they found 23 children who had been forced to weave carpets for two and a half years for little more than inadequate food and abuse. The *Kathmandu Post* (1998) reported that two 13-year-old girls tearfully asked to be returned to their homes, and the 20 year-old who escaped the factory to inform police told them they had not been paid since arriving at the factory, despite a promise of 1,200 rupees for migrating to the city.

This story is well rehearsed in Nepal, where reports of the exploitation and abuse of young children by the carpet industry are common. The minimum age for full-time employment in Nepal is 16; 14 years for limited employment (36 hours a week and less). Thus, most of these weavers were not children, by legal definition. They were described as such in the story because the confinement and coercion they suffered was analogous to forms of child labor exploitation reported throughout South Asia in the 1990s.

There is evidence that carpet factory owners *(saahu-ji)* or labor contractors *(thekadaar)* exploited child weavers in the Nepalese carpet industry in the early 1990s. In 1992, a Nepalese nongovernmental organization (NGO), Child Workers in Nepal (CWIN 1993), estimated that 150,000 migrant children wove carpets in appalling conditions at a time when carpet production and export to Europe had more than tripled from a decade earlier. Many of these children worked with their siblings' parents or their brothers and sisters, but almost half were lured from their families in mountain villages by labor brokers with promises that a portion of their wages would be remitted to their parents. Once alone in Nepal's metropolis, they were compelled to rely on their adult employers for food, clothing, health care, and work. Frequently, that reliance was in turn abused by adult carpet producers and labor contractors who provided only minimal care and failed to pay either the child weaver, or their parents, the full value for their labor. Children were, moreover, bonded to their employers through debts that prevented them from escaping to find work elsewhere.

Migrant carpet weavers of periurban Kathmandu work in the service of a global export industry. Currently most are adults, yet many accounts of carpet weavers have been of child workers (CWIN 1993; NASPEC 1994; Onta-Bhatta 1997; Sattaur 1993). The kind of exploitation reported in the *Kathmandu Post* is familiar to many who have been following the development of the carpet industry in Kathmandu, but it does not necessarily reflect the experience of most carpet weavers. An "analytical confusion" (James, Jenks, and Prout 1998:111) between unfree labor and the labor market dynamics of carpet work has precluded analysis of their actual condition. Do all weavers, like the children among them, fall victim to powerful interlopers who extract an unreasonable and unsustainable portion of their earnings? Does the coercive and oppressive treatment of weaving children differ only by degree from the treatment of all carpet weavers?

Most carpet weavers are recent migrants to the urban area, coming from agricultural hill and lowland regions bordering India that have, until recently, been poorly served by educational infrastructure and only partially articulated with the state and its emerging capital economy. For many migrants, finding work and negotiating wages in the city is an onerous task, and they are at a disadvantage in both education and experience. In direct dealings with employers, this disparity of knowledge and experience may be sufficient to increase the risk of wage and debt bondage, something that Thaker (1993) and the Nepal Independent Carpet Workers' Union (1996) claim is accomplished by granting wage advances *(peskii)* to workers. Because advance wages are cut directly from salaries, weavers are caught in a cycle of debt that can significantly constrain their autonomy and mobility and render them more dependent upon their saahu-ji.

Although migrant weavers have left their villages to work in the Kathmandu Valley, for the majority of them Kathmandu is only a place of work. They identify with the villages from where they migrated and to which many will return, having no permanent stake in the urban expansion of the capital. Capitalist urban expansion is usually understood to pull in migrants who become separated from their kin groups and communities, but for many carpet weavers village and household claims on family labor remain. Just as labor contractors and factory owners control weaving labor by manipulating wage allocation, so too, it is thought, do household authorities. Parents receive a fee for sending children to weaving work, and they depend on a flow of money from Kathmandu to their cash-poor households. The importance of allocations of child labor in developing countries has recently been recognized as critical to household reproduction in South Asia (see, for example, Chandrashekar 1997 and Nieuwenhuys 1994), but my research suggests that intergenerational claims on migrant wages in Nepal extend to adult wages as well.

Conditions of debt bondage and coercion are not necessarily what brings young weavers to work in the Nepalese industry. I will discuss two strategies of coercive labor control: 1) the wage advances carpet saahu-ji are said to deploy to bind weavers to their looms; and 2) the practice of remitting wages to the weaver's family that ensures that young weavers, as one critic put it, "are exploited even by their own families, who use them as workhorses to earn money which they control" (Sattaur 1993:34). Migrant participation in the wage economy erodes traditional idioms of domination and substitutes for them the discipline of a market where labor is negotiated between ideally free agents. Young Nepalese carpet weavers are not free, but they are victimized less by traditional labor practices than by the capricious cycles of global capitalism.

METHODOLOGY

Estimates of the number of carpet weavers in the Kathmandu Valley are frequently outdated, overstated, or inaccurate. Given the shifting fortunes of the industry throughout the 1990s, and a large, flexible, and unorganized sector of small subcontracting shops that supply carpets to the more visible and accountable carpet-export sector, the exact figure is nearly impossible to give. CWIN (1993) gave an initial estimate of 300,000 weavers in 1992, when carpet exports to Europe were at an all-time high. It claimed 150,000 were children under the age of 16. By 1994, the United States Agency for International Development (USAID) put the number at about 108,000, at a time when carpet sales were beginning to slump due to export overproduction and stockpiling by European buyers and the broadcast of a "Panorama" documentary in Germany that condemned child labor practices in the carpet industry. From a survey of 300 carpet factories in the summer of 1995, I put the number of weavers at 13,183 for the research area and only 88,000 for the entire industry.

Industry sales fell further between 1995 and 1998, when I collected the data for this paper. By 1998, many carpet exporters had instituted the "Rugmark" program in their factories, in which they were frequently and randomly monitored for child labor. Export reductions put pressure on the many small subcontracting units I found in 1995, and many had closed altogether. This also reduced the number of weavers required, and only trained and experienced weavers found work in most factories. Therefore, the widespread exploitation of child labor reported by CWIN and in the "Panorama" documentary did not exist in 1998.

The research for this paper was conducted between September and December of that year. Because of the relatively short field period, I decided to gather detailed information from a small sample of carpet weavers that was obtained purposively from contacts at the Nepal Independent Carpet Workers' Union (NICWU) and from within the unorganized sector with which I had worked in 1995. I conducted focus group interviews with 106 carpet workers (encompassing occupations other than weaving) and collected corresponding survey data from the same sample. Only data from the 68 carpet weavers in the sample are reported here. Nonweavers and former weavers were removed so that those working under similar conditions and earning similar wages could be compared. I wrote the survey and interview instruments in romanized Nepali.

They were tested for accuracy and reviewed by both NICWU staff and a research assistant with experience with Nepali–English translations.

Focus groups were used because of the short research period available and because they afford an opportunity for informants in a similar occupational class to reflect and elaborate on each other's experience. Focus groups were normally held to five participants to maintain an intimate dynamic that fostered optimal participation, though on occasion weaver enthusiasm, happenstance, and time constraints increased group size. In addition, interviews and informal discussions took place with union activists, both from the NICWU and the rival Nepal Trade Union Congress. I recorded and transcribed all interview data in collaboration with a research assistant and used NUD*IST qualitative research software in my analysis.

Survey data were similarly cotranscribed before analysis. Every weaver was surveyed for basic demographic information, including age, family size, caste, and place of origin, as well as a bounded recall of the previous month's expenses according to basic categories including food, clothing, education, family remittance, discretionary expenses, and medical expenses. Survey and interview data were collected beginning in September and continuing through October and early November. Nepal's annual Dasain festival, which is a time when Nepalese traditionally purchase clothing and gifts and spend much money on feasting, fell in mid-October. Most schools, businesses, and government offices shut down for at least the official five-day festival period. The export sector of the carpet industry is an exception, as exporters had to meet a spike in carpet orders that comes at the end of the summer. Union weavers were interviewed before and during this festival. Nonunionized subcontractors, however, frequently sent their staff home for the holiday, often for as long as two weeks, and survey data from nonunion workers were collected after the holiday.

Although the sample size is limited, it is balanced between unionized and nonunionized weavers. Unionized weavers in Kathmandu tend to work in large organized export companies where wages are higher and job security is better. Nepalese labor law does not permit organized labor units with less than 10 employees. Most nonunion subcontractors, for whom carpet orders fluctuate drastically from month to month, work in these smaller units. I take care not to read too much into these results, but survey data triangulated with interview and observational data present a representative picture of the overall condition of carpet weavers and their wages.

WEAVING WAGES, EXPENSES, AND SALARY ADVANCES

Table 1 compares age and pay for union and nonunion weavers in the sample. The youngest weaver surveyed was 16, the oldest 39. This is not to say that younger workers do not exist elsewhere in the industry, but it does suggest that they are in a minority. Contrary to what has been written about other south Asian carpet industries, the Nepalese industry in 1998 did not rely on child labor, although it clearly did in 1992 (NASPEC 1994; Onta-Bhatta 1997).

Table 1. Union and nonunion weavers by age and piece rate (N = 66)

	Age	Piece Rate*
Union (n = 30)**	24.53	411.33
Nonunion (n = 36)	22.78	365.69

(Piece rates given in Nepalese rupees; 60 NRS = $1.00)
* t = 6.23; p < .0.001
** Two cases in which weavers received higher piece rates for
100-knot carpets were eliminated from this table.
Source: Field survey, 1998.

Parental claims on their child's earnings are not extinguished when a weaver reaches the age of majority, however.

Table 1 also shows that weaving piece rates, the standard by which weavers are paid, vary significantly between union and nonunion weavers. Weavers thus stand to earn much more in the union sector because they work in export factories, which pay a higher piece rate than subcontractors.

Earnings may not be sufficient to provide migrant weavers with the basic necessities of life, and they frequently must go into debt to their employers to subsist. The need for informal credit exposes weavers to deception and exploitation aimed at securing continued labor, but it also exposes carpet saahu-ji to the risk of being cheated by disgruntled workers. Carpet weavers in Kathmandu have cause to be disgruntled, as increasing living costs continually erode their ability to make a living weaving carpets.

Carpet weavers were paid by the piece in 1998. For each square meter of carpet woven, weavers received a fee that was paid by different factories at different intervals, but usually when a carpet was completed. Much anthropological literature has associated piece rate with exploitation of peasant weavers in economic modes thought to be in transition from petty commodity production to modern capitalist production (Nash 1993; Schneider 1988). Piecework means that what a weaver earns is directly related to what is produced. Hourly wages, advocated by many in Nepal for carpet workers, render that relation abstract by separating time from space (literally, in this case, a square meter of space), thus producing a distinction thought to be central to modernity (Giddens 1990). Scott Cook (1993) points out that a product of piecework is alienated from the weaver as it must be turned over to middlemen, who extract a profit when the woven product is sold in the market. Nepalese carpet weavers, too, must depend on their saahu-ji to find a market for their labors and receive remuneration that pales when compared to the high prices some of their products fetch on the European market.

Cook (1993:67) also points out that piecework allows the worker "to essentially be in charge of the labor process and, therefore, the output that will determine his or her wage". Weavers set their own pace, but the low wages they receive keep them at their looms for long working days. The shift from piece to time rates would be optimal from the point of view of industrialist control over productivity, but carpet saahu-ji cannot resort to this because of the cyclical and precarious nature of export carpet orders. Export saahu-ji, in particular, are often distanced from the activities of the weaving floor, describing them as "open spaces" into which labor comes and goes at will. One saahu-ji told me in 1995:

> Some people have also complained about this. We are not responsible for this. For us it is better to weave daytime because they are not paying electricity. Weavers are not paying electricity bill. The company pays. When you visit during the daytime, you will see the weaving hall is half empty. OK, during nighttime, say after, before dinner if you go, everyone is on the loom, weaving carpets. After 8, 10, 11, 12 o'clock [at night]. Even 12 o'clock. Some people want to weave, and sometimes we restrict them, "OK, don't weave" because he is using all the light in the factory just to complete his work. Quota, you know. It's a financial loss to us. So these kinds of concepts are mistranslated as labor abuse, you know.

> **Tom**: So, in fact, the workers have a lot of freedom in the factory to keep their own hours.

> **Saahu-ji**: Yeah. See, our factory is, you know, an open space. They go in and sometimes I don't recognize who is who. They go out, come in so long, on their own.

Although the picture here is of a working space where weavers set their own pace, most weavers reported they typically worked 12 or more hours a day. If they leave their looms for shopping, medical care, or even to "stroll around" (*gumma jaane*), they have to make up the time later to earn enough to meet basic needs in Kathmandu.

The average daily wage for weavers is about 85 rupees (although there is considerable variation between weavers), and the average daily wage for agricultural work in the central hill region, where many weavers come from, is 40 rupees, which in part explains migration decisions.[1] But the average daily wage in the Kathmandu Valley, where many jobs in the commercial, government, and tourist sectors are found, is 118 rupees (HMG 1997:48). Living costs are much higher in Kathmandu, and weavers fall seriously behind if they are not working. In addition, the declining number of carpet exports since 1995 has meant that weaving jobs are harder to obtain, and weavers who do not weave to an acceptable rate may not get an order again from the same factory.

Weavers measure their progress in centimeters, not in hours. Carpet masters mark 10-centimeter intervals on the cotton weft before weaving begins, and weavers describe their productivity in "centis". The carpets they work on are of Tibetan construction and follow the "cutting loops" tradition, where Tibetan or imported New Zealand wool is looped around a one-meter-long iron rod, or *gipsi* (Denwood 1974; Eiland 1992). Once the "line" is fully looped, the gipsi is hammered down to join the partially completed carpet and the loops are cut away to achieve the pile. Most weavers report their productivity at between 30 and 35 centis a day. Theoretically, they could complete one square meter in three days. But most weavers reported various completion rates and hours worked:

Tom: How long did you take to weave one square meter?

Male Weaver 1: It takes 25 days. If we weave very fast, it takes only two days. We can finish in three days, well, it takes four, five, six, seven days for one square meter.

Tom: How many hours do workers have to work in one day?

Male Weaver 2: We have to do for 10 hours, at least. Some of us have to work for 12 hours, or 13, 14 hours a day.

Tom: How long is the weaving room open?

Weaver: From 5:00 A.M. to 12 midnight.

Female Weaver: It is open. It opens for 18 hours. How long we want to weave, that is how long the room is open. Some weavers weave for 6 hours, some weavers weave for 5 hours, some weavers weave for 18 hours.

Tom: Can they go out if they get sick?

Female Weaver: They can go out if they are sick, but we have to survive with our money. The owner does not give us money. In case they gave us money, we have to pay it back after working.

The various times given here for completing one square meter may reflect differences in weaving ability, but they also indicate that production is often due to external factors. Delays affect piece workers particularly hard – they must produce to earn, but they still have to subsist during any delay. Nepal's frequent and busy holiday schedule is one reason work stops; another is the politically motivated curfews (*bandhs*) that increasingly shut down the valley. Delays in the weaving process are also common, and weavers are left languishing without pay while they wait for carpet orders or materials:

Male Weaver 1: We had many problems. People go to Kathmandu to find a job but they can't get one on time. They have to wait four or five days to get a job. So, they wait without doing anything.

Female Weaver: They sometimes say that there is no more string left.

Male Weaver 2: Sometimes we have to wait for a month without working. Sometimes we can't get all the colors. If they can't get all the colors, we can't weave. So, our money will be finished.

Tom: Did you go back to the village or stay in Kathmandu at that time?

Female Weaver: We stayed in Kathmandu.

Weavers who stay in Kathmandu are fortunate because most factories provide modest rooms for them to stay in free of charge. In one case, a subcontractor did not have enough rooms for all of his weavers, so he provided a subsidy of 200 rupees a month toward rent. These rooms vary in quality and they are crowded, often with visiting relatives from their home village. Saahu-ji provide only the room and perhaps basic furniture, weavers must supply the rest from their own salary. Meals are cooked on a single-burner kerosene stove placed in one corner of the room, where a few simple pots and dishes are kept. Female weavers cook in addition to their weaving, and preschool children are often found with them at their looms while they work.

Living expenses in Kathmandu are very high, and even this housing subsidy does little to enable weavers to save. Basic foodstuffs, in particular, have increased sharply. In 1998, many weavers complained about a sudden and, to them, inexplicable rise in the price of onions, a staple in dhal and curry. Unlike the cash-poor villages from which they came, all foodstuffs, clothing, utensils, and other supplies must be purchased with cash. Structural adjustment policies put in place in the early 1990s fueled inflation (Dixit 1995). For example, the price of rice and lentils, two main components of their daily diet, increased by about 20 percent between 1994 and 1995 and between 1996 and 1997 (HMG 1998: table 12.2). Weaving piece rates increased only by 11 percent over the same period.[2]

Table 2 gives an indication of the mean expenses for each of six basic categories of expenditure. As both union and nonunion weavers must subsist in the same urban area, there are few significant differences between them. Union weavers did appear to spend more on education ($t = 2.175$, $p = .034$), which is not surprising as they are an older work force and likely to have more school-aged children. Nonunion weavers spent more on discretionary expenses ($t = -2.65$, $p = .043$), which likely reflects the timing of their survey after the Dasain holiday, when more discretionary spending than usual takes place.

Table 2. Expenditure means and range by union and nonunion, N = 68

Mean	Union	Nonunion
Food	950	900
Clothing	630	735
Education	163	57
Family remittance*	275	231
Discretionary spending*	273	393
Medical**	422	174
Sum of expenses	2,713	2,495
(range)	(1,600–7,900)	(1,400–5,700)

In Nepalese rupees, 60 NRS = $1.00 US in 1998.
* sig. <0.050
** mode is 0 rupees
Source: Field survey, 1998.

Despite the visible differences of means, other expenses did not significantly differ between the union and nonunion groups. What these data do show, however, is that some union and nonunion weavers live beyond their means. The range of the sum of expenses (the sum of these six categories) for both indicates that a number of weavers spent far more than they earned. For example, one weaver reported spending 7,900 rupees in the previous month. He would have had to have completed over 16 square meters of carpet to earn this much. At 3.5 days per square meter in the best of circumstances, this would have taken 56 days to accomplish.

While it might be tempting to eliminate this and other high-value cases as outliers, assuming reporting error on the survey instrument, those who reported an extraordinarily high sum of expenses also frequently reported high expenditures for health care. The weaver in the example above reported spending 5,000 rupees for medical services. Allopathic health care is generally on a fee-for-service basis, so weavers who need medical help for themselves or family members must pay much more than their monthly earnings allow. Many weavers reported that this was a principal reason for taking salary advances.

The high range of the sum of expenses indicates that many weavers are taking salary advances (peskii) from their saahu-ji. As the saahu-ji see it, migrant carpet weavers arrive in the Kathmandu Valley with few possessions. They must acquire the basic necessities through an advance payment from the saahu-ji or from the labor contractor (thekadaar) who trains, maintains, and ultimately controls weavers and their labor. A 1995 survey of 300 carpet factories revealed that 165 gave peskii to new workers, and an additional 64 gave advances for such things as weddings or festivals such as Dasain, which involve enormous outlays of cash for gifts and feasting (O'Neill 1997). Two hundred twenty-three saahu-ji said they provided for the medical needs of their workers. Some saahu-ji offer fully equipped health clinics or sponsor workers at private or government clinics, but the most common method was to advance money for medical treatment and "cut the sum" – subtract the advance from a weaver's overall piece rate when the carpet was finished. Salary advances thus make up for weaver shortfalls when large one-time expenses occur. Many saahu-ji view these shortfalls as evidence of a lack of fiscal responsibility among many weavers, but others view salary advances as a means of "short-term bondage" – they create a debt cycle that constrains weaver mobility (Thaker 1993:31; NICWU 1996).

The ethnographic record is replete with examples of wage advances being used to bind workers to their masters, particularly in South Asia. The most cited case in Nepal is the kamaiya (bonded labor) system, which is prevalent in portions of the western terai (a lowland region on the Indian border). Landlords loan funds to low-caste households, which are then compelled to agricultural work with no real hope of ever paying off their debt (NESAC 1998:111). The pattern also exists in India, where Breman (1993:104) describes how agricultural labor recruiters (mukudam) advance payments to laborers during the nonproductive monsoon season against harvest wages, thus attaching them to their employers when the work begins. The peskii of the Nepalese carpet industry is similar to other forms of wage bondage. It compels weavers to work for low wages and prevents a truly free labor market from emerging. Weavers validated this view in interviews:

> We are told that you have this much money, which should be paid before leaving. Although the carpet is good he puts in "B". They made us take peskii and we could work there. Those who didn't want to take the peskii, the saahu-ji would not hire. They made us work hard and we were dominated. So workers tried to run away. We could never pay it back. The saahu-ji is not good. If he had not cheated us, we would never have run away. The saahu-ji should have been very nice.

This weaver is describing a factory he left for an organized factory where the union prevents such exploitation. He describes two methods of domination: 1) compulsory salary advances; and 2) the classification of finished carpets as "B" grade. Such second-rate carpets are paid at a lower piece rate, thus making it more difficult to repay the debt.[3]

Other weavers shared this same experience. One 20-year-old weaver said the saahu-ji gave him an advance of 1,600 rupees when he started to weave in his factory, but it had been recorded falsely as 3,400 rupees in the ledger book and later cut from his salary. Being unable to read or "do the sums" himself, he was unaware of the discrepancy until well afterward. There is evidence that some saahu-ji manipulate wage advances to control their workers, but this manipulation alone is insufficient as a mechanism of "bondage" in the noisy and malleable carpet labor market.

Many weavers also spoke of others who had run away from a job without repaying their salary advance to the saahu-ji, something the NICWU (1996:26) both confirms and deplores when it claims that a "get advance payment and run away kind of lumpen attitude has discouraged the workers to relate their livelihood with the industry and employment stability, and . . . also gives negative effect for the institutional development of the industry and for . . . self reliance". For many saahu-ji, particularly those in smaller factories, salary advances are also seen as a risk. Several reported they had lost considerable sums of money when weavers left without repaying their advances, usually after a labor contractor, who is given the money, runs off leaving both his weavers and the saahu-ji. The weavers they are supposed to be dominating, too, can occasionally cheat the labor contractor. One weaver interviewed in a subcontracting factory said she and her husband lost a large amount when 11 weavers who they had "recommended" to the saahu-ji left with their advances. Because the couple was responsible for the weavers, they had to repay the debt, but once the sum had been repaid, they quickly left for another factory.

Leaving a factory without repaying a salary advance may be evidence of a "lumpen attitude", but it may also be the rational act of a desperately poor weaver. Some saahu-ji demand unsustainable terms of repayment, either as a means of domination or because of a lack of trust in their weavers. The high costs of living detailed above lead many weavers to run away:

Weaver: We have to go to the hospital when we get sick. I was sick and I had to pay 2,000 rupees. What the saahu-ji gives is not enough. And the saahu-ji cuts all the peskii, the saahu-ji should cut slowly, but they don't. When they cut all the peskii, we cannot get food. So that is why the workers run away from the factories. When we pay back all of the peskii, we cannot get enough food. We have to look for our children. If they cut 1 or 200 rupees, the workers would not run away. If they cut all of the peskii, of course they will run away.

Tom: You mean workers have to run away?

Weaver: If they give us food and cut our peskii little by little, they stay. If they cut all the peskii, they cannot stay here. They go to another factory. It becomes a mess. It has been done by the saahu-ji. There are no rules.

Debt alone is a necessary, but not a sufficient, condition for debt bondage. For bondage to be truly effective, there must be no alternative for the bonded worker, and the wage-labor market in Kathmandu presents many opportunities for run-away weavers: work in another factory, another menial job, or return to their village, something many weavers have done since the slowdown in carpet production that began in 1994.

Cash advances exist because weavers need them. They subsidize initial set-up costs for migrant workers, provide them with much-needed money for marriages and festivals as well as for medical treatment in the free-market health sector. The Carpet and Wool Development Board, a government agency, and the Nepal Trade Union Congress have offered carpet weavers access to free clinic care in return for registering as carpet weavers. Neither scheme has been universally successful because of competing union and management interests and the dramatic fluctuations in the carpet market. Both labor and management are attempting to organize and control weaving labor by meeting needs met by the peskii.

INTERGENERATIONAL WAGE REMITTANCES: "KEEPING YOUR PARENTS' STOMACHS"

Weavers are dominated by the industry, but the conditions of child labor exploitation often reported in the media do not describe their general condition. Erroneous claims continue to circulate in the media and among international NGOs. This is a serious matter for an industry that relies on export sales to the West, and it is also a serious matter for adult weavers who are the first to suffer as exports fall off. In February 2000, for example, an International Labor Organization report was summarized in *The Daily Telegraph* on the continued use of child weavers in Kathmandu:

In Kathmandu Valley, the carpet industry absorbs a large number of children whose average age is 13 years. Children of the Bhote clan like Tamang, Lama and Sherpa comprise 85 percent of the child laborers in the carpet industry. The remaining 15 percent come from the Newar, Chettrai, Brahman and Magar communities. Child laborers in the carpet industry have migrated mainly from Ramechap, Kavre, Dolkha, Nuwakot, Makwanpur, Sindhupalchowk, Banke, Bardia, Dang, Rasua and Sunsari districts.

Two things are remarkable about this claim. First, that the industry "absorbs large numbers of children", which is contradicted not only by my research but also by Onta-Bhatta (1997) who claims that most child weavers were released from employment in 1994, after the "Panorama" documentary aired (see also Graner 2001). Second, the predominant *jaat*[4] origin of child weavers is given as *bhote*, a pejorative reference to the Buddhist minority communities who inhabit the hills and mountains immediately adjacent to the Kathmandu Valley (Campbell 1997; Desjarlais 1992). Thirty-one of the 68 weavers I interviewed were Tamang or Lama and came from the mountain regions around Kathmandu, while the rest were hill Brahmins and Chetris, eastern Rai and Limbu, or claimed to be Sherpa, though only one of these reported coming from Solu-Khumbu, the main Sherpa region. The ILO report's estimate of ethnic composition is exaggerated, but more accurate than the estimate of the average age of "child" weavers. In 1995, I found that many of the mid-level carpet subcontractors and "stock weavers", who produced carpets on a speculative basis for the local "spot" market, were Tamang in origin (O'Neill 2001).

The use of "bhote" in the ILO report is significant because Tamang constitutes a cultural "Other" in Nepal. In contradistinction to the educated and developed Brahmin–Chetris elite, "bhotes" are uneducated, poverty-stricken, and backward peoples who routinely send their own children to work in the carpet factories that largely benefit coreligionist Tibetan refugee owners. This characterization is partly accurate: Tamang make up a large portion of carpet weavers, and Tamang households continue to control the labor of unmarried children. Thomas Fricke (1990) argues that Tamang decisions to deploy non-family wage labor are shaped by both gender and life-course factors. Not only are unmarried family members deployed in gender-appropriate nonfamily work, but married sons, who break off to establish independent households, continue to contribute to their native household.

The lure of the carpet industry for young Tamang weavers has been strong. The main previous waged occupation was as load bearers (*beriya*) (Campbell 1997). Contemporary carpet weavers often articulated their work in comparison with load bearing. As one man put it: "We are uneducated, so we cannot get government jobs. We would have carried loads, been porters. We would have done the dishes at a hotel, plates . . . things like that. This job [carpet weaving] is easier than others. We don't get wet. And we don't have to walk in the sun."

Carpet weaving also provides an appropriate occupation for unmarried women, and the proximity of the Tamang homelands to the Kathmandu Valley means that kin and village ties need not be wholly extinguished by urban migration (Fricke 1990). As one Lama saahu-ji admitted when he described how he enticed young laborers to come to the Kathmandu Valley to work:

> In the beginning we took poor villagers, they have got trouble. If they
> live there they won't have enough food. If you marry in Kathmandu,
> we told them, and if you weave carpets you will get a little benefit.
> They can send a little to the village. You can keep your parents'
> stomachs. I did like that.

This enticement contains two contradictory elements of appeal. First, weavers
are lured by the promise of shop-floor romance and the possibility of engaging in
their own relationships without parental interference. Tamang prefer to preserve
social reciprocity through bilateral cross-cousin marriages that are held as
ideal, and marriages are strategically arranged to form ties to distant, and more
prestigious, families (Fricke 1989). In the Tamang regions of Sindhupalchok,
for example, women are said to marry "uphill" into the higher status Tamang
and Yolmo, or Helambu Sherpa, households (Clarke 1980). Migrant carpet
weavers who marry in the Kathmandu Valley are decidely marrying "down",
both in elevation and in status, and in doing so escape familial marriage
arrangements.

Migrant weavers are also lured by the potential for contributing to their
native household, and maintaining reciprocal relationships with it, by being able
to "keep their parents' stomachs". This can most readily be accomplished by
making cash transfers back to the family, done either when they return to their
village households or when family members visit the Kathmandu Valley. Most
of the weavers in my sample (54 of 68) returned to their villages at least once in
the previous year – minimally, for the Dasain festival – and many returned more
than once (mean of 1.63 return trips).

The importance of family remittances to cash-poor villages thus raises a
question about the continued claims of village adults on the wages of their
children at work in the Kathmandu Valley. Remittances are an important
element in the economies of some households in the regions that produce
weaving labor. The most lucrative source of remittances is from other countries,
such as those from Nepalese Gurkha troops in the employ of Great Britain, a
source that has declined in recent years and was never available to the Tamang
because of their caste designation (Campbell 1997; Tamang 1992). Remittances
from urban to rural areas are second, however, and the Nepal Living Standards
Survey of 1996 reports that 44.75 percent of all remittances pass from son or
daughter to parent (HMG 1997: Table 7.6). Investigation about the uses of wage
remittances by rural households was not included in this study, but much
research from other areas of the developing world show that urban–rural
international wage remittances play an important role in subsidizing marginal
agriculture. Leinbach and Watkins (1998), for example, show that remittances
from nonpermanent, circulatory migrants diversified household responses to
production losses in dry seasons by allowing cash investment in other
enterprises.

In my sample of 68 carpet weavers, land inadequacy at the household
level determined wage remittances between migrant weavers and their village
household, suggesting that marginal agriculture is a factor in the Nepalese case as
well (chi square = 7.264, p = .007). These data are drawn from a qualitative

assessment by the weaver and not any empirical measure of land capacity. Remittances were paid more frequently by Tamang weavers, then weavers from all other castes, since Tamang weavers were more likely to report an inadequate household land base (chi square = 5.783, p = .016). Wage labor in the urban carpet industry, then, can be seen as at least in part articulated to hill agriculture, both by relieving surplus household members from hill households and by bringing some much-needed cash into an agricultural economy that is unevenly monetized. This process is described in terms of intergenerational reciprocity or, at the very least, as an intergenerational obligation made necessary by a lack of food:

> **Tom**: Do you have to give some money to your parents from your salary?

> **Weaver**: We have to. We don't have enough land. They have to eat.

> **Tom**: And you?

> **Other Weaver**: A little. About 100 or 150 rupees. It is not enough for myself.
>   We have to save a little money without eating outside. We have to be misers. If we have 500 rupees, we send 200 rupees for our parents.

> **Tom**: The saahu-ji's price is not higher than before. Did you send much more money than now?

> **Weaver**: I used to. Now everything is expensive, and we get the same rate. Things were cheaper before. Now things are expensive and the rate is the same so I can't send money home.

Remitting weavers sent, on average, about 22 percent of their wages home in the previous month surveyed, for an estimated yearly sum of between 5,000 and 6,000 rupees. As one of the weavers above suggests, this "saving" represents a significant burden on their own budget and their ability to establish a separate household. As prices for basic necessities have risen over the past few years, their ability to make even that "saving" is jeopardized, straining urban–rural and village relations in the process. "Keeping their parents' stomachs" is more difficult, too, when weavers have their own children to feed, clothe, and educate. Given this, it might be expected that the remittance burden would fall disproportionately on young and unmarried weavers, who are more easily controlled by household authorities.

Significantly, neither age nor marital status is a reliable predictor of remittance payment. The large number of married remitters suggests that in some cases weavers are remitting to spouses who do not live in Kathmandu, rather than to parental households. Among Tamang weavers, however, residency practices shape urban–rural remittance behavior. Most weavers in my sample worked alongside their spouses in the same factory – often at the same loom – and pooled their wage earnings to meet monthly expenses. One young couple, for example, collectively earned 3,500 rupees in the previous month. The 20-year-old husband completed four square meters and his 17-year-old wife six. Both reported spending 600 rupees each for food and 200 for discretionary spending, but she reported spending a hefty 800 rupees for clothing (consistent with Dasain festival practice) and he 200. The husband also reported sending between 400 and 500 rupees home to his family, while she sent nothing. This is consistent with patrilocal residency patterns – the remittance goes to the husband's family, from both of them.

In another case, a 31-year-old woman reported sending between 800 and 1,000 rupees to the village home of her husband's parents, even though she and her husband had separated. One of her three children lived with her in Kathmandu to attend a government school, for which she reported spending 300 rupees in the past month. Her other two children lived in the village with her ex-husband and his parents, making her remittance more a child-care payment than a happily met obligation. The burden of these expenses meant she was constantly in debt, forcing her to take peskiis from her saahu-ji and slowly try to pay them off before her next major expense. Remittances are a part of the household economy when members are dispersed between villages and the Kathmandu Valley where wage labor is comparatively more valuable. As this case shows, however, household economies do not always fully reciprocate, and individuals may not necessarily give freely of their resources.

A number of weavers in my sample did not send remittances home, and it would be convenient to conclude from this that weavers are becoming alienated from their origins by the wages they earn and by the lure of big city consumption. The duration of recall required by the survey, however, excluded many weavers who sent remittances home, but not in the past month, or those who wanted to remit but could not because of budget pressures. That they did not remit is less because they no longer regarded intergenerational obligations as important than because the inflated cost of living in Kathmandu and shifting life course obligations in the nuclear family subject traditional reciprocity to the calculus of day-to-day priorities. Other weavers have taken to carpet work as individuals, escaping the hardships of hill life for the chance to make a new life in what is for them a periurban frontier. Remittances are not a case of external control over weaving wages, but they are an important practice in the maintenance of a marginal and, from the saahu-ji's point of view, disposable work force.

CONCLUSION

I began this paper with an account of child labor exploitation not because I wished to question the validity of such claims. Child labor is pervasive in Nepal and visible in most sectors of the economy. The exploitative treatment of weavers in that factory was, however, not symptomatic of the kind of mistreatment all weavers faced. My concern was not so much with that specific case of coercive labor control, but rather with the validity of it as a metonym for an entire industry. I was not interested in championing the reputation of that industry nor in suggesting that the position of its workers was not problematic. To characterize that position as "unfree" labor, however, is inaccurate – carpet weavers are as free as possible in a context in which they are compelled to sell their labor to entrepreneurs for whom the only way to extract surplus value is to make weaving labor as cheap, efficient, competent, and predictable as possible.

I have discussed the practices of salary advances and wage remittances as potential mechanisms of coercive labor control. Wage advances were not an unambiguous mechanism of domination, and there is much evidence that weavers are sometimes able to use the practice to their own ends. Wage remittances appeared to be an element of intrahousehold reciprocity, an obligation that many weavers, notably those from the Tamang jaat who make up a majority of carpet weavers in the Kathmandu Valley, see as necessary input into village households. Many weavers no longer gave remittances, or never gave them at all, and the obligation to give was coming under stress from the increased cost of living in the city. Peskii advances, in which wages are received in a form of credit, did send some weavers into a spiral of debt from which it was difficult to escape. But, even though some weavers claimed to have taken peskii under coercion, the usual practice was for weavers to take them only when they chose. The wage remittance, which is an expenditure paid out to a collective pool of resources, was a burden on the ability of some weavers to sustain themselves in the city. Other weavers, however, chose to drop this obligation when it was no longer viable. As different as these two practices were, both appeared to interfere with the autonomy of weavers to freely engage their labor, and thus seemed incompatible with a modern, capitalist labor market.

Both practices are linked, however, in another way. They are economically necessary for workers whose wage is insufficient for sustained life in the Kathmandu Valley. Peskiis are necessary, initially, because migrant weavers have little in the way of material goods to set up a household in Kathmandu. Later, they are necessary when weavers have to meet large expenses, such as medical costs, that their wage does not cover. Remittances are a flow of resources to village households, indicating the continued membership and obligation of weavers with their originating village, or, as in the case of the Tamang women, with their husband's household. That membership is an important resource for urban weavers because it provides a place to return when weaving work ends and a place where families the weaver cannot sustain in the city can be housed. Although many weavers continue to live and work in Kathmandu, many others have given up and returned to their villages because working in the carpet factories was untenable and much-needed social networks were lacking.

The Tibeto-Nepalese carpet industry has all the outward signs of a modern industry, with professional organizations, trade unions, and government regulation, but it remains reliant on weaving hands to fashion its product for the world market. Global concern that the industry exploited child workers contributed to the rapid market contraction that diminished profitability and any real improvement in weaving wages. The fruits of globalization, however, were never fairly distributed, as carpet workers have been hard pressed just to earn a basic livelihood in Kathmandu. Maintaining those weavers at the lowest possible cost is instrumental to the success of this industry, and this is partly accomplished by keeping its work force on the margins of urban life without the means to fully integrate as permanent residents.

NOTES

1   The figure of 85 rupees a day is calculated by dividing the average piece rate by the average number of working days taken to complete the work, as reported in interviews. The figure of 40 rupees a day for hill agricultural work is taken from the 1996 National Living Standards Survey (HMG 1997).
2   Based on data collected in 1995 and in 1998. The mean rate for 60-knot carpets in 1995 was 348.3 rupees per square meter. By 1998, this had increased to 386.4.
3   Grading of carpet quality is used to distinguish between those carpets competently woven and ready for export ("A"), and those with varying weaving flaws that require additional repairs ("B" and "C"). Grades are usually determined by the saahu-ji and ostensibly protect them from high repair costs.
4   Jaat is Nepali, roughly a gloss for "caste", but indicating more distinctions between Hindu Pahari peoples and Nepal's numerous minority ethnic groups.

REFERENCES

Breman, Jan. 1993. Beyond Patronage and Exploitation: Changing Agrarian Relations in South Gujerat. Oxford: Oxford University Press.

Campbell, Ben. 1997. The Heavy Loads of Tamang Identity. *In* Nationalism and Ethnicity in a Hindu Kingdom: The Politics of Culture in Contemporary Nepal. David Gellper, Joanna Pfaff-Czarneeka, and John Whelpton, eds. Pp. 205–35. Amsterdam: Harwood Academic Publishers.

Chandrashekar, C. P. 1997. The Economic Consequences of the Abolition of Child Labour, Journal of Peasant Studies 24(3):137–79.

Child Workers in Nepal (CWIN). 1993. Misery Behind the Looms, Kathmandu: Child Workers in Nepal Concerned Centre.

Clarke, Graham. 1980. A Helambu History. Journal of Nepal Research Centre 4:1–38.

Cook, Scott. 1993. Craft Commodity Production, Market Diversity, and Differential Rewards in Mexican Capitalism Today. *In* Crafts in the World Market: The Impact on Global Exchange on Middle American Artisans. June Nash, ed. Pp. 59–83. Albany, NY: State University of New York Press.

Daily Telegraph The. 2000. Situation Analysis of Child Labour in Nepal URL: <http: www.nepalnews.com> (February 23, 2000).

Denwood, Philip. 1974. The Tibetan Carpet. Warminster: Aris & Philips.

Desjarlais, Robert. 1992. Body and Emotion: The Aesthetics of Illness and Healing in the Nepal Himalayas. Philadelphia, Pa: University of Pennsylvania Press.

Dixit, Praveen M. 1995. Economic Reform in Nepal: A Cursory Assessment. Institutional Reform and the Informal Sector (IRIS) Country Report No. 17. College Park: University of Maryland, Center for Institutional Reform and the Informal Sector.

Eiland, Murray. 1992. Cutting Loops: The Unique Weaving of the Tibetan Carpet. The Nepalese–Tibetan Carpet, Kathmandu: Nepal Traveller.

Fricke, Tom. 1989. The Family Contexts of Marriage Timing in Nepal. Ethnology 29: 135–58.

Fricke, Tom. 1990. Family Organisation and the Wage Labour Transition in a Tamang Community of Nepal. Human Ecology 18: 283–313.

Giddens, Anthony. 1990. The Consequences of Modernity. Stanford, Calif.: Stanford University Press.

Graner, Elvira. 2001. Labour Markets and Migration in Nepal: The Case of Workers in Kathmandu Carpet Manufactories. Mountain Research and Development 21: 253–9.

His Majesty's Government of Nepal (HMG). 1997. Nepal Living Standards Survey Report: Main Findings (Volume Two). Kathmandu: His Majesty's Government Central Bureau of Statistics.

His Majesty's Government of Nepal (HMG). 1998. Statistical Pocket Book. Katmandu: His Majesty's Government Central Bureau of Statistics.

James, Allison, Chris Jenks, and Alan Prout. 1998. Theorizing Childhood. New York: Teacher's College Press.

Kathmandu Post. The 1998. Twenty-Three Children Rescued from Sweatshop URL.: <http: www.nepalnews.com> (December 30, 1998).

Leinbach, Thomas R., and John F. Watkins. 1998. Remittances and Circulation Behaviour in the Livelihood Process: Transmigrant Families in South Sumatra. Indonesia. Economic Geography 74: 45–63.

Nash, June. 1993. Introduction. In Crafts in the World Market: The Impact of Global Exchange on Middle American Artisans. June Nash. ed. Pp. 1–22. Albany, NY State University of New York Press.

National Society for Protection of Environment and Children (NASPEC). 1994. Status of Child Labour in Carpet Industry. Kathmandu: Institute of Trade and Development.

Nepal Independent Carpet Workers' Union (NICWU). 1996. Proceeds from the First Carpet Workers' Convention. Kathmandu: General Federation of Nepalese Trade Unions.

Nepal South Asia Centre (NESAC). 1998. Nepal Human Development Report 1998. Kathmandu: Nepal South Asia Centre.

Nieuwenhuys, Olga. 1994. Children's Lifeworlds: Gender, Welfare and Labour in the Developing World. London: Routledge.

O'Neill, Tom. 1997. Carpets, Markets and Makers: Culture and Entrepreneurship in the Tibeto-Nepalese Carpet Industry. Ph.D. dissertation, Department of Anthropology, McMaster University.

O'Neill, Tom. 2001. Nepalese Entrepreneurial Communities and the European Hand-Knotted Carpet Market. In Plural Globalities and Multiple Localities. Martha Rees and Josephine Smart, eds. Pp. 149–65. Lanham, Md: University Press of America.

Onta-Bhatta, Lazima. 1997. Political Economy, Culture and Violence: Children's Journey to the Urban Streets. Studies in Nepali History and Society 2: 207–253.

Sattaur, Omar. 1993. Child Labour in Nepal. London: Anti-Slavery International, Child Labour Series No. 13.

Schneider, Jane. 1988. European Expansion and Hand-Crafted Cloth: A Critique of Oppositional Use-Value vs Exchange Value Models. Journal of Historical Sociology 1: 431–7.

Tamang, Pashu Ram. 1992. Tamangs Under the Shadow. Himal. May/June: 25–7.

Thaker, Prabba. 1993. Technology: Women's Work and Status. Kathmandu: International Centre for Integrated Mountain Development.

United States Agency for International Development (USAID). 1994. The End of the Carpet induced Boom? Kathmandu: USAID ECON Internal, June 16.

Carol Saunders, Craig Van Slyke and Douglas R. Vogel

MY TIME OR YOURS? MANAGING TIME VISIONS IN GLOBAL VIRTUAL TEAMS

A S TECHNOLOGY TRANSCENDS SPATIAL, temporal, and organizational boundaries, Global Virtual Teams (GVTs) are becoming increasingly popular. This popularity is a result of several factors: (1) organizations increasingly rely upon virtual teams to accomplish organizational goals as the knowledge required to solve problems expands beyond the capacity of any single individual; (2) increases in telecommunication bandwidth promote the use of networks that link individuals inside and outside the organization; and (3) advances in collaborative technologies such as groupware make virtual teams increasingly effective for collaborating and decision-making.[1] As the popularity of GVTs increases, it becomes more important to understand those factors that affect the way they function. Time is one of those factors.

GVTs can leverage time to their advantage. Performing work asynchronously helps global organizations effectively bridge different time zones so that the teams are productive over more than one work period. For example, London team members of a GVT of software developers at Tandem Services Corporation initially coded the project and transmitted their code each evening to US team members for testing. US members forwarded the code they tested to Tokyo for debugging. London team members started their next day with the code debugged by their Japanese colleagues, and another cycle was initiated.[2] This is only one example of how GVTs can increase team-member productivity and reduce development time.

Unfortunately, positioning GVT members across different time zones also extends the workday and creates work delays and coordination difficulties. Normal working hours for one team member may be midnight for another. GVTs may also need to work through coordination difficulties created by national holidays and other slower-paced periods of work in the team members' different countries. One such slower period is the summer season when vacations frequently occur. In the Northern Hemisphere, summer occurs between June and August, while in the Southern Hemisphere it is between December and February. Thus, GVTs with members in both hemispheres need greater coordination among team members. Unlike more traditional teams, GVTs must coordinate distally separated team members using electronic and computer-mediated communication.

Finally, time works more subtly on GVTs due to different time visions that must be managed in order for the full potential of the team to be realized. *Time visions* are different perceptions of time across sets of time dimensions. They are based on different ethnic and national orientations about time that affect team-member perceptions of deadlines and team success[3] that are described below. Certain time visions may be more likely to encourage creativity.[4] Yet other time visions, especially in combination, may impede other aspects of GVTs. Thus, it is important, and challenging, to manage time visions to enhance GVT effectiveness across a range of tasks.

Understanding how individuals differ in their perceptions of time requires awareness of different temporal dimensions; these dimensions combine to form an individual's time vision. In the following section, we discuss several of these dimensions.

WHAT IS TIME?

Time is an extremely complex concept, as demonstrated by the descriptions of the various time dimensions in Table 1. Each culture develops a dominant conception of time by developing along these dimensions, many of which are interwoven. Merging a number of these dimensions results in four time visions, which we discuss in the next section.

DIFFERING TIME VISIONS

These various notions of time can help us understand the disparate time visions found in GVTs. Time visions differ across countries, longitudinal status (i.e., Eastern vs. Western), and even latitudinal status (i.e., southern vs. northern cultures).[5] Because of their cultural and religious foundations, time visions clearly can transcend national boundaries. Further, many different time visions can be held by the individual citizens of a single country.

Although our focus is on the cultural aspects of time visions, we recognize that individuals have an innate sense of time that is hidden in the more primitive reaches of their minds. In spite of its omnipresence, time is curiously invisible, taken for granted, and hard to explain. None the less, psychologists have often attempted to map "objective" time to "subjective" time and to find conditions (e.g., fatigue, mental disorders, drugs, etc.) that distort or otherwise affect an

Table 1. Time factors and associated dimensions

Dimension[6]	Description
Continuity	*Continuous* – time is viewed as a whole
	Discontinuous – time is viewed as a series of divisible, very small time units strung together and separated by temporal lacunae
Homogeneity	*Homogeneous* – each second is like another second; for example, a second is the duration of 9,192,631,770 periods of the radiation that corresponds to the transition between two hyperfine levels in the basic state of the atom of caesium$_{133}$[7]
	Epochal – units of time differ qualitatively, such as when focusing on events
Linearity	*Linear* – time is directional and flows from past to present to future
	Cyclical – time is seen in the recurring cycles such as annual seasons, life cycles, or circadian rhythms
Dimensionality	*Uni-Dimensional* – time flows in one, irreversible direction
	Bi-Directional – movement is forward or backward, as in mathematics and classical physics
	Cyclical – flow is recurrent
Abstraction	*Abstract* – time is viewed as the medium in which events occur; no reference is made to "past", "present", or "future"
	Concrete – not all parts in the sequence of events can be experienced at the same time (e.g., gestation or metamorphosis unfolds over time)
Subjectivity	*Objective* – time is based upon the oscillations of subatomic particles; is independent of consciousness
	Subjective – time must be experienced; involves an individual's awareness of a transient state of affairs
	Intersubjective – time involves the agreement of individuals on the meaning of time; must be experienced
Long-term/Short-term	*Long-term* – society values future rewards; the time span of discretion extends far into the future
	Short-term – society fosters values related to the past and present; time span of discretion focuses on the "here" and "now"
Chronicity	*Monochronicity* – events are scheduled separately, and only one thing is done at a time
	Polychronicity – multiple activities occur at the same time; transactions are handled together rather than completed separately according to strict schedule.

individual's estimation of time. For example, time seems to pass much more quickly when one is having a good time than when one is bored. Relevant individual traits include one's personal sense of time urgency (i.e., concern with the passage of time) and time perspective (i.e., orientations toward past,

Table 2. Examples of time visions

Dimension	Clock	Event	Timeless	Harmonic
Continuity	Discontinuous	Continuous	Continuous	Continuous
Homogeneity	Homogeneous	Epochal	Epochal	Homogeneous
Linear/Cyclical	Linear	Cyclical	Cyclical	Cyclical
Direction	Uni-Dimensional	Recurrent	Recurrent	Recurrent
Abstraction	Abstract	Concrete	Abstract	Concrete
Objectivity	Relatively Objective	Subjective	Subjective	Intersubjective
Time Horizon	Short-term	Long-term	Long-term	Long-term
Chronicity	Monochronic	Formal–Monochronic; Informal–Polychronic	Polychronic	Monochronic

present, or future).[8] However, even though individuals' sense of time is psychologically based, it is refined by participation in society and culture. Thus, it is virtually impossible to separate time from culture at some level. Table 2 offers four common examples of types of time visions that are held by large numbers of people: clock, event, timeless, and harmonic.

Clock

American, Anglo-Saxon, Germanic, and Scandinavian countries often hold a clock time vision, or a view of time as a scarce commodity.[9] This time vision draws heavily from the concept of time as linear – a concept that had its birth in the Judaic religion. This view of time also is partially based on Isaac Newton's view of time as abstract, mathematical, quantifiable, and flowing by itself, independently of man. But, the clock time vision, in contrast to that held by Newton's classical physics, considers time to be uni-dimensional, and irreversible. Further, it is often short term and monochronic.

Adopting a clock time vision that is linear and divisible into distinct homogenous units allows one to adopt metaphors of time as a commodity that can be lost, spent, or wasted. This conceptualization of time, sometimes referred to as the economicity of time, is recognized as a significant contributor to the development of the Industrial Revolution.[10] It fostered specialized jobs broken into time units that allowed organizations to pay employees for the time they worked rather than on a piecework basis. With this conceptualization, time is a resource that can be measured and manipulated to make organizations more efficient or productive by shortening the amount of time it takes to complete a given amount of work.[11]

Event

An event time vision offers a marked contrast to time as a scarce commodity. An event time vision perceives time as cyclical, continuous (holistic), and epochal.

As is often the case when time is viewed as cyclical, time is recurrent. Thus, there would appear to be an unlimited supply of time, and wasting it is not a concern. This time vision is common in Japan where there is a keen sense of the unfolding of time. In Japan, there is an emphasis on passing from one phase of an activity to another, rather than on the total time involved.

Consider, for example, the mandatory, two-minute exchange of business cards between Japanese executives meeting each other for the first time. This time-activity segment marks the beginning of a relationship phase. Many other events are characterized not only by well-defined beginnings and endings, but also by unambiguous phase-switching signals (e.g., cherry blossom viewing, gift-giving routines, sake-drinking sessions, etc.). This concrete, epochal, event-driven, long-term, holistic view of time is consistent with the Japanese love of compartmentalization of procedure, tradition, and ritual. The Japanese compartmentalized view of time is consistent with the monochronic way in which they approach the impersonal, official business side of their lives.[12] However, in their personal lives, when the Japanese look inward, toward themselves and their integrated system of relationships, they tend to be polychronic and long term in their orientation. This culturally based long-term orientation influences how Japanese organizations undertake strategic planning.[13]

Timeless

Regions where Hinduism or Buddhism predominates tend to adopt the timeless view of time. Hinduism views the world in terms of simultaneous creation and destruction. In such a world the passage of time is insignificant. The world is seen as timeless, even though time may be viewed as real for trivial tasks like daily chores. Thus, the timelessness of Hinduism is long term, abstract, and epochal. It is also continuous, cyclical, polychronic, and recurrent. Buddhism, which arose from a sixth-century reform movement of Hinduism, is based on a similar concept of timelessness, especially in its view of the soul reaching a timeless state of Nirvana. For Buddhists, only the instantaneous sensation is real, while duration, in contrast, is a construction of the imagination.[14] In a Buddhist culture, both life and time go round in a circle: generation follows generation; seasons follow seasons; monsoons, earthquakes, and other catastrophes recur; and the sun and moon rise and set day after day. With this time vision, it makes little sense to make a quick decision since opportunities, risks, and dangers eventually reappear when the decision-makers are so many days, weeks, or months wiser. People with a timeless vision may become so engrossed in their work that they are likely to develop and apply creative ideas.[15]

Harmonic

In contrast to the timelessness of Hinduism and Buddhism, Confucianism and Taoism promote a time vision based on harmony. These latter religious systems that predominate in China and other parts of the world seek temporal harmony within the person, among individuals, and between society and nature.[16] Time is very concrete for the Chinese mind, and it is perceived as an aspect of dynamic, living systems that needs to be explored qualitatively. Hence, this time vision is intersubjective since it takes into account the perceptions of others in the society, as well as the individual. Like the event and timeless time visions, it is long term, cyclical, continuous, and recurrent. However, it is also homogeneous to the extent that each second has value and is monochronic in its focus on working on one task at a time. In China, where the harmonic time vision is common, it is customary to thank participants for contributing their valuable time. Punctuality is considered so important that it is not unusual for Chinese to arrive 15 to 30 minutes early for a two-person meeting "in order to finish the business before the time appointed for its discussion" to keep from stealing the other person's time.[17]

TIME VISIONS AND ORGANIZATIONS

The way that the dimensions of time are combined into time visions depends upon the society and work organization of the individuals holding these time visions. It has been argued all members of a particular society share a common temporal consciousness, or social time. Social time is a product of society, and the "units of time are often fixed by the rhythm of collective life".[18] The time visions of all individuals are shaped by the society in which they live and refined by the organizations in which they work. Thus, time visions are the product of a social construction about time that varies tremendously between and within societies.

In modern organizations, social time offers a means of ordering and co-ordinating activities. Factory and office employees order their work within the parameters and constraints of the workday. The high degree of functional specialization that first emerged during the Industrial Revolution requires the temporal coordination of the many-segmented activities within the organization. Temporal coordination requires planning and predictable schedules. Thus, formal organizations need to *schedule* activities in time, *synchronize* functionally specialized, time-segmented activities, and *allocate* the total amount of time among the total set of activities that need to be performed so as to maximize the organization's goals/priorities.[19]

Not surprisingly, organizations adopt a clock time vision to the extent that schedules are developed to make reliable predictions of the points in time at which specific actions will occur and to ensure temporal meshing. Schedules highlight priorities when allocating the scarce temporal resource and synchronizing employee activities. However, conceptualizing time as only objective, linear, homogenous, and divisible is neither inevitable, culturally universal, nor always desirable. Such an approach may be especially undesirable in GVTs.

VIRTUAL TEAMS AND TIME VISIONS

Like organizations, teams have social time around which their activities are organized. Teams, groups, and subcultures each develop social times that compete with one another in the selection of their society's dominant time. This article focuses on the mélange of conflicting time visions found in GVTs. Team members and managers face challenges when trying to reconcile and integrate the members' different social times. For example, active members of Baha'i and Jewish communities need to reconcile their religious calendar with their secular one. Holidays and practices are based on their religious holidays, while their children's school timetables and their work schedules are based on secular calendars.[20]

Do different time visions affect the performance of GVTs? We believe that they do. They create alternate views of scheduling and consequently impact meeting deadlines. They affect synchronizing member activities into an underlying rhythm. Further, the differing visions impact the allocation of resources to the extent that they affect how performance is measured and rewarded. In the following section, we address three issues (i.e., deadlines, rhythms, and performance measures) typically associated with clock time vision and demonstrate how other time visions can be used in managing these issues.

Scheduling time: deadlines

GVT members who hold a clock time vision view time deadlines in terms of the completion of a series of activities along a timeline. The timelines that they use are divided into intervals with homogeneous units of measure. The needed tasks are performed in a sequence with prescribed milestones. This enables planning using such tools as Gantt or PERT charts. But the focus on deadlines and schedules hampers polychronicity[21] or the ability to handle multiple tasks at one time. It also tends to eliminate interpersonal and nontask communication and interactions as team members focus on their assigned task.[22] These types of interactions help build a cohesive team identity.

In contrast, a timeless time vision allows a more holistic view of deadlines. With this time vision, neither the time requirements for various activities nor their sequencing is considered. Rather, each activity is epochal and has a value of its own. One finds performing each activity in the present moment to be very wholesome.

When studying GVTs from a clock time vision, Jarvenpaa, et al., found that the most successful virtual teams in their study used their time well and had few purely social exchanges.[23] In contrast, it is unlikely that holders of cyclical time visions would be too excited about using their time well. Further, the focus on scheduled production may not be as pronounced when holding a cyclical time vision. Temporary teams rarely exhibit dysfunctional group dynamics, such as dealing with jealousy and hurt feelings, because they do not have enough time to do so.[24] They must concentrate on the primary task assigned to their team. But, would someone who does not view time along a timeline but lives in the moment be concerned about completing an assigned task by the deadline set for the temporary virtual team? For example, those who hold a timeless time vision may unintentionally ignore the passing of time if it means that conversations would be left unfinished. They may consider reality of the moment as something that can be molded or stretched, irrespective of schedules. Therefore, one would be unlikely to hear an individual with a timeless, or any cyclical, time vision bemoaning time as wasted, spent, or used.

Synchronizing time: team rhythms

Clock time vision was clearly evident in Gersick's[25] work on punctuated equilibrium, or alternating periods of inertia and activity. Using this perspective, a team's rhythm develops in response to its deadline. At the midpoint between the starting point of a project and its scheduled completion time, team members transition from preliminary activities to a more hectic pace undertaken to complete the project on time. When viewed from a clock time vision, the team members consider time as linear and divisible. At the halfway point, their actions change to allow them to meet the deadline by effectively pacing and synchronizing their activities. Thus, they synchronize their activities by segmenting time into homogeneous units and temporally segregating their team's activities.

Though a clock time vision often predominates in organizations and teams such as those studied by Gersick, time visions that are based on cycles cannot be ignored when looking at a team's rhythms. Team members need to mesh their individual cycles into a synchronized pattern of activities. To be successful, a GVT needs to establish a rhythm that recognizes the repeating cycles inherent in its tasks or characteristics.[26] In one study of GVTs, the repeating cycles of activity were structured around intense face-to-face meetings. These meetings served as the team's heartbeat that rhythmically pumped new life into the team's processes. Most team communications occurred around the face-to-face meetings. In between the meetings, team members interacted in response to previous meetings or in anticipation of the next meeting. The beat speeded up when the task became more complex or interdependent and slowed when tasks were unambiguous and roles were well defined.

Toyoda Kiichiro, the founder of Toyota Motor Company, viewed synchronization as the critical aspect of manufacturing efficiency. In order to make production at Toyota more efficient in the 1930s, he purchased the latest and most sophisticated machines. But dramatic increases in efficiency were not realized because each machine completed jobs at a different speed. It was then that Kiichiro designed a just-in-time manufacturing process where each phase was synchronized with every other phase in a smooth coordinated flow. Synchronization took into account the rhythms of the whole production system – humans, machinery, and equipment. Kiichiro's approach contrasts with the approach used at Ford and other American automobile manufacturing companies which makes manufacturing more efficient by squeezing wasted time from each individual task in the sequence.[27] Typically the entire system is not synchronized.

Allocating time: performance measures

Time visions also play a role in measuring GVT performance. Because a clock vision makes it easier to estimate and account for labor costs, most accounting systems are based on a clock time vision. Time spent on a particular task can be broken into units of time and costed out. With a clock vision, the work of GVTs can be assigned to team members using a rational allocation scheme, and progress can be monitored with completion targets derived from accounting-based guidelines. However, approaches to time management based upon accounting practices with a clock time vision are inadequate for understanding project-based team processes.[28] With the clock time vision, work is perceived to follow an orderly, managerially imposed timeline and timetable comprised of discrete, measurable activities with predictable durations, sequencing, and interactions.

However, this is not always the case. For example, an Executive Information Systems (EIS) development project did not always have discrete, measurable activities with predictable durations and sequencing. Rather, project work was often socially organized and characterized by routine activities and unexpected interruptions that both recurred in a cyclical manner. Multiple cycles existed within the project and included daily report updates, weekly team meetings, annual budgeting rounds, and occasional software upgrades. Project members needed to negotiate how these cycles would be handled. Further, since project members were assigned to several different projects, they were often forced to choose among a number of projects as they packed activities into their time-constrained schedules. They actually ended up using a relaxed and informal time management approach rather than one based on detailed time-planning or record-keeping. Thus, an event time vision was much more appropriate for measuring performance with cyclical (but changing) routines, interruptions, and uneven changes in the pace of the project. We believe that, like this project, GVTs can benefit from an event time vision, especially when the GVT members are assigned to several different projects at the same time.

MANAGING TIME VISIONS

Each of these issues (i.e., deadlines, rhythms, and performance measures) can be mapped back to management problems experienced around the globe: temporal uncertainty, conflicting temporal interests and requirements, and the inherent scarcity of temporal resources.[29] Temporal uncertainty arises from differences in time vision. It also arises from unexpected complications. Scheduling and synchronizing reduce temporal uncertainty to the extent that the starting and ending points can be specified. Thus, scheduling and synchronizing may both be linked to deadlines. Synchronization is the mutual adjustment of various social units. This adjustment reduces conflicts and coordinates activities so that they can be executed smoothly. Understanding and generating the underlying rhythms promote this synchronization. Finally, efficiently matching available time with required activities is the focus of allocation. This requires assigning priorities or values to tasks. The performance measurement system should reflect these priorities or values.

Because team members are separated by time and space, virtual teams, especially global ones, often acutely experience these three problems. We believe that, although time visions cannot easily be changed, they can and should be managed. Some approaches to managing different time visions include:

- creating awareness of the differences,
- facilitating the development of team norms,
- creating an intersubjective time vision,
- matching technology to time visions,
- avoiding time language traps, and
- applying the appropriate measures of performance.

Table 3 applies these approaches to the three problem areas.

Creating awareness

Teams that are unable to manage differences in time visions regarding deadlines may be unable to work well collaboratively.[30] The first step in managing time visions is to make GVT members aware of differences in time visions. For example, if some GVT members with a clock time vision are not aware of the perceptions of other members with an event time vision, they are likely to be frustrated when their team members do not hold deadlines in the same high regard and, consequently, fail to meet them. Team members whose views of time differ markedly from those of their teammates may exhibit withdrawal behaviors such as low satisfaction, absenteeism, and turnover.[31] Becoming aware of differences in time visions helps team members understand the practices and traditions related to alternative time visions, thereby decreasing withdrawal behaviors.

Just as the Myers–Briggs test identifies the cognitive styles of team members, a test could be devised to uncover different time visions. In the absence of such a test, managers may take special pains to watch for and address possible misunderstandings related to different time visions. They could meet privately with employees to bring up time-sensitive issues related to their understanding of deadlines and ways to meet those deadlines. Team members and managers alike could initiate discussions to gain a better understanding of members' time visions. This is difficult because team members may not be able to articulate – or even know – their time visions. Yet, it can be done. At least one study demonstrated that managers who had worked with team members for some time were able to identify the extent of polychronicity in their subordinates.[32] Training may help them identify differing time visions and articulate their own.[33]

When imposing deadlines, work times, and physical monitoring, managers should take into account the differing rhythms evolving from the members' time visions. For instance, effective flight crews adapted to the different temporal perspectives of other crew members during time-constrained, high-workload

Table 3. Examples of solutions to problems in managing time visions

Solutions	ISSUE (Associated Problem)		
	DEADLINES (Temporal uncertainty)	RHYTHMS (Conflicting temporal interests and requirements)	PERFORMANCE MEASURES (Scarce temporal resources)
Creating Awareness	Awareness of differences helps team members understand why some members are not as concerned about deadlines as others, reducing withdrawal behavior.	Appropriate timing (neither too loose or tight) promotes consensus and coordination of non-routine activities.	Individuals with clock time vision may be assigned to production-oriented or scheduling tasks.
Developing Team Norms	Norms on punctuality, attendance, and scheduling help in establishing and meeting deadlines and reducing uncertainty.	Norms help coordinate each activity; norms about temporal aspects of standard operating procedures reduce conflict among team members.	Individuals with harmonic time vision may be helpful in balancing and mediating tensions generated by other time visions.
Creating an Intersubjective Time Vision	Team members with clock time vision may be more vocal in proposing and forcing agreement on deadlines.	Team members with event time vision may bring focus to special activities, transitions, and cycles.	Intersubjective time vision must not stifle non-clock time visions when team is assigned creative tasks to perform.
Matching Technology to Time Visions	Automated scheduling tools make priorities and deadlines explicit, as well as offering reminders of approaching deadlines.	Automated scheduling tools assist in sequencing activities; asynchronous media help synchronize rhythms; asynchronous media allow monochronic individuals feeling the stress of meeting deadlines the ability to reschedule conflicting activities.	Automated scheduling tools assist in monitoring and tracking activities that cross multiple time visions.
Avoiding Time Language Traps	Precise understanding about deadlines and differences in uses of verb tenses and nouns reduces uncertainty.	Sensitivity to rhythms with different degrees of timeliness eases tensions.	Focus on harmony may encourage multiple shared appreciations and interpretations of time.
Applying Appropriate Performance Measures	Accounting systems need to reflect both deadlines and milestones on a well-defined timeline with individual accountability.	Team rhythms, cyclical routines, interruptions, uneven changes in pace, and aggregated team performance bear consideration.	Reward systems may be applied on the basis of time orientation and time scales.

flight simulations.[34] Crew members needed to overcome conflict and reach a consensus about team-level activities before they could jointly adapt to non-routine problems.

Considering different time visions may allow GVT managers to use limited resources more effectively. For example, GVT managers may take time visions into account when assigning individuals to teams, or when assigning tasks to individuals within a team (i.e., production-oriented or scheduling tasks may be best assigned to individuals who hold a clock time vision).

Facilitating the development of team norms

Managers of GVTs should avoid viewing cultural diversity as threatening or harmful. Rather, they need to fully appreciate all time visions. In particular, they need to realize that clock time vision prescriptions may not be the most appropriate for all GVTs. Instead, managers must take advantage of different time visions when they are responding to temporal uncertainty, reducing temporal conflicts, and dealing with scarce temporal resources.

Managers who anticipate incongruent time visions among team members can reduce ensuing uncertainty by arranging for them to participate in exercises (for example, brainstorming) that ensure they all have the same time perspective. Managers can also ask a person who is part way between the team members in polychronicity, time horizons, etc., or team members with harmonic time visions, to serve as intermediary at critical points of the team's development and decision making. Of course, in some cases the differences in time visions may be beneficial to the team. For example, GVTs composed of members with different time visions may be less likely to experience "groupthink".

GVT leaders should lay the groundwork for developing norms, or unwritten and often implicit rules, about how the team members should interact with one another. Norms are critical in synchronizing the actions of the team members to reduce temporal conflict and in establishing schedules to reduce temporal uncertainty. Without norms, team members would need to coordinate each activity with one or more of their teammates. This coordination becomes more demanding as the size of the team increases. Eventually implicit norms become translated into explicit rules, regulations, and standard operating procedures, with formalized sets of expectations about how team members are supposed to behave in each of their roles.[35]

As team members interact to establish team norms concerning the use of information and communication technologies, time vision differences may be highlighted and, hopefully, understood. In particular, norms on punctuality, conferencing etiquette, and scheduling should reflect differences in time vision. Norms should be established concerning telephone, email, and video conferencing etiquette (e.g., warning team members when a person will be out of town, guidelines for returning phone calls, etc.), meeting attendance and scheduling, work to be performed, punctuality, and constructive feedback.[36] Development of shared norms is more dynamic and achievable than many would initially suspect.[37]

Creating intersubjective time vision

Being aware of differences in time vision may not be enough. For example, individuals with cyclical time visions may not only place low priority on completing their tasks in a timely fashion, but they may also be difficult to train to work faster or be more focused on deadlines.[38] A view of time as linear and objective may be excellent for tight deadlines and well-organized schedules, but it is at odds with a vision of time as cyclical, epochal, polychronic, and subjective. GVT members cast the tone for their group in their first few message exchanges. This has clear implications for scheduling activities in team projects with specific deadlines. Team members, cognizant of differing time visions, may need to create a team vision of time early in the life of their project. In so doing, the vision will, of necessity, be intersubjective.

In creating an intersubjective time vision, individuals possessing a clock time vision may more actively seek to have the team time vision reflect their personal time vision. Time-urgent individuals who have a heavy focus on meeting deadlines (and who consequently have a linear, monochronic orientation to time) may persuade other team members to perform key tasks in a sequential manner.[39] A clock time vision in which the members focus on doing one thing at a time within a scheduled timeline may be especially appropriate for many production tasks. In other situations, however, it may be more efficient for teams working under tight deadlines to form subgroups, divide large tasks into subtasks, and allow the subgroups to perform the subtasks simultaneously.[40] Deadlines may need to be relaxed, and loose schedules may need to be employed to adapt to their varying rhythms.

Creating an intersubjective time vision may be especially important in tasks requiring creativity. Creative tasks may be hampered by over-concern with deadlines. Because of limited attention to resources, the more one's consciousness focuses on succession, the less attention it invests into the task itself. Full involvement in the task, or timelessness, increases the likelihood of creativity in regard to the task. Thus, for creative tasks, a cyclical time vision may be more desirable, whereas a clock time vision is more appropriate for straightforward production tasks.

All time visions may be highly desirable depending upon the task. Organizations can proactively take advantage of differing time visions to maximally support multi-cultural virtual teams.[41]

Matching technology to time visions

By definition, virtual teams rely heavily upon information and communications technology. That very technology may help accommodate different time visions:

- Automated scheduling tools, such as Gantt and PERT charts, make team members, especially team members with cyclical time visions, aware of team schedules. An example of this is the prototype of an "operation book" for scheduling surgery in a clinic. The tool is used to plan surgeries, decide upon and administer ad hoc changes for scheduled operations, communicate among clinical staff, and provide information for individual and team planning. The built-in planning function keeps track of the availability of operation theaters and personnel, medical–technical conditions which influence the timing of surgeries, and the compatibility of scheduled operations with personnel's working hours. Hence the tool promotes synchronization, the allocation of temporal resources, and coping with temporal uncertainty.[42]

- For GVT members with monochronic time visions who feel the stress of trying to do two or more things at the same time, technology can be used to reschedule one or more of the conflicting activities. For example, an individual can videotape an event (such as a meeting) so that it can be viewed at the individual's convenience. Or, asynchronous communication media such as email may be used to defer communication to a later time when the team member is less busy.
- Technology can make work events occur in a more predictable, regular sequence. For example, a new technology increased the monochronicity of radiologists' work by making the recurring events in their working day more structured and predictable. Further, radiologists and technicians experienced less conflict among themselves when their work patterns were synchronized.[43]

Other technological aids for time management can be conjectured: Automated tools for applying critical-path methods can identify a project's critical path and the possibility of simultaneous performance of tasks by subgroups; group collaboration tools with multi-channeling capabilities can expand the creativity abilities of team members with clock time visions; knowledge-management technologies may encourage GVTs to create shared time visions; collaboration systems and discussion forums are promising technologies for helping members of virtual teams understand each other's time visions, and consequently to move toward a shared, intersubjective time vision for the team; dynamic workflow systems help GVTs deal with differences in time vision, particularly if those systems are adaptive in terms of the time vision underlying the systems' design; and, intelligent agents can be programmed to recognize the different time visions of team members and to perform accordingly.

Avoiding time language traps

Problems are often created through the language traps about time and how that language is used. An objective, linear, clock time vision translates expressed time units into the appropriate action. On the other hand, Chinese employees often view units of time holistically and work to create an intersubjective meaning that extends beyond individual units of time. For example, an American boss in Hong Kong says to an employee "Wait a minute" without giving specific attention to how long that minute might really be but expecting the employee to leave after a short time. The Chinese employee may interpret this instruction literally and wait outside the boss's office door, not wanting to disturb him or her. This can go on for many minutes to an hour, depending on the circumstances. "Give me a minute" can be confusing to a non-westerner. Whose minute is it to give and who wants (or gets) it? Needless to say, the expression "I'll be with you in a minute" has many interpretations and expectations relative to different time visions. However, these are all metaphors we live by that, in the relative non-ambiguity of a single culture or a shared understanding of that culture, allow us to function effectively.[44] In multi-cultural GVTs, these ambiguous situations relating to the language of time should be avoided. Awareness of the problem is a major step in avoiding time language traps.

Precise language becomes particularly important in conveying expectations about deadlines. A deadline may specify (1) the latest time an activity must start; (2) the time before which an activity may not start; (3) the earliest time an activity may cease; (4) the latest time an activity must be completed; and (5) the precise time an event must start or cease. The meaning of deadlines is conveyed both in the wording and the underlying expectations in the following examples:

> If the next bus is due to leave a certain station at 6:03 p.m., this does not so much predict that it will leave at precisely 6:03 as it insures that it won't leave before that moment and offers a loose prediction that it will leave as soon thereafter as conditions permit. Similarly, if a store says it closes at 5:00 p.m., we expect it to be open at 4:50 but would not be surprised if it had not closed up by 5:01. If a ballgame is scheduled to start at 2 p.m., we would expect to see the opening kickoff by arriving in our seat at 1:59:55 but would not be surprised if it had begun at 2:01. On the other hand, a summons to the boss's office at 2:00 p.m. probably means that you had better be there at or before 2, although the boss may not be ready to see you until after 2. Starting time for a class, or a work shift, implies arrival at least by that time; and a starting time for a party often means "don't show up until sometime later than that".[45]

Of course, the meanings about deadlines vary to an even greater extent when the deadlines are specified in different cultures. For example, in Latin countries, the party begins when the partygoers converge – which is often hours after the specified starting time. In other cultures, guests are expected to arrive at the time when the host told them that the party would start.

Finally, the level of detail specified when talking about the future has been linked to improved planning.[46] Managers who use the future perfect tense (i.e., set goals in the future perfect tense; e.g., I *will have completed* the top five activities on my to-do list) plan more effectively than those who speak in the future tense (I *will complete* the top five activities on my to-do list). Here the language reflects the way that these managers think about time. Of course, this is an example in English, a language that has 22 simple and continuous verb tenses. Not all languages have similar tenses. For example, the languages of Indonesia and Malaysia have no verb tenses. Rather, time is conveyed through the use of time adverbs (e.g., yesterday) or time indicators (e.g., already).

Temporal uncertainty arises from language differences not only because of varying uses of verb tenses but also from the use (or lack of use) of appropriate nouns. For example, the Nuer tribe in Sudan has words for month and day but not for any unit of time in between.[47] And whereas the seasons are nouns in many languages, the Hopi seasons are treated like adverbs. "The Hopi cannot talk about summer being hot, because summer is the quality hot, just as apple has the quality red. Summer and hot are the same! Summer is a *condition*: hot. There is nothing about summer that suggests it involves time."[48] GVT managers may reduce temporal uncertainty by being aware of language differences in the use of nouns and verbs.

Applying appropriate performance measures

Good evaluation and compensation systems motivate task- and team-related behaviors. New evaluation systems may be needed for GVTs to assess both individual contribution to the team and the nature of team performance as a whole. Nandhakumar and Jones found that traditional management accounting approaches with strictly enforced deadlines and individual accountability were too mechanistic to capture the complexity of the process of an executive information system (EIS) project development team.[49] Instead they suggested target cost management applied to the team as a whole, or a team-budget approach. Applying their findings to GVTs, team performance and budget allocation should be reviewed systematically, and team activities should be coordinated using an event or harmonic time vision. A simple accounting approach based on the regular review of an aggregated team budget may have advantages over an individual, project-based approach grounded in a clock time vision.

Organizations may also need to switch between different accounting systems to accommodate different time visions. An example comes from a mountain resort that keeps two sets of accounts: one for its cyclical, seasonal businesses (golfing in summer and skiing in winter) and the other to provide annual financial reports to its parent company, which operates on a regular fiscal year.[50]

GVT managers may also use knowledge of subordinates' time visions to guide procedures for rewarding performance. Subordinates holding time visions with shorter time orientations may be more responsive to frequent and immediate rewards than those with longer time orientations. Those with longer time orientations may be willing to sustain high levels of job performance if they perceive significant prospects for future rewards.[51]

Finally, GVT managers may wish to consider time-scales when measuring performance. A typical feature for a unit or system is its lifetime, or the duration of a process or of an occurrence. A typical lifetime determines the appropriate time-scale for a system.[52] For a mayfly the time-scale is one day, while a human's time-scale is approximately 70 years. When using an annual time-scale to assess the efficiency of banks in Cyprus, coastal banks in tourist areas were found to be less efficient than banks in other parts of the country. However, when using a

TIME VISIONS IN GLOBAL VIRTUAL TEAMS 313

finer time-scale, the month of July (which is the peak tourist season), the coastal banks were significantly more efficient. Apparently, coastal banks carried some slack over the entire year. While this decreased their efficiency on an annual basis, it allowed the coastal banks to cater to the huge tourist influx in July.[53] Thus, time-scales can help determine what period of time to use in measuring performance.

GVTs: CHALLENGES AND OPPORTUNITIES

It is clear that GVTs offer a number of managerial challenges in addition to opportunities. With this article we introduced more subtle issues that plague GVTs. Perceptions of time may be so innate that many managers may not be conscious of their potential to influence GVT performance. But even though the perceptions are innate, managers need to be aware of and respond to underlying value systems based on time visions. Fortunately, steps can be taken to manage diverse time visions in GVTs. Managers and members of GVTs should:

- Create awareness of different time visions among team members
- Facilitate the development of time-related team norms
- Create an intersubjective time vision
- Match information and communication technologies to time visions
- Avoid time language traps
- Apply multiple, appropriate performance measures that reflect sensitivity to differing time visions

Creating awareness among managers about different ways of considering time and its consequences is important for GVT success. Sensitivity to time visions presents many opportunities for productively creating and managing GVTs. Synergism within a multi-time vision GVT can lead to creative ways of dealing with schedules and tensions and generate new ways of addressing complex issues that might not emerge in a GVT with only a single time vision. Many issues about time visions remain to be explored – but, unfortunately, we are out of time.

ACKNOWLEDGMENTS

We would like to thank Pam Carter, Rusty Saunders, Johanna Vogel, and the attendees of seminars at National University of Singapore, Nanyang Technical University, and Virginia Polytechnic Institute and State University for their comments on earlier versions of this paper. An earlier version of this paper was presented at the Tenth Annual Cross Cultural Workshop in Barcelona, Spain in December, 2002.

NOTES

1   Townsend, A. M., DeMarie, S., and Hendrickson, A. R. 1998. Virtual teams: technology and the workplace of the future. *The Academy of Management Executive*, 12(3): 17–28.

2   Boudreau, M. C., et al. 1998. Going global: using information technology to advance the competitiveness of the virtual transnational organization. *The Academy of Management Executive*, 12(4): 120–8.

3   Waller, M. J., et al. 2001. The effect of individual perceptions of deadlines on team performance. *Academy of Management Review*, 26(4): 586–600.

4   Mainemelis, C. 2001. When the muse takes it all: a model for the experience of timelessness in organizations. *Academy of Management Review*, 26(4): 548–65.

5   See Hofstede; Lewis, R. D. 1996. *When cultures collide: managing successfully across culutres*. London: Nicholas Brealey Publishing; Vatsyayan, S. H. 1981. *A sense of time: an exploration of time in theory, experience and art*. Delhi: Oxford University Press.

6   To learn more about Continuity, Homogeneity, Linearity, Dimensionality, Abstraction, and Subjectivity, see McGrath, J. E., and Kelly, J. R. 1986. *Time and human interaction*. New York: Guilford Press; Orlikowski, W., and Yates, J. 2002. It's about time: temporal structuring in organizations. *Organization Science*, 13(6): 684–700. Time orientation is studied by Hofstede, G. 1991. *Cultures and organizations: software of the mind*. London: McGraw-Hill; also Jaques, E. 1979. Taking time seriously in evaluating jobs. *Harvard Business Review*, September–October: 124–32. Chronicity is discussed in Hall, E. T. 1989. *The dance of life: the other dimension of time*. New York: Anchor Books; also Bluedorn, A. C., and Denhardt, R. 1988. Time and organizations. *Journal of Management*, 14(2) 299–320.

7   Jönsson, B. 2001. *Unwinding the clock: ten thoughts on our relationship to time*. Bruno, Calif.: Audio Literature.

8   Waller, et al.

9   Lewis.

10 Ancona, D. G., Okhuysen, G. A., and Perlow, L. S. 2001. Taking time to integrate temporal research. *Academy of Management Review*, 26(4): 512–29; Clark, P. 1985. A review of the theories of time and structure for organizational sociology. *Research in the Sociology of Organizations*, 4: 35–79.

11 Lee, H., and Liebenau, J. 2002. A new time discipline: Managing virtual work environments. In Whipp, R., Adam, B., and Sabelis, I. (eds.), *Making time: time and management in modern organizations*: 126–39. Oxford: Oxford University Press.

12 Hall.

13 Hay, M., and Usunier, J.-C. 1993. Time and strategic action: a multi-cultural view. *Time and Society*, 2(3): 313–33.

14 Vatsyayan.

15 Mainemelis.

16 Fraser.

17 Lewis.

18 Bluedorn, A. C., and Denhardt, R. 1988. Time and organizations. *Journal of Management*, 14(2): 299–320; Durkheim, E. 1976. *The elementary forms of the religious life*, 2nd edn. London: George Allen & Unwin.

19 McGrath, J. E., and Rotchford, N. L. 1983. Time and behavior in organizations. *Research in Organizational Behavior*, 5: 57–101.

20 Orlikowski and Yates.

21 Conte, J. M., Rizzuto, R. E., and Steiner, D. D. 1999. A construct-oriented analysis of individual polychronicity. *Journal of Managerial Psychology*, 14(3/4): 269–87; Waller, M. J., Giambatista. R. C., and Zellmer-Bruhn, M. 1999. The effects of individual time urgency on group polychronicity. *Journal of Managerial Psychology*, 13: 244–56.

22 McGrath, J. E., et al. 1990. Intellectual teamwork. In McGrath, et al. (eds.), *Social technological foundations of cooperative work*: 23–61.

23 Jarvenpaa, S. L., Knoll, K., and Leidner, D. E. 1998. Is anybody out there? Antecedents of trust in global virtual teams. *Journal of Management Information Systems*, 14(4): 29–64.

24   Meyerson, D., Weick, K. E., and Kramer, R. M. 1996. Swift trust and temporary groups. In R. M. Kramer and T. R. Tyler (eds.), *Trust in organizations: frontiers of theory and research*: 166–95. Thousand Oaks, Calif.: Sage Publications.

25   Gersick, C. J. G. 1988. Time and transition in work teams: toward a new model of group development. *Academy of Management Journal*, 31: 9–41; Gersick, C. J. G. 1989. Marking time: predictable transitions in task groups. *Academy of Management Journal*, 32: 274–309.

26   Maznevski, M. L., and Chudoba, K. 2000. Bridging space over time: global virtual team dynamics and effectiveness. *Organization Science*, 11(5): 473–92.

27   Nishimoto, I. 2002. Cooperation engineered: efficiency in the "just-in-time" system. In Whipp, Adam, and Sabelis (eds.), 104–14.

28   Nandhakumar, J., and Jones, M. 2001. Accounting for time: managing time in project-based team working. *Accounting. Organizations and Society*, 26(3): 193–214.

29   McGrath and Rotchford.

30   Vinton, D. E. 1992. A new look at time, speed, and the manager. *The Academy of Management Executive*, 6(4): 7–16.

31   Schiber, J. B., and Gutek, B. A. 1987. Some time dimensions of work: measurement of an underlying aspect of organization culture. *Journal of Applied Psychology*, 72(4): 642–50.

32   Conte, Rizzuto, and Steiner.

33   Bluedorn and Denhardt; Beldona, S., Inkpen, A. C., and Phatak, A. V. 1998. Are Japanese managers more long-term oriented than United States managers? *Management International Review*, 38(3): 239–56.

34   Waller, M. J. 1999. The timing of adaptive group responses to nonroutine events. *Academy of Management Journal*, 42: 127–37.

35   Hassard.

36   Kiser, K. 1999. Working on world time. *Training*, 36(3): 28–34; Duarte, D., and Snyder, N. 1999. *Mastering virtual teams: Strategies, tools and techniques that succeed*. San Francisco, Calif.: Jossey-Bass; Furst, S., Blackburn, R., and Rosen, B. 1999. Virtual team effectiveness: a proposed research agenda. *Information Systems Journal*, 9(4): 249–70.

37   Rutkowski, A., et al. 2002. E-collaboration: the reality of virtuality. *IEEE Transactions on Professional Communication*, 45(4): 219–30.

38   Waller, et al., 2001.

39   Hall; Waller, M. J., Giambatista, R. C., and Zellmer-Bruhn, M. 1999. The effects of individual time urgency on group polychronicty. *Journal of Managerial Psychology*, 13: 244–56.

40   McGrath and Rotchford; Waller, M. J. 1997. Keeping the pins in the air: how groups juggle multiple tasks. In M. Beyerlein and D. Johnson (eds.), *Advances in interdisciplinary studies of work teams*. 4: 217–47. Greenwich: JAI Press.

41   Qureshi, S., and Vogel, D. 2001. Organizational adaptiveness in virtual teams. *Group Decision and Negotiation*, 10(1): 27–46.

42   Egger, E., and Wagner, I. 1992. Time management: a case for CSCW. *CSCW Proceedings*, 249–56.

43   Barley, S. R. 1988. On techology, time and social order: technologically induced change in the temporal organization of radiological work. In Dubinskas, F. A. (ed.), *Making time: ethnographies of high-technology organizations*: 123–69. Philadelphia, Pa: Temple University Press.

44   Lakoff, G., and Johnson, M. 1980. *Metaphors we live by*. Chicago, Ill.: University of Chicago Press.

45   McGrath and Rotchford, 77.

46   Bluedorn and Denhardt.

47   Adam, B. 1995. *Timewatch: and the social analysis of time*. Cambridge: Polity Press.

48   Hall, 37.

49   Nandhakumar and Jones.

50   Orlikowski and Yates.

51   Ebert, R. J., and Piehl, D. 1973. Time horizon: a concept for management. *California Management Review*, 15(4): 35–41.

52   Kümmerer, K. 1996. The ecological impact of time. *Time & Society*, 5(2): 209–35.
53   Zaheer, S., Albert, S., and Zaheer, A. 1999. Time scales and organizational theory. *Academy of Management Review*, 24(4): 725–41.

Roger Hallowell, David Bowen and Carin-Isabel Knoop

FOUR SEASONS GOES TO PARIS

Europe is different from North America, and Paris is very different. I did not say difficult. I said different.

A senior Four Seasons manager

THE LINKAGE BETWEEN SERVICE CULTURE AND COMPETITIVE ADVANTAGE

THE ENDURING SUCCESS OF service organizations such as Southwest Airlines, The Walt Disney Company, Wal-Mart, and USAA (among others) is frequently attributed in no small degree to their corporate cultures. These companies have built and maintained organizational cultures in which everyone is focused on delivering high customer value, including service, and individuals behave accordingly. The culture influences how employees behave, which, in turn, shapes the value that customers receive, in part through the thousands of daily encounters between employees and customers.

Corporate culture has been linked to competitive advantage in companies, for better or worse,[1] and in service companies, in particular.[2] Culture is so important in service companies because of its effect on multiple factors affecting customer value, factors as critical as employee behavior and as mundane (but important) as facility cleanliness. These aspects are especially visible to customers, who often co-produce a service with employees. In many services employee and customer interactions take place continually, in many parts of the organization, so that no realistic amount of supervision can ever exercise sufficient control over employee behavior. Under these circumstances, culture becomes one of management's most effective, if unobtrusive, tools to influence employee thoughts, feelings, and, most important, behavior.

UNDERSTANDING CORPORATE CULTURE

Our model of corporate culture, which uses Schein[3] as a point of departure, consists of the following four components: underlying assumptions, values, employee perceptions of management practices, and cultural artifacts.

Underlying assumptions

These are basic assumptions regarding the workplace, such as the assumption that subordinates should fulfill their job requirements as a condition of employment.

Values

These are those things that are viewed as most important in an organizational setting, such as cost control, customer satisfaction, and teamwork.

Values exist in two forms in organizations. The first is what can be termed "espoused values", which are what senior managers or company publications say the values are.

The second form is "enacted values", which are what employees infer the values to be. Although enacted values, *per se*, are invisible, employees infer what they are by examining the evidence found in the next two components of culture: management practices and cultural artifacts. These two components are more readily observed than assumptions and values.

Employee perceptions of management practices (particularly relating to human resources): policies and behaviors

Employees' views of practices such as selection, training, performance appraisal, job design, reward systems, supervisory practices, and so on shape their perceptions of what values are actually being enacted in a setting. For example, although customer service may be an espoused value, if job applicants are not carefully screened on service attitude, or if employees who provide great service are not recognized and rewarded, then employees will not believe that management truly values service. In short: culture is what employees perceive that management believes.

Cultural artifacts

These include heroes, rituals, stories, jargon, and tangibles like the appearance of employees and facilities. Again, given the espoused value of customer service, if jargon used to characterize customers is usually derogatory, then a strong service culture is unlikely to emerge.

In contrast, if espoused values are enacted – and thus reflected in policies, management behaviors, and cultural artifacts – then a culture may emerge in which senior management and employees share similar service-relevant thoughts, feelings, and patterns of behavior. This behavior has the potential to enhance customer value and contribute to competitive advantage.

EXPORTING CORPORATE CULTURE: CAN CULTURE TRAVEL ACROSS BORDERS?

If a company succeeds in creating a corporate culture that contributes to competitive advantage in its home country, can it successfully "export" that corporate culture to another country – particularly if that country's national culture is strongly distinct, as is the case in France?

The issue of flexibility versus consistency

Will an organization's *corporate* culture "clash" or "fit" with a different *national* culture? The key consideration here is what components of corporate culture link most tightly to competitive advantage and, as a consequence, must be managed *consistently* across country borders – even if they seem to clash with the culture of the new country. Alternatively, are there components of culture that are not critical to the linkage? If so, *flexibility* may enhance the competitiveness of the corporate culture given the different national culture.[4]

One way to frame this analysis is around whether the potential clash between corporate and national culture is over the corporate values themselves, i.e., *what* they are, or over the manner of their implementation, i.e., *how* they are enacted (specifically, management practices and cultural forms). Is there a clash between core corporate values and core country values? If so, and if those core values are critical to competitive advantage, then perhaps the company cannot be successful in that setting. If the clash is over how values are enacted, then some management practices or cultural forms can be modified in the new setting. However, this requires managers to ask which practices or forms can be modified, enhancing the competitive advantage of the corporate culture, and which practices, if modified, will undermine corporate culture.

In short, all of the elements of corporate culture can be thought of as the threads in a sweater: when a thread sticks out of a sweater, sometimes it is wisely removed, enhancing the overall appearance. However, sometimes removing a thread will unravel the entire sweater. Managers must determine which aspects of their corporate cultures will "stick out" in a new national environment and whether modifying or eliminating them will enhance the organization or weaken it.

FOUR SEASONS HOTELS AND RESORTS: OVERVIEW

In 2002, Four Seasons Hotels and Resorts was arguably the world's leading operator of luxury hotels, managing 53 properties in 24 countries. Being able to replicate "consistently exceptional service" around the world and across cultures was at the heart of the chain's international success and sustained advantage.

For Four Seasons, "consistently exceptional service" meant providing high-quality, truly personalized service to enable guests to *maximize the value of their time*, however guests defined doing so. Corporate culture contributed to the firm's success in two ways. First, through the values that the organization espoused. For Four Seasons, these were personified in the Golden Rule: "Treat others as you wish they would treat you." Second was the set of behaviors that employees and managers displayed, in effect the enactment of the firm's values. The organizational capability of translating core values into enacted behaviors created competitive advantage at Four Seasons. Doing so required managers to address a central question as they expanded into new countries: What do we need to keep consistent, and what should be flexible, i.e., what should we adapt to the local market?

Performance

Four Seasons generally operated (as opposed to owned) mid-sized luxury hotels and resorts. From 1996 through 2000 (inclusive), Four Seasons increased revenues from $121 million to $347.5 million and earnings from $55.7 million to $125.8 million, a 22.6 percent compounded annual growth rate (CAGR). Operating margins increased from 58.8 percent to 67.9 percent during the same period. Four Seasons' 2001 revenue per room (RevPAR), an important hospitality industry measure, was 32 percent above that of its primary United States competitors and 27 percent higher than that of its European competitors. Growth plans were to open five to seven new luxury properties per year, predominantly outside of North America.

Four Seasons entered the French market by renovating and operating the Hotel George V, a historic Parisian landmark. The hotel was renamed the Four Seasons Hotel George V Paris (hereafter, "F. S. George V").

International structure

Each Four Seasons property was managed by a general manager responsible for supervising the day-to-day operations of a single property. Compensation was in part based on the property's performance. Hotel general managers had a target bonus of 30 percent of base compensation. Twenty-five percent of the bonus was based on people measures (employee attitudes), 25 percent on product (service quality), and 50 percent on profit.

Four Seasons' management believed that the firm's regional management structure was a key component of its ability to deliver and maintain the highest and most consistent service standards at each property in a cost effective manner. General Managers reported directly to one of the 13 Regional Vice Presidents or directly to one of the two Senior Vice Presidents, Operations. A Regional Marketing Director, an Area Director of Finance, and a Regional Human Resources Director completed each support team. The majority of these individuals were full-time employees of a Four Seasons-managed property, with a portion of their time devoted to regional matters including both routine management and deciding how to customize Four Seasons operating practice to the region.

Management

Four Seasons' top management team was noted for its longevity, many having been at the firm for over 25 years. Characteristics which executives attributed to their peers included an international flair, a respect for modesty and compassion, and a "no excuses" mentality.

Italian in Italy, French in France

The firm's top managers were very comfortable in a variety of international settings. Antoine Corinthios, President, Europe, Middle East and Africa, for example, was said to be "Italian in Italy, French in France". Born and educated in Cairo, Corinthios then spent 20 years in Chicago but described himself as a world citizen. He was as much of a cultural chameleon as he wanted Four Seasons hotels to be. "When I speak the language of the environment I am in, I start to think in the language I am in and adapt to that culture. If you are going global, you cannot be one way," he explained.

No bragging, no excuses

Modesty, compassion, and discipline were also important. A manager who stayed with Four Seasons from the prior management of the George V described the Four Seasons due diligence team that came to the property as "very professional and not pretentious; detail oriented; and interested in people. They did not come telling me that all I did was wrong," he remembered, "and showed a lot of compassion. The people are good, but still modest – many people in the industry can be very full of themselves." Importantly, excuses were not tolerated at Four Seasons. "Oh, but we have just been open a year" or "The people here do not understand" were not acceptable statements.

Strong allegiance to the firm

Both corporate and field managers often referred to the firm as a "family", complete with rules, traditions, and tough love. There was a strong "one-firm sentiment" on the part of managers in the field; they worked for the firm, not for the individual property to which they were assigned. For example, a general manager explained, "We are happy to let stars go to other properties to help them."

Service orientation

Customer service extended to all levels in the organization. Managers sometimes assisted in clearing restaurant tables in passing. "If I see that something needs to get done," a manager explained. "I do it."

FOUR SEASONS' APPROACH TO INTERNATIONAL GROWTH

> Today, we have opened enough properties overseas that we can go into any city or town and pull people together to fulfill our mission.
>
> *Isadore Sharp, Founder and CEO*

Diversity and singularity

One of the things Four Seasons managers were wary about was being perceived as an "American" company. They found it useful in Europe to position Four Seasons as the Canadian company it was. One noted, "The daughter of a property owner once told us. 'I do not want you to be the way Americans are.' She assumed that Americans say 'Do it my way or take the highway.' Canadians are seen as more internationally minded and respectful of other value systems."

According to Corinthios, "Our strength is our diversity and our singularity. While the essence of the local culture may vary, the process for opening and operating a hotel is the same everywhere." He continued:

> My goal is to provide an international hotel to the business or luxury leisure traveler looking for comfort and service. The trick is to take it a couple of notches up, or sideways, to adapt to the market you are in. Our standards are universal, e.g., getting your message on time, clean room, good breakfast; being cared for by an engaging, anticipating and responding staff; being able to treat yourself to an exciting and innovative meal – these are global. This is the fundamental value. What changes is that people do it with their own style, grace, and personality; in some cultures you add the strong local temperament. For example, an Italian concierge has his own style and flair. In Turkey or Egypt you experience different hospitality.

As a result, "Each hotel is tailor made" and adapted to its national environment, noted David Crowl, Vice President Sales and Marketing, Europe, Middle East and Africa:

> Issy Sharp once told me that one of our key strengths is diversity. McDonald's is the same all over. We do not want to be that way. We are not a cookie cutter company. We try to make each property represent its location. In the rooms, we have 40 to 50 square meters to create a cultural destination without being offensive. When you wake up in our hotel in Istanbul, you know that you are in Turkey. People know that they will get 24-hour room service, a custom-made mattress, and a marble bathroom, but they also know that they are going to be part of a local community.

According to David Richey, president of Richey International, a firm Four Seasons and other hotel chains hired to audit service quality, "Four Seasons has done an exceptional job of adapting to local markets. From a design perspective, they are much more clever than other companies. When you sit in the Four Seasons in Bali, you feel that you are in Bali. It does not scream Four Seasons at you."

A manager explained Four Seasons' ability to be somewhat of a cultural chameleon with an analogy to Disney: "Unlike Disney, whose brand name is so strongly associated with the United States, Four Seasons' brand doesn't rigidly define what the product is. The Four Seasons brand is associated with intangibles. Our guests are not looking to stay in a Canadian hotel. Our product has to be 100 percent Four Seasons, but in a style that is appropriate for the country."

According to Crowl, Four Seasons learned from each country and property: "Because we are an international hotel company, we take our learning across borders. In Egypt, we are going to try to incorporate indigenous elements to the spa, but we will still be influenced by the best practices we have identified at our two spas in Bali."

Globally uniform standards

The seven Four Seasons "service culture standards" expected of all staff all over the world at all times were:

1. SMILE: Employees will actively greet guests, smile, and speak clearly in a friendly manner.
2. EYE: Employees will make eye contact, even in passing, with an acknowledgment.
3. RECOGNITION: All staff will create a sense of recognition by using the guest's name, when known, in a natural and discreet manner.
4. VOICE: Staff will speak to guests in an attentive, natural, and courteous manner, avoiding pretension and in a clear voice.

5. INFORMED: All guest contact staff will be well informed about their hotel, their product, will take ownership of simple requests, and will not refer guests elsewhere.
6. CLEAN: Staff will always appear clean, crisp, well-groomed, and well-fitted.
7. EVERYONE: Everyone, everywhere, all the time, show their care for our guests.

In addition to its service culture standards, Four Seasons had 270 core worldwide operating standards (see Appendix 1 for sample standards). Arriving at these standards had not been easy; until 1998 there were 800. With the firm's international growth, this resulted in an overly complex set of rules and exceptions. The standards were set by the firm's senior vice presidents and Wolf Hengst, President, Worldwide Hotel Operations, who explained: "We had a rule about the number of different types of bread rolls to be served at dinner and number of bottles of wine to be opened at lounges. But in countries where no bread is eaten at dinner and no wine is consumed, that's pretty stupid."

"While 270 standards might seem extensive," Richey noted, "if there are only 270, there are thousands of things that are not covered over which the general manager and local management team have a lot of control."

In addition, exceptions to the standards were permitted if they made local sense. For example, one standard stated that the coffee pot should be left on the table at breakfast so that guests could choose to refill their cups. This was perceived as a lack of service in France, so it was amended there. Standards were often written to allow local flexibility. While the standards require an employee's uniform to be immaculate, they do not state what it should look like. In Bali, uniforms were completely different from uniforms in Chicago. Managers underlined the fact that standards set *minimum expectations*. "If you can do something for a client that goes beyond a standard," they told staff, "do it." As a result, stories about a concierge taking a client to the hospital and staying with that person overnight were part of Four Seasons lore, contributing to cultural artifacts.

To evaluate each property's performance against the standards, Four Seasons used both external and internal auditors in its measurement programs. "Our standards are the foundation for all our properties," a senior manager noted. "It is the base on which we build." "When you talk to a Four Seasons person," Richey concluded, "they are so familiar with each of the standards, it is astonishing. With many managers at other firms this is not the case."

"We have been obsessed by the service standards," Hengst concluded. "People who come from the outside are surprised that we take them and the role they play in our culture so seriously. But they are essential. Talk to me about standards and you talk to me about religion." Another manager added, "Over time, the standards help to shape relationships between people, and those relationships contribute to building our culture."

Delivering intelligent, anticipatory, and enthusiastic service worldwide

A manager stated: "We decided many years ago that our distinguishing edge would be exceptional, personal service – that's where the value is. In all our research around the world, we have never seen anything that led us to believe that 'just for you' customized service was not the most important element of our success." Another manager added, "Service like this, what I think of as 'intelligent service', can't be scripted. As a result, we need employees who are as distinguished as our guests – if employees are going to adapt, to be empathetic and anticipate guests' needs, the 'distance' between the employee and the guest has to be small."

There were also tangible elements to Four Seasons' service quality. The product was always comfortable – so much so that at guests' requests, the company made its pillows, bedspreads, and mattresses available for sale. Guests could also count on a spacious bathroom, which was appreciated by the world traveler, especially in Europe where bathrooms tended to be small. "However there are differences in the perception and definition of luxury," explained Barbara Talbott, Executive Vice President of Marketing. "In the US our properties have public spaces with a luxurious, but intimate, feeling. In the Far East, our properties have large lobbies enabling guests to see and be seen. People around the world also have different ways of using a hotel – restaurants, for example, are more important in hotels in Asia, so we build space for more restaurants in each property there."

Human resources and the Golden Rule

Four Seasons' managers believed that human resource management was key to the firm's success. According to one senior manager. "People make the strength of this company. Procedures are not very varied or special. What we do is fairly basic." Human resource management started and ended with "The Golden Rule", which stipulated that one should treat others as one would wish to be treated. Managers saw it as the foundation of the firm's values and thus its culture. "The golden rule is the key to the success of the firm, and it's appreciated in every village, town, and city around the world. Basic human needs are the same everywhere," Sharp emphasized. Appendix 2 summarizes the firm's goals, beliefs and principles.

Kathleen Taylor, President, Worldwide Business Operations, provided an example of how Four Seasons went about enacting the Golden Rule as a core value. "We give employees several uniforms so they can change when they become dirty. That goes to their dignity, but it is uncommon in the hospitality industry. People around the world want to be treated with dignity and respect, and in most organizational cultures that doesn't happen."

Managers acknowledged that many service organizations made similar statements on paper. What differentiated Four Seasons was how the chain operationalized those statements. Crowl noted, "A service culture is about putting what we all believe in into practice. We learn it, we nurture it, and most important, we do it."

In 2002, for the fifth year in a row, Four Seasons was among *Fortune* magazine's list of the top 100 best companies to work for in North America. While turnover in the hospitality industry averaged 55 percent, Four Seasons turnover was half that amount.

GOING TO PARIS

However it developed its approach and philosophy, Four Seasons management knew that entering France would be a challenge.

The George V opportunity

The six hotels in Paris classified as "Palaces" were grand, historic, and luxurious. Standard room prices at the F. S. George V, for example, ranged from $400 to $700. Most palaces featured award-winning restaurants, private gardens, and expansive common areas. For example, the Hotel de Crillon, a competitor to the F. S. George V, was an 18th-century palace commissioned by King Louis XV. The nine-story George V was designed in the 1920s by two famous French art deco architects. The property was located in one of Paris's most fashionable districts. For comparative data on Parisian palaces, please refer to Appendix 3.

Observers of the Paris hotel scene noted that by the 1980s and 1990s, the George V, like some of its peers, was coasting on its reputation. In December 1996, HRH Prince Al Waleed Bin Talal Bin Abdulaziz al Saud purchased the hotel for $170 million. In November 1997, Four Seasons signed a long-term agreement to manage the hotel. "We needed to be in Paris," John Young, Executive Vice President, Human Resources, explained. "We had looked at a new development, but gaining planning permission for a new building in Paris is very hard. Since we look for the highest possible quality assets in the best locations, the George V was perfect. It established us very powerfully in the French capital."

In order to transform the George V into a Four Seasons, however, an extensive amount of effort had to be placed into both the tangible and experiential service which the property and its people could deliver.

Physical renovations

Four Seasons' challenge was to preserve the soul of the legendary, almost mythical, George V Hotel while rebuilding it for contemporary travelers. Four Seasons closed the hotel for what ended up being a two-year, $125 million total renovation. Because the building was a landmark, the façade had to be maintained. The interior of the hotel, however, was gutted. The 300 rooms and suites were reduced to 245 rooms of larger size (including 61 suites). Skilled craftsmen restored the façade's art deco windows and balconies, the extensive wood paneling on the first floor, and the artwork and 17th-century Flanders tapestries that had long adorned the hotel's public and private spaces.

The interior designer hired by Four Seasons, Pierre Rochon, noted: "My main objective was to marry functionality with guest comfort, to merge 21st-century technology with the hotel's 'French classique' heritage. I would like guests rediscovering the hotel to think that I had not changed a thing – and, at the same time, to notice how much better they feel within its walls."[5] The fact that the designer was French, Talbott pointed out, "signaled to the French that we understood what they meant by luxury".

While Four Seasons decided to build to American life-safety standards, it also had to adhere to local laws, which affected design and work patterns. For example, a hygiene law in France stipulates that food and garbage cannot travel the same routes: food and trash have to be carried down different corridors and up/down different elevators. Another law involved "right to light", stipulating that employees had the right to work near a window for a certain number of hours each day. As a result, employees in the basement spa also worked upstairs in a shop with a window for several hours a day, and as many windows as possible had to be programmed into the design.

The new Four Seasons Hotel George V opened on December 18, 1999 at 100 percent effective occupancy (occupancy of rooms ready for use). Managers credited extensive publicity, the millennium celebration, and the profile of the property for that success. The opening was particularly challenging because Four Seasons only took formal control of operations on December 1, in part due to French regulations. "The French are very particular about, for example, fire regulations, but the fire department would not come in and inspect until everything else was complete," a manager said.

BECOMING A FRENCH EMPLOYER

Entering the French hospitality market meant becoming a French employer, which implied understanding French labor laws, business culture, and national idiosyncrasies.

Rules

France's leaders remained committed to a capitalism that maintained social equity with laws, tax policies, and social spending that reduced income disparity and the impact of free markets on public health and welfare.[6] France's tax burden, 45 percent of GDP in 1998, was three percentage points higher than the European average – and eight points higher than the OECD average. A further burden on employers was the 1999 reduction of the work week to 35 hours. Unemployment and retirement benefits were generous. Importantly, Four Seasons' management was not unfamiliar with labor-oriented government policy. "Canada has many attributes of a welfare state, so our Canadian roots made it easier to deal with such a context," Young explained.

The country was known for its strong unions.[7] "In France, one still finds a certain dose of antagonism between employees and management," a French manager underlined. The political party of the Force Ouvrière, the union that was strongest at the F. S. George V. garnered nearly 10 percent of the votes in the first round of the 2002 French presidential election with the rallying cry, "Employees fight the bosses!"

"If you look at the challenges of operating in France," noted Corinthios, "they have labor laws that are restrictive, but not prohibitive. The laws are not the same as, for example, in Chicago. You just need to be more informed about them." The law did give employers some flexibility, allowing them to work someone a little more during peak business periods and less during a lull. A housekeeper, for example, might work 40-hour weeks in the summer in exchange for a few 30-hour weeks in the late fall. Furthermore, French employers could hire 10 percent to 15 percent of staff on a "temporary", seasonal basis.

A particularly tricky area of labor management in France involved terminations. "Wherever we operate in the world," a Four Seasons manager explained, "we do not fire at will. There is due process. There is no surprise. There is counseling. So, Paris isn't that different, except to have the termination stick is more challenging because you really need a very, very good cause and to document *everything* carefully. If you have one gap in the documentation, you will have to rehire the terminated employee."

National and organizational culture

Geert Hofstede's seminal work, *Culture's Consequences*,[8] indicates a great disparity between North American (US and Canadian) national culture and that of France. While Hofstede's work has been criticized for the construction of the dimensions along which cultures differ,[9] there is general agreement with the principle that cultures do differ. Further, Hofstede's work and that of other scholars indicate that the differences between North American and French organizational culture are large. Corinthios identified attitudes surrounding performance evaluation as one difference:

> European and Middle Eastern managers have a hard time sitting across from people they supervise and talking about their weaknesses. The culture is not confrontational. It is more congenial and positive. It is very important to save face and preserve the dignity of the person being reviewed. Some Four Seasons managers using standard forms might even delete certain sections or questions or reprogram them in different languages.

For Didier Le Calvez, General Manager of the F. S. George V and recently appointed Regional Vice President, another significant difference was the degree to which middle and front-line managers felt accountable. "The greatest challenge in France is to get managers to take accountability for decisions and policies," he said. "In the French hierarchical system there is a strong tendency to refer things to the boss."

Le Calvez was also surprised by managers' poor understanding of human resource issues. In France, when a manager has a problem with an employee, the issue generally gets referred to the human resources department. "We, at Four Seasons, on the other hand, require that operating managers be present, deal with the issue, and lead the discussion."

"Seeing is believing"

When reflecting on their experiences with employees in France, several Four Seasons managers mentioned Saint Thomas ("doubting Thomas"). "They must see it to believe it," Le Calvez explained. "They do not take things at face value. They also tend to wait on the sidelines – once they see that something works, they come out of their shells and follow the movement." A Four Seasons manager continued: "Most of the workforce in France did not know what Four Seasons was all about. For example, they did not think we were serious about the Golden Rule. They thought it was way too American. Initially there were some eyebrows raised. Because of this skepticism, when we entered France, we came on our tip toes, without wanting to give anyone a lecture. I think *how* we came in was almost as important as *what* we did."

More differences

For several Four Seasons managers, working in France required a "bigger cultural adjustment" than had been necessary in other countries. "In France, I always knew that I would be a foreigner," a manager explained. "It took me a while to adjust to the French way." "There is simply an incredible pride in being French," added another. "The French have a very emotional way to do things," an F. S. George V manager explained. "This can be good and bad. The good side is that they can be very joyous and engaging. On the bad side, sometimes the French temper lashes out."

According to Four Seasons managers, what was referred to in the cultural research literature as the French "logic of honor"[10] was strong. While it would be degrading to be "in the service of" (*au service de*) anybody, especially the boss, it was honorable to "give service" (*rendre service*), with magnanimity, if asked to do so with due ceremony. In this context, management required a great deal of tact and judgment.

Managing differing perceptions of time could also be a challenge for North Americans in France. North Americans have been characterized as having a "monochronic" culture based on a high degree of scheduling and an elaborate code of behavior built around promptness in meeting obligations and appointments.[11] In contrast, the French were "polychronic", valuing human relationships and interactions over arbitrary schedules and appointments. These differences created predictable patterns summarized in Appendix 4.

Specific areas where Four Seasons and French national culture differed often related to either (French) guest expectations of a palace hotel, including its physical structure and tangible amenities, or manager–employee relationships. For example, in France, hotel guests expected a palace hotel to have a world-class gastronomic restaurant. They also expected exquisite floral arrangements and to be wowed by the décor. In contrast. Four Seasons hotels generally have excellent, although not necessarily world-class, restaurants and are known for their understated, subtly elegant look. An example of differences in employee–manager relationships can be found in the French managerial practice of being extremely cautious in providing employee feedback to the degree that, according to Four Seasons' managers, the practice is unusual. In contrast, Four Seasons management practice involved a great deal of communication, including feedback on an individual employee's performance, which managers believed critical to solving problems and delivering superior service.

Cultural renovation at the F. S. George V

Awareness and management of French cultural patterns were especially important to Four Seasons managers in Paris because a significant portion of the former operator's management and staff remained. Young explained:

> When we explored options for refashioning the George V into a Four Seasons hotel, we realized that without being able to start from scratch, the task would be Herculean. The existing culture was inconsistent with ours. In a North American environment you can decide whom to keep after an acquisition at a cost you can determine in advance on the basis of case law. In France, the only certainty is that you cannot replace the employees. You are acquiring the entity as a going concern. Unless you do certain things, you simply inherit the employees, including their legal rights based on prior service.

To be able to reduce headcount, by law an enterprise had to plan to be closed for over 18 months. Because the F. S. George V owner wanted the renovation to be complete in 12 months, staff were guaranteed a position with Four Seasons unless they chose to leave.[12] "Many of the best employees easily found other jobs, while the most disruptive were still there when the hotel reopened," Young said. "The number of people we really did not want was somewhere in the region of 40 out of 300 coming back on reopening."

Managers uniformly noted that the cultural renovation necessary to enable Four Seasons to be able to deliver its world-class service was on par with the extent of the physical renovation. Young provided an example. "During the due diligence process, the former general manager went to lunch with one of our senior staff. Even though guests were waiting, the maitre d' immediately tried to escort the general manager and his party to the general manager's customary table. At Four Seasons this is seen as an abuse of privilege. For us, 'the guest always comes first'."

Fortunately, in taking over The Pierre in New York, Four Seasons had been through a somewhat similar process. The scale of change necessary in each situation was enormous, as illustrated by this quotation from a senior Four Seasons manager: "Shortly after we bought The Pierre in 1981, a bell captain lamented that the times of the big steamer trunks were over. The staff had not adjusted to jet travel, despite its prevalence for two decades. This is the same kind of recalibration we had to do at the George V."

Apples and oranges

Young described the firm's approach to cultural transformation in acquired properties with existing staffing:

> If we can achieve a critical mass of individuals among the work-force who are committed to doing things differently, to meeting our standards, that critical mass overcomes the resistance of what becomes a diminishing old guard. Progressively, that old guard loses some of its power. If one rotten apple can ruin the barrel, then you have to seed the organization with oranges that cannot be spoiled by the apples. As a result, a departing old-guard employee is very care-fully replaced. Concurrently, individuals with the right culture and attitude are promoted. That creates a new culture, bit by bit by bit. At the F. S. George V, we also appealed to the national pride of our staff to help us restore a French landmark – to restore the pride of France.

"UN BOSS FRANCO-FRANÇAIS"

To effect this cultural change, Four Seasons picked Le Calvez to be general manager. Le Calvez was described as both demanding and "Franco-Français",[13] an expression used in France to describe someone or something "unequivocally French". At the same time, Le Calvez brought extensive Four Seasons and North American experience. Prior to opening the Regent Hotel in Singapore, he spent 25 years outside France, including 11 years at The Pierre. "He is very inter-national, yet also very French, very attached to his country and its culture," an executive explained. "He knows everyone and has an unbelievable memory for names and events (what happened to so-and-so's mother-in-law, etc.). He is very visible and accessible to the staff, eating in the staff cafeteria."

An F. S. George V manager noted, "The hotel's culture is embodied in the general manager – he shows a lot of love and respect for others and promotes social and cultural and ethnic integration." In a country where people typically referred to each other as Monsieur and Madame with their last name, Le Calvez encouraged the use of the first name. "It is more direct, relaxed, and straightforward. It represents the kind of relationship I want to have with my staff," he stated.

Young commented on the choice of Le Calvez: "The choice of senior leadership is absolutely critical. Adherence to our values and operational goals has to be extremely strong. Hotel openings require a lot of patience and tolerance because results are likely to be less positive as you manage through periods of major change."

The task force – "culture carriers"

To help Le Calvez and his team "Four Seasonize" the F. S. George V staff and ensure a smooth opening, Four Seasons assigned a 35-person task force, as it did to every new property. A manager noted:

> The task force helps establish norms. We help people understand how Four Seasons does things. Members listen for problems and innuendoes and communicate the right information to all, and squash rumors, especially when there are cultural sensitivities. The task force also helps physically getting the property up and running. Finally, being part of the task force exposes managers who may one day become general managers to the process of opening a hotel.

The task force, composed of experienced Four Seasons managers and staff, reflected the operating needs of each property. For example, if an experienced room service manager had already transferred to the opening property, those skills would not be brought in via the task force.

"The task force is truly a human resource, as well as a strong symbol," a manager explained. "The approach supports allegiance to the firm and not just one property – because members of the task force are not associated with one hotel. We are excited to participate, even if it means working long hours for weeks away from home." Most task force members, who typically stayed three weeks for an opening, stayed seven to eight weeks at the F. S. George V.

Strong tides

After working 25 years abroad, Le Calvez admitted that he was hesitant to return to work in France in light of the general tension he sensed between labor and management. However, he was encouraged by what he had seen at The Pierre, where Four Seasons managers noted that they had fostered a dialogue with the New York hospitality industry union. Le Calvez felt he could do the same in Paris. "When I arrived I told the unions that I did not think that we would need them, but since the law said we had to have them, I said 'Let's work together.' I do not want social tensions. Of course, this is not unique to me; it is Four Seasons' approach. We have to be pragmatic. So we signaled our commitment to a good environment."

Le Calvez communicated this commitment by openly discussing the 35-hour work week, the Four Seasons retirement plan, and the time and attendance system, designed to make sure that staff would not work more than required.

At the outset of negotiations, in preparation for the reopening, Le Calvez took the representatives of the various unions to lunch. As work progressed, he organized tours of the site so that union representatives could see what was being done and "become excited" about the hotel. He noted that "Touring the property in hard hats and having to duck under electric wires builds bonds. Witnessing the birth of a hotel is exciting." Managers stated that the unions were not used to such an inclusive approach in France.

Young felt that dealing with unions in France was easier than in New York: "In France, you are dealing with an institution backed by stringent, but predictable, laws. In the United States you are dealing with individuals in leadership who can be much more volatile and egocentric."

Four Seasons' experience with The Pierre proved invaluable. According to Young:

> In New York, we redesigned working spaces, and trained, and trained, and trained staff. But we also burned out a couple of managers. The old culture either wears you down or you wear it down. In an environment with strong labor laws, management sometimes gives up the right to manage. At some point managers stop swimming against the tide. If that continues long enough, the ability to manage effectively is lost. The precedents in a hotel are those that the prior managers have permitted. If the right to manage has been given up, standards are depressed, productivity decreases, margins decrease, and eventually you have a bad business. Regulars are treated well, but many guests are not. Reversing this process requires enormous management energy. It is very wearing to swim against a strong tide. You are making decisions that you believe reasonable and facing reactions that you believe unreasonable.

The 35-hour work week

Managers believed that Four Seasons' decision to implement the 35-hour work week at the F. S. George V to meet the letter and spirit of French law was a major signal to the unions and workforce about the way the company approached human resource issues. "When we hire staff from other hotels, they are always surprised that we obey the law," an F. S. George V manager noted. "They were working longer hours elsewhere."

A 35-hour work week yielded 1,820 annual workable hours per full-time staff equivalent. But since the French had more holidays and vacation, an employee provided 1,500 to 1,600 workable hours. This compared to about 2,050 hours in the United States for a full-time equivalent. The manager added, "We did not really understand the impact of the 35-hour work week. Each of our

Table 1. Employees-to-room ratios at selected Four Seasons properties

Property	Employees-to-Rooms Ratio
Four Seasons worldwide average	1.6
The Pierre New York	2.3
Four Seasons Hotel New York	1.6
Four Seasons Hotel George V Paris	2.5
Four Seasons Hotel Berlin	0.9
Four Seasons Hotel London	1.2
Four Seasons Hotel Canary Wharf, London	1.4
Four Seasons Hotel Milano	2.2

Source: Four Seasons.

80 managers has to have two consecutive days off a week, and each of the staff can work 214 days a year. Not 215, Not 213. But 214."

In 2002, 620 staff covered 250 rooms, or 2.5 staff per room. On average, Four Seasons hotels had 1.6 employees per room. Depending on food and banquet operations, that average could rise or fall significantly. Table 1 shows employees-to-room ratios at selected Four Seasons properties.

Young felt that labor laws explained about 15 percent of the need for increased staff ratios in Paris; vacations and holidays, 10 percent; with the rest explained by other factors including some logistics of the operation, e.g., a historic building, all compared to US norms. Corinthios elaborated:

> In Paris, you have six palaces competing for the same clients. It is a more formal operation. Guest expectations are very high, as is the level of leisure business (which requires higher staffing). People stay four to six days and use the concierge extensively. The concierge staffing at the F. S. George V is as big as anything we have in the chain. Then there is more emphasis on food and beverage. We have a fabulous chef and more staff in the kitchen for both the restaurant and room service – expectations of service in the gastronomic restaurant are very high.

RUNNING THE F. S. GEORGE V

Recruitment and selection

Four Seasons wanted to be recognized as the best employer in each of its locations. In Paris, F. S. George V wages were among the top three for hotels. Salaries were advertised in help wanted ads, a first in the industry in Paris according to F. S. George V managers, who believed doing so would help them attract high quality staff.

At the F. S. George V, as across the firm, every potential employee was interviewed four times, the last interview with the General Manager. According to one executive, "In the selection process, we try to look deep inside the applicant. I learned about the importance of service from my parents – did this potential employee learn it from hers?" "What matters is attitude, attitude, attitude," Corinthios explained. "All around the world it is the same. Without the right attitude, they cannot adapt." Another manager added, "What we need is people who can adapt, either to guests from all over the world, or to operating in a variety of countries." One of his colleagues elaborated on the importance of hiring for attitude, and its challenges:

> You would think that you would have a lot of people with great experience because there are so many palace hotels in Paris. But because we hire for attitude, we rarely hire from the other palaces. We hire individuals who are still "open" and tend to be much younger than usual for palace hotels. Then we bet on training. Of course, it takes much longer to train for skills when people do not have them. We look for people persons, who are welcoming and put others at ease, who want to please, are professional and sincerely friendly, flexible, smiley, and positive. At the F. S. George V, people apply for jobs because they have friends who work here.

To spread the culture and "de-demonize" the United States, the new F. S. George V management recruited staff with prior Four Seasons and/or US experience to serve as ambassadors. A manager noted, "Staff with US experience share with other staff what the United States is about and that it is not the terrible place some French people make it out to be." Several managers had international experience. About 40 individuals had prior US experience.

"Anglo-Saxon" recognition, measurement, and benefits

Le Calvez and his team launched an employee-of-the-month and employee-of-the-year program. "This had been controversial at Disney. People said it could not be done in France, but we manage to do it quite successfully. It all depends how it is presented," Le Calvez noted. "We explained that the program would recognize those who perform. Colleagues can tell who is good at their job."

Le Calvez used the same spirit to introduce annual evaluations, uncommon in France:

> People said evaluations would be unpopular, but the system seems to work. We told the staff that it would be an opportunity for open and constructive dialogue so that employees can know at all times where they stand. This allows them to adapt when need be. We wanted to make clear that there would be no favoritism, but rather that this would be a meritocracy. Here your work speaks for itself. The idea that your work is what matters could be construed as very Anglo Saxon!

In another "Anglo Saxon" action, a "Plan d'Epargne d'Entreprise" was set up for George V employees. This was a combination tax-deferred savings account and 401(k) type retirement plan. "This is totally new in France," Le Calvez claimed. Employees could contribute up to 4 percent of their salary, and the hotel would match it with 2 percent, to be raised based on profitability. The unions signed the agreement, although they were opposed to the principle of a non-government-sponsored retirement plan.

IMPLEMENTING THE GOLDEN RULE

The Golden Rule was at work at the F. S. George V, as its human resource director illustrated: "Cooks, before joining Four Seasons, used to have very long days starting in the morning to prepare for lunch, having a break during the afternoon, and coming back to prepare dinner. Today they work on either the morning or afternoon shift, enabling a better organization of their personal lives."

"All these gestures take time to work," Le Calvez summarized. "At first employees do not think we mean it. Some new hires think it's artificial or fake, but after a few months they let their guard down when they realize we mean what we say."

Managers believed that the effect of Four Seasons' human resource practices was reflected in customer satisfaction. Indeed, Le Calvez proudly reported that guest cards often included comments on how friendly and attentive the staff were. "All the other palace hotels in Paris are beautiful, but we believe that we have a special focus on friendly and personable service." He continued, "We offer friendly, very personal service. We have a very young and dynamic brigade with an average age of 26, spanning 46 different nationalities."

Communication

To promote communication and problem solving, the F. S. George V management implemented a "direct line". Once a month the general manager met with employees, supervisors, and managers in groups of 30. The groups met for three consecutive months so that issues raised could be addressed, with results reported to the group. Managers believed that the F. S. George V was the only palace hotel in France with such a communication process. It was important to note that the groups met separately – that is, employees met separately from supervisors – because subordinates in France did not feel comfortable speaking up in front of superiors.

French law mandated that a *comité d'entreprise* (a staff committee) be established in organizations with more than 50 employees. It represented employees to management on decisions that affected employees (e.g., salaries, work hours). At the F. S. George V, Le Calvez chaired the committee's monthly meeting, which included union representatives. "We would do these things anyway, so it is easy to adjust to these laws," Corinthios said. "We do it in France because it is required by law. But we do the same around the world; it just has a different name."

Every morning the top management team gathered to go over glitches – things that may have gone wrong the day before and the steps that had been, or were being, taken to address the problem. "Admitting what went wrong is not in the French culture," a French Four Seasons Manager explained. "But the meetings are usually very constructive."

Finally, about three times a year, Le Calvez and his team hosted an open-door event inviting employees and their families to spend some time at the hotel. "This is to break down barriers," he explained. "We take people around the hotel, into the back corridors. Try to remind, people of a notion that is unfortunately being lost – that of the '*plaisir du travail*' – or enjoying one's work. Furthermore, we celebrate achievement. Good property rankings, for example, are recognized with special team celebrations."

The property also cultivated external communication with the press in a way that was culturally sensitive. Le Calvez and his team felt that they had been very open and responsive to the press (which they stated was unusual in France) and that as a result, "Not a single negative article had been written about Four Seasons Hotel George V since its opening". A colleague added, "The press appreciated that they were dealing with locals. It was not like Disney where everyone was American."

CULINARY COUP D'ÉTAT

In a significant diversion from typical Four Seasons practice, a non-Four Seasons executive chef was hired. "In France having a serious chef and serious food is important," the F. S. George V food and beverage director noted. "You cannot be a palace hotel without that." "We knew that what mattered in Paris was food and décor," Talbott added. Although only 7 percent of room guests were French, most restaurant patrons were French.

Chef Philippe Legendre from the world famous Parisian restaurant Taillevent was recruited. "Didier came to get me through a common friend," Legendre explained. Legendre accepted Four Seasons' offer because "there was something exciting about being part of opening a hotel". He also liked their language which he described as "optimistic" and "about creating possibilities".

Legendre felt that Four Seasons' real strength was around relationship management (with clients and among staff), which "is not something that we are that good at in France, or place particular emphasis on. We have a lot to learn in the social domain. Everything at Four Seasons is geared towards the needs of the guest. At first it was hard, especially the training. Perhaps because in France we think we know everything."

He continued: "After three years I might not talk the Four Seasons talk, I might not use the same words, but I have the same view and adhere to the same system."

Despite Legendre's success (earning two Michelin stars), a colleague added that "bringing in such an executive chef was problematic. The challenge is that with this chef you have someone with extraordinary talent, but who must still adjust to the way service is delivered at Four Seasons." Coexistence was not always easy. Legendre described a situation illustrating miscommunication and cultural differences that required tremendous patience on the part of the restaurant, guests, and management:

> Recently a man ordered an omelet and his wife ordered scrambled eggs. The man returned the omelet because he decided he wanted scrambled eggs. We made them. Then he sent them back because they did not meet his expectations. Of course, we realize that our oeufs brouillés are different from scrambled eggs, which don't contain cream. Because we are Four Seasons we cooked the eggs as he wanted them, like American scrambled eggs, and didn't charge for them. But cooking is about emotion – if you want to please someone, you have to do it with your heart. *We live differently in France.*

RESULTS

A cultural cocktail

The F. S. George V was, in effect, a cultural cocktail. Le Calvez explained, "The F. S. George V is not *only* a French hotel – it is French, but it is also very international. We want to be different from the other palaces that are oh so very French. We want to project the image of a modern France, one that does not have to be dusty. We want to be a symbol of a France that is in movement, a European France, a France that stands for integration and equality."

The cultural cocktail also contained a number of elements unusual in France. At the time of the opening, journalists asked about the "American" smiling culture, which was referred to in France as "la culture Mickey Mouse". Le Calvez replied, "If you tell me that being American is being friendly and pleasant, that is fine by me. People tell me everyone smiles at the Four Seasons George V."

The spectacular flowers in the lobby of the F. S. George V (a single urn once contained 1,000 roses) were both very French and extremely international. "Paris is a city of fashion and culture, artistic and innovative," Le Calvez explained. "That is why, for example, we have the flowers we do. We can do that here." However, the flowers were designed by a young American. Another departure from French standard was the decision to hire women as concierges and men in housekeeping. These were viewed by managers as revolutionary steps in Paris.

Service quality

Richey summarized the results of the first F. S. George V service quality audit in October 2000, identifying some differences between French and North American business culture:

Keep in mind that this occurred less than one year after opening, and it takes at least a year to get things worked out. There were three things we talked to Four Seasons' executives about, mostly related to employee attitude. First, the staff had an inability to apologize or empathize. I think that could be construed as typically European, and especially French. Second, the team had a very tough time doing anything that could be described as selling. This is also typically European. For example: say your glass is empty at the bar. In Paris, they may not ask you if you want another drink. Third, the staff were rules and policy oriented. If something went wrong, they would refer to the manual instead of focusing on satisfying the guest.

Things had changed considerably by Richey's second audit in August 2001, when "they beat the competitive market set". The scores showed a significant improvement, raising the property to the Four Seasons system average.

More good news came in July 2002 with the results of an Employee Opinion Survey, in which 95 percent of employees participated. The survey yielded an overall rating of 4.02 out of 5. The questions that ranked the highest were: "I am proud to work for Four Seasons Hotels and Resorts" (4.65) and "I would want to work here again" (4.61).

The property also received several industry awards including Andrew Harper's Hideaway Report 2001 and 2002, World's Best Hotels and Resorts, Travel & Leisure Readers' Choice Awards 2001, #2 Best Hotel in Europe, and #5 World's Best Hotel Spa.

CONCLUSION: CULTURE, CONSISTENCY, AND FLEXIBILITY

The Four Seasons Hotel George V case illustrates how a service firm with a strong, successful organizational culture expanded internationally into a country with a distinct, intense national culture. When Four Seasons entered France, some elements of organizational culture were held constant, while others were treated flexibly. Managers never considered altering their *organizational values*, whether related to the service provided to guests which had to be engaging, anticipating, and responding; the property which had to be beautiful, luxurious, and functional; or how managers would treat employees, insisting that employees be treated as managers would like to be treated if they performed those jobs. While these values remained constant despite considerable differences in operating environments, the ways those values were enacted did sometimes change. This required changes in policies, management practices, and the use of cultural artifacts.

The tangible elements of service provide clear evidence of flexibility. Like all Four Seasons properties, the F. S. George V is luxurious. However, in France the first floor of the hotel is adorned with gilt and 17th century tapestries. No other Four Seasons property is decorated this way. The hotel elected to have a two-Michelin-star restaurant, despite the challenges of working with a famous chef in a country where there may be no more distinguished form of celebrity. More subtly, non-tangible elements of service quality changed, requiring changes in policies. For example, a coffee pot is never left on the table for guests to help themselves. This change enables the hotel to meet the standard for service set by a Four Seasons' organizational value ("anticipatory") as interpreted in France, where one should not have to pour coffee oneself.

Management practices also changed. In order to have an engaging, anticipating, and responding staff, managers relied upon employee selection even more heavily than at other properties. In this way management practice was intensified in response to a new national culture. However, the goal of those intensified selection efforts was to hire a less experienced staff than typical for other palace hotels and the chain. This was because of underlying, inflexible assumptions which many more experienced workers in France have about employment and how they should treat guests. Less experienced individuals are less set in attitudes and cultural stereotypes contrary to delivering the service for which Four Seasons is renowned. Management therefore focused more sharply on hiring based on attitudes rather than prior work experience. Thus this management practice changed in France to enable Four Seasons to remain true to its organizational values.

The use of cultural artifacts also changed. While a typical Four Seasons property opening would be accompanied by information to the press on the world-renowned service for which the chain is famous, including legendary service stories, in France this was an afterthought to the glory of the property and the appropriateness of the renovations for a *French* architectural landmark.

Many management practices did not change upon arrival in France. Employee of the month and year recognition programs, feedback practices, and meetings to discuss problems were implemented despite a general belief that they would be found incompatible with the French environment. Yet they were successful because of *how* they were implemented – using the words of one manager, "on tip toes". Their more awkward (from a French perspective) elements were amended, and their purpose was communicated gently, but repeatedly. The individuals carefully selected into Four Seasons' environment did not object to their use because they understood the intent of the practices, as well as their effect. The practices ultimately contributed to achieving the changes in organizational culture that Four Seasons managers believed were necessary, helping to ensure that the "oranges" (new employees) carefully selected into the property become the dominant culture carriers, overwhelming the leftover "apples" who refused to change, creating an environment in which those apples no longer fit comfortably.

Perhaps the most important element of management practice contributing to Four Seasons' success in France was management discipline. This took two forms, both of which can be viewed as contributing to the enactment of organizational values. First, discipline can be seen in the way Four Seasons managers lived the values they espoused; allowing guests to be seated first in the dining room; treating employees with dignity; adhering to local labor laws and internal policies designed to protect employees. Second, Four Seasons managers had the discipline to insist that employees deliver outstanding service to guests.

This occurred through adherence to the core service-culture standards and 270 operating standards (as occasionally amended). Meeting these standards has resulted in customer loyalty. Thus discipline acts as a glue, ensuring that organizational values actually *drive* a culture, which in turn *contributes* to competitive advantage.

Managers in widely diverse service industries can benefit from Four Seasons' approach to global management when entering countries with distinct, intense national cultures. To do so they must understand their own organizational culture: What are their (1) underlying assumptions, (2) values, (3) employee perceptions of management practices (policies and behaviors), and (4) cultural artifacts? Managers must then ask what elements of their culture are essential to competitive advantage in existing environments, and how the new environment will change that linkage. When there is a change, does the element of culture itself need to change (coffee pot no longer left on the table), or does the way the element is implemented, the way a value is enacted, need to change, such as the implementation "on tip toes" of an employee-of-the-month recognition program. In general, *values core to the organization's "value proposition" (what customers receive from the firm relative to what they pay for it) will not change, but elements of how they are enacted may.*

While organizations eventually come to understand how to operate in a new national environment, successful organizations cannot afford the type of negative publicity and poor financial performance that accompany blundering into a new national culture, as Disney discovered after opening Euro Disney in France. The Four Seasons case study is a single case, based on a single organization. As such we do not claim that its findings are necessarily applicable to other firms. However, it illustrates an approach to global management that managers of other services may find useful, but which they must customize to their own organizational and cultural needs.

APPENDIX 1: SAMPLE CORE STANDARDS

RESERVATIONS

Mission: To provide crisp, knowledgeable, and friendly service, sensitive to the guest's time, and dedication to finding the most suitable accommodation.
- Phone service will be highly efficient, including: answered before the fourth ring: no hold longer than 15 seconds; or, in case of longer holds, call-backs offered, then provided in less than three minutes.
- After establishing the reason for the guest visit, reservationist automatically describes the guest room colorfully, attempting to have the guests picture themselves in the room.

HOTEL ARRIVAL

Mission: To make all guests feel welcome as they approach, and assured that details are well tended; to provide a speedy, discreet, and hassle-free arrival for business travelers: to provide a comforting and luxurious arrival for leisure travelers.

- The doorman (or first contact employee) will actively greet guests, smile, make eye contact, and speak clearly in a friendly manner.
- The staff will be aware of arriving vehicles and will move toward them, opening doors within 30 seconds.
- Guests will be welcomed at the curbside with the words "welcome" and "Four Seasons" (or hotel name), and given directions to the reception desk.
- No guest will wait longer than 60 seconds in line at the reception desk.

HOTEL DEPARTURE

Mission: To provide a quick and discreet departure, while conveying appreciation and hope for return.
- No guest waits longer than five minutes for baggage assistance, once the bellman is called (eight minutes in resorts).
- No guest will wait longer than 60 seconds in line at the cashier desk.
- Staff will create a sense of recognition by using the guest's name, when known, in a natural and discreet manner.

MESSAGES AND PAGING

Mission: To make guests feel that their calls are important, urgent, and require complete accuracy.
- Phone service will be highly efficient, including: answered before the fourth ring; no longer than 15 seconds.
- Callers requesting guest room extensions between 1 a.m. and 6 a.m. will be advised of the local time and offered the option of leaving a message or putting the call through.
- Unanswered guest room phones will be picked up within five rings, or 20 seconds.
- Guests will be offered the option of voice mail: they will not automatically be routed to voice mail OR they will have a clear option to return to the operator.

INCOMING FAXES AND PACKAGES

Mission: To make guests feel that their communications are important, urgent, and require complete accuracy.
- Faxes and packages will be delivered to the guest room within 30 minutes of receipt.

WAKE-UP CALLS

Mission: To make certain that guests are awakened exactly on time in a manner which gently reassures them.
- When wake-up calls are requested, the operator will offer a second reminder call.
- Wake-up calls will occur within two minutes of the requested time.

GUEST ROOM EVENING SERVICE

Mission: To create a sense of maximum comfort and relaxation. When meeting guests, to provide a sense of respect and discretion.

- Guest clothing which is on the bed or floor will be neatly folded and placed on the bed or chair – guest clothing left on other furniture will be neatly folded and left in place; shoes will be paired.
- Newspapers and periodicals will be neatly stacked and left on a table or table shelf in plain view; guest personal papers will not be disturbed in any way.
- Guest toiletries will be neatly arranged on a clean, flat cloth.

LAUNDRY AND VALET

Mission: To provide excellent workmanship and make guests feel completely assured of the timing and quality of our service.
- Laundry service will include same-day service; express four-hour service; and overnight service (seven days per week).
- Dry cleaning service will include same-day service; express four-hour service (seven days per week).
- Pressing service will be available at any time, and returned within one hour; and can be processed on the normal laundry schedule.

ROOM SERVICE

Mission: To provide a calm, competent, and thorough dining experience, with accurate time estimates and quick delivery.
- Phone service will be highly efficient, including: answered before the fourth ring; no hold longer than 15 seconds; or, in the case of longer holds, call-backs offered, then provided in less than three minutes.
- Service will be prompt and convenient; an estimated delivery time (an hour and minute, such as "nine-fifteen PM") will be specifically mentioned; and the order will be serviced within five minutes (earlier or later) than that time.
- Continental breakfast will be delivered within 20 minutes, other meals within 30 minutes, and drinks-only within 15 minutes.
- Table/tray removal instructions will be provided by a printed card, and tables will be collected within twelve minutes of guest call.

APPENDIX 2: FOUR SEASONS GOALS, BELIEFS, AND PRINCIPLES

Who We Are: We have chosen to specialize within the hospitality industry, by offering only experiences of exceptional quality. Our objective is to be recognized as the company that manages the finest hotels, resorts, residence clubs, and other residential projects wherever we locate. We create properties of enduring value using superior design and finishes, and support them with a deeply instilled ethic of personal service. Doing so allows Four Seasons to satisfy the needs and tastes of our discriminating customers, to maintain our position as the world's premier luxury hospitality company.

What We Believe: Our greatest asset, and the key to our success, is our people. We believe that each of us needs a sense of dignity, pride, and satisfaction in what we do. Because satisfying our guests depends on the united efforts of many, we are most effective when we work together cooperatively, respecting each other's contribution and importance.

How We Behave: We demonstrate our beliefs most meaningfully in the way we treat each other and by the example we set for one another. In all our interactions with our guests, business associates, and colleagues, we seek to deal with others as we would have them deal with us.

How We Succeed: We succeed when every decision is based on a clear understanding of and belief in what we do and when we couple this conviction with sound financial planning. We expect to achieve a fair and reasonable profit to ensure the prosperity of the company, and to offer long-term benefits to our hotel owners, our shareholders, our customers, and our employees.

APPENDIX 3: COMPARATIVE DATA ON PARISIAN PALACES

Property	Construction/Style	Capacity (Rooms and Suites)	Amenities	Price (Dollar/Single Room)	Owner	Lessee/Operator
Bristol	Built in 1829 Louis XV-XVI style	180	1 restaurant: Le Bristol 1 interior garden 1 swimming pool 1 fitness center 1 beauty salon	480–600	Société Oetker[c] (1978)	Independent
Crillon	Built in the 18th century Louis XV-XVI style	152	2 restaurants: L'Ambassadeur and L'Obélix 1 fitness center Guerlain Beauty Institute	460–550	Groupe Hôtels Concorde[a] (1907)	Groupe Hôtels Concorde[a] (1907)
Four Seasons Hotel George V Paris	Built in 1928 Art Deco style	245	1 restaurant: Le Cinq 1 swimming pool 1 fitness center 1 beauty salon	670	Prince Al Waleed Bin Talal[d] (1996)	Four Seasons Hotels and Resorts (2000)
Meurice	Built in the 18th century Louis XV-XVI style	161	1 restaurant: Le Meurice 1 fitness center Caudalie Beauty Institute	470–550	The Sultan of Brunei (1997)	The Dorchester Group[b] (2001)
Plaza Athenée	Built in 1889 Belle Epoque style	144	2 restaurants: Le Relais Plaza	490–508	The Sultan of Brunei (1997)	The Dorchester Group[b] (2001)

APPENDIX 3—*continued*

Property	Construction/Style	Capacity (Rooms and Suites)	Amenities	Price (Dollar/ Single Room)	Owner	Lessee/ Operator
Ritz	Built in 1898 Louis XV-XVI style	139	1 restaurant: L'Espadon Escoffier-Ritz cooking school 1 fitness center 1 beauty salon 1 swimming pool	From 580	Mohammed Al Fayed (1979)	Independent

Source: "Four Seasons Hotels and Resorts," Brian D. Egger, et al., Crédit Suisse First Boston, April 5, 2002, page 21. *http://meuricehotel.com, http:// www.hotel-bristol.com, http://www.ritz.com, http://www.fourseasons.com/paris/vacations/index.html, http:// www.plaza-athenee-paris.com, http:// www.crillon.com.* Accessed June 2002.

[a] Groupe Hôtels Concorde was created in 1973 to regroup the luxury hotels such as the Crillon, the Lutetia, and the Hôtel Concorde Saint-Lazare (all in Paris) owned by La Société du Louvre.

[b] The Dorchester Group, a subsidiary of the Brunei Investment Agency, was established in 1996 as an independent United Kingdom registered company to manage luxury hotels, including The Dorchester in London, The Beverly Hills Hotel California and the Hotel Meurice in Paris.

[c] The Oetker Group is a German agribusiness group which owns four luxury hotels in addition to the Bristol: the Cap Eden Roc in Antibes, France; the Park Hotel in Vitznau, Switzerland; the Brenner's Park Hotel in Baden-Baden, Germany; and the Château du Domaine Saint-Martin in Vence, France.

[d] Al Waleed Bin Talal owns 21.9 percent of Four Seasons' stocks. Investments by Prince Al Waleed in Four Seasons' properties include F. S. George V and Riyadh (100 percent); London (majority); Cairo, Amman, Alexandria, Sharm El Sheikh and Beirut (unspecified); and Aviara (minority).

APPENDIX 4: PREDICTABLE PATTERNS OF MONOCHRONIC AND POLYCHRONIC CULTURES

Monochronic people (Americans)	Polychronic people (French)
Do one thing at a time	Do many things at once
Concentrate on the job	Can be easily distracted and manage interruptions well
Take time commitments (deadlines, schedules) seriously	Consider an objective to be achieved, if possible
Are low-context and need information	Are high-context and already have information
Are committed to the job	Are committed to people and human relationships
Adhere religiously to plans	Change plans often and easily
Are concerned about not disturbing others; follow rules of privacy and consideration	Are more concerned with those who are closely related (family, friends, close business associates) than with privacy
Show great respect for private property; seldom borrow or lend	Borrow and lend things often and easily
Emphasize promptness	Base promptness on the relationship
Are accustomed to short-term relationships	Have strong tendency to build lifetime relationships

Source: Adapted from Edward T. Hall, *Understanding cultural differences, German, French, and Americans*. Yarmouth: Intercultural Press, 1990.

NOTES

1   Kotter, J. P. and Heskett, J. L. 1990. *Corporate culture and performance*. New York: The Free Press.
2   Heskett, J. L., Schlesinger, L. A., and Sasser, W. E., Jr. 1997. *The service profit chain*. New York: The Free Press; Schneider, B., and Bowen. D. E. 1995. *Winning the service game*. Boston, Mass.: Harvard Business School Press; and Berry, L. L. 1995. *On great service*. New York: The Free Press.
3   Schein, E. H. 1990. Organizational culture. *American Psychologist*, 45(2): 109–19.
4   The theory behind this discussion finds its roots in the contingency work of scholars such as Lawrence and Lorch; see Lawrence, P., and Lorsch, J. 1967. *Organization and environment*. Boston, Mass.: Harvard Business School Press. Other scholars, including James Heskett, have used the contingency perspective as a starting point for theories of internationalization of services; see Loveman, G. 1993. *The internationalization of services*. Harvard Business School Module Note No. 9–693–103, Boston, Mass.: Harvard Business School Publishing. Heskett's views have influenced ours considerably. We are indebted to Professor Caren Siehl, Thunderbird, for much of the framework on managing the potential clash between organizational culture and country culture, which she developed for her organizational behavior MBA classes. In turn, Caren always acknowledges an intellectual debt to Professor Joanne Martin, Stanford University.
5   *Interior Design*, March 2000, p. S24.
6   For example, maternity leave for a salaried employee's first child was six weeks of prenatal leave and 10 weeks of paid leave after birth; for a third child it was eight weeks off before and 18 weeks after birth.

7   Communist-controlled labor union (Confédération Générale du Travail) or CGT, nearly
     2.4 million members (claimed); independent labor union or Force Ouvrière, 1 million
     members (est.); independent white-collar union or Confédération Générale des Cadres,
     340,000 members (claimed); Socialist-leaning labor union (Confédération Française
     Démocratique du Travail) or CFDT, about 800,000 members (est.). Source: *http://www.
     cia.gov/cia/publications/factbook/geos/fr.html*, accessed June 10, 2002.

8   Hofstede's work was based on a survey conducted by questionnaire with IBM employees
     in 50 different countries; see Hofstede, G. 1982. *Culture's consequences: international
     differences in work-related values*. Thousand Oaks, Calif.: Sage.

9   Hofstede's approach has not been without its critics but, as Hickson comments, Hofstede
     had "frail data, but robust concepts"; see Hickson, D. 1996. The ASQ years then and now
     through the eyes of a Euro-Brit. *Administrative Science Quarterly*, 41(2): 217–28.

10   See d'Iribarne, P. 1996/97. The usefulness of an ethnographic approach to the inter-
     national comparison of organization. *International Studies of Management and Organisation*,
     18(4): 32.

11   Van der Horst, B. Edward T. Hall – a great-grandfather of NLP, *http://www.cs.ucr.edu/
     gnick/bvdh/print_edward_t_hall_great_htm*, accessed April 20, 2002. The article reviews
     Hall, E. 1959. *The silent language*. New York: Doubleday.

12   One alternative was to give the staff a significant enough severance package to encourage
     them to go. However, as Young explained. "The government deplores that approach".

13   Usually used to describe a meal – say a first course of fromage de tête (pig's head set
     in jelly) or bouillabaisse (fish soup), followed by a main course of blanquette de veau (veal
     stew with white sauce) and rounded off with a plateau de fromage (cheese platter) or tarte
     aux pommes (apple tart).

Joyce S. Osland and Pedro Ferreira

ANATOMY OF A PARAGUAYAN STRIKE[1]

Two labor union leaders were sitting in a café in Asunción, the capital city of Paraguay, looking back on the tumultuous events of recent months and wondering if it had all been worthwhile. Oscar Martinez and Roberto Ugarte were president and vice president (respectively) of the Engineers Labor Union (UIA) of ANDE, the parastatal electric power utility for the entire country. ANDE has four different labor unions for its 4500 employees. Oscar is an idealistic, engaging man in his early thirties. He is extremely bright and recently graduated at the head of his Executive MBA class. He teaches engineering classes on the side and is involved in numerous community projects to help the poor. Roberto is an intense man in his forties, who is known for his dedication to his work and family.

Both men hold prestigious jobs on two counts. First, engineers in Latin America are so highly regarded that, like doctors, they are addressed using the name of their profession – "Engineer Gonzalez" rather than "Mr." (Señor) Gonzalez. Second, the electricity utility in most Latin American countries is often the most respected and well-run government agency, perhaps due to its well-educated work force and its importance to the citizenry.

Labor Day, *el Dia del Obrero*, is a holiday celebrated on May first throughout Latin America. Work places are closed, employers host parties for workers, and labor unions organize parades and sometimes more serious forms of protest to improve worker conditions. Sometimes, there are "general strikes", which attempt to shut down an entire country or city by persuading sympathizers to stay home and show their solidarity with union demands. Even if citizens do not support a general strike, it is usually too difficult or dangerous to transport themselves to work. In Paraguay, May 1, 1996 was a special occasion since four labor union federations had convoked a two-day general strike for May 2 and 3. They were protesting government economic policies that they deemed harmful to the poor and government inaction in areas where they felt reform was needed.

The anatomy of this strike can only be understood within the broader context of the Paraguayan political situation and the events that led up to it within the UIA.

NATIONAL SITUATION

Paraguay lived through a dictatorship headed by Alfredo Stroessner from 1954–1989. During much of this time Stroessner enjoyed the popular support of the people. He accomplished this via pronounced economic growth, social mobility (the lower classes could improve their lot by obtaining government jobs), control and manipulation of information, and convincing the public that other needs were more important than liberty.

In 1989, a coup d'etat was engineered by General Rodriguez, the father-in-law of Stroessner's son. Rodriguez had been Stroessner's right hand man. When he assumed power, Rodriguez initiated a period of democratic progress, with broad guarantees of freedom of expression and functioning opposition parties. As often occurs when totalitarian regimes fall, raised expectations and a particular set of hopes and beliefs flourished. Many Paraguayans began to attribute all the country's problems to Stroessner's dictatorship and believed that democracy would soon resolve these problems. They also believed that the corruption that was part and parcel of the dictatorship would be eliminated or at least reduced once freedom gave people the courage to denounce unethical practices. With corruption eliminated, people believed there would be a more equal distribution of wealth. If they just had patience and hope, the general welfare of the people would improve. These expectations were not realized, in part because corrupt practices continued in the democratic governments that followed the dictatorship. The only difference is that Paraguayan newspapers now have the freedom to publish numerous articles about corruption.

In 1993, the Engineer J. C. Wasmosy was elected president in an election that was considered to be fraudulent by the majority of the population. A businessman who became wealthy during the dictatorship, Wasmosy was the first civilian Paraguayan president in almost half a century. He enacted a series of economic measures, which were applauded by liberal sectors and by business. However, his actions were also criticized by those who believed that he was simply looking out for the interests of his fellow capitalists.

In contrast to the business sector, the economic expectations of people at the lower end of the social strata were not fulfilled. Paraguay has a set minimum wage that applies to most workers. The buying power of the minimum wage had decreased by 20 percent compared to the levels that existed prior to the coup d'etat in 1989. The *campesinos* (people who live in the country, usually small farmers or ranchers) are forced to sell products at lower prices, which caused problems of land ownership, unemployment, health and education. Although inflation has decreased from 30–40 percent annually to approximately 10 percent, interest rates are still very high (50 percent).

Since 1992, there have been a series of protests, strikes, road closures, and demands for political justice, mostly aimed against government policies, which were perceived as conflicting with the interests of the common people. A few people died in these protests, usually *campesinos*, but these actions had little impact on the government. In late 1995, the *campesinos* organized a march that was widely considered to be an admirable example of a peaceful protest. Nevertheless, the government did not know how to respond to their concerns in a timely fashion. When the government finally invited the *campesino* leaders to a dialogue, the latter said they were not interested. The purpose of their march was not to solicit solutions from a government that made promises it did not fulfill. Their purpose was to convict the government of a lack of interest in social problems and the diversion of resources to other priorities.

One of the most influential figures in Wasmosy's government, until April 1996, was General Lino Oviedo. The army general was very popular after the military coup of 1989 due to the bravery he demonstrated at that time and to the subsequent leadership he exerted over the military rank and file when he eventually succeeded General Rodriguez. In 1992, however, General Oviedo's image was beginning to deteriorate among some groups in light of his increasingly evident political aspirations. According to one Paraguayan, much of the populace was "fed up with having two presidents – one who held the reins of power and the other who had the tanks". This further increased the dissatisfaction of the populace.

On Monday, April 22, 1996, relations were ruptured completely between the President and General Oviedo. There are differing versions about what actually occurred. Wasmosy claims he asked Oviedo for his resignation, and the General refused. According to Oviedo, Wasmosy asked him to take measures that would disempower the Congress, but the General refused. Everyone agrees that Oviedo threatened to take over the government, and there was widespread concern that armed force and violence would result. Shortly thereafter, the US embassy and Brazilian officials announced their support for Wasmosy. The university students staged a peaceful demonstration against a military takeover, and the danger of a military coup was defused. The middle and upper class, the media, the intellectuals, and a large part of the population hoped that this would be a positive turning point for Wasmosy's government. The unions, however, did not think Oviedo's removal would produce deep-seated changes; in their eyes, the displacement of the military leaders simply meant greater power for the business leaders controlling the government. Right upon the heels of the heady drama of the attempted coup came Labor Day and the general strike.

MEETINGS OF THE UIA UNION LEADERS PRIOR TO THE STRIKE

The UIA leaders had a series of meetings and decisions prior to the strike when they were trying to decide whether or not they should go along with the other unions and strike. Snippets of these meetings follow.

UIA executive meeting – April 10, 1996

The leaders of UIA met, as they did every Wednesday. Among other agenda items, they needed to discuss an invitation from the federation of unions to participate in a congress to be held the following Saturday. At that meeting, the union representatives would decide whether or not to hold the threatened general strike. Five members were seated around a table in the union headquarters.

Oscar: It sounds like we're all in agreement that the officers should attend the congress this Saturday. Then our next decision is – do you think we should strike?

Roberto: Several of our members weren't happy with the position we took during the last strike. They didn't think it was enough to simply write a manifesto agreeing with the workers and then go to work as if it were "business as usual". It's the easy way out.

Miguel: Well, at least we published a manifesto proposing structural changes and things the government should do to avoid a civilian outburst. [Please see Appendix 1.] You'll never get all the engineers to go on strike when so many of them are managers.

Roberto: If we want to wake up the government, manifestos aren't enough. The social situation is deteriorating, and the moment will arrive when there won't be anything left to do.

Victor: I agree with Roberto. Besides, if we are in agreement that the government is neglecting the lower classes, why don't we pledge ourselves to the strike?

Miguel: Don't forget though that in the six years of the UIA's existence, we have only participated in two strikes – one against the unethical privatizations and the other against corruption. In both cases, the participation of our members was pretty luke-warm, because there is always a lot to lose in these situations.

To strike or not to strike?

After more debate, the group decided to call a general assembly meeting for all their members to decide what stance the UIA should take at the congress. At the assembly, the union members agreed to join the strike. Their reasons can be divided into two categories. The first category were ethical reasons. The members believe it is wrong to ignore the needs of the majority of the population. What use is it for some people to have a great deal of money when others are suffering for lack of resources? Furthermore, it is not fair for the government to focus only upon the interests of the politicians and their friends.

The second set of reasons were practical ones that touched upon the general welfare of the citizenry and self interest. The union did not perceive that it was benefiting from government policies, and the government was not living up to its side of their agreement on a previous labor contract with the union. The country's economic difficulties caused an increase in crime, particularly robberies and assaults, which affected everyone. If the poor eventually were to lose patience and rebel, everyone would suffer with the exception of the wealthy capitalists who would simply leave the country and live on money they have stashed overseas. Members of the UIA did not have this option.

UIA executive meeting – April 17, 1996

Oscar began the meeting by reporting on the congress held by the union federation.

Oscar: As you know from reading the newspaper, the federation has decided to go forward with the strike on May 2nd and 3rd. If there is not a favorable response from the government, there will be another week-long strike before the end of the year.

Miguel: The business owners will not like that!

Oscar: I have a copy here of the main points the federation is asking for in connection with the strike. [See Appendix 2] There are more than twenty on the list, some of which are rather strange. The most important ones are a salary increase, improving the Instituto de Prevision Social (the social security institute) which, as we all know, is currently a disaster, and avoiding privatizations that benefit politicians or government officials who buy public resources at lower than market value. I don't agree with all these demands, but I think we have to show solidarity with the other unions so the government takes notice.

Victor: I wanted to report that we've received a note from the Ministry of Justice and Work inviting us to a meeting the day after tomorrow. We made inquiries and none of the unions, other than the *amarillos*,[2] are planning to go. The invitations only went to unions like us that are not associated with any federation. This looks like a ploy to give the impression that the government wants to dialogue, but the unions don't. If they had wanted to discuss things, they should have done so before the deadline set by the Federation, which ran out on April 8. Now that the strike is irreversible, they are trying to discredit this pressure tactic and divide the unions.

UIA meeting – April 30, 1996 (last meeting prior to the strike)

Miguel: Some people called to complain about the decision taken in the assembly to go on strike. I told them that if they wanted to discuss it, they should meet and explain their point of view.

Roberto: Some of them believe that public opinion is in favor of the government after last week's failed coup and Oviedo's ouster.

Carlos: In my area the people from SITRANDE (a union for workers and technicians at ANDE) are commenting that we aren't going to have the necessary mass that we're hoping for. The danger of all this is that if the government thinks its position is stronger because of the failed coup and believes that the worker movement is losing steam, they might take advantage of the situation to get even with groups that have been protesting against them.

Roberto: In my department they are saying that we all have to agree on the strike, because there is a certain threat that this strike will be bloody, unlike the last one. Business can't allow this strike to be successful, because it will result in the week-long strike planned for the end of the year. Victor, what happened at the meeting between the ANDE executives and the Strike Committee?

Victor: I thought the attitude of the ANDE executives seemed irresponsible. They refused to talk about how we'd keep the system going with fewer people on the job. They just wanted to make sure all the engineers would be at work. They kept insisting that *all* positions were vital for the operation of the power system, even the administrative ones.

Miguel: How did the meeting end up?

Victor: No agreements were reached. Management said they would continue operating the system with the people who come to work – but without "subordinating" themselves to a strike committee.

Carlos: The situation is dangerous because the SITRANDE members only take orders from their own strike committee. We need to help organize this and figure out what workers are needed to keep the system operating during the strike. We should elect Victor as president of the strike committee of UIA, because he works in operations and will be informed about everything that occurs. All in favor, say aye.

A chorus of ayes followed Carlos' suggestion.

Oscar: SITRANDE has invited us to join them at the crossroads of Route 1 and the highway, which will be the principal point of friction between the strikers and the police. Any strike that is successful in blocking all traffic at this point is guaranteed at least a 50 percent success rate, because no one can get into downtown Asunción otherwise.

Roberto: I heard a police announcement on the radio warning that if the strikers tried to take this intersection, they were going to prevent it with violence if necessary.

Victor: The quantity of strikers at that point is usually so large, added to the throngs of people who are waiting at the various bus stops there, that it is impossible to clear the road. When the police clear out one side of the street, the other is already blocked again. The best the cops can hope for is an intermittent flow of traffic, and the resulting traffic jam will be so large that there will be no way into the city.

Carlos: The union delegate in my department, Samuel, will carry a cellular phone and keep us posted on what is going on. He'll be at the intersection early in the morning. I will have another cellular phone just in case the telephone service is cut off in our meeting place.

Discussion between Oscar and Roberto – May 2, 1:10 a.m.

Shortly after midnight in the early hours of May 2nd, Oscar Martinez and Roberto Ugarte visited one of the sites in Asunción where union members gathered to make strike plans. Oscar and Roberto were concerned that only a handful of strikers were present. Those in attendance assured them, however, that the others would show up at five in the morning. On their way home they discussed their concerns about the coming strike.

Oscar: Roberto, what kind of turnout do you think we'll have?

Roberto: Well, the fact that last year's strike was peaceful has given the union members more confidence. There should be more protesters on the street as a result. What do you predict?

Oscar: I think people here in Asunción will not go to work, but I don't expect many of them to join the protest. Since the two days of general strike follow a holiday, some people may just treat this as a long weekend.

Roberto: SITRANDE can probably count on having between 300–500 strikers of their 2500 members at the main meeting point.

Oscar: I was calculating the numbers for our own union last night. Of our 140 members, thirty are senior managers, thirty are in jobs that are crucial to providing power service, and twenty are out of town or on vacation. I'll be happy if 25 of the remaining fifty show up at the union hall.

Roberto: APROANDE [the non-engineering professionals union] is the only union that is not going out on strike. Maybe they think they'll gain something later on by not participating.

Oscar: It would have been better if all the ANDE unions had formed a united front.

Roberto: True, but you know how hard it is to get that many people to agree. At least SITRANDE is committed to the strike, and there's no way management can replace their technicians since ANDE is the only electricity company in Paraguay.

Oscar: Let's get some rest; tomorrow may be a long hard day.

UIA assembly meeting – May 2, 7:00 a.m.

Some of the UIA members and the leaders gathered to monitor the strike's progress at the union hall. Because of their status, they did not protest in the streets. In horror, they watched and listened to live TV and radio coverage of a strike that had quickly turned violent. The police began harassing and attacking protesters at 4:00 a.m. in an effort to prevent the strikers from blocking the intersection of Route 1 and the highway. According to reporters, the police were beating members of the press as well as observers. People were calling the radio stations to complain about police brutality. Some of the SITRANDE protesters were beaten without provocation before they even reached the intersection. The police fired shots at them, and the protesters had to take refuge in a private home. The principal leaders of the union federation were arrested, beaten, and loaded into a truck heading to an unknown destination. Since union leaders have sometimes figured among the *desaparecidos* (people who simply disappear, apparently murdered by enemies, paramilitary groups, or the military, etc.) in Latin America, this caused a great deal of alarm. The general secretary of SITRANDE appeared on TV warning that if the leaders were not freed within an hour, ANDE technicians and workers on duty would leave their posts, essentially cutting off the electricity supply.

Oscar: Is there any word on the federation leaders?

Carlos: The mobile unit of the radio station is following the truck they were loaded into, since their lives might be in danger.

Victor: I just heard that the power line from San Lorenzo to Itaugua is out of service. They can't find any technical reason for the blackout. The instruments in the stations outside Asunción are not giving us the correct readings, so we're working blind. I think it's best that I go to the office in case the problem gets any more complicated.

Carlos: I have a cell phone call from SITRANDE members who are right in the middle of the protest. They are requesting some type of help from us. I can hear shots in the background. They say the shots are not being fired into the air but right over their heads. The police are beating people with clubs, and they are stampeding.

Oscar: Tell them to be careful and to give us a little time to see what we can do.

Carlos: Now the police are corralling them. They want a communication or something from us right away.

Oscar: Give me a moment to think.

A ringing telephone broke the tense silence in the room. It was Oscar's mother-in-law, saying, "The entire family is supporting you!" Oscar thanked her for calling and returned to weighing his options. "What's the right thing to do?" he muttered.

Oscar and his fellow officers decided to write a communiqué. Carlos suggested calling the president or senior management of ANDE. Oscar responded, "See if you can get them on the phone, but I don't think we have enough time. We have to do something that freezes the situation and avoids a power shutdown." Roberto and Oscar began to work over a legal pad at one end of the table. The other officers continued with their conversation.

Carlos: I think that supporting SITRANDE at this moment when they are threatening to cut off the power would be an unpopular move. We'll lose public support if we go along with them. Worse yet, we're going to look like SITRANDE's caboose – they get involved in a fight and then drag us in after them.

Danilo: If the SITRANDE workers walk off the job and cause a blackout, the consequences will be enormous.

Victor: I just heard that the technicians in the distribution department handed a note to their boss and immediately left their positions. They are going to the intersection to help their fellow union members. The only people left on duty are two workers and the supervisor.

Miguel: A friend of mine called from headquarters saying that everyone believes the breakdown in the San Lorenzo line was intentional. The maintenance workers were told to repair it, but they have refused until SITRANDE's strike committee approves the request.

Carlos: This is getting worse and worse. Why don't we just let SITRANDE continue with their own fight? Why get involved in a conflict like this?

Miguel: Don't you realize that people could be killed or wounded? If there is a blackout, things will be that much worse. There are hospitals in the country that don't have backup generators.

Carlos: If you get involved in a strike, you have to be willing to pay the consequences.

Oscar: We're wasting valuable time, and everything indicates that the situation is getting out of hand. Why don't we send out a forceful communiqué. A half-hearted gesture on our part at this point won't have any impact. We have to be aware of the danger we're courting, but this should give everyone more time – the police, the unionists, and the administrators of ANDE. Here's the draft we wrote just now. What do you think of it?

The officers all read and agreed to the communiqué. After several tries, they were successful in getting a telephone line to one of the largest local radio stations. Oscar read the following communiqué over the telephone in a solemn tone of voice, and his statement was broadcast over the air. (The first communiqué appears in Appendix 3.)

REACTIONS TO UIA'S COMMUNIQUÉ

Reactions to UIA's announcement came fast and furious. The radio station that aired the broadcast interpreted the statement as irresponsibility on the part of the UIA for failing to guarantee electrical service to hospitals without backup generators.

Meeting with SITRANDE – May 2, 1996, 8:20–10:00 a.m.

SITRANDE immediately called the officers of UIA and asked for a meeting where they would plan out the next steps. The UIA officers jumped into a car and went to the meeting location, devising their strategy and position en route. Upon entering the meeting room, they found the SITRANDE members in a highly emotional state. Some men had been harassed by the police, beaten, and threatened with death. A policeman had aimed his gun and discharged the bullet right over the head of one of the leaders. These well-respected civil servants had never experienced this type of treatment before; they were in shock and appeared to be much more nervous than the UIA members.

As a result, the initial positions of the two unions were very different. The engineers did not want to endanger the country electricity system in any way, whereas SITRANDE wanted to fight back and demonstrate the force and cohesion of the electricity sector.

The meeting was a cauldron of conflicting ideas. Some wanted vengeance, others worried about the imprisoned leaders and the people who'd been injured. Still others vowed to take a firm stance with the government and yield nothing in what was now a full-fledged fight. Those who wanted to escalate the conflict made the following statements.

> "We should contact the union at Itaipú, [the enormous dam that is the main source of electricity for both Paraguay and the neighboring region of Brazil], and get them to go on strike too."
>
> "In this instance, cutting off the electricity is a matter of self defense until the federation leaders are released."
>
> "Why should we be concerned about the life-threatening consequences of a blackout? The police were not worrying about human life when they were shooting guns at us this morning!"
>
> "How many times has Paraguay had blackouts due to technical problems and no negative consequences resulted? Why would an intentional black- out be any different?"
>
> "The San Lorenzo line should not be repaired or tested."
>
> "We should knock out the large power cables, because this would force an immediate solution."
>
> "Let's cut off power in the areas where the army is quartered!"

Others argued more calmly for considering the negative consequences to escalating the conflict:

> "We can't put innocent lives at risk."
>
> "Public opinion will be against us."
>
> "Cutting off the power will give ammunition to those who want to privatize ANDE."
>
> "Pulling the power plug should be the last and not the first weapon in the fight."
>
> "We can't make a decision like this without the full vote of the general assembly."

After an hour and a half of discussion, the combined unions made the following decisions:

1.   There will be no unilateral actions.
2.   The two unions would send out a joint communiqué.

The purpose of the first resolution was to ensure that decisions would be made in a rational manner, taking all factors into consideration. No union or a subgroup would unilaterally cause a blackout. The purpose behind the second resolution was to present the two unions' side of the situation to the public, thereby pressuring the police to release the federation leaders and showing a united front to encourage the strikers in the streets.

The leaders of the two unions hammered out a joint communiqué which was released to the radio stations. (See Appendix 4.)

After leaving the meeting, the UIA officers turned on the radio to hear that a rumor was circulating that two of the arrested federation leaders would be released shortly. The rest of the news, however, was disheartening.

- The president of ANDE, Ricardo Alvarez, had called the UIA irresponsible, citing Oscar and Roberto by name. He also announced that even if the technicians went out on strike, ANDE had an emergency plan that would guarantee service. Alvarez is an electrical engineer with an MBA from the same alma mater as Oscar. He has a relaxed, pleasant personality and good political skills. Union members griped that while they were worrying about trying to prevent more violence and blackouts from happening, Alvarez was concentrating on protecting his own image.
- A doctor complained that there was no electricity in the Sanatorio Cristian clinic, and ANDE had failed to restore service, thereby threatening innocent lives.
- Rumor had it that two of the arrested federation leaders would be released shortly.
- Some radio announcers began a slander campaign against the unions in the electricity sector.

As soon as they returned to their headquarters, the UIA officers checked on the clinic and discovered that it had not suffered a power outage and the doctor's claims were false. Their next call went to the ANDE engineers who specialized in operations to ask about Alvarez's claim that ANDE had an emergency plan. A plan did exist, which relied primarily upon army personnel, to run a station that was refusing to operate. The success of the plan would depend upon whether or not the workers on duty would leave peacefully and whether the problem with the inaccurate instrument readings could be resolved. It was never determined whether the instrument system was sabotaged (and if so, by whom) or whether it was simply another technical problem that looked suspicious. The engineers were doubtful that the emergency plan would be successful; some worried that if the entire system went down it could be extremely difficult to get it up and running again.

The UIA officers figured that the negative publicity campaign was being orchestrated by ANDE itself. The radio station that led the campaign was the major recipient of ads and program support from ANDE. Therefore, the officers decided to go directly to this station and try to inform the public about the true facts of the situation and reassure them that there were no health clinics without electricity.

When they arrived at the station, however, the announcer/owner would not let them speak. Instead, he proudly told his listeners that he would not give air time to "traitors like these". The union leaders regrouped and sent faxes to all the radio stations.

General UIA assembly meeting – May 2, 11:00–14:00

The UIA members met at their headquarters and heard a recount of the events of the day. Many of the members were unhappy about the efforts to discredit them by some of the radio stations. There was some good news however: the violence in the streets was virtually over by 8:00 a.m.; there were no major locations without electricity; and two of the federation leaders had been released, but refused their freedom until all the other leaders were released. For a moment, it looked as if things were returning to normal. Oscar breathed a sigh of relief – but this was just the calm in the eye of the storm.

- A radio news flash announced that the workers at Itaipú were threatening to shut down the largest hydroelectric plant in the world if the federation leaders were not immediately released. Since the workers did not specify whether only Paraguay would be affected, there was the possibility that Brazil would also be dragged into the conflict. It appeared as if SITRANDE had asked the Itaipú workers to take this measure without consulting UIA.
- Once again, Alvarez went on the air, complaining that the union leaders were irresponsible. He also went to court and obtained a restraining order that was served upon both unions.
- In response, another player entered the game. The Electricians' Association, with 3000 members, issued a manifesto supporting the ANDE unions and attacking its president, Alvarez.
- At noon, Oscar received a phone call from his wife, who said, "Oscar, don't you realize that you are endangering everyone?"
- The unions extended the deadline they had given the government to release the federation leaders by 1:00 p.m.

Meanwhile, the UIA assembly agreed upon the following conclusions. They had achieved their goals in the conflict. SITRANDE, however, was escalating the conflict unnecessarily. After a few phone calls to the dam, they concluded that the Itaipú workers would probably not shut down the turbines, and it was unwise to keep the populace on edge worrying about a blackout. Furthermore, it looked as if the federation leaders would be released very soon. Therefore, they decided to release a third communiqué clarifying their position and trying to calm the public. (See Appendix 5.) This was read on radio stations around noon.

The conflict continued to escalate during the afternoon.

- Disaster struck again at 12:50 when the lights went out in an area that contained two large hospitals. The cause was a common technical problem concerning overheated cables, which was unrelated to the strike. Nevertheless, this produced a deluge of criticism against the UIA and SITRANDE. Alvarez went back on the air accusing the unions of slowdown tactics, a purposeful delay in restoring service to the hospitals. He said their leaders were criminally responsible for any loss of human life. Oscar called the same radio station to clarify that this was simply a technical problem that was repaired in forty minutes.

- The newscaster at Radiomundo, a friend of Alvarez, read a phony curriculum vitae that portrayed Oscar as a "*Stronista*", a term applied to Stroessner supporters, collaborators, and/or profiteers.
- A representative of SITRANDE called Radiomundo to back up the veracity of Oscar's radio announcement and denounce Alvarez's actions. He also accused Alvarez of supporting General Oviedo, claiming Alvarez had ordered two generators to be delivered to the general's headquarters during the failed coup attempt.
- Alvarez called back the radio station, denying this charge and lashing out again at the unions. Some of Oscar's friends said he should clear his own name and attack Alvarez. He refused, explaining that the UIA's objectives had been met and the radio fight was distracting attention from more important issues. Instead, Oscar called the person on Alvarez's staff who was friends with both of them. This person got Alvarez to agree to Oscar's suggestion that neither of them would speak on the radio again to keep ANDE from losing further prestige.

THE AFTERMATH

- According to Oscar, just about everyone lost as a result of the strike. Two workdays were lost and in the following two days not much was accomplished. The unions were weakened, because it became obvious that a strike lasting longer than a day would require more public support than they could muster. The government did not change anything, but they became even less popular. They also lost whatever momentum they might have gained after removing Oviedo from the scene. Social instability has increased, prompting the popularity of more authoritarian leaders, which may threaten the evolution of democracy in Paraguay. Wasmosy was not reelected by his party.
- Alvarez never did meet with Oscar. A week after the strike, the president initiated a criminal lawsuit against Oscar and the leaders of SITRANDE, but, as frequently occurs in Paraguay, nothing came of it.
- Just prior to the strike, Oscar had been selected for a faculty job at an industrial engineering school (professors in Paraguay have "day jobs" and moonlight as professors). A week after the strike, the job search was reopened. Oscar was tied with another candidate. A member of the faculty committee who was a friend of Wasmosy suggested that the other candidate be named, given Oscar's actions in the strike.

- Six months after the strike, Oscar lost out on yet another professorship. This happened in spite of the fact that he was more qualified than the person who was appointed and had been teaching this course for four years, waiting for a vacancy to open.

- For a while after the strike, Oscar felt uncomfortable with some of his friends. In particular, he felt that his MBA classmates, who are business people who don't think much of the working class, did not approve of his actions.

- There have been no apparent negative repercussions for Alvarez. Oscar believes that people generally believed Alvarez's version of what occurred rather than his own. Oscar regrets channeling their communiqué through Radiomundo, which took attention away from the union demands to engineer a conflict between Alvarez and the union and its leaders. Alvarez enjoyed an advantage in this arena because he is friends with several radio announcers and the newspaper is anti-union. The unions believe this is because the newspaper owner wants to buy state businesses and the unions are against privatization.

- Oscar does not think his career has suffered within ANDE. He was promoted to a management job in Human Resources shortly after the strike by placing first on the selection exam. A month later a huge storm knocked out several towers in an isolated part of the country. Since Oscar had been responsible for maintaining high tension lines in the past, he went to the trouble spot without being asked. The president was also there; for 48 hours they worked together almost nonstop to repair the line. Both were grateful for the other's help. In Oscar's opinion, there is no rancor between them.

- Oscar's actions in the strike have helped him in his relations with the workers and technicians within ANDE. They trust him and are more willing to share information and problems with him.

In Oscar's opinion, the one positive outcome of the strike is that the engineers stood behind the workers and technicians when the strike became dangerous and helped prevent a country-wide blackout.

APPENDIX 1: MANIFESTO OF THE ENGINEERS LABOR UNION OF ANDE DECEMBER 1995

(This manifesto was released on the occasion of the first general strike, in which UIA did not participate.)

For the time being we manifest our deep concern for the lack of attention given by the National Government to the serious problems facing this country:

1. Lack of buying power of salaries given the cost of the *canasta familiar* (family basket of necessities)
2. The worker, rural farmer, and middle classes are indebted due to interest rates higher than the level of inflation and the decrease in their income
3. Lack of work, land and resources oriented to production

4.   Deficient infrastructure and human resources
5.   Lack of internal and external credibility of our legal justice system
6.   Deficient handling of citizen complaints and state powers
7.   Personal interests placed before the interests of the nation
8.   A permissive climate towards corruption

The general strike and the *campesinos'* march are eloquent symptoms of the critical social situation of the country. The National Government should accept these legitimate complaints with wisdom and self-criticism.

Therefore, the Engineers Labor Union of ANDE proposes the following:

1.   Reorient national politics towards the solution of social problems
2.   Execute bipartisan policies
3.   Implement plans for cultural revolutions of short, medium and long term, that will permit us to compete more effectively, a current requirement of market economies
4.   Firmly brake the efforts of those, including the government, who try to destabilize reform
5.   Dialogue and commitment to the public will, as evidenced in the last elections
6.   Respect for public institutions and their officials for their role as servants of the people and not for political interests or sectarian economies

Finally, we express our confidence that people in power in the government will be reminded of their patriotic and moral values, so they can orient their minds and actions for the common good. The Paraguayan people will acknowledge and be grateful for these acts.

Steering Committee

APPENDIX 2: DEMANDS[3] OF THE LABOR UNION FEDERATIONS APRIL 13, 1996

1.   Increase the minimum salary by 31 percent
2.   Salary readjustment (increases) for public employees
3.   Protection and reform of the Social Security Institute (IPS)
4.   Benefit coverage for self-employed workers
5.   Fulfillment of contracts signed with public and private workers
6.   Fulfillment of specific contracts signed with transportation workers
7.   Convocation of a referendum on privatization
8.   Adoption of a policy of full employment
9.   Support for the demands of the rural farmer organizations
10.   Full participation of all social classes in the process of regional integration of the Mercosur (trading bloc of the southern Latin American countries)
11.   Distribution of the National Labor Code
12.   Repeal of Decree No. 6.478/94 regarding positions of trust

APPENDIX 3: FIRST COMMUNIQUÉ ENGINEERS LABOR UNION OF ANDE (UIA) MAY 2, 1996 7:50 A.M.

In light of the serious repercussions reported this morning and the arrests and beatings of union leaders, and protesters, we declare the following:

1. We send an urgent plea to the police to release the union leaders and protesters so they can freely exercise their constitutional rights.
2. SITRANDE (syndicate of workers of ANDE) has notified us of their decision to not guarantee the provision of electrical energy service, including the abandonment of key posts.
3. The UIA appeals to the common sense and wisdom of the police, because this could result in serious consequences – not only the possible loss of electrical power but extensive damage to the electrical system itself.
4. Since the members of UIA find themselves in a strike of solidarity with the working class, we will not guarantee the provision of electrical power as of 8:15 a.m. If SITRANDE pulls workers off the job, it will be physically impossible to guarantee service.

APPENDIX 4: SECOND COMMUNIQUÉ SPECIAL GENERAL ASSEMBLY OF UIA AND SITRANDE MAY 2, 1996 10:00 A.M.

Given the serious acts of violent repression and detention of union leaders, protesters, journalists, and workers in general, the strike committee of SITRANDE and UIA inform the general public of the following:

ANDE workers who respond to customer complaints throughout the country are no longer on the job.

Service complaints from hospitals and other essential services will be handled rapidly by the strike committees of both unions.

Neither union will be responsible for power cutoffs that are the result of acts of sabotage and/or the operation of the national electricity system by people who do not work for ANDE.

The operators of the stations, substations, and Acaray Central Hydroelectric plant will remain at their jobs until the strike committees deem otherwise.

If the national government does not release our unfairly detained colleagues, the strike committees of both unions reserve the right to take whatever measures they consider necessary.

Other decisions to be decided will be communicated solely to the media and the ANDE authorities.

STRIKE COMMITTEES OF SITRANDE AND UIA

APPENDIX 5: THIRD COMMUNIQUÉ ENGINEERS LABOR UNION OF ANDE (UIA) MAY 2, 1996

In light of the misinformation with respect to the electrical power service, the Engineers Labor Union of ANDE informs the general public of the following:

1. At no time has our union caused or will cause a cutoff in the provision of electrical energy.
2. This union promises to take care of energy outages that affect hospitals, clinics or other essential services where there is direct or indirect danger to human life. We will respond immediately and diligently repair the problems.

We have the technical means to accurately and immediately identify when outages affect the essential services mentioned above.

NOTES

1   All names have been changed to protect the identity of the protagonists.
2   The *amarillos* or "yellow ones" support management in return for certain advantages like promotions, paid trips, etc., rather than fight for the workers' conditions.
3   Some of these demands concerned previous contractual agreements that the government had not honored.

Ngo Minh Hang

THE CASE OF ABB TRANSFORMER
IN VIETNAM

Sitting behind his desk, Eric Nylund, general director of the joint venture ABB Transformer Ltd. in Vietnam, was staring blankly through a window, thinking hard about
how to overcome his difficult situation. The joint venture was being sued by some
recently laid off employees, who managed to get support from the mass media to
publicize their plight. Numerous articles on the case had been published making Eric
out to be irresponsible toward his employees in the public's eyes. He was accused of
creating big losses and blaming this on the market. Trying hard to build persuasive
arguments for the coming court case, he was recalling when ABB International first
came to Vietnam to look for investment opportunities, and the origins of the joint
venture.

THE BUSINESS ENVIRONMENT IN VIETNAM

After Vietnam launched an open-door policy in 1990, investment started to come
into the country. Before that time, the country's economy had been centrally planned,
and demand for goods always far exceeded available supply. Many foreign companies
decided to set up business in Vietnam, as they saw the country as a market with good
potential. The open-door policy attracted foreign investors, boosting the country's
economy to grow at an unprecedented rate of 7–8 percent per annum, creating
many jobs for local people and stimulating local markets. This contributed to making
Vietnam even more attractive to subsequent potential investors.

   While trying to attract foreign investment, the government of Vietnam also tried
to protect local companies, because they were inexperienced and so much weaker

than their foreign competitors in all respects except knowledge of the local culture. The protection often took the form of preferential selection of tenders for work on government-funded projects.

The implementation of foreign investment proved not to be easy: foreign investors faced many difficulties. One such difficulty was finding qualified Vietnamese employees: the labour market lacked all kinds of skills and experience, such as: human resource management, public relations management, accounting, operations management, IT, technical skills, problem-solving skills, English-language skills, and so on. They had to train newly hired staff almost from scratch.

Vietnam is relatively hierarchical in many aspects of its society, especially in management. The degree of delegation is very low, and decision-making takes time. In addition, in many cases personnel decisions are made based on personal preferences and relationships, causing inefficiencies and opportunities for pragmatists to get things done in their own way.

Difficulties were also caused by employee attitudes. People who had worked for state-owned companies had never had to worry about losing their job, and nobody had ever been fired for poor performance before. The only justification for firing had been such things as being absent from work without reason, or stealing state-owned property, etc. This proved to be a crucial problem for companies. In state-owned organizations, the common culture had been "binh quan chu nghia", meaning an equal share of everything: equal share of income, of effort, of performance, and so on, and all at an average level. If someone was considered average, then they felt safe. There was not much difference in the way poor and excellent performers were treated. Therefore people were not motivated to go for high performance. In such an environment, seniority was the most important factor affecting one's income, promotion and respect in an organization.

All of these phenomena were rooted in the way people thought, and were embedded in their culture, causing frustration amongst foreign investors requiring government approval. Foreign investors considered that the business environment was neither transparent nor clear: to be successful in certain cases, they had to do a significant amount of lobbying. In effect, businessmen quite often complained about corruption in the government.

As a result, most foreign companies recruited new graduates, because it was easier to educate young people than it was to change the habits of older workers.

LABOR REGULATIONS IN VIETNAM

One of the reasons for this ingrained culture was that people had always been protected by law: the Personnel Organization Law, and later the Labor Code of 1995. These contained many vague articles (hence the requirement for by-laws to guide their implementation). According to the Employment Law, foreign companies and joint ventures had to recruit through Vietnamese labor-supply organizations. They had to use contract forms designed by the Ministry of Labor, Invalid and Social Affairs (MOLISA), and they had to register new hires with the ministry.

The Trade Union Law stipulated that all joint ventures were encouraged to set up an internal union, and had to sign collective labor agreements with the unions. Also, their internal labor rules must be agreed by the trade unions. Collective labor agreements and internal labor rules had to be registered with the provincial representative of MOLISA (DOLISA) and had to conform to the Labor Code. The various Vietnamese government bodies kept a very close eye on the implementation of the Labor Code in foreign companies and the joint ventures.

Employee protection was especially strong in the case of mass lay-offs. Article 17 of the Labor Code states:

> Where, as a result of organizational restructuring or technological changes, an employee who has been employed in the business for a period of one or more years becomes unemployed, the employer shall have the responsibility to retrain and assign the employee to another job within enterprise; if a new job cannot be created, the employer must pay an allowance for loss of work . . .

and

> . . . the employer must submit a list of employees to be retrenched, and on the business requirements, seniority, skills, family conditions and other factors of each employee provided, the employer shall gradually retrench the employees, provided that the Employee Committee of the Trade Union of the enterprise is consulted in accordance with the procedures stipulated in clause 2 of article 38 of this Code.

Clause 2 of article 38 goes on to say:

> . . . the employer must discuss and reach an agreement with the Employee Committee of the Trade Union. Where there is a disagreement, both parties should submit the report to the competent body or organization. After a period of 30 days as from the date of the labor office is notified, the employer shall have the right to make a decision and be responsible for such a decision

and

> An employer shall only be permitted to retrench employees after notifying the local labor office.

Moreover, the law required that employers inform people to be laid off 45 days in advance of the actual date. Employers were also required to pay salaries for the notice period, to pay one month's salary for each year worked as part of a severance package, and to pay an additional allowance to allow laid-off employees to look for another job.

THE ABB TRANSFORMER JOINT VENTURE LTD. (VNTRA)

Before ABB came to Vietnam, there were only five transformer producers in Vietnam, and they were all state-owned. Three of them reported to the Electricity Authority of Vietnam (EVN), and the other two belonged to the Ministry of Industry. They all used Russian technology and standards, which were relatively outdated. Because of the nature of the economy, there had been no competition among the different transformer producers: production targets were set by the government. Marketing, both as a term and as a concept, was unknown.

Among the five producers, CTBT (Transformer Manufacturing Company) was the most successful, having about 70 percent of the total transformer market in northern Vietnam. The company's main products were distribution transformers.

In the rest of the world, transformer manufacturing is a mature industry. Market shares are well established amongst major competitors, such as ABB, Alstom, Schneider and others. Apart from some development in the materials used and optimization of the design, there had been few changes in the technology and the nature of utilization in recent years. Customers cared more about the cost than about technical features. To expand, producers therefore tried to penetrate new markets, such as Vietnam.

In 1994, ABB, an international group in the field of electrical engineering, and CTBT formed ABB Transformer Ltd., a joint venture. The joint venture was seen as a good fit: ABB had up-to-date technology, financial resources, worldwide management experience and reputation; and CTBT had the local venue, nationwide distribution networks, local business experience and cheap labor. Before the foundation of the joint venture, a feasibility study was carried out in 1993. According to the study's results, approved by both parties, the joint venture would first start producing distribution transformers, then medium voltage switchgears (1996), and finally power transformers (1997). At the time the feasibility study was conducted, there were only three EVN transformer producers. The joint venture intended to produce 1,600 distribution transformers per year, and it predicted 14 percent annual growth of the market in Vietnam.

When the joint venture (JV) was formed, ABB contributed 65 percent of the total investment, in the form of cash, machinery and equipment. CTBT contributed the balance, in the form of buildings, infrastructure and machinery (the last of which was sold in 1997 as salvage). ABB agreed that the JV would hire all of CTBT's 475 staff members, aged 45 on average, even though the joint venture predicted that it would need only 270 employees by the time it would be expanding its operation to produce all three kinds of products. In the JV plan, both sides agreed to gradually reduce the number of staff to 270 by 1998. The joint venture agreed to pay its workers about US$80 per month, even though the regulated minimum for JVs was US$50, and the market average wage was quite a bit lower. Because of this, ABB was reputed to be very generous to local people. Finally, ABB also agreed to license all of its technologies and designs to be used by the JV. The advantage of ABB technology was the low power losses and low material consumption per transformer.

The JV management board (MB) consisted of six members; four of them from ABB. There were two other persons from ABB, all holding key management positions, except in the personnel sector. The chairman of the MB and the general manager were all ABB people. There was a Vietnamese MB vice chairman, Mr. Duong Lac, responsible for personnel issues. According to the joint venture's charter, the chairman's position was to alternate between the two sides. Thus, Mr. Duong Lac would take his turn in the next period. As per the feasibility study, the management role was to be gradually transferred to the Vietnamese side, so that by 1998 only two foreigners would remain in the distribution transformer factory. Compared to other joint ventures in the country, the Vietnamese side was successful in the negotiation process.

THE MARKET AND COMPETITION

The joint venture's mission was to meet the need for dependable electrical energy, and thus to assure sustainable growth, while fully respecting environmental demands. Its objectives were to manufacture transformers and other electric equipment using ABB advanced technology, initially for electrification of Vietnam and subsequently for export in the future. The joint venture started producing distribution and power transformers as planned. In 1996, it started producing medium voltage switchgears. However, the production of switchgears stopped in 1998 because the market was too small.

By 1997–8, there were six transformer producers in the country, including VNTRA. Two of them were subsidiaries of EVN. Another one was a joint venture with a Japanese company. In terms of technology, all used relatively current equipment. Still, VNTRA's products had the best reputation for quality. Unfortunately, the demand for transformers was only half of what had been estimated in the feasibility study.

The JV's customers could be classified into four major groups, comprising: power companies, power construction companies, internal ABB group companies, and others. Power companies were the most important customers, but they were the most difficult to handle. Compared to the other groups, these customers were more technically competent. ABB Transformers Ltd. and its products managed not only to cater to customers' requirements, but also to call for their awareness of its superior design. This was done through intensive customer interaction including technical seminars, customer training and customers' visits to the factory. The company was successful in a number of projects funded by the World Bank and the Asian Development Bank (ADB).

Unfortunately, as all the Vietnamese power companies belonged to the same giant entity (EVN), and two of its subsidiaries manufactured the same products as VNTRA' s, albeit at a much weaker level, EVN selected them in tenders whenever possible, so as to support them. This process was unfair to VNTRA. So VNTRA found it difficult to win projects funded by, or through, the government. VNTRA only tended to win those projects requiring very high quality products, or in cases where the tendering process was transparent, or had strict evaluation procedures by donor organizations such as the World Bank and the ADB.

The second and the third VNTRA customer groups were the power construction companies and the industrial customers (including processing industries like cement, steel, paper, consumer manufacturers, OEMs, hotels, etc.). VNTRA was the most successful amongst the competitors in dealing with this group, thanks to its good customer technical support and brand name.

The fourth group of VNTRA's customers was people in rural areas. Owing to an electrification movement in the countryside, many districts and communes looked to buy transformers for their own needs. This group, however, could not afford high investment up front, so as to enjoy lower total life-cycle costs. Therefore the joint venture was losing market share in this sector.

By 1998, the joint venture had fewer than 40 percent of the national market, and was working at under capacity. It aimed to reach a target of 40 percent of the local market by the year 2000, but the competition became more and more fierce. Since its foundation, the joint venture had been operating at a loss, and this had increased to US$7 million by 1998. However, its workers were still generously paid, at nearly four times the national minimum. In addition, the workers had two days off a week compared to the common practice of just one day off per week.

THE STORY OF VNTRA – PART ONE

As the joint venture was operating at a loss, and the market was not as big as first projected, the JV could not expand its operations and invest further in production, as initially planned. Moreover, employees working in the closed-down units with old Russian technology were redundant. Therefore, the JV needed to take measures to cut costs, in order to reduce losses.

From August 1996 to August 1998 the joint venture introduced an "early retirement scheme" for factory workers. This retirement campaign first focused on those employees who were close to retirement age and could not be retrained to cope with new technologies. Each volunteer early retiree was paid two types of allowances: an early retirement allowance, and an allowance for time worked for CTBT. The joint venture paid US$500 for each early retirement year for those workers having from 1–5 such years, and US$350 for those having 5–10 years. Those who had worked for CTBT for more than 20 years were paid US$100 for each year after the 20th year. On average, each volunteer received about US$1,700, depending on the length of his/her service with CTBT – a handsome bonus in Vietnamese eyes. This compensation package was very good in Vietnam, and much higher than that required by the Labor Code. In all, the costs for the volunteer retirement were VN$6.2 billion (about US$480,000). Because of the generosity of the package, all 121 workers targeted agreed to take voluntary retirement, and the first mass staff reduction went smoothly.

After that, VNTRA continued to operate at a loss, as the market remained small and the degree of industry competition was still tough. VNTRA had to reduce its operating costs again. Upgrading technology to achieve higher productivity, closing ineffective units (two post-sale service centers) and outsourcing unimportant services (such as the canteen) were realized. That helped rationalize operating costs and improve services, thus reducing costs. On November 12th, 1998, the joint venture announced a lay-off of 92 workers, owing to technology updates and organizational restructuring. This was in accordance with the feasibility study, although somewhat delayed.

Before the official announcement of the list of the laid-off workers, Mr. Duong Lac, then chairman of VNTRA, had promised to let all workers discuss and vote on who should go, and to then publicly announce the list of those laid off. However, this did not happen: the announcement was received individually by laid-off employees at the end of the lunar year (1998). They were informed that they would receive their salaries up to the date of termination of their employment with the JV. Unlike the previous early retirement scheme, under this redundancy package each person was to be paid a monthly salary for each year worked for VNTRA, plus a retraining allowance of three months' salary, and pay in lieu of annual leave. Thus, the joint venture paid lower allowances than the previous time, and it also failed to follow its earlier pledge on the manner in which workers would be selected for redundancy. The workers were very angry, and sixteen of them brought the case to the Hanoi Labor Court, asking to get back their jobs, and accusing the management of unfair treatment and violating retrenchment laws. In addition, they succeeded in getting loud and sympathetic support from the local newspapers, asking the public to protect national employees.

On February 5th, 1999 many of those laid off received empty envelopes for their January pay. It was explained that they would receive no salary owing to the termination of their employment, and that they would be paid only if they agreed to take the redundancy package. This angered the workers even more because they felt insulted. Later, the management did apologize for this, explaining that the accountant had put salaries in envelopes following the salary list, without consulting with his manager. This event again provoked many newspaper articles against the joint venture's management.

Several days later, some 30 of the laid-off workers staged a sit-in at the office, to protest the termination of their labor contracts and irrational application of rules on early retirement. They went to various governmental and social organizations, such as the Office of the Central Committee of the Communist Party, reputed newspaper premises, the Office of the Government, etc. There were many articles in various newspapers, describing and commenting on the case. Most of them supported the case of those laid off. The Ministry of Planning and Investment stepped into the fray, ordering the "managers of VNTRA to do a serious self-criticism about the disrespectful judgment and to search for a solution to re-use as many as possible of those laborers".[1]

By early September 1998, the joint venture was stung by a special interministerial inquiry, which examined why it had laid off the workers and made large losses. ABB Transformer Ltd.'s directorate offered various reasons for the lay-off: improved production technology, shrinking domestic markets as big projects were delayed, and an adverse foreign exchange rate. "Our losses have gone way over the predicted figures, and at the same time there are no signs of the market improving," said Mr. Nylund. "We have to do this to guarantee we can stay here during the difficult times, so we will be in good shape when the market takes off again. Keeping the workers on would put the whole operation in jeopardy."

The dispute between VNTRA and those laid off lasted for more than a year. During that time, VNTRA did not pay their salaries, even though the workers were fighting to get paid. Although many meetings were held between the management of the joint venture and its union, neither side could come to an agreement.

Thinking hard about his difficult situation, Mr. Nylund knew that they had no choice but to lay off those who were made redundant, and he was confident that his company's compensation package was more than that required by law. But he was very hesitant, because most newspapers appeared to be very critical of him. Should he withdraw his lay-off decision, or should he defend his opinion in the up-coming court case?

NOTE

1   *Lao dong* newspaper, "Phai tim moi bien phap de su dung lao dong", Le Huan – Quang Chinh.

Joseph J. DiStefano

JOHANNES VAN DEN BOSCH
SENDS AN EMAIL

Professor Joe DiStefano prepared this mini-case as a basis for class discussion rather than to illustrate either effective or ineffective handling of a business situation.

The mini-case reports events as they occurred. The email exchanges in both cases are reported verbatim, except for the names, which have been changed. Professor DiStefano acknowledges with thanks the cooperation of "Johannes van den Bosch" in providing this information and his generous permission to use the material for executive development.

After having had several email exchanges with his Mexican counterpart over several weeks without getting the expected actions and results, Johannes van den Bosch was getting a tongue-lashing from his British MNC client, who was furious at the lack of progress. Van den Bosch, in the Rotterdam office of BigFiveFirm, and his colleague in the Mexico City office, Pablo Menendez, were both seasoned veterans, and van den Bosch couldn't understand the lack of responsiveness.

A week earlier, the client, Malcolm Smythe-Jones, had visited his office to express his mounting frustration. But this morning he had called with a stream of verbal abuse. His patience was exhausted.

Feeling angry himself, van den Bosch composed a strongly worded message to Menendez, and then decided to cool off. A half hour later, he edited it to "stick to the facts" while still communicating the appropriate level of urgency. As he clicked to send the message, he hoped that it would finally provoke some action to assuage his client with the reports he had been waiting for.

He reread the email, and as he saved it to the mounting record in Smythe-Jones's file, he thought, "I'm going to be happy when this project is over for another year!"

Message for Pablo Menendez

Subject: IAS 1998 Financial statements

Author: Johannes van den Bosch (Rotterdam)

Date: 10/12/99 1:51 p.m.

Dear Pablo,

This morning I had a conversation with Mr. Smythe-Jones (CFO) and Mr. Parker (Controller) re the finalization of certain 1998 financial statements. Mr. Smythe-Jones was not in a very good mood.

He told me that he was very unpleased by the fact that the 1998 IAS financial statement of the Mexican subsidiary still has not been finalized. At the moment he holds us responsible for this process. Although he recognizes that local management is responsible for such financial statements, he blames us for not being responsive on this matter and inform him about the process adequately. I believe he also recognizes that we have been instructed by Mr. Whyte (CEO) not to do any hand-holding, but that should not keep us from monitoring the process and inform him about the progress.

He asked me to provide him tomorrow with an update on the status of the IAS report and other reports pending.

Therefore I would like to get the following information from you today:

- *What has to be done to finalize the Mexican subsidiary's IAS financials;*
- *Who has to do it (local management, B&FF Mexico, client headquarters, B&FF Rotterdam);*
- *A timetable when things have to be done in order to finalize within a couple of weeks or sooner;*
- *A brief overview why it takes so long to prepare and audit the IAS f/s;*
- *Are there any other reports for 1998 pending (local gaap, tax), if so the above is also applicable for those reports.*

As of today I would like to receive an update of the status every week. If any major problems arise during the finalization process I would like to be informed immediately. The next status update is due January 12, 2000.

Mr. Smythe-Jones also indicated that in the future all reports (US GAAP, local GAAP and IAS) should be normally finalized within 60 days after the balance sheet date. He will hold local auditors responsible for monitoring this process.

Best regards and best wishes for 2000.

Johannes

Index

Note: page numbers in *italic* denote references to figures/tables.

What was most
interesting Monday?

What would you like to
learn about in IHRM?

What do you see as top 5 IHRM
challenges
    - as Org leader ⎫
                     ⎬ 2 teams
    - as HR PROF ⎭

have students discuss how
to make HR practices +
policies more consistent
across countries

1. should this be a goal
    why or why not
2. what steps should be
    taken + what results are
    expected